No Trade Is
FREE

No Trade Is
FREE

CHANGING COURSE, TAKING
ON CHINA, AND HELPING
AMERICA'S WORKERS

ROBERT LIGHTHIZER

BROADSIDE BOOKS

HarperCollins books may be purchased for educational, business, or sales promotional use. For information, please email the Special Markets Department at SPsales@harpercollins.com.

Broadside Books™ and the Broadside logo are trademarks of HarperCollins Publishers.

FIRST EDITION

Library of Congress Cataloging-in-Publication Data

Names: Lighthizer, Robert E., 1947 - author.
Title: No trade is free : how to change course, take on China, and help our workers / Robert Lighthizer.
Description: New York, NY : Broadside, [2023] | Includes index.
Identifiers: LCCN 2023013187 (print) | LCCN 2023013188 (ebook) | ISBN 9780063282131 (hardcover) | ISBN 9780063282148 (ebook)
Subjects: LCSH: United States—Commerical policy. | United States—Foreign economic relations. | Free trade—United States.
Classification: LCC HF1455 .L48 2023 (print) | LCC HF1455 (ebook) | DDC 382/.30973—dc23/eng/20230508
LC record available at https://lccn.loc.gov/2023013187
LC ebook record available at https://lccn.loc.gov/2023013188

24 25 26 27 28 LBC 7 6 5 4 3

To Bob and Claire and to every American
worker who makes our country great

When the facts change, I change my mind. What do you do, sir?

—*attributed to John Maynard Keynes*

Failure is not fatal, but failure to change might be.

—*John Wooden*

CONTENTS

Part Five: Moving Forward

INTRODUCTION

In Washington, DC, it was an overcast day on June 9, 2010, and, by local standards, on the cool side. Seventy degrees is a comfortable temperature there in the summer. I was in a taxi on my way to the Dirksen Senate Office Building to testify before the US-China Economic and Security Review Commission. This was a group of twelve men and women appointed by the bipartisan congressional leadership and tasked with assessing US relations with China.

By the time my panel began, the temperature had risen a bit, and it had started to rain. I thought, "Perfect, depressing report on a depressing day." I was appearing on a panel with a couple other trade law experts. A group from Congress including Senators Lindsey Graham of South Carolina and Chuck Schumer of New York was on right before us. My task for the commission was to evaluate the impacts of China's joining the World Trade Organization (WTO) ten years on.

The commission invited me to speak because by that point I was well known in Washington circles as a skeptic not only of trade relations with China but also of the international trade system writ large. I had been a trade lawyer for more than thirty years—working for the US Senate, in the Reagan administration, and in private law practice representing American manufacturers in front of administrative agencies and courts. By the time of the hearings in 2010, I was one of a small handful of Washington commentators willing to openly argue against the negative effects of Washington's one-sided free trade agenda.

My testimony on American trade relations with China that day was thirty-five single-spaced pages. It showed in great detail what a disaster the 2000 decision to grant China "Most Favored Nation" (MFN) status had been for America—and particularly for our workers. It listed all the commitments that China had made back then and showed how they hadn't kept them, presented the economic calamity that these ten years had been for us, and highlighted the giddy pronouncements that our politicians had made, including President Clinton, Republican presidential candidate George W. Bush, and many leaders in Congress. The testimony quoted their unparalleled optimism—this was a "hundred to nothing deal" proclaimed then President Clinton. And then my testimony gave the butcher's bill. We had lost millions of jobs and thousands of factories while wages had stagnated. This ultimate concession to Communist leaders, free trade, and multinational corporations had been an unmitigated disaster for working people.

Finally, I predicted it was only going to get worse for our workers if we stayed on the same course, and I made specific policy recommendations, including imposing tariffs on Chinese imports, to correct the problem. After the hearing, two of the commissioners told me it was the most important testimony they had heard in their tenure, but little to nothing changed over the following half decade. My warnings over China went largely unheeded, just as they had throughout the 1990s, when I editorialized and fought against allowing China to join the WTO, the ratification of the North American Free Trade Agreement (NAFTA), and Washington's radical free trade agenda.

..

Well before 2010, it was clear to me that the issue of American trade relations with China was not an isolated problem but was instead emblematic of larger issues in US trade policy. The political establishments of both the Republican and Democratic parties, under the influence of multinational corporations and importers, were unwilling or unable to recognize their mistakes. Instead, they remained convinced that rather than protect American workers and manufacturers, government policy had to put them at risk amid a quest to maximize corporate profits and economic efficiency while minimizing consumer prices.

The result of this effort today is a starker, more indisputable failure than even I could have predicted. While corporate profits soared for a select group of importers and retailers, many of America's manufacturing companies were hollowed out—forced either into bankruptcy or into moving their factories abroad. And what about ordinary Americans?

Though prices for some products declined, wage growth in this country has utterly stagnated since the 1980s—driven in large part by the decline of manufacturing sector employment. As a result, increasingly, working-class families must rely on two full-time incomes in lower-end service sector jobs to maintain the same quality of life one manufacturing sector income once provided. It is no exaggeration to say that American leaders traded the health of the US industrial base and the good-paying manufacturing jobs it supported for current consumption and little more.

A look at the specifics emphasizes the problem:

- We have had fifty straight years of trade deficits with Japan, annual deficits of more than $300 billion with China for years, and enormous and sharply growing deficits with Europe (primarily Germany and Ireland), and a whopping 27 percent of Vietnam's entire economy is exports to the United States.
- The first personal computer was rolled out by Apple in 1976, made in America. Today, the vast majority of our personal computers are imported, and those few that are made domestically are assembled largely with imported parts. In 2020, almost $90 billion worth of computers were imported.
- In 1995, America was the largest producer of solar cells globally, with 45 percent of world production. Today, virtually no solar cells are made in America, and 78 percent of world production is in China.
- From the 1960s through the 1980s, the United States was the lead source of rare earth materials, largely from Mountain Pass Mine in California. Today, because of Chinese industrial policy, the United States accounts for just 12 percent of global production, while China accounts for 62 percent.
- North Carolina had a vibrant furniture manufacturing sector with ninety thousand middle-class jobs. Within ten years of China's joining the WTO, imports flooded our market, and half the workforce lost their jobs. Now 73 percent of all furniture sold in America is imported.[1]

- In 1990, the United States imported about $40 billion worth of cars. That number exploded to more than $180 billion by 2020, and for the first time in our history, less than half the cars sold in America may be assembled here.
- In the 1970s and 1980s, the United States was the world's leading producer of critical semiconductors. Today, we manufacture only 12 percent of global supply, and we cannot make any of the most advanced chips.
- For the first time in our history, the United States is on track to import more food than we export.

..

Donald Trump was elected president in 2016 in substantial part because he opposed the failed policy that got us such miserable results and promised to change it. He asked me to head up his trade policy and negotiation effort because I had spent my professional life fighting against these same forces. For nearly forty years, I had litigated, negotiated, and editorialized against the failed policies of hyper free trade.

My philosophy of international trade—and the philosophy that undergirds this book—is starkly at odds with the radical free trade theology that got us here. Simply put, I believe that American trade policy should revolve around helping working-class American families. Enhancing corporate profits, increasing economic efficiency, and lowering consumer prices are important but, in my view, secondary to this goal. When I look at the world today, the only practical way to help working people I see is to support the American manufacturing sector.

We must never forget that international trade, like all economic policy, is beneficial only if it contributes to the well-being of most of our citizens, if it makes families stronger, and if it makes our communities better. These broader goals are the real objective. In this context, it is imperative to remember that our citizens are first producers and only second consumers. Producing things is crucial to citizens' capacity to enjoy the dignity of work, support their families, and actively contribute to society. When all citizens—including those without college degrees—have a chance to be productive, it's good for the country.

American trade policy in the 1990s and early 2000s ignored this reality, and its failures are why, when I took over running American trade policy in early 2017, I knew we needed to follow a new trajectory aimed at advancing America's workers. Our success explains why the Biden administration has continued many of the changes in US trade policy that President Trump and I began.

The Trump administration had two historic accomplishments in the area of international trade policy. First, we changed the objective. Previous presidents had too often chased big trade deals that made it easier for companies to import products into the United States and that effectively encouraged manufacturing overseas. The decisions of bureaucrats at the WTO, meanwhile, were regarded as sacrosanct. President Trump changed all that. He was committed to bringing manufacturing jobs back to America. He wanted to reduce imports and to increase exports of manufactured goods and agricultural products. He judged success by the creation of new jobs, wage increases, the movement of factories back to America, and the reduction of the trade deficit. With this new objective as our lodestar, we increased tariffs on imports and fought unfair practices. We insisted that our trading partners grant us more market access. Finally, we took on the WTO and largely stopped its unfair, undemocratic appellate body.

The Trump administration's second great contribution was to awaken the country and ultimately the world to the danger of our growing economic dependence on China. China is an adversary of the United States. Regardless of its rhetoric to the contrary, its actions—and, increasingly, its words as well—show that China views us as a foe. It poses a military, diplomatic, and economic threat. Prior to the Trump administration, China was often portrayed as a friendly partner. This is an illusion. The reality is that it is a mercantilist nation that wants to impose its system on the world. It is opposed to the liberal democratic order and wants to put an end to American hegemony. Trump's policies reversed the trend of economic dependence and the transfer of trillions of dollars to our adversary in the form of trade deficits. This policy was also a success. Leading up to the onset of COVID-19, the trade deficit with China was reduced from the year before in five straight quarters. Dependence on China was declining. Supply chains were shifting away from China to the United States and other countries. The historic "Phase One" trade agreement with China maintained our tariffs, brought about substantial systemic change there, and created new markets for our products here at home.

..

I have two goals in this book. First, I want to challenge the way you think about trade policy. I want to lay out the reasoning behind my philosophy of trade and the underlying data that support the major course correction we took under the Trump administration. Second, I want to describe what we did in the Trump administration to implement this philosophy. Through doing this, I hope to show you how a more assertive US trade policy aimed at helping US workers can actually work in practice.

In the first part of the book, I will explain in detail how I think about international trade. I feel strongly that the course we set for trade policy must rest on a more complete and nuanced understanding of the effects of international trade in the United States—and throughout the world— than can be captured by the question of how much we pay for televisions and toys. So, throughout the first four chapters I will explain why I care about trade policy (chapter 1), my overarching philosophy on international trade (chapter 2), how this philosophy is a part of the American tradition (chapter 3), and how the WTO has failed (chapter 4).

In the second part of the book, I will focus on how the Trump administration pursued a worker-focused trade policy by resetting our economic relationship with China. It has become increasingly clear that China is the United States' major adversary in the world, militarily, diplomatically, and economically. And yet in trade policy we don't treat them as an adversary. Indeed, we give them Most Favored Nation status. While we criticize Germany for sending billions of euros to Russia for natural gas, some think it is okay for us to send hundreds of billions of dollars to China for televisions and other consumer goods. Indeed, trade is the Achilles' heel of our relationship with China—a weakness that has sapped our strength and that continues to distort our actions across a range of different arenas on the world stage. We need to understand the threat we face from China. We must understand its economic policy. This is a country that is fundamentally different from ours in ways that we have long ignored to our detriment. We need to see the subtexts and implications of Chinese actions and rhetoric, rather than solely the deeds done and words spoken out loud.

I feel this issue is so important that I have devoted three chapters to explaining the threat China poses to American security (chapter 5), how the Chinese economic model works (chapter 6), and how this model threatens American economic vitality (chapter 7). With this foundation established, I then explain how the Trump administration used tariffs to negotiate with China (chapters 8 through 10). Finally, I conclude the China section with my thoughts on how the United States must develop a policy of strategic decoupling with China (chapter 11).

China, of course, is not the only complex trade issue facing our country. In the third part of the book, I will explain how we renegotiated the North American Free Trade Agreement with Mexico and Canada (chapters 12 through 14). In the fourth part of the book, I will discuss various international trade issues with other major trading partners and in the global economy (chapters 15 through 17). Finally, in the last part of the book, I will conclude with my thoughts on the path forward for America's approach to international trade.

..

By now, it is clear to me that the once nearly unanimous Washington consensus on free trade is dead. In the final days of the Trump presidency, some Republicans in Congress who had disagreed with me for decades confided that I had changed the way they thought about trade, and the few staunch free trade holdouts remaining in the party are slowly retiring. President Biden, despite supporting most of the failed trade policies of the past during his time in the Senate, essentially adopted the Trump trade policy during his 2020 campaign. The Biden administration's subsequent decisions to keep most of the China tariffs in place, to continue to ignore the World Trade Organization, and to support American semiconductor and electric vehicle production show that the shift in priorities that we started has become entrenched across both parties.

Understanding why and how this happened is imperative for anyone seeking to find a new path forward. During the course of the Trump presidency, I was often asked to recommend one book that would give the history and philosophy of our worker-oriented trade policy. This is that book.

Part One

FOUNDATIONS

Chapter 1

Where It Started

When I arrived at Mar-a-Lago in December 2016 to meet with President-elect Donald Trump, I anticipated I would be offered the job of United States Trade Representative, and indeed I was. Sitting there in the walnut-paneled former library across the table from the president-elect, I knew that what I was being offered was not just a job. It was the chance to fight a battle that I had been preparing for my whole life: the battle to build trade policy that supports a society in which American workers, including those without college educations, can build better lives for themselves and their families through the stable, well-paying jobs that no healthy country can do without.

I knew what I was signing up for. I was facing four years of eighteen-hour days and seven-day weeks. Along with my team, I'd be fighting big business. I'd be fighting globalists and nationalists of all stripes from China, Mexico, Canada, and Europe whose interests diverged from those of American workers. I'd be at odds with upholders of the orthodox free trade position of the Republican Party. Indeed, some of those people would be my colleagues in the Trump administration. That didn't faze me particularly. I was up for the fight. And I had already been developing a philosophy on trade—based on practice rather than theory—for almost thirty-five years at that point.

I am often asked how I developed my concern for this issue. Why have I dedicated so much of my life to this fight?

In large part, the answer lies in my upbringing in Ashtabula, Ohio—a small industrial city in the uppermost northeastern corner of Ohio on Lake Erie. Ashtabula was thriving when I grew up in the 1950s and 1960s. It had a port that brought in iron ore from the Minnesota Iron Range and then shipped it by rail down to Pittsburgh to be made into steel. It had a vibrant railroad industry. Off of Bridge Street near the harbor, you could see hundreds of hopper cars of iron ore in the process of unloading. Ashtabula also had a lot of small manufacturing jobs, many based at companies that were suppliers to the auto industry in Detroit. These days, the hopper cars aren't unloading much iron ore, as many of the steel industry jobs that relied on that supply have moved overseas. The manufacturing jobs supporting the auto industry in Detroit have also dwindled to a comparative trickle. But back when I was growing up, my hometown was an ordinary, prosperous, bustling American city—one of many such places.

My father was a doctor. His story is an interesting one. Our family—the Lighthizers—originally came to America in 1748. George Lighthizer fought for independence in the American Revolution alongside his sons. According to our family history, he was illiterate and of humble origin. Over the nineteenth century and into the twentieth, the life and livelihood of the Lighthizers was woven into the fabric of American history. My ancestors on that side were farmers and smelters of pig iron. Then, as the industrial revolution transformed the country, many of them became blue-collar workers. My father was born early in the twentieth century and raised in a small town near Steubenville, Ohio. He and his brother were the first in our family to go to college. Their hometown, Mingo Junction, had one steel mill that was the center of economic activity and employed much of the population. My grandfather, the son of a farmer, was a bricklayer. My father worked in the steel mills and then gradually worked his way through college. After graduating from the University of West Virginia in 1933 at the relatively old age of twenty-nine, he went on to medical school—first at West Virginia, then at NYU in New York City. He built a good life for our family.

Like my father, my mother was also the first in her family to attend college—in her case, at the University of Kentucky. Her family was Irish with some Scottish mixed in. My brother and I are thus Irish, Scottish, and German, with a little of everything else. We went to Mother of Sorrows Catholic School in Ashtabula, in the district near the harbor. Our friends were the children of families with blue-collar jobs. Ashtabula had many immigrants from many places—notably, sizable communities from Italy and, interestingly, Finland. There were three Catholic parishes when I was growing up. Our parish had been built in the 1890s by the rapidly growing immigrant community who worked in Ashtabula Harbor. Mount Carmel was a parish largely of Italian immigrants, and nearby there was Saint Joseph's. Now all three parishes are combined into one. Mother of Sorrows Catholic School closed long ago. The building stands empty.

Our house was a couple of miles away—across the street from Lake Erie. I can remember watching the boats heading down Lake Erie toward Ashtabula Harbor. Like most of my friends, I had a summer job every year from the time that I was maybe twelve years old. I worked in the first automated car wash in town. Other years, I bagged groceries in a grocery store. I sometimes caddied at our country club when I got the chance. From my last year in high school through my first year of law school, I spent my summers painting what seemed like an endless series of apartments.

Ashtabula was a good place to grow up in the middle of the twentieth century. I'm reminded of the line from Wilbur Wright (of Wright Brothers fame), who mused, "If I were giving a young man advice as to how he might succeed in life, I would say to him pick out a good father and mother, and begin life in Ohio."[1] But growing up in Ashtabula doesn't hold as much promise these days as it did back then. The city's population peaked in 1970 at about 24,000 people. Since then, many of the jobs have left. A lot of the people left, too, in search of greener pastures somewhere else. Many of those who remain are struggling. Nearly a third of the people of Ashtabula live in poverty. Less than 10 percent of its residents have a college degree. The vast majority have only a high school education or less.

What happened to Ashtabula, and indeed much of the industrial heartland of the Midwest, has several causes but among the largest is poor international trade policy, helped along by the waves of technological change that transformed the nature of many jobs. Surging steel imports hurt the port, the flood of imported Japanese cars cost auto parts manufacturing jobs, and so on. Our country simply does not make many of the things we need anymore. Instead, we buy things from other countries and have them shipped here in an endless flow of container ships.

Think about the things you use every day. How many of them were made in this country by people who live here? Increasingly few.

In the 1960s, I packed up for college. For me, Georgetown University—and later Georgetown Law School—in Washington, DC, was a world far removed from Ashtabula. Both academically and socially, it was exciting and invigorating. I had the sense that my horizons were expanding in every direction. But the disconnect from the concerns of people I knew well was disconcerting and disturbing. In the early 1970s, the currents of trade were already shifting fast. When I went back home during the summers, I could see those effects beginning to play out in people's lives, and I didn't like what I saw. But it was tough to convey the reality of that perspective to the fast-paced world of Georgetown, where resistance to the tides of free trade was largely seen as untenable and antediluvian.

In that elite world, the benefits of globalization were very much in the forefront, while the concerns of those hurt by it were far away and easy to dismiss. The reasoning of the free trade advocates was perfectly clear, but from my viewpoint, their relative priorities on the costs versus benefits seemed seriously askew. Advocates for free trade seemed to accept the growing distress in so many manufacturing-centered communities with the easy assurance of those whose understanding of the calamity was wholly theoretical. It was also hard to dismiss the sense that the proponents of free trade whose voices were heard the most were not trying very hard to see the reality of those costs in the context of the people and families whose lives were affected. Impersonal, inexorable market forces provided an acceptable fig leaf for the turn to globalization that was always the preferred course regardless.

After law school I practiced law at the law firm of Covington and Burling in Washington for a few years. In 1977, after his run for vice president, Senator Robert Dole decided he wanted to hire a young conservative lawyer to help him put together his Senate Finance Committee staff. Elizabeth Dole called a friend of hers at the law firm and that partner recommended me. I met Senator Dole and we liked each other from the start. Few encounters have proved more consequential in my life. A few months later, he offered me the job of staff director for the Republicans and entrusted me with hiring a staff. Over the following years, I worked closely with him, initially on his staff and later in many different forums.

During the time that I worked with Senator Dole (December 1978 to April 1983), he was approaching the peak of his career. He was the ranking member of the Senate Finance Committee, and in 1981 he became its chairman. I became the staff director of the committee. Senator Dole was a smart, tough legislator. We helped write the economic plan of the Reagan administration and then helped get it passed through Congress.

In 1983, I left Senator Dole's staff to accept an appointment as deputy US trade representative (USTR) under Bill Brock in the Reagan administration. Brock was a smart Tennessee politician. He had been a congressman and a senator and had served as the head of the Republican Party that organized the across-the-board sweep of the 1980 election.

By this time, trade was well on its way to becoming a passion for me. The staff at USTR was getting started on a major multilateral round of trade negotiations (the Uruguay Trade Round), and we were also in the throes of negotiating trade agreements on major issues with Japan, including steel and autos. While Ronald Reagan spoke in favor of free trade, in his heart he was always a strong advocate for American national interests. And one prior assumption was always understood: free trade could be a force for our prosperity only if it rested on a level playing field. In a speech on September 23, 1985, President Reagan said:

> Above all else, free trade is, by definition, fair trade. When domestic markets are closed to the exports of others, it is no longer free trade. When governments subsidize their manufacturers and farmers so that they can dump goods in other markets, it is no longer free trade. When governments permit counterfeiting or copying of American products, it is stealing our future, and it is no longer free trade. When governments assist their exporters in ways that violate international laws, then the playing field is no longer level, and there is no longer free trade. When governments subsidize industries for commercial advantage and underwrite costs, placing an unfair burden on competitors, that is not free trade.[2]

President Reagan distinguished between free trade in theory and free trade in practice. He imposed quotas on imported steel, protected Harley-Davidson from Japanese competition, restrained imports of semiconductors and automobiles, took on the overvalued dollar, and pursued similar steps to keep American industry strong during the 1980s. Indeed, after he left office, one group of rabid libertarian free traders said that he was the most protectionist president since Herbert Hoover.[3] I can't hide the fact that I always took that as a compliment.

From 1983 to 1985, I was one of two deputies to the USTR. My colleague had responsibility for the geographic offices—those, for example, that dealt with Asia, Europe, and the Middle East. My responsibilities were the sectoral offices. That means that I was responsible for industry, agriculture, investment, services, and trade policy. It's easy to see that, given that kind of division, both deputies could claim responsibility for almost everything that came into the office. However, in our case, the division of responsibilities worked out well. While my colleague was coordinating our efforts on a multilateral level, I handled most of the actual negotiations with our trading partners. And it was in the process of those trade negotiations that I truly found my wheelhouse.

Under the Reagan administration, our office undertook a number of actions to enforce US rights and fairness in our trading relationships. My first major negotiation was the long-term grain agreement between the Soviet Union and the United States. This corrected President Carter's unfortunate decision to stop our grain sales to the Soviets after they invaded Afghanistan. These were the "Evil Empire" days, and I was among the first senior US officials to travel to Moscow.

My next negotiations involved steel. President Reagan made the strategic decision to take action to limit the imports of specialty steel from a variety of countries around the world because of the threat they posed to American industry. I negotiated those bilateral deals with a team of career staffers from USTR. The president then decided to impose similar limits on carbon steel imports. My team and I negotiated several agreements here as well. Overall, I led the negotiations of about twenty international deals while deputy. During my time at USTR, I focused more and more on negotiations, the unfair practices of our trading partners, growing trade deficits, and the problem of Japanese industrial policy and its effect on US jobs. For a period, I negotiated on a bilateral investment treaty with China. This was 1984, and of course China was not what we see today. We never did come to an agreement, but I had my initial up-close experience with the Middle Kingdom.

One lesson that became crystal clear throughout those trade negotiations: no one gives up anything valuable for nothing. The strategic use of leverage was essential to successful negotiating. It was the potential to impose costs that allowed us to demand action on issues of unfair trade. And a key point of leverage was the credible threat to act unilaterally to impose tariffs. Our bilateral voluntary restraint agreements (VRAs)—that is, agreements in which our trading partners decide to restrain their imports in order to create breathing space for American companies—with Japan and other countries on steel and cars rested on this leverage. We would block their imports if we could not reach a deal. This was a lesson that was to stand us in good stead in the Trump administration, which differed from that of the Reagan administration in significant ways with respect to trade.

The most noteworthy distinction between the Reagan years and the Trump years was that President Trump cared enormously about trade issues. It was one of the major reasons why he chose to run for president. Taking action in this area was something that he thought about every day, whereas for President Reagan, trade had not been a top-level priority—he had many critical domestic and international policy issues on his mind. President Reagan didn't talk about trade or have meetings on it more than a few times a year. The same thing could be said of President Bush and President Obama. But for President Trump, issues of international trade were a key priority that dominated his thoughts, and I quickly came to know the depth of his level of engagement firsthand when I assumed my role as USTR.

The Post-Reagan Years

On September 2, 1987, I was paging through my usual stack of newspapers when I came across a full-page ad on issues of foreign policy and trade. "There's nothing wrong with America's Foreign Defense Policy that a little backbone can't cure," it declared. It was addressed, "To the American People," from Donald J. Trump.

"For decades, Japan and other nations have been taking advantage of the United States," Trump observed. "The world is laughing at American politicians as we protect ships we don't own, carrying oil we don't need, destined for allies who won't help." The letter noted the costs for America of acting as de facto policeman to the world, but it also touched on trade issues because these costs coincided with vast trade deficits. "Over the years, the Japanese, unimpeded by the huge costs of defending themselves (as long as the United States will do it for free), have built a strong and vibrant economy with unprecedented surpluses. . . . It's time for us to end our vast deficits by making Japan, and others who can afford it, pay."

I had been aware of Donald Trump through the 1980s. His larger-than-life personality ensured that. As a young lawyer, I often took the Trump shuttle into New York City. And I was familiar with Trump Towers and his other property interests in New York City. But that letter to America, published in the *New York Times*, the *Washington Post*, and the *Boston Globe*, and paid for by Trump personally at a cost of close to $100,000, was one of the first times I paid serious attention to him on the issue of trade. I realized that his instincts were similar to mine. For the decades afterward, I cheered on his pronouncements on trade and the harm done to our country by unfair imports.

One thing I had begun to realize very early after my arrival at Georgetown was that standing up for American interests on trade was often not a popular opinion in Washington, DC. That rule applied even more so to New York and its financial and investing interests. We had labor advocates in our corner but sometimes few others. The enlightened position was the standard neoclassical case for free trade. This was still the case as late as the 2016 campaign. Anything other than full-throated support for free trade was regarded as a throwback to protectionism and isolationism, as well as an invitation to trade wars. "Isolationism is a recipe for total failure," Harvard professor and Clinton adviser Nicholas Burns said at the time regarding Trump's trade policy.[4]

Proponents of free trade reassure us that the United States is much better off and stronger on balance by opening ourselves to trade. Concern about American workers and communities, as they see it, is shortsighted. New jobs would develop in new industries that would grow. Workers would move to new locations. Government job training would fix any remaining problems. Everything will work out, they said and continue to say. By the time that it became apparent that everything was not working out and that there were devastating costs to many communities, most people in DC didn't worry very much, because it was all happening someplace far away to people they didn't know. Nothing useful could be done to hold back the tides of inexorable market forces. This was all aided, of course, by the fact that many in the Washington business trade associations had become far more concerned with the interests of importers than those of US manufacturers. The lobbying money was on the side of free trade.

Over the years of following Trump's pronouncements on trade, I came to believe that he had good instincts. In the run-up to the 1988 presidential election, there was discussion about the possibility of Donald Trump running for president. I was vice chairman of Senator Dole's campaign that year, and in that capacity, I was keeping track of the issue. I was very much aware of Trump and his criticism of our unfair trade with Japan. I advocated for a similar track for Senator Dole on issues of trade. In 1989, Trump had a well-known interview with Diane Sawyer in which he called for 15 percent to 20 percent tariffs on imports from Japan to get the trade deficit under control. Trump's 1990 book, *Surviving at the Top*, laid out his trade philosophy as well, and his books after that time, including *The America We Deserve* (2000), expanded this philosophy along similar lines.

As the problem with international trade shifted in the 1980s and 1990s from Japan to China, Trump's focus shifted as well. My focus on trade also changed at this time. It was obvious to those of us who were concerned about workers' job losses and trade deficits that the growing problem with China was a much larger issue than the existing issues with Japan. On that topic, I increasingly followed what Trump had to say. He not only understood the underlying issues that we were facing with trade at the time, but he was a practical problem solver. He was knowledgeable, articulate, and passionate on the issues of trade that I considered pivotal.

My law practice in the 1990s and 2000s was largely focused on representing US manufacturers (mostly steel companies) in actions against foreign manufacturers who flooded our market with low-cost, unfairly traded products. We used laws that penalized dumping and subsidization by foreign producers. Essentially, after a litigation process, a duty would be put on the imported product to offset the unfair advantage. These cases were appealed to domestic US courts but also to the dispute resolution process at the WTO in Geneva. It became increasingly obvious that WTO decisions too often were not founded on the trade agreement text and went against our national laws. Problems of unfair trade would not be solved at the WTO. Indeed, it was making matters worse.

After 2000, China became a growing problem, with extensive state ownership, enormous state subsidies, a closed home market, currency manipulation, rampant government-sponsored theft of intellectual property, and every other mercantilist practice. Trade deficits skyrocketed to unprecedented levels. We were allowing China, a foreign adversary, to use all forms of state-sponsored, government-organized unfair trade to run up a more than $270 billion trade surplus with us and to take US jobs in the process. These were the years that American workers were hit by what economists later called the "China shock."[5] It was so severe that even the usual advocates for trade started to get a little nervous.

The deep recession after the financial crisis of 2008 was the only thing that put a dent in the massive trade deficits. But it wasn't enough. We were on an unsustainable path, and no one had a plan to deal with it at the time—except possibly Donald Trump. In 2011, when there was talk of a Trump presidential run, I wrote an op-ed in the *Washington Times* making the case that his "get tough on China" views very much reflected the historical roots of American conservatism and of the Republican Party. (We'll discuss that history in chapter 3.) In the end, of course, we had to wait until 2016 for the presidential run that would end up changing this country's history on trade and, in effect, bringing us back to our roots.

The Trump Candidacy and Presidency

Over the course of the 2016 campaign, Donald Trump spoke about trade at every stop. He talked about the problems with China. He talked about the rip-off that was NAFTA. And he talked about trade deficits and how they were hurting working people. He summed up his position in a definitive speech just outside Pittsburgh in Monessen, Pennsylvania. Working people could see that, as president, Donald Trump would be on their side and that their concerns would no longer be treated as the necessary cost of economic progress.

When Donald Trump first laid out his objectives for trade policy on the presidential campaign trail, a long road lay ahead. Once in office, he faced the enormous challenge of putting the plan into practice with me as USTR. Despite the predictable bends in the road, the hand-wringing from advocates of free trade, the pushback from our trading partners, and the occasional setback in negotiations, we largely stuck with the road map that he had laid out back on that June day in Monessen. And our major trade partners were placed on notice.

President Trump was a great boss, and together we fought to keep his promises. At a cabinet meeting on May 19, 2020, after we had finished most of the milestone agreements, he said: "And one of the people I wanted to get when I was elected was Bob Lighthizer because he had the record and really had the reputation as being the best trade negotiator anywhere in the world that everybody respected. He was the authority. So I got him and you've lived up to your reputation."[6] I said thank you and started to think about that day at Mar-a-Largo three and a half years earlier. The long days had been worth it.

Chapter 2

Where We Are Now

Having spent most of my life thinking about trade policy, I've come to a few basic conclusions. First, the post–World War II strategy of reducing barriers to imports in return for the hope of new exports seriously went off the rails in the 1990s. The United States placed an all-or-nothing bet on free trade in the form of three consecutive deals. Since that time, we have seen the loss of millions of jobs and exploding trade deficits. Second, the United States needs to insist on fair trade in our market and reciprocal access in foreign markets. Decades of poor trade deals have produced neither. Third, we need a policy that assures balanced trade. We cannot afford to continue to transfer our wealth to foreign countries in return for consumer products. These are the realities. The more fundamental questions are, how did we get to this place, and what is the philosophy of trade that will achieve these objectives?

For some, trade is mostly a way to engage on the world stage. One hears about the need for America to use its economic prowess to gain friends and to influence events. We need to trade more—read: import more—so that other countries will like us instead of, say, China. For others, trade is really about obtaining the cheapest products for our consumers. For these people, if the result is the loss of manufacturing and related jobs, that is a fair exchange. Cheap televisions trump American factories.

I feel that most Americans reject both these approaches. For most average people, economic policy and thus trade policy should be about improving the prosperity of our communities, not high-minded foreign policy maneuvering or getting cheap stuff. They want to have better jobs, stronger families, and safer, more prosperous communities. They believe that America's strength is its people as producers. A trade policy that pursues these goals is what we call a trade policy for the common good, and it is what we tried to carry out in the Trump administration. Our objective was no less than to turn around a failed policy that had been prevalent for sixty years. The disconnect between the elites who think primarily about foreign policy or economic efficiency and the vast majority of our people is great. It was time for the people to take back the policy. And for the most part they did.

Common Good Economics

The Trump administration broke with the orthodoxies of free trade religion at times, but contrary to what critics have charged, it did not embrace protectionism and autarky. Nor did it engage in a reactive tit-for-tat approach. Instead, it sought to balance the benefits of trade liberalization with policies that prioritized the dignity of work and more generally the common good. The goal was increasing the number of high-quality jobs paying higher wages in the United States.

Under this policy, the Office of the US Trade Representative took aggressive and, at times, controversial actions to protect American jobs. But it did so without sparking unsustainable trade wars and while continuing to expand US exporters' access to foreign markets. The United States–Mexico–Canada Agreement (USMCA), which was first signed in 2018 and entered into force on July 1, 2020, offers the best and most comprehensive illustration of a trade policy oriented toward the common good. (We'll discuss the negotiations for this agreement in chapters 12–14.) This new way of thinking also motivated the Trump administration's policies toward China and the World Trade Organization (WTO), as we'll discuss in chapter 4. In addressing other challenges, the administration always had the same goal: a balanced, worker-focused trade policy that served the common good for Americans and, where possible, achieved a bipartisan consensus.

I want to be clear. It is certainly not my position that post–World War II trade orthodoxy has been uniformly bad for America. Our country is the second largest exporting nation after China, and overseas markets help support millions of American jobs. Global competition is essential to maintaining technological superiority. Our companies must go head-to-head with foreign companies to remain sharp, and they must often integrate cutting-edge overseas technology to improve their own.

Further collaboration in research and development with friendly, secure nations is important. The profitability of the American agriculture sector depends on exports. Our services sectors run substantial surpluses every year, and we lead in technology, financial services exports, and a number of other areas. America has a number of competitive advantages, and we make them count.

The US services surplus is very significant for our country. However, it is important to understand what that means. First, compared to the goods deficits, the services surpluses are small. Second, the services numbers are much less reliable than the goods numbers. By their nature they are more difficult to count than goods crossing a border. To create this data, the Department of Commerce sends out a survey to businesses in these industries and then it guestimates the imports and exports based on the responses. Many things that readers may not think are exports are still counted as exports. For example, foreign students coming to our universities and foreign tourists are both large services export categories. Finally, it is important to know that over 80 percent of our services surplus is accounted for by royalty payments for the use of intellectual property paid back to US companies by their foreign subsidiaries and financial services in which the United States has a large competitive advantage, but which also produce relatively more employment overseas than they do at home. In fact, the royalty payments are often part of a US tax-avoidance scheme that has no positive effect on our employment or the well-being of our country.

Further, trade policy has helped build our great American economy and contributed to making the world safer. Exports to US consumers rapidly helped Japan and West Germany rebuild and become responsible members of the world community. The tearing down of trade barriers within Europe, starting with the establishment of the European Coal and Steel Community in 1951, brought the democracies of Western Europe closer together, setting a template for future cooperation. Despite the benefits of our post–World War II trade policy to Western Europe, the US commitment to free trade in this period was not so unbridled as to produce neglect of Cold War challenges. Rather, the costs and benefits of trade liberalization were calibrated relative to national interests and changing political circumstances. No one would have argued for free trade and economic interdependence with the Soviet Union.

The Berlin Wall Falls . . . and So Does Our Guard

After the fall of the Soviet Union in 1989, however, the United States began to throw caution to the wind. Many believed that the end of autocracy and the triumph of democratic market capitalism was inevitable. This post–Cold War push for unfettered trade liberalization did yield some benefits. For example, lower trade barriers and the proliferation of free trade agreements (FTAs) in recent decades swelled the profits of many multinational corporations. That benefited not only CEOs but also middle-class Americans who hold equities in their retirement accounts. Trade also helped revive many of the country's great urban centers. Cheap imports and the rise of big-box and online retailers have made an ever-expanding class of consumer goods available to the masses. And in China, India, and throughout the rest of the developing world, millions of people have been lifted out of poverty.

The thinking at the time was that this trade liberalization had no downside and that with the fall of the Soviet Union in the rearview mirror, the whole world, including Communist China, was being swept up on a rising wave of liberal democracy. Unlike most waves, however, this one was somehow never supposed to crash back down to earth. There was no need for caution about the prospects of the proposed plan of trade liberalization on steroids, the end goal of which was access to low-wage Chinese workers and the emerging middle class of Chinese consumers.

The policies of the 1990s and early 2000s embodied this free trade mentality. Under the Clinton administration, the United States doubled down on free trade in a way that served the interests of global corporations and foreign countries at the expense of American workers and US national interests. The United States ended up with the North American Free Trade Agreement (NAFTA), which went into effect on January 1, 1994. This agreement allowed for the removal of most trade barriers to goods and services flowing between the United States, Mexico, and Canada. Presidents George H. W. Bush and Clinton fought hard for it, but it was never popular. Next came the Uruguay Round trade agreement, which was also unpopular. Among other things, it produced the WTO. And to complete the trifecta in 2000, the United States gave China permanent Most Favored Nation treatment. The following year, China joined the WTO. This was a riverboat gamble—dramatically opening our markets would supposedly lead to prosperity and world peace. Thank you, Mr. Clinton and America's elites.

First cracks and then holes soon started to appear in the wall of globalist delusions that could not be plastered over by rhetoric. Between 2000 and 2016, the United States lost nearly five million manufacturing jobs. Median household income stagnated. And in the places that prosperity left behind, the fabric of society frayed. Since the mid-1990s, the United States has faced an epidemic of what the economists Anne Case and Angus Deaton have termed "deaths of despair." They have found that among white middle-aged adults who lack a college education—a demographic that has borne much of the brunt of offshoring—deaths from cirrhosis of the liver increased by 50 percent between 1999 and 2013, suicides increased by 78 percent, and drug and alcohol overdoses increased by 323 percent. From 2014 to 2017, the increase in deaths of despair led to the first decrease in life expectancy in the United States over a three-year period since the 1918 flu pandemic.[1]

Trade has not been the sole cause of the recent loss of manufacturing jobs or of the attendant societal distress. Automation, productivity gains, foreign currency manipulation, and the financial crisis of 2008 have played key roles as well. But it cannot be denied that the offshoring of jobs from high- to low-wage places has devastated communities in the American Rust Belt and elsewhere.

There Was Never Such a Thing as "Free Trade"

Today, the tide has turned against the argument for unfettered free trade, in no small part because of the changes we made in the Trump administration. More broadly, evidence and experience have shown us that free trade is a unicorn—a figment of the Anglo-American imagination. No one really believes in it outside of countries in the Anglo-American world, and no one practices it. After the lessons of the past couple decades or so, few believe in it even within that world, save for some hardcore ideologues. It is a theory that never worked anywhere.

All the great economies were built behind a wall of protection and often with government money. The British industrial revolution was aided by a wall of tariffs. Likewise, the late-nineteenth-century explosion of American industry was the product of protectionism and often subsidies. Can anyone imagine the great American railroads being built without the grant of free land per mile? Similarly, the manufacturing countries of Japan, Germany, and now China all benefited during their development from tariffs, other barriers, and subsidies of one kind or another. It is important to remember that no country became great by consuming. They became great by producing.

The Limits of Interdependence

Advocates of free trade frequently argue that enhanced international trade corresponds with greater international peace. This point of view traces back to the post–World War II period. Before World War II, tariffs were high by contemporary standards. From the 1820s until the late 1940s, the weighted average US tariff (which measures duties collected as a percentage of total imports) rarely dipped below 20 percent. President Franklin Roosevelt and the New Deal Congress ushered in a period of relative tariff liberalization in the 1930s, but even then the tariff rate remained in the mid- to high teens throughout the decade. After the war, however, both Democrats and Republicans came to champion tariff reduction as a means of preventing yet another conflict, arguing that trade fostered interdependence between nations. Trade liberalization came to be seen not just as a tool of economic policy but also as a path to perpetual peace. Indeed, Cordell Hull, the secretary of state from 1933 to 1944 in the Roosevelt administration and lead architect of its trade policy, claimed that his philosophy centered on the idea that "unhampered trade dovetailed with peace; [and] high tariffs, trade barriers, and unfair economic competition, with war."[2]

The need for the United States to temper the often uncritical post–World War II enthusiasm for interdependence at all costs has never been greater than it is now, in the face of the Chinese threat. We need to remember that, historically speaking, interdependence does not always lead to peace. In the United States, economic ties between the North and the South did not prevent the Civil War. Global trade grew rapidly in the years right before World War I; exports as a percentage of global GDP peaked at nearly 14 percent in 1913, a record that would hold until the 1970s. Likewise, it would be hard to argue that the rise of Germany as a major exporter in the late nineteenth century helped pacify that country in the first half of the twentieth. Japan's dependence on raw materials from the United States motivated its attack on Pearl Harbor. More recently, as we will discuss in chapter 4, China's accession to the WTO in 2001—which was supposed to make the country a model global citizen—was followed by massive investments in its military capabilities and territorial expansion in the South China Sea. And certainly the great trade between Ukraine and Russia did not stop Putin's invasion in 2022.

On the flip side, conflict over trade is not always destabilizing or a threat to broader foreign policy objectives. The North Atlantic Treaty Organization (NATO) alliance survived the tariff hikes associated with both the 1960s "chicken war," when the United States clashed with France and West Germany over poultry duties, and the 1970s "Nixon shock," when the United States effectively abandoned the Bretton Woods system. The United States and Japan fought about trade in the 1980s, but their bilateral security alliance stayed strong.

Countries, like people, compartmentalize between separate issues. There may be situations when it is appropriate to make concessions on trade to achieve broader diplomatic aims, but one should keep in mind that such bargains can prove costly in the long run. Letting India join the General Agreement on Tariffs and Trade (the precursor to the WTO) in 1948 with nearly a third of its industrial tariffs unbound, for example, no doubt made sense to Cold Warriors, who thought that it would help bring India into the US camp. Yet the negative repercussions of that decision persist to this day, now that India has become one of the world's largest economies and, at times, a troublesome trading partner for the United States. Over the years, such concessions have piled up.

Sometimes the tendency to view trade through the lens of diplomacy has led to excess timidity and passivity. The most vivid example is the failure of the George W. Bush and Obama administrations to meaningfully confront China's market-distorting subsidies and policy of forcing foreign companies to share their technology. But there are many others. For instance, until the Trump administration took office, the United States had never invoked the procedures for enforcing environmental commitments it had bargained for in its free trade agreements. The Trump administration used those tools to crack down on illegal timber harvesting in Peru and illegal fishing in South Korea.

Although the United States should not wield its economic leverage blithely, fear of rocking the diplomatic boat cannot be an excuse for inaction. Despite the "sky is falling" rhetoric that greeted many of the administration's policies, the United States remained the most open of the world's major economies throughout Donald Trump's presidency. Even with the tariffs imposed against China, along with efforts to rescue the domestic steel, aluminum, and solar power industries, the United States' weighted average tariff was only 2.85 percent in 2019 (and 1.3 percent for imports from countries other than China). That's slightly higher than the 1.5 percent rate that prevailed during the last year of the Obama administration but still lower than a comparable figure for the European Union: the 3.0 percent weighted average rate it imposes on imports from other WTO members.

History will judge the ultimate effectiveness of the Trump administration's targeted duties. But experience has already proven wrong those who said that the administration's actions would inevitably lead to a 1930s-style trade war. Broadly speaking, the geopolitical case for free trade is anachronistic. Tariffs don't necessarily prompt trade wars, and removing tariffs often does little to prevent actual war.

The Efficiency Obsession

Some cite efficiency as a rationale for free trade. For adherents of this faith, the sole objective of trade policy is market efficiency. Lower tariffs and nontariff barriers reduce the costs of producing and distributing goods and services; that, in turn, makes society as a whole better off—or so the argument goes. Of course, there are advantages to lower prices when considering Americans as consumers. The problem is that adherents of this view seldom consider how this single-minded pursuit of efficiency affects the men and women who actually do the producing.

According to the definitions preferred by these efficiency-minded free traders, the downside of trade for American producers is not evidence against their approach but rather is an unfortunate but necessary side effect. That's because free trade is always taken as a given, not as an approach to be questioned. Rather than envisioning the type of society desired and then, in light of that conception of the common good, fashioning a trade policy to fit that vision, economists tend to do the opposite: they start from the proposition that free trade should reign and then argue that society should adapt. Most acknowledge that lowering trade barriers causes economic disruption, but very few suggest that the rules of trade should be calibrated to help society better manage those effects. On the right, libertarians deny that these bad effects are a problem, because the benefits of cheap consumer goods for the masses supposedly outweigh the costs, and factory workers, in their view, can be retrained to write computer programs. On the left, progressives promote trade adjustment assistance and other wealth-transfer schemes as a means of smoothing globalization's rough edges.

As I discuss in the next section, neither response really solves the problems of free trade for the working class. A big part of elites' misunderstanding of the situation is that they have no appreciation for the social component of work. Those obsessed with efficiency tend to see employment simply as a means of allocating resources and ensuring production. In so doing, they greatly undervalue the personal dignity that individuals derive from meaningful work. Commentators from Pope Leo XIII in the nineteenth century to Arthur Brooks and Oren Cass today have written eloquently about the central role of work in a well-ordered society. Doing honest work for a decent wage instills feelings of self-worth that come from being needed and contributing to society. Stable, remunerative employment reinforces good habits and discourages bad ones. That makes human beings into better spouses, parents, neighbors, and citizens. By contrast, the loss of personal dignity that comes from the absence of stable, well-paying employment is not something that can be compensated for either by increased consumption of low-cost imported goods or by welfare checks.

None of this is to suggest that efficiency should be irrelevant. But it should not be the sole factor in trade policy, and certainly not an object of idolatrous devotion, as some have made it. When it comes to taxes, health care, environmental regulation, and other issues, policy makers routinely balance efficiency with other competing goals. They should do the same for trade. As with everything else, there are trade-offs involved in the context of trade.

In recent years, however, the fixation on efficiency has caused many to ignore the downsides of trade liberalization. Particularly as elites came to accept free trade as an article of faith, businesses found that they could send jobs abroad without attracting much negative publicity. In fact, General Electric's hard-charging CEO from 1981 to 2001, the late Jack Welch, told suppliers at one point that his company would stop doing business with them if they *weren't* outsourcing jobs. "Supply chain relocation" became a cure-all peddled by management consulting firms. Unfortunately, as COVID-19 has made painfully apparent, many companies caught up in the outsourcing frenzy failed to appreciate the risks. They ignored possible transportation problems, input disruptions, and the real possibility of foreign government policy shifts and instability.

Why Retraining, Services, and Technology Jobs Aren't the Answer

Those that claim that the benefits of interdependence or efficiency justify the costs free trade places on the American working class often argue this negative impact can be offset by retraining that helps workers move into new service sector or technology jobs. In theory, retraining may sound attractive, but this phenomenon has failed to materialize. Compared with those who lost their jobs in earlier periods of economic change, displaced workers in modern, developed economies typically have fewer and less attractive options. Historically speaking, this was not always the case. In the United Kingdom in the nineteenth century, for example, the repeal of the protectionist Corn Laws prompted agricultural workers to flee the countryside for industrializing urban areas where factory jobs were waiting. By contrast, the American factory workers who were displaced beginning in the 1990s either had nowhere to go or ended up working in low-skill, low-paying service jobs.

Rather than attempt to reverse these trends, some argue that mature economies should increase their reliance on services, the digital economy, and research and development. These sectors contribute greatly to the United States' competitive edge, and the service sector employs most Americans today and will likely continue to do so for the foreseeable future. At the same time, however, it is difficult to imagine that the US economy can serve the needs of working people without a thriving manufacturing sector.

The technology sector, for all its virtues, is not a source of high-paying jobs for working people. Over half of the United States' roughly 250 million adults lack a college diploma. Historically, manufacturing jobs have been the best source of stable, well-paying employment for this cohort. Perhaps with massive new investments in education, former autoworkers could be taught to code. Even so, there probably wouldn't be enough jobs to employ them all. Apple, Facebook, Google, and Netflix collectively employ just over 300,000 people—less than half the number that General Motors alone employed in the 1960s.

Moreover, the service and technology jobs most accessible to working people, such as data entry and call center jobs, are themselves vulnerable to offshoring. Economists have estimated that nearly forty million service sector jobs in the United States could eventually be sent overseas.[3] That's more than three times the number of current manufacturing jobs in the country. People without college degrees face increasingly steep obstacles to obtaining stable, well-paying jobs. In sum, the United States has not taken adequate measures to put its own workers first.

Why Persistent, Long-term Trade Deficits Matter for the United States

On a different front, our long-term massive deficits tell the story of a country that has failed to protect its own interests. The deterioration in America's trade balance since the early 1990s has been precipitous. The pace of decline accelerated after the birth of the WTO in 1995 and again after China's accession in 2001. From a starting goods deficit of less than $80 billion in 1991, the deficit reached $1.1 trillion in 2021 and has deteriorated further in 2022. Our trade deficit grew by a factor of fourteen, while our GDP grew by a factor of four. The win-win situation promised by advocates of free trade has never materialized.

The United States has run huge consecutive trade deficits for decades. All told, we have accumulated more than $11 trillion in trade deficits since just 2000. None of this is free. We are trading our assets for short-term consumption. Yet incredibly there is a debate about whether this matters. Ordinary Americans know on a commonsense level that deficits matter in life. If you make more than you spend, you get richer. If you spend more than you make, you get poorer. Only some economists seem to have trouble with this simple concept.

Free trade enthusiasts, and those influenced by their arguments, take comfort in the following trope: "I run a trade deficit with my barber; since both of us are better off as a result, even though he gave me no money back, this shows why trade deficits are benign." However, a deficit with the barber is one thing, but if I run a deficit with the barber, the butcher, the baker, and everyone else, including my employer, the situation is altogether different. Moreover, long-term trade deficits must be financed through asset sales, which can prove unsustainable over time. The man paying his barber can pay with a cash surplus, but what if he starts trading assets—that is, things he owns that he expects to lead to future wealth? The trade deficit that he runs with providers of goods and services he consumes is benign if it is offset by the surplus he runs with his employer through the sale of his labor. But the situation may prove unsustainable if he's funding his consumption by taking out a second mortgage on his home. And that is essentially what the United States has been doing over the past three decades by running a trade deficit year after year.

It is not my position that all trade deficits are harmful. Clearly, if a country runs a deficit one year and a surplus the next, no harm is done. The surplus will offset the deficit, and all is good. Likewise, for one country to run a bilateral trade deficit with a second country and a surplus with a third is fine. They offset each other. Indeed, all three countries could benefit by increasing efficiency and maximizing the allocation of resources among them. What concerns me, and motivated our work in the Trump administration, is running huge trade deficits with the entire world year after year for decades.

There are two exceptions to the understanding that bilateral deficits don't matter. First, the content of trade can be important. For example, it is not in the interest of a large manufacturing economy such as the United States to ship basic materials overseas in exchange for manufactured goods. This makes the United States less developed and less rich, and it costs millions of high-paying manufacturing jobs. Historically, this is the colonial relationship. The United States should not be the miner and forester for other countries. We benefit from having value added in our country. Also, of course, we can't be dependent on other countries for the manufacturing of products that are critical for national security.

The second exception to the principle that bilateral deficits don't matter is that running up gigantic trade deficits with one's geopolitical adversary is particularly stupid. In our case, the United States ships hundreds of billions of dollars' worth of our wealth to China every year. This helps them build up their economy, build up their military, and have leverage over the political situation in the United States. It makes them more powerful in the eyes of all world leaders. I'm not sure there's an example in world history in which two rivals—indeed, some would say enemies— have had such a lopsided economic relationship. It is fair to say China is challenging us because we gave them the money to do it. Clearly, during the Cold War with the Soviet Union, we never transferred such money. Had we done so, we might have lost to them.

Free trade economists counter our concern about these persistent huge trade deficits by arguing that these deficits don't matter because they are just the other side of the capital account. Their notion is that dollars earned in these surpluses must come back to the United States in the form of investment. Some economists even go so far as to argue foolishly that this is an indication of a strong economy. Running up big deficits means that our consumers are spending more than the consumers of other countries. This of course assumes that free trade actually exists and that foreign government practices aren't keeping our products out (but that is an argument for later in the book).

The real problem with this line of economic analysis is that it assumes that it doesn't matter who owns the assets of our country. Indeed, these surplus dollars do come back to the United States. But those dollars aren't purchasing goods and services, they're purchasing our assets. They come back when foreigners buy US equity, debt, and real estate. When they buy these assets, the new owners get the future earnings of those assets, as well, for all time.

As Warren Buffett pointed out in his famous 2003 article about "Thriftville and Squanderville" ("America's Growing Trade Deficit Is Selling the Nation Out from under Us"), there is a compounding effect in huge trade deficits.[4] That is something we could call negative compounding. The people in the foreign country who buy our assets own those assets forever, with the obvious effect that they get the profit from those assets year after year. That profit compounds, and the effects of even one year's trade deficit multiply over time as profits continue. Added to this is the fact that we have seen huge $500 billion to $1 trillion trade deficits year after year, so we have both an accumulation of trade deficits and a compounding negative multiplier on each trade deficit.

So how big is the problem? There is something called the net investment position of a country. That is how much a country owns in all other countries (all-inclusive—stocks, bonds, real estate) compared to how much all other countries own in that country (all-inclusive). For the

United States, it would be how much US citizens own around the world compared to how much foreign citizens own in the United States. It's not a stretch to say that the country with the most positive net investment is the richest.

The net investment position of the United States was positive and very high for decades. Indeed, we were the richest country in the world by this measure for most of the twentieth century. In the last thirty years, however, that number has changed very dramatically. When Mr. Buffett made his complaint about our rising persistent trade deficits back in 2003, the negative net investment of the United States was about $2.5 trillion. It is now $18 trillion. In other words, foreign interests own $18 trillion more of American debt, equity, and real estate than we own within them. That means that their children will receive and can invest all of that wealth and that our children cannot. With $18 trillion, you could buy most of the top hundred companies in America and get some change.

Now keep in mind that none of this was supposed to be possible. In the days when gold facilitated trade, a country would run out of gold before they had a big deficit. In the current period of floating currencies, the assumption, most famously articulated by Milton Friedman while advocating for a transition to such a system in the 1950s, has always been that a country's currency would adjust to reflect its trade position and to move it back toward balance.[5] So a country that ran large trade deficits for a few years would find less demand for their currency and their currency's value would drop. This would then make it very difficult for that country to import and easy for it to export in terms of its domestic currency. Therefore, the weak currency would help correct the trade imbalance. Indeed, we see this occurring regularly around the world.

The problem is that this self-correcting mechanism has not applied to the US dollar. We have run trillions of dollars of trade deficits over a relatively brief period of time without our currency weakening substantially. We can debate what the cause of this is. One possible cause is currency manipulation by our trading partners, and surely this is at least among the reasons. Japan weakened its currency to gain competitive advantage.

China certainly has. Likewise, other Asian countries have followed the example. A second reason is that the dollar, at least now, has an elevated status among currencies. It is the reserve currency, and it is often the safe-haven currency. That means that in times of political or economic crisis, people around the world will buy dollars so that they will maintain their personal wealth. We have most recently seen this with the Russia-Ukraine war, where the dollar surged and was at parity with the euro and there are 137 yen to the dollar. This puts upward pressure on the price of the dollar and also keeps it from adjusting. The high dollar makes imports cheaper and contributes to the trade deficit.

Contrary to what some might say, none of this is inconsistent with the basic understanding of classical economists. Adam Smith and David Ricardo both did their analysis about trade with the assumption that trade with other countries would ultimately be balanced. The same is true if you look at the great debate between John Maynard Keynes and Friedrich Hayek. None of these men would have assumed that a country could ever run decades of gigantic trade deficits and survive.

Another consequence of these persistent deficits is that they contribute to financial booms and bubbles. When we run these huge deficits, the dollars come back but not necessarily to the most productive investments. They often go disproportionately into particularly liquid assets, thus running up the price. For example, foreign central banks looking for "safe" assets to buy in the early 2000s bought up the obligations of government-sponsored enterprises, such as Fannie Mae and Freddie Mac, which were major guarantors of subprime home mortgages. Eventually, the fundamentals catch up and the bubble bursts. Many think this phenomenon was a contributing factor to the housing bubble and its disastrous collapse in 2008.

Huge persistent trade deficits are making the United States poorer. The real question is, what can we do about it? There have been three prominent suggestions. Mr. Buffett proposed requiring an import certificate to import goods into the United States. These certificates could only be obtained from exporters. Another idea is to put a surcharge on inward investment. So when these dollars come back, they will buy less. This would essentially lower the value of the dollar. My solution is that we should put in place tariffs on imports to offset what would be the over-valuation of our currency. These tariffs could come or go depending on the size of the deficit. They could also be flexibly applied to avoid unduly regressive effects on American consumers.

It is important to note that huge persistent trade imbalances make the entire global economy worse off. As Professor Michael Pettis of Peking University and the coauthor of *Trade Wars Are Class Wars* argues, countries should export in order to import and increase consumption and the standard of living for their people. This is how comparative advantage and the added economic value of trade is supposed to work. Over time in a properly functioning global market, all countries will be near balance. When a country runs huge, persistent trade surpluses, its domestic policies are taking resources away from its own citizens by reducing their consumption and giving the resources to its manufacturing sector to increase exports and ultimately their ownership of trading partners' assets.[6] Indeed, in 2021, China's household expenditures (consumption) as a percent of its GDP was just 38 percent, as compared with a global average of 63 percent. This is one of the weakest consumption levels of a major economy.[7] Policies that create this result include currency manipulation, targeted government spending on production capacity and related infrastructure, import restraints, an exploitative banking system, labor immobility, wage suppression, and similar schemes. This is unfair trade. It results in the workers of the surplus country being worse off because of decreased consumption and reduced wages and the workers in the deficit country also being worse off because of lost jobs and lower income. Of course, the owners of production in the surplus country (such as the Chinese Communist Party and its affiliates) get richer, as do the importers in the deficit country.

These persistent surplus countries are the real protectionists. Actions taken by a deficit country to reduce these surpluses, such as the Buffett plan, the investment surcharge, or imposing tariffs, actually help the market function by reducing the impacts of unfair trade by surplus countries. This can be thought of as an application of the famous economic "theory of the second best," which asserts that in a situation where a particular distortion cannot be removed in an interdependent market, the most efficient possible outcome can be achieved only by introducing other, countervailing distortions that bring the system to a higher overall equilibrium.[8] My proposed flexible regime of offsetting tariffs by the United States would improve long-term global market efficiency, not reduce it. Small groups of wealthy American importers may be worse off, but the trading system as a whole benefits, and American workers are better off because of increased employment and wages.

Why Free Trade Agreements Don't Necessarily Work Well for the United States

Free traders regularly complain that the United States is not pursuing more free trade agreements. An FTA, in the words of the International Trade Administration, is simply "an agreement between two or more countries where the countries agree on certain obligations that affect trade in goods and services, and protections for investors and intellectual property rights, among other topics."[9] The perception of those who argue for FTAs is that more agreements mean more trade, and that is good. The reality is quite different. Granting easier access to our market with tariff reductions has often not been helpful to us. We are the biggest market in the world, and often the result of an FTA has been more imports into the United States and no real increase in our exports. This is because most FTAs fail to address the unfair trade practices of our trading partners in a meaningful and enforceable way. Many of our FTA partners manipulate their currency, give subsidies to their manufacturers, and maintain extensive non-tariff barriers, such as discriminatory regulatory requirements, which are harder to detect than traditional protectionism. All these things make American producers less competitive in those markets. This is compounded by the chronically overvalued US dollar discussed earlier. Furthermore, the fact that other countries use a value added tax (VAT) helps their exporters and protects their domestic production (this is covered in chapter 17). For all these reasons, promised increases in US exports from new FTAs have repeatedly failed to materialize.[10]

When we were considering an FTA with the United Kingdom in 2020, I called several manufacturing CEOs and asked what I could do to increase our exports to Britain. The short answer was that, for the most part, tariffs are already low and patterns of trade are set. They could not identify any significant potential for new sales. I always tried to analyze specifically where improvements would come from proposed changes. Generally, staff would just look at tariff models (most of which have repeatedly been proven wrong[11]) and then come up with presumed benefits without tying them to real products.

The one exception is that in some cases we could see new agricultural sales. This sector has been so protected around the world that market opening can help. The numbers are not large, but the sales can help specific products. We reasoned that rather than sacrifice manufacturing jobs to obtain new farm sales, we should just go to the countries keeping our competitive products out and demand more access. This was our approach in the Trump administration. Countries with enormous trade surpluses with the United States have a lot more to lose from our taking concessions away. We have leverage and should use it.

There is very little actual trade benefit to the United States in the form of real efficiency gains from trade agreements. Back in the early 1990s, economist Dani Rodrik of Harvard explored why developing nations had turned to trade liberalization and what they stood to gain in terms of efficiency and redistribution.[12] His results showed that the redistribution of income resulting from the turn to free trade in developing countries outweighed the efficiency gains. In a later work, he invoked the example of the United States to explain the ramifications of his earlier finding, remarking that "in an economy like the United States, where average tariffs are below 5 percent, a move to complete free trade would reshuffle more than $50 of income among different groups for each dollar of efficiency or 'net' gain created!"[13] Essentially, new free trade agreements help consumers by about $1 and take $50 from producers and give it to importers. There is no way that is in the national interest. We need to prioritize producers, and that means reversing the hollowing out of our manufacturing capabilities.

Why Manufacturing Makes a Difference

In places where editorial boards, economics faculties, and other clever people meet to ponder the future, there is near consensus that the United States is heading toward post-industrialization, that manufacturing was just a passing phase in economic development, and that we'll happily be a services economy. Like so many things that they talk about at their gatherings, this myth is complete nonsense. No great economy in the world has ever given up on manufacturing. To the contrary, they are all for the most part based on it. The vast majority of international trade is in manufactured goods and agriculture. The best jobs for high school graduates are in manufacturing. Most innovation in our economy is in this area. A prosperous, successful future needs a flourishing manufacturing sector.

The underestimation of manufacturing has been going on for a long time. Back in 2010, former Intel CEO Andrew Grove wrote an article titled "How America Can Create Jobs."[14] In it, he raised a red flag about our "general undervaluing of manufacturing—the idea that as long as 'knowledge work' stays in the U.S., it doesn't matter what happens to factory jobs." Grove's point was that in losing manufacturing jobs, the United States also "broke the chain of experience that is so important in technological evolution. As happened with batteries, abandoning today's 'commodity' manufacturing can lock you out of tomorrow's emerging industry." In every economy, a great deal of innovation comes from manufacturing, and this innovation usually takes place very close to the place of manufacturing. The engineers on the ground are the ones who incorporate much of what we call productivity gains.

Today the lively debate about the importance of manufacturing in our economy continues, but, increasingly, those who argue that manufacturing does not matter are on the defensive. Of course, all jobs matter, and the other sectors of our economy beyond manufacturing also received an enormous amount of attention in our administration.

In the United States, while manufacturing represents about 11 percent of GDP, it is far more important as a driver of the economy than that number might suggest. According to a McKinsey Global Institute report, manufacturing is responsible for 20 percent of the country's capital investment, 30 percent of productivity growth, 60 percent of exports, and 70 percent of business research and development.[15] Innovation disproportionately comes from the manufacturing sector. Further, the GDP number understates the impact of manufacturing, because estimates show that each new manufacturing job helps create up to seven additional jobs in services and related industries.[16]

Here, as I often do in analyzing a problem, I would ask the commonsense question: What creates wealth in a country?

In large part, prosperity comes from the agriculture, manufacturing, and mining (including oil production) industries. These add value to the country in a real sense, and in a prospective sense because it is hard for a country to innovate with respect to products that it doesn't even make. Many services industries largely move wealth around within the country. Think of health care. While it is enormously important, it doesn't create wealth for the nation. The same could be said of the retail industry. It can make some people rich, but it cannot sustain a people.

We need to create value to buy things from importers. Of course, some services are exportable, such as banking or professional services, but most are not (think food services or health care). In all likelihood, the actual manufacturing employment number is much larger. A lot of what used to be called manufacturing—such as the back-office work of plant- and production-related accounting, public relations, and other manufacturing-related services—is now often outsourced and therefore don't count in the manufacturing numbers. So many of what we call services jobs would not exist in the United States if it were not for the foundation provided by manufacturing.

The fact is that all of the world's large prosperous economies have, and have long had, a substantial manufacturing element. This is true of the four biggest economies in the world—the United States, China, Germany, and Japan.

Manufacturing is also particularly important for the employment of high school educated men and women. It is very often their most likely ticket to the middle class. Manufacturing jobs generally pay higher wages, as was detailed by Susan Helper, Timothy Krueger, and Howard Wial in a major Brookings report on the value provided by the manufacturing sector.[17] Stable manufacturing jobs are a primary way for people without college degrees to comfortably support themselves and their families, while enjoying the sense of dignity and pride that comes from making things. In Trenton, New Jersey, which used to be notable for its manufacturing, there is a bridge featuring large letters reading "Trenton Makes—The World Takes." No bridge would ever boast of a city or, for that matter, a country that takes rather than makes, and for good reason.

The notion of citizens as producers—and owners—is vital not just to people's standard of living at any given moment but also to the civic pride, civilizational confidence, and prudent management of productive assets that all play a role in the long-term common good. Here, we must emphasize the difference between short-term good and long-term good. Consumption offers short-term gains in the form of things such as new cars and the latest appliances. Production, however, is about the long-term economic capacity of the country, which bears directly on our capacity to defend ourselves militarily.

The United States must have the ability to manufacture its own military equipment. This includes high-tech military equipment. Any country that cannot manufacture its own such equipment is vulnerable to interruptions of equipment supply during times of conflict. Similarly, we need to control the manufacture of the pharmaceuticals and medical supplies that are particularly needed during health care crises, such as the COVID-19 pandemic. We also need ready and sustainable access to core industrial inputs, such as steel, that are essential to any rapid military buildup or other government response in a crisis situation such as war or a major natural disaster.

Even in ordinary times, manufacturing is invaluable for national economic health beyond its own sector. Importantly, manufacturing is responsible for productivity increases in the services sector. It is innovation in manufactured products such as computers and semiconductors, for example, that has allowed our economy to become more efficient both directly and by providing a platform for software and other tools that rely on such improvements in underlying hardware. Manufacturing-driven innovation thus helps all the services sectors from health care to travel.

Additionally, manufacturing is also key to trade deficit reduction. While services exports are important, they are only a small fraction of our international trade. Exports in manufacturing are nine times bigger than services exports. Further, manufacturing exports even proportionally create more jobs at home. Services exports, in contrast, often create jobs in the export market with limited employment impact domestically.

Finally, manufacturing is particularly important because it makes a disproportionately large contribution to environmental sustainability. According to analysis in the Brookings manufacturing report, the "clean economy" is nearly three times as dependent on manufacturing as the overall economy is. Further, of the clean economy's 2.7 million jobs in 2012, Brookings estimates that 26 percent are in manufacturing, and overall manufacturing is a much smaller percent of jobs. This is particularly true, the report points out, in specific clean technologies such as electric vehicle technology, energy- and water-efficient appliances and machinery, green chemicals, and renewable energy generation.[18]

The Challenge of Dealing with China

No discussion of our trade policy would be complete without considering China. I discuss US trading relations with China in depth later in this book, but for now it is sufficient to say that the United States made a crucial mistake when it decided to treat China's non-market, Communist economy the same way it treats the economies of our democratic, free market allies. As part two of this book will show, a nation cannot treat its chief geopolitical adversary as just another market participant. In the Trump administration, we began the process of changing our economic relationship with China through a series of tariffs put in place to counteract their economic predation.

The Challenges Ahead

We changed the course of trade policy during my time working for President Trump by focusing on American workers and innovation. We aggressively used trade enforcement tools that had sat on the shelf for decades. We negotiated massive trade agreements to force manufacturing back to America. We put tariffs on imports from China. We put the interests of working people first in every decision we made. Our critics said the world would blow up if we did any one of these things. But they were wrong. Before the onslaught of COVID-19, millions of new jobs had been created—including hundreds of thousands of manufacturing jobs. These were the same jobs that President Obama had proclaimed gone forever. One would need a "magic wand" to bring them back.[19] I guess President Trump found that wand.

Ours was an America First trade policy. The real family income in the United States rose in the year before COVID-19 by 6.8 percent, the largest gain in our history. American workers had a raise. The trade deficit was down, and the bilateral deficit with China was trimmed from the year before in six consecutive quarters. In fact, our course correction away from blind adherence to the tenets of free trade has steered us in a positive direction that the Biden administration has to some extent continued to follow. The fact is that trade is an issue on which it is possible to achieve broad, bipartisan consensus in an otherwise divided time. After all, the USMCA deal transforming trade relations with Mexico and Canada won the support of 90 percent of both the House and the Senate, Republicans and Democrats.

This powerful consensus should last, because it is rooted in deeply held values. Where trade is concerned, most Americans want the same thing: balanced outcomes that keep trade flows strong while ensuring that working people have access to steady, well-paying jobs. Neither old-school protectionism nor unbridled globalism will achieve that. Instead, as the United States confronts future trade challenges, it should chart a sensible middle course—one that, at long last, prizes the dignity of work and affirms a shared vision of the common good. Such visions are not self-executing. They require concerted and often aggressive courses of action.

Chapter 3

A Short and Selective History
of US Trade Policy

From the beginning, we in the Trump administration were told that we were reversing a long history of successful American trade policy. We heard of the "post–World War II consensus" and how our America First policies would threaten our prosperity and that they were radical and unique. But actually, the opposite is true. Protecting American trade interests was one of the very reasons for our revolution. Further, the America First policies of President Trump really were the natural heirs of the "American System" policy that guided our nation for decades and indeed that made it great. Tariffs and subsidies were an important part of the recipe that made us the largest economy in the world by 1890 and that created the strong middle class of workers and farmers that populates our states. During those days I often thought of that old expression that the only thing new in the world is the history that one doesn't know.

The moment our Constitution was written, it was clear that the federal government—not state governments or international bodies—would make trade policy for the United States. Article I, section 8, clause 3, of the Constitution states plainly that "the Congress" shall have power "to regulate Commerce with foreign Nations." Article I, section 10, clause 2, provides that "no state shall, without the Consent of Congress, lay any Imposts or Duties on Imports or Exports, except what may be absolutely necessary for executing its inspection Laws." Article I, section 8, clause 1, states that Congress does have power to lay and collect "Taxes, Duties, Imposts, and Excises," but that "all Duties, Imposts and Excises shall be uniform throughout the United States." In other words, the Constitution shows that while the United States is a free trade zone for Americans, Congress can restrain the access of other countries to this market.

One likely reason the Founders were determined to keep the trade policy of the new nation under the control of the federal government and, in particular, under the control of Congress was the colonists' frustration with the mercantilist policies of imperial Britain. This experience had made clear to the new Americans the cost of severing trade policy from domestic control and democratic legitimacy. Because they had no representation in Parliament, the colonists had no voice in the policies that largely confined them to producing raw materials to be sold to Great Britain and then buying back those materials in the form of manufactured goods. The colonies had to pay taxes (customs duties) on shipping and transportation. But "taxation without representation" wasn't going to work for the soon-to-be Americans. And this discontent was a major cause of the American Revolution.

The history of British mercantilism is a long one. Until 1651, the British had lagged behind the Dutch and the Spanish in trade. But that year Parliament passed navigation acts designed in part to stop the Dutch from storing imported goods to be shipped elsewhere and to control its own colonial trade. Additional navigation acts were passed in 1660, 1663, 1673, and 1696. Then came the Sugar and Molasses Act of 1733, which levied duties on molasses imports from any country outside the British empire into "any of the colonies or plantations in America, which now are or hereafter may be in the possession or under the dominion of his Majesty."

The American colonists would have none of it. They promptly engineered novel, covert ways of trading with European nations, all of which were illegal. They refused to serve solely as an export market for an empire that was, in the words of the Declaration of Independence, committed to "cutting off our Trade with all parts of the world."

While the colonists resisted being victims of unfair mercantilist practices by the British empire, as founders of the new American nation, they recognized the need to protect their own developing economy. As historian Alfred Eckes has observed, they "regarded tariffs not only as effective instruments for raising domestic revenue but also as powerful tools for fashioning a diversified manufacturing base."[1] From 1776 onward, American trade policy was distinctive not only for its insistence upon freedom from international control but also for a realistic awareness of the connection between foreign commerce and the common good.

Reviewing the history of US trade policy will help us understand the challenges that we faced when President Trump was elected—and why so many voters wanted a change in US policy that would put the common good of Americans first. Commentators regularly act as if President Trump had been trying to bring about an unprecedented approach. But this claim is upside down. The dangerous change actually took place in the early 1990s, when American policy makers effectively decided to let the rest of the world make our trade policy. This crazy experiment had never been tried before—and, one hopes, will never be tried again. The catastrophic results of that experiment helped drive the populist movement that led to President Trump's election—and one of President Trump's major goals was to return US trade policy to its realistic and pragmatic roots. In short, US history shows that the extreme free traders in both parties are the true radicals. The Trump administration was simply trying to return the country to the commonsense principles that made America rich and powerful in the first place.

The Privileges of Our Markets

The Founders plainly intended for the new federal government to use the leverage of the US market to obtain favorable terms in trade negotiations with other countries. They understood that unilaterally opening our market was naive and that trade had to be structured to our benefit. In the first decades of the republic, however, it became clear that just pursuing this kind of trade reciprocity would be insufficient. Instead, by the early 1800s American leaders from across the aisle came to believe that even as the government pursues reciprocity, it also must act to protect manufacturing for national security reasons.

No American understood the importance of supporting American manufacturing more than Alexander Hamilton. Even before the Constitution's ratification, in number 11 of the *Federalist Papers*, Alexander Hamilton warned that powerful European countries were trying to prevent Americans from using their own merchant ships for trade with Europe. After the Constitution was implemented, and Hamilton became secretary of the treasury, he issued his famous *Report on the Subject of Manufactures* (1791). In it, Hamilton pointed out that "the regulations of several countries, with which we have the most extensive intercourse, throw serious obstructions in the way of the principal staples of the United States." In other words, major foreign powers were blocking US exports. Hamilton warned that without a strong response, Americans would remain dependent on foreign manufactured goods. This would have disastrous consequences for the US economy because, as he put it, "the wealth . . . independence and security of a Country appear to be materially connected with the prosperity of manufactures." Hamilton recognized that mere complaints would not convince our trading partners to change their ways. Thus, he concluded, "'Tis for the United States to consider by what means they can render themselves least dependent, on the combinations, right or wrong, of foreign policy." He then described a series of options—including both trade regulations and government support where necessary—that would "tend to render the United States, independent on foreign nations, for military and other essential supplies."

At the time, Thomas Jefferson did not share Hamilton's enthusiasm for industrial policy, but he nonetheless recognized the importance of reciprocity in trade policy. Jefferson—the founder of the Democratic Republican Party—believed America should be a predominantly agrarian nation supported by a policy of free trade and low tariffs. Yet Jefferson understood that reciprocity was a necessary precondition to ensure Americans received fair trading terms and prices for their agricultural products. Should they not receive such terms, Jefferson argued in his 1793 *Report on Commerce*, it would behoove "us to protect our citizens, their commerce, and navigation by counter-prohibitions, duties, and regulations." Thus, the two antagonists of early American economic policy, one a proponent of an industrial policy to promote manufacturing and the other the banner carrier for agriculture and trade, both realized that reciprocity and using domestic market access as leverage were the keys to trade policy.

The War of 1812 helped to expand this early bipartisan trade policy consensus to include some protection for American manufacturing.

England's wartime blockade and invasion turned America's prewar dependence on British manufactured goods into a perilous weakness that frustrated its wartime mobilization and caused widespread shortages. As a result, even the most agrarian focused politicians, such as Jefferson, came to realize that an independent country such as the United States needed to manufacture some goods on its own in order to preserve its security. While Jefferson wrote in 1774 that "free trade with all parts of the world" was a "natural right," by 1816, he openly changed his mind, saying that "experience has now taught me that manufactures are now as necessary to our independence as to our comfort," and anyone "now against domestic manufacture, must be for reducing us either to dependence on [Britain] or to be clothed in skins, and to live like wild beasts."[2] Unsurprisingly then, a year after the war ended, Congress enacted its first serious protective tariff—set at a temporary 25 percent.

The debate between Hamilton, Jefferson, and their successors over tariffs was by no means settled. While agrarian Southern Democratic Republicans saw the security needs for some tariffs, they sought to keep them low to ensure Southern farmers could buy the cheapest manufactured goods possible. The Federalist Party—and later the Whig Party—on the other hand, sought even higher tariffs for both security and economic reasons. Despite these disagreements, however, the Founding period established a consensus around basic principles that dominated American thinking on trade for most of the next two centuries:

1. *US trade policy is made by the federal government and applies to the entire country.* In the 1830s, John C. Calhoun of South Carolina suggested that a state could refuse to collect certain tariffs if it disagreed with the federal government's trade policy. But President Andrew Jackson informed South Carolina that he would use force, if necessary, to overturn any such policy—and ever since then, there has been no question that the United States acts as a union in matters of trade.

2. *The United States can, and should, use its leverage in trade negotiations to get favorable terms from other countries.* Anyone familiar with the mu-

sical *Hamilton* knows that Alexander Hamilton and Thomas Jefferson had many disagreements. But as shown above, Hamilton and Jefferson both recognized that the United States should not accept unfair or discriminatory trade practices from other countries. They both argued that the United States should, when necessary, limit the access of major trading countries to the US market to obtain better trade terms.

3. *The United States can, and should, decide for itself what sort of a manufacturing base it wants.* While the political parties of early America did not agree on how and when the government should support domestic manufacturing, they both agreed that America could not be wholly dependent on foreign manufactured goods. Further, as Hamilton (and later Jefferson) recognized, US policy makers could not just wish an American industrial base into existence, especially since other countries' policies put American manufacturers at an unfair disadvantage. Instead, the federal government needed to act to ensure America made certain national defense–relevant goods for itself.

The Founders launched the United States into a world of complex trade rules that gave older and richer countries an unfair advantage over Americans. Rather than simply accepting those disadvantages, they wanted US policy makers to use the tools available under the Constitution to obtain the best deals possible for American workers and businesses.

Over the next two hundred years, US policy makers held countless debates over trade policy—and during that time frame, the United States tried many different types of trade policy, as Americans repeatedly adapted their policies to changing circumstances. The results are summarized in the following chart, which shows US average tariff rates from 1821 to 2016. The solid line—the higher of the two lines—shows the average tariff rate across all dutiable imports. The dotted line shows the average tariff rate for total imports, including those that entered duty-free pursuant to some type of trade deal.

US Average Tariff Rates (1821–2016)

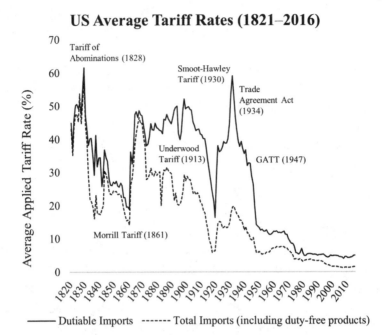

Source: Federal Reserve Bank of St. Louis; US Department of Commerce, Bureau of the Census, "Historical Statistics of the United States Colonial Times to 1970"; US International Trade Commission, "U.S. Imports for Consumption, Duties Collected, and Ratio of Duties to Value, 1891–2016."

Before the Civil War, tariffs regularly accounted for over 80 percent of the revenues collected by the federal government. Under these circumstances, eliminating tariffs was not feasible—tariffs were necessary to fund the government. However, as shown on the chart, tariff rates generally fell between 1830 and 1860—a fact that reflected the strong power of the Democratic Party and its agricultural supporters during this period. The slaveholding economy of the South depended on agriculture, exports, and European manufactured goods. Southerners such as Calhoun generally advocated for low tariffs.

But Henry Clay of Kentucky advocated for a very different approach. In 1832, Clay defended what he referred to as the "American System." He contended that the supporters of "free trade" were dangerously naive:

> The call for free trade, is as unavailing as the cry of a spoiled child, in its nurse's arms, for the moon or the stars that glitter in

the firmament of heaven. It never has existed; it never will exist. Trade implies at least two parties. To be free, it should be fair, equal, and reciprocal. But if we throw our ports wide open to the admission of foreign productions, free of all duty, what ports, of any other foreign nation, shall we find open to the free admission of our surplus produce? We may break down all barriers to free trade on our part, but the work will not be complete until foreign powers shall have removed theirs.[3]

Clay argued that a policy of "free trade" would harm US manufacturing and "lead substantially to the recolonization of these states, under the commercial dominion of Great Britain." He further argued that a protective tariff—that is, a tariff high enough to discourage imports and encourage manufacturing in the United States—would allow the United States to become less dependent on Great Britain and other sources of manufactured goods.

As shown from the previous chart, Clay's arguments did not prevail in his lifetime. Between the election of Andrew Jackson in 1828 and the 1850s, the Jacksonian Democrats were generally stronger than Clay's Whigs. But the Whigs collapsed in the 1850s and were replaced by a new Republican Party that agreed with Clay's American System and Hamilton's admonitions. In their 1860 platform, the Republicans stated that "sound policy requires such an adjustment of these imports *as to encourage the development of the industrial interests of the whole country.*"[4] Abraham Lincoln, who led the new party to victory in 1860, thought of Clay as "my beau ideal of a statesman, the man for whom I fought all my humble life."[5] Even before Lincoln entered office, the departure of many Southern members of Congress allowed the passage of the Morrill Tariff of 1861 (named after its chief sponsor, Representative Justin Morrill of Vermont), which launched a new era of protectionism. As the Civil War continued—and with the departure of many Southerners who had supported free trade and slavery—the Republicans continued to raise tariffs in a manner designed to encourage US manufacturing.

These policies were popular with most Americans. By 1872, the Republican Party—on the verge of winning its fourth consecutive presidential election—stated in its platform that except for taxes upon tobacco and liquors, the federal revenues "should be raised by duties upon importations, *the details of which should be so adjusted as to aid in securing remunerative wages to labor, and to promote the industries, prosperity, and growth of the whole country.*"[6]

Under these policies, the United States enjoyed the economic and manufacturing boom that Henry Clay had predicted. Immigrants poured into the United States, driving our population from 31.4 million in 1860 to 92.2 million in 1910. But that's not all. By 1890—only thirty years after the Republicans first captured the White House—the United States had the largest economy in the world. According to a 2004 study, US industrial production soared by 1,030 percent from 1860 to 1910.[7]

Given this record, it is hardly surprising that many Americans viewed their trade policy as a success—particularly in contrast to the free trade model of the United Kingdom, which was steadily losing ground to the United States. William McKinley, one of the most popular presidents of this era, achieved national fame through his strong and successful support of high tariffs as chairman of the House Ways and Means Committee. It is no surprise then that President Trump spoke often and favorably of President McKinley. Theodore Roosevelt, McKinley's vice president and successor, captured the mood of the country when, in 1895, he wrote to Henry Cabot Lodge as follows: "Thank God I am not a free-trader. In this country pernicious indulgence in the doctrine of free trade seems inevitably to produce a fatty degeneration of the moral fiber."[8]

One year later, the 1896 GOP convention—which nominated McKinley for president—included a ringing defense of Republican trade policy in its platform: "Protection builds up domestic industry and trade and secures our own market for ourselves; reciprocity builds up foreign trade and finds an outlet for our surplus."[9]

William Jennings Bryan and populist Democrats opposed the GOP in vain, in large part because urban workers—including many of the new immigrant voters—believed that Republican policies led to good jobs and high wages. In fact, between Lincoln in 1860 and the 1932 election, there were only two Democratic presidents, Grover Cleveland and Woodrow Wilson. Most of the Republican victories were by landslides.

A split between Theodore Roosevelt and President William Howard Taft led to a Democratic victory in 1912 and gave the Democrats the opportunity to lower average tariff rates from approximately 40 percent to approximately 25 percent—the lowest rates since before the Morrill Tariff was approved. But the Democrats were buried under a GOP landslide in 1920, and the Republicans returned tariffs to protectionist levels. In its 1924 platform, the GOP stated, "We reaffirm our belief in the protective tariff to extend needed protection to our productive industries." The voters responded by giving Republicans two more huge victories in the presidential elections of 1924 and 1928. Every one of those twelve Republican presidents during this time of massive economic growth would proudly call themselves protectionists.

By 1932, however, the US economy was suffering the effects of the Great Depression, and voters were ready for a change. In 1930, months after the stock-market crash that signaled the beginning of the depression, the GOP-led Congress passed the Smoot-Hawley Tariff Act, which was highly controversial at the time—and has been ever since. As a matter of economic policy, it seems clear that the new tariff law had little if any impact on the economic crisis of the early 1930s. Douglas Irwin, a trade historian, has summarized the evidence as follows: "Given the overriding importance of monetary and financial factors in bringing about the Great Depression, the Hawley-Smoot tariff almost surely played a relatively small role in the economic crisis."[10] Irwin points out that in 1929, dutiable imports constituted only 1.4 percent of US gross domestic product, while the money supply decreased by one-third. Furthermore, Smoot-Hawley did not represent a dramatic change in US trade policy; it merely increased the average tariff from 40 percent to 46 percent. Given these facts, it simply isn't credible to blame any increase in tariffs for the catastrophic effects of the Great Depression. While the economic effects of the Smoot-Hawley Tariff may not have been significant, the political effects were profound. One of the chief opponents to the Smoot-Hawley Tariff was Cordell Hull, a Tennessee Democrat on the House Ways and Means Committee. By March 1933, Hull was the secretary of state under the new president Franklin Roosevelt. Hull would hold that position for eleven years, making him the longest-serving person to hold that vital role. And he would drive US trade policy in a very different direction.

Significantly, Hull did not push for what many commentators now think of as "free trade" in the sense of a unilateral decision to revoke all restrictions on imports. He did, however, argue for free trade as a geopolitical strategy aimed to protect peace:

> Toward 1916 I embraced the philosophy that I carried throughout my twelve years as Secretary of State. . . . Though realizing that many other factors were involved, I reasoned that, if we could get a freer flow of trade—freer in the sense of fewer discriminations and obstructions—so that one country would not be deadly jealous of another and the living standards of all countries might rise, thereby eliminating the economic dissatisfaction that breeds war, we might have a reasonable chance for lasting peace.[11]

While New Deal Democrats generally opposed the type of protectionism that dominated US policy from 1861 to 1932, they were not willing to simply let imports overrun the US market. Instead, their views were generally aligned with Jefferson's belief in reciprocity. This fact can be seen in the following excerpt from the Democratic platform of 1936:

> We shall continue to foster the increase in our foreign trade which has been achieved by this administration; to seek by mutual agreement the lowering of those tariff barriers, quotas and embargoes which have been raised against our exports of agricultural and industrial products; *but continue as in the past to give adequate protection to our farmers and manufacturers against unfair competition or the dumping on our shores of commodities and goods produced abroad by cheap labor or subsidized by foreign governments.*[12]

These principles—reciprocal treatment for countries that treat us fairly, but restrictions on unfairly traded imports—would remain the primary drivers of US trade policy through the end of the Cold War. It is also important to note that while Republicans and Democrats disagreed on tariff levels, even those who wanted lower tariffs generally advocated for tariffs much higher than we see today. Essentially no one on the political scene advocated for zero tariffs.

The Reciprocal Trade Agreements Act of 1934 gave the president power to negotiate bilateral, reciprocal trade agreements with other countries. Each agreement included an unconditional Most Favored Nation clause—meaning that concessions made in any bilateral negotiation would apply to all other countries that had MFN trading status with the United States. The RTAA would come up for renewal before Congress every three years, but Congress would not vote on agreements negotiated by the president. This was an extremely important step. It began the process of the Congress delegating some of its constitutional authority over tariffs to the executive. This delegation would be expanded over the years.

GATT: The Forerunner to WTO

In April 1947, US representatives negotiated the General Agreement on Tariffs and Trade, a pact negotiated in Geneva and eventually signed by twenty-three nations. This agreement spawned a bureaucracy-laden organization in Geneva, Switzerland, to facilitate the negotiation of international trade deals. The United States entered into the GATT as a contracting party through executive order of the president. Congress did not vote on it. While the GATT fell well short of the postwar dream of a full-fledged international trade organization, it was thought that the pact would at least avoid a return to the trade wars of the 1930s and, more broadly, that it would promote "peace and stability through interdependence" through the promotion of international trade.

The GATT contained the following critical provisions:

• Each GATT member would provide MFN treatment to all other
  members. This provision meant that, with certain exceptions,
  any trade liberalization offered by one member to another would
  automatically extend to all other members.

- GATT members would negotiate their tariff schedules, and members agreed that they would not raise tariffs above the negotiated level—unless certain exceptions applied.
- GATT members would provide each other with "National Treatment"—that is, they would generally avoid using internal taxes and regulatory provisions "to afford protection to domestic production."

Significantly, GATT members largely accepted these principles—and other principles contained in the GATT—on faith. It was as if a new great religion had been started. Like most religions, it was based not on science but on belief—and also like most religions, many of its adherents failed to follow its precepts.

The GATT did not introduce an era of unregulated trade. Instead, US policy makers regularly used their constitutional authority to ensure that efforts to lower tariffs and encourage trade with US allies would not disrupt the US economy and hurt American workers.

GATT benefits were limited to US allies. Throughout the Cold War, the United States maintained significant barriers to trade with the Soviet Union and other countries whose interests were opposed to those of the United States. For example, Cuba was an original party to the GATT, but after Fidel Castro created a Communist government in that country, the United States effectively blocked all trade with Cuba. During the Cold War, the whole notion that our adversaries should have unlimited access to the US market—or that we would encourage US companies to invest in countries hostile to us—would have been regarded by almost all US policy makers as bizarre.

Trade liberalization was negotiated over many decades. After 1947, the GATT system grew slowly and cautiously. Between 1948 and 1960, the United States and its allies negotiated four separate rounds of tariff reductions. The next round of trade negotiations—the so-called Kennedy Round—began in May 1964 and took thirty-seven months to complete. And the Tokyo Round, which came next, began in September 1973 and took more than six years to finish. The caution showed by policy makers during the GATT era gave US workers and businesses time to adjust to changes in trade rules.

President Nixon intervened when trade deficits threatened US interests. By the early 1970s, freer trade meant that the United States—which had enjoyed trade surpluses during most of the twentieth century—was facing a trade deficit. At that time, the US dollar was still tied to gold at a price of thirty-five dollars per ounce, and other countries were pressing the Americans to redeem dollars for gold. There was a legitimate fear that the United States would run out of gold. In response, President Nixon ended the practice of allowing dollars to be exchanged for gold. Significantly, he also imposed a 10 percent tariff on imports to prevent foreign producers from gaining a significant advantage in the US market. In response, major US trading partners agreed to revalue their own currencies, thus making US production more competitive in global markets. Nixon's actions plainly interfered with free trade but were essential to preserving our manufacturing economy and to maintaining US support for the GATT system.

Congress created new tools to prevent imports from harming the US economy. Section 232 of the Trade Expansion Act of 1962 empowered the president to adjust imports when necessary to address national security concerns. Section 301 of the Trade Act of 1974 gave the president broad authority to use tariffs and other trade restrictions in response to unfair or discriminatory trade practices. And in 1979, Congress significantly strengthened US anti-dumping and anti-subsidy duty laws to give US workers and businesses a more effective response to unfairly traded imports. Each of these measures was designed to ensure that freer trade did not lead to US workers and businesses being harmed by a flood of imports.

After the initial Geneva Round of 1947, seven more rounds of trade talks took place over the ensuing decades: Annecy (1949), Torquay (1950–51), Geneva (1956), Geneva (1960–61), Kennedy (1964–67), Tokyo (1973–79), and Uruguay (1986–93). For the most part, these rounds involved tariff reductions. The Kennedy Round, which was named for our president who had been assassinated the year before, was also notable for producing an anti-dumping agreement and for grappling with the question of how to help developing countries—an issue that would prove to be contentious from that point onward.

The Tokyo Round sought pointedly to reduce nontariff barriers, regulations, and other actions taken by countries to make it more difficult to sell by foreign countries in their market, as well as to promote some systemic reform. I worked on the Tokyo Round as the Republican chief of staff for the Senate Finance Committee with Senator Dole, and this was my first in-depth exposure to trade. At the time, the USTR was Robert Strauss, the famous Democrat lawyer and statesman. I remember watching him before the committee and thinking that while he didn't know very much about trade laws, as an operator, he was in the hall of fame.

Generally speaking, US policy makers during the GATT era were no mere cheerleaders for globalization. Instead, they balanced concerns about helping US allies with efforts to prevent other countries from taking unfair advantage of the US market.

Ronald Reagan's trade policy illustrates this balance. President Reagan certainly believed in efficient markets, and he supported lowering taxes and eliminating unnecessary regulations. But he was also willing to respond to import surges that were causing problems in the United States. For example, he used tariffs to block certain motorcycles from Japan in order to give Harley-Davidson a chance to become more competitive. When Japan violated an agreement with the United States on trade in semiconductors, President Reagan imposed punitive tariffs of 100 percent on a wide variety of goods produced by Japanese electronics companies. When American steel producers and automakers were harmed by imports, he directed the Office of US Trade Representative to negotiate "voluntary restraint agreements"—that is, agreements in which our trading partners agreed to restrain their imports to create breathing space for American companies. As a deputy USTR in the Reagan administration, I negotiated many of these agreements. Other countries came to the table because they knew that President Reagan was prepared to take stronger action if they did not.

President Reagan also acted to bring down rising trade deficits. During his presidency, a booming US economy and a strong US dollar drew in large volumes of imports, and our current account deficit grew from 0.15 percent of GDP in 1981 to almost 3 percent of GDP in 1985. By September 1985, Democrats in Congress were clamoring for a more aggressive US trade policy, with Representative Dick Gephardt, an economic nationalist who would become House Democrat leader, stating: "We're at the crossroads. We have a choice to make whether we'll be a winner in the world economy—or a loser."[13] Gephardt and other Democrats were pushing legislation that would have imposed a 25 percent surcharge on imports from countries that had "excessive" trade surpluses with the United States and who dealt in unfair trade practices.[14]

But by the time Representative Gephardt made those comments, the Reagan administration had already acted. On September 22, 1985, at the Plaza Hotel in New York City, Secretary of the Treasury James Baker negotiated the so-called Plaza Accord with France, West Germany, Japan, and the United Kingdom. Under the Plaza Accord, the United States and its allies agreed that major non-dollar currencies would appreciate— and thus make US products relatively more competitive. The US current account deficit peaked at 3.3 percent of GDP in 1987 but fell rapidly thereafter.

Reagan's actions were strongly criticized by free traders at the time. In 1988, the libertarian Cato Institute published an article claiming that "Ronald Reagan by his actions has become the most protectionist president since Herbert Hoover, the heavyweight champion of protectionists."[15] This statement was nonsense—President Reagan was charting a pragmatic path to ensure that US workers and businesses had a fair chance to take full advantage of a stronger US economy and that wages and jobs were not lost to unfair trading practices from abroad. But the mere fact that Cato accused President Reagan of protectionism belies the myth that he was a simpleminded free trader who never interfered with imports.

One other point should be made here about President Reagan's trade policy. The key trade disputes of his time did not involve our political adversaries—our trade with the Soviet bloc was very limited. Indeed, no one would have advocated strong economic relations with the Soviet Union. Instead, the major trade issues of the 1980s involved our major allies, especially Japan. But President Reagan understood that there are situations in which the United States must stand up for its economic interests even against its friends.

Decades of prudent US trade policy during the GATT era paid enormous dividends. By the early 1990s, the United States held one of the strongest economic and geopolitical positions of any nation in history. We had won the Cold War. We had solved the inflationary trials of the 1970s and were coming off the economic boom of the 1980s. Perhaps most importantly, by responding to concerns about unfair trade, and saving key industries such as steel and autos, US policy makers maintained the popular support they needed to prevail over the Soviet Union.

To this day, supporters of globalization try to defend their views by pointing to the success of the GATT era. But they are wrong. The United States abandoned the pragmatism of the GATT era in 1994, when US policy makers decided to replace the GATT system with a new set of agreements that would be enforced by a new international body: the World Trade Organization.

The Era of Globalization

There had been serious negotiations about creating an international trade organization as part of the GATT system in the late 1940s, but the idea failed because of opposition from Congress. But with the end of the Cold War, policy makers in the United States and the European Union saw a chance to create a new multilateral institution with responsibility for enforcing trade obligations. For years, US politicians had complained—and not without reason—that our trading partners were not living up to their obligations under the various deals negotiated under the GATT. Many of the disputes between the United States and Japan during the 1980s, for example, grew out of Japanese practices (such as closed home markets) that Americans regarded as unfair. Many US policy makers hoped that by creating a new multinational organization—and giving that organization the power to rule upon trade disputes—we could obtain better cooperation from our trading partners.

But our trading partners in Japan and Western Europe had a very different agenda. They were looking for ways to stop Americans from using the leverage of our huge market in trade negotiations. As shown above, President Reagan repeatedly used tariffs—or the threat of tariffs—to press our trading partners to change their behavior. It's hard to believe that other countries would have agreed to the Plaza Accord if they had not been concerned about the possibility that Congress would raise tariffs. By creating the WTO and pressing the United States to rely on multilateral trade litigation rather than unilateral action, these countries understood that they could significantly weaken the leverage of US policy makers. Faced with assurances from President Clinton that the dispute settlement provisions of the WTO would allow the United States to effectively defend its interests, Congress approved our entry into the WTO in 1994. Significantly, this congressional vote took place during a lame-duck session of Congress, a few weeks *after* the Democratic-led Congress had been annihilated in the 1994 midterm elections. In other words, our entry into the WTO was approved by a Congress that had been overwhelmingly rejected by the American people. The same Congress had previously approved the new North American Free Trade Agreement in 1993.

On paper, neither the WTO nor NAFTA prevented US policy makers from using our leverage in trade negotiations. But until Trump, none did. In fact, the Trump administration would prove that the US government still had legal power to defend our national interest. But from 1995 through 2016, US presidents from both parties put all their faith in globalization. Time and time again, they acted as if they could do nothing to help US workers and businesses facing tough—and often unfair—import competition. The old Hamiltonian concerns about using US trade policy to promote a strong and effective industrial base were abandoned. The old Jeffersonian concerns about reciprocity were largely ignored. The United States did bring dozens of complaints to the WTO and won or partially won many of them. But nothing meaningful ever changed. Our trading partners brought even more cases against us and won almost all of them. And the US government made serious detrimental changes to our laws in order to comply. Remarkably, the United States—which has run significant trade deficits almost every year since the WTO began—

has consistently been treated by the WTO as the world's scofflaw, as the great protectionist when it comes to trade.

From the beginning, it was obvious that the WTO system placed US companies and workers at a significant disadvantage in global markets. In 1995, the US current account deficit amounted to 1.486 percent of US GDP. By 2000, that figure had soared to 3.92 percent—larger even than the trade deficits that had led Democrats to call for tariffs back in the mid-1980s and that had eventually resulted in the Plaza Accord.

This time, however, the US government decided not to prevent US workers and businesses from being overrun by imports. Instead, US policy makers—a lame-duck president and leaders in Congress—decided to double down on globalization. In 2000, the United States made one of the worst mistakes in its history by giving Permanent Normal Trade Relations (PNTR) status to Communist China, as part of US efforts to bring China into the WTO.

Consider what a radical notion this was. China was, and is, a Communist dictatorship, and its geopolitical interests obviously clash with ours. The United States had previously engaged in some trade with China— but China had not been part of the GATT system. Indeed, during the 1990s, Congress had to vote each year on whether to grant Most Favored Nation status to China. While Congress consistently refused to revoke MFN status for China, the mere fact that the vote existed put pressure on China to avoid offending US policy makers—and discouraged companies from moving their factories to China or becoming dependent on China for their supply chains. After all, it would be risky to rely on a country that required annual approval from Congress to retain its MFN status.

Letting China into the WTO changed all this. Supporters of China argued that the term "Most Favored Nation" was no longer appropriate—we were simply granting China "normal trade relations" on a permanent basis. But whatever term is used, by granting PNTR to China, we were making an extraordinary concession to a geopolitical adversary—and we were clearing a path for companies to use China as a global manufacturing center.

Unfortunately, the leaders of both parties pushed for PNTR for

China—and in the process made claims that later proved embarrassingly false. In March 2000, President Clinton argued that letting China into the WTO was "a hundred-to-nothing deal for America when it comes to the economic consequences."[16] Two months previously, then presidential candidate George W. Bush claimed that granting PNTR to China would "provide American businesses and farmers access to China's growing market and narrow our trade deficit with China."[17] Congress agreed and, in 2000, voted to grant PNTR for China. How could so many of our leaders be so wrong?

As the new century began, therefore, the United States had completely abandoned the prudent trade policies that had served us through most of our history and instead placed our trust in an international body. We had also given our chief geopolitical adversary free access to the US market. The results were disastrous. Many companies, no longer concerned about trade tensions between the United States and China, quickly abandoned US workers and concentrated supply chains in China. In 2000, the United States had over seventeen million manufacturing jobs—roughly the same figure as in the early 1970s. By 2009, we had fewer than twelve million manufacturing jobs, and the great majority of those lost jobs have never returned. Our current account deficit surged—rising to 6 percent of GDP in 2006 and falling below 4 percent only after the catastrophic recession of 2009.

US exports of goods to China did increase from $16.185 billion in 2000 to $115.594 billion in 2016. But over the same period, US imports of goods from China soared from $100.018 billion to $462.42 billion. Our trade deficit in goods with China went from $83.833 billion in 2000 to $346.825 billion in 2016. Of course, that flood of dollars helped to transform China into a superpower that could mount a serious geopolitical challenge to the United States. Both President Bush's prediction that granting PNTR to China would lower our trade deficit and President Clinton's assessment that the deal was a "hundred-to-nothing" in our favor were proven false.

As we will discuss in chapters 12, 13, and 14, our other trade deals fared little better. NAFTA was supposed to help US workers. Instead, our trade in goods with Mexico went from a surplus of $1.35 billion in 1994 to a deficit of $63.271 billion in 2016. Our trade in goods with Canada—which was already showing a deficit of $13.967 billion in 1994—reflected a deficit of $10.985 billion in 2016. Automobile factories were moving to Mexico at an alarming rate. Auto parts makers created hundreds of thousands of jobs in Mexico in just a few short years. Then candidate for president Ross Perot even published a book on the threat posed by NAFTA, in which he argued that "NAFTA is really less about trade than it is about investment. Its principal goal is to protect US companies and investors operating in Mexico. . . . Large portions of it are written in the type of obscure legal terms found on the back of an insurance policy. Buried in the fine print are provisions that will give away American jobs and radically reduce the sovereignty of the US."[18]

The devastation caused at least in part by NAFTA suggests that contemporary critics were onto something with respect to the threat to American jobs. In a paper titled *NAFTA's Impact on the States*, economist Robert E. Scott identified the following industries as having been most affected by NAFTA: electrical electronic machinery (108,773 jobs lost); motor vehicles and equipment (83,643 jobs lost); textiles and apparel (83,258 jobs lost); and lumber and wood products (48,306 jobs lost).[19]

While the following chart does not identify causal factors, it should provide food for thought.

It became obvious over time that, beyond NAFTA, "globalization"—which had been greeted with such enthusiasm by the leadership of both parties—was not delivering the type of results Americans had come to expect. Remember that our trade and economic policies before we joined the WTO had generally been successful—there's a reason why we were the richest and most powerful country on earth in the early 1990s. In the sixteen years before China joined the WTO, real median household income in the United States (measured in 2019 dollars) rose from $53,337 in 1984 to $63,292 in 2000. But then real median household income fell below the 2000 level in every year until 2016—and even in that year, it only reached $63,683 (an increase of less than $400 in sixteen years).[20] In other words, during the whole period marked by the Bush and Obama administrations the median US household saw virtually no improvement in its standard of living. (After only three years of

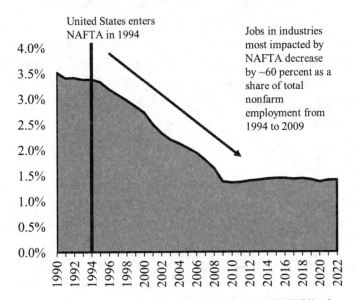

**Share of Non-Farm Employment in
Industries Most Impacted by NAFTA***
(percent of total nonfarm employment)

* Based on Economic Policy Institute analysis; Data from Bureau of Labor Statistics "B" Tables of the Employment Situation Release; Industries included are Wood Products, Electrical Equipment and Appliances, Motor Vehicles and Parts, Textile Mills, Textile Product Mills, and Apparel.

President Trump, this figure reached $69,560 in 2019. Even in 2020, when the economy was suffering under COVID-19, real median household income was $67,521—almost $4,000 above 2016 levels.)

The Obama administration knew that US trade policies weren't working. In 2008, candidate Obama had threatened to pull out of NAFTA, if necessary, to get better terms in that agreement.[21] The Obama administration repeatedly complained that the WTO's dispute settlement system interpreted WTO texts in a manner that did not reflect the US understanding of those agreements. For years, the Obama administration pleaded with our trading partners for new deals that would benefit US workers and businesses.

But the Obama team was hamstrung by the principles of globalization. For most of American history, certain basic concepts of trade policy were obvious: (1) don't allow your geopolitical adversaries to benefit from

the US market; (2) use access to the US market as leverage in trade negotiations; (3) don't hesitate to use trade policy as necessary to create the
type of economy that you want Americans to have; and (4) act unilaterally when needed. Under the WTO system, however, US policy makers
abandoned each of these concepts. They believed that China had significant rights as a WTO member, despite its hostility to our interests. They
believed that it was wrong to use the US market as leverage in trade talks.
Obama abandoned his promise to use our ability to opt out of NAFTA.
And finally, the Obama team trusted "the market" to determine what
sort of jobs would exist in America—even when that "market" was so
heavily distorted by unfair trading practices abroad that it was not really
"free" at all.

Given these principles, Obama's team only had two realistic options
to address trade concerns. First, they could—and did—bring trade cases
against China at the WTO. But many of China's most egregious practices, such as its policy of forcing US companies to share technology
to access the Chinese market, were not necessarily violations of WTO
rules. And even when the United States won a trade case against China,
it was quite easy for China (or any dictatorship) to appear to bring itself
into compliance with that WTO decision while simply adopting new
policies to achieve the same market-distorting effect.

Second, the Obama administration could—and did—seek to rewrite
trade rules through negotiation. But here the administration ran into
the obvious problem that other major economies, most of whom were
happily enjoying large trade surpluses with the United States, had no incentive to make any concessions to us. Under the old GATT system, the
United States negotiated round after round of tariff reductions and other
changes to global trading rules, largely because (1) we were negotiating
primarily with our allies and (2) other countries wanted more access to
the US market. But under the WTO system, other countries had no
incentive to make significant concessions to the United States. They already had tremendous access to the US market—and to the extent they
wanted the United States to change any of its trade policies, they could
simply use the WTO dispute settlement process to sue us. (For example,
in 2001, the Bush administration imposed emergency tariffs to help save

American steel producers from a flood of imports—but revoked those tariffs soon after losing a dispute at the WTO.) The last serious effort to negotiate a major trade deal inside the WTO—the so-called Doha Round—collapsed in 2007. And with any major WTO deal requiring buy-in from China, there was no chance for the Obama administration to accomplish much in that forum.

Recognizing that major negotiations at the WTO were a waste of time, the Obama administration tried to reach new trade deals with our allies in Europe and Asia. But our allies are also unwilling to make trade concessions to the United States—unless we give them compelling reasons to do so. The Obama administration's effort to negotiate a major trade deal with the European Union—known as the Transatlantic Trade and Investment Partnership—failed because the European Union had no interest in agreeing to the type of deal that could win support in Washington. The Obama administration did complete a deal with a group of countries in the Pacific region—the Trans-Pacific Partnership. But the other TPP countries agreed to this deal only after winning concessions from the Obama administration that would have encouraged companies to move more good jobs out of the United States and left American workers and manufacturers in an even weaker position in global markets. The TPP was so unpopular that Congress never even brought it up for a vote. Even Hillary Clinton opposed it in the end, and President Trump withdrew us from it entirely almost as soon as he took office.

In short, the experience of the Obama administration proved the wisdom of Jefferson's statement that "*free commerce and navigation are not to be given in exchange for Restrictions and Vexations: nor are they likely to produce a relaxation of them.*" During the WTO era, US policy makers abandoned over two hundred years of wisdom on trade and hoped that giving free commerce to other countries—including our geopolitical adversaries—would produce a relaxation on "*Restrictions and Vexations*" that block our trade. As Jefferson predicted, those efforts failed.

By 2015, it was clear that we needed a very different approach—we needed a president who knew how to get and use leverage in trade negotiations, who would not be intimidated by support for globalization in the press, and who would return US trade policy to its traditional focus on reciprocity and defending our national interest. We needed a president who would reaffirm the Republican commitment to use tariffs to force development, fairness, and balance.

And then, on June 16, 2015, Donald Trump announced that he was running for president.

Chapter 4

How the WTO Has Failed America

Many equate the Geneva-based World Trade Organization with the rules-based international trading system itself. But as we have seen in the previous chapter, that system existed for nearly five decades before the establishment of the WTO. And it functioned quite well. That period saw a massive expansion of global trade—a roughly fifteen-fold increase between the end of World War II and 1995—and eight successful rounds of multilateral trade negotiations. The system was not anarchic, but countries retained flexibility to impose trade-restrictive measures when it was in their interest to do so. When disputes arose, the GATT dispute settlement process provided a framework for resolving them with the assistance of a neutral (but non-binding) arbitration panel. But most disputes were resolved in the end through political negotiations.

Yet caught up in the heady days of the Cold War's end, trade policy elites in the United States and elsewhere thought the existing system untidy and set about to perfect it. Their solution was the WTO and, in particular, its Appellate Body.

During my tenure as USTR, I found confusion even among senior government officials about what the WTO actually did. Many thought that it set tariff rates and wrote trading rules. In reality, it is a member-controlled organization that does only what all its members in consensus want it to do. It is much more like a trade association than a corporation. I like to tell people that when you think of the WTO, you should think of two things. One is a place, a room, where countries can come together and negotiate new rules on subsidies, fisheries, or any other trade matter. The other is a courtroom, where countries can resolve trade disputes.

As we've seen, the negotiating room existed before the WTO. The key innovation in the 1994 Uruguay Round Agreement was the courtroom—

the WTO dispute settlement system. This was the great hope of the WTO's founders. No longer would trade disputes be settled in country-to-country negotiations by "grubby politicians." Instead, such matters would be delegated to panels of "dispassionate" and "enlightened" experts, whose decisions would be binding on the parties. At the center of this new judicial branch of the international trading system was the Appellate Body, charged with reviewing the decisions of dispute resolution panels to ensure fidelity to the WTO rules and consistency across decisions.

The Appellate Body—and by extension the WTO itself—was both a colossal and tragic failure, not only for the United States but for the world trading system as a whole. Let's consider what Americans were told we were getting out of the Uruguay Round Agreement and what we actually got. The comparison provides a damning indictment.

We were told the WTO would level the playing field for American workers, farmers, and businesses; what we got in exchange for lowering our own tariffs and surrendering part of our sovereignty were exploding trade deficits.

We were told the dispute settlement system would empower the United States to open markets for our goods and services; instead, we won very little of consequence in cases we brought yet became the most frequently sued country at the WTO and suffered at least partial losses in 90 percent of the cases brought against us.

We were told the Appellate Body's role would be a relatively modest one of ensuring only that the most egregious decisions of dispute settlement panels would be corrected; what we got was a self-aggrandizing institution that saw its role as to perfect and expand rather than simply apply rules agreed to by the WTO's member states.

We were told the WTO posed no threat to US sovereignty because our laws were fully consistent with its rules; what we got were repeated decisions by the Appellate Body finding fault with US laws, which pressured Congress to repeal those laws.

When we acquiesced to China's joining the WTO five years after its founding, we were told the dispute settlement process gave us the tools necessary to ensure China played by the rules, abandoned its non-market predilections, and transformed itself into a "responsible stakeholder" in the rules-based international system; what we got instead was an institution that not only failed to discipline China but in fact has enabled its rise for over two decades.

We were told the Appellate Body would simply complement, not supplant, the WTO's negotiating function; what we got instead was a hopeless stalemate in serious multilateral trade negotiations as many countries, most notably China, found they could best advance their interests in litigation, rather than negotiation. As a result, inequitable rules and exceptions built into the Uruguay Round Agreement have undermined the international trading system and damaged US interests.

In short, we were promised a golden age in global trade; what we got was a big hot mess.

A Bad Deal for America

As discussed in chapter 3, during the Uruguay Round, which ran from the mid-1980s to the early 1990s, the GATT was absorbed into the WTO. The WTO carried over the GATT's Most Favored Nation and National Treatment principles. But it included new disciplines and set up a new, binding dispute settlement system. This arrangement was supposed to be more effective than the GATT. And from the perspective of the United States, it was supposed to expand markets, help level the playing field, and generally make things better for workers, farmers, and businesses. As President Clinton remarked when the Uruguay Round Agreement passed Congress, "The real victors [in the agreement] are the autoworkers, the accountants, the engineers, the farmers, the communications workers, the people who will now have a chance to be more rewarded for their labors."[1]

How did things work out? The following chart speaks for itself.

Following the creation of the WTO in January 1995, the US trade balance plummeted. While part of the sharp decline in balance for goods trade was offset by surpluses in trade for services, the net deterioration in the total trade balance in the post-1995 era is striking.

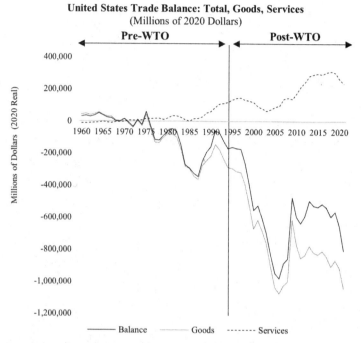

United States Trade Balance: Total, Goods, Services
(Millions of 2020 Dollars)

Sources: Bureau of Economic Analysis; U.S. Census Bureau, Economic Indicators Division; Federal Reserve Bank of Minneapolis.

Drawn out as a line on a graph, the goods trade balance falls off a cliff right after US entry into the WTO. After controlling for the effects of inflation, the total trade deficit increased by a factor of six from 1994 to its temporary peak in 2006. There was a temporary drawback in the deficit at the time of the financial crisis in 2008–9; however, the improvement was not sustained. The average real trade deficit for 2010 through 2020 was four times the pre-WTO deficit in 1994. The numbers are even worse if one factors in 2021, where the goods and services deficit soared to $860 billion and the goods deficit alone was more than $1 trillion.

At the same time, after a brief spike in the late 1990s, median household income in the United States plateaued and then dipped over the next fifteen years.[2] So much for workers having "a chance to be more rewarded for their labors."

I don't mean to suggest that the WTO is the sole or even the primary cause of these trends. And there were some positive provisions in the Uruguay Round on services, technical barriers to trade, intellectual property, and agriculture that benefited the United States and likely off-set the trade deficit to some extent. But we were led to believe that the Uruguay Round Agreement would *improve* the balance of trade by giving us new tools to level the playing field, increase exports, and raise wages. By that standard set by President Clinton and other WTO boosters, the institution at best has been a major disappointment for America. And, in fact, it has done major damage.

A Restraint on American Power

The supposed "crown jewel" of the Uruguay Round—and the top priority for US negotiators—was a new and supposedly improved dispute settle-ment system. The very first seeds of this idea had been sown back when I was the deputy USTR under President Reagan. At the time, my boss, Ambassador Brock, was quite concerned with the non-binding nature of GATT dispute settlement. The United States would win a case, and nothing would happen. He wanted that fixed.

I remember asking whether one's position on binding dispute set-tlement should not be determined by whether one anticipated being a plaintiff or a defendant in most future cases. I said that if we would likely be a defendant under a putative binding system, we would proba-bly be better off with the then current non-binding process. I feared that we were far more likely to be sued than to sue. Brock didn't agree. And so the fateful US position was set. We wanted a "court system."

So did many other countries, particularly in Europe. But their rea-sons didn't exactly overlap with our own. Indeed, in selling the system to their own citizens, European officials were quite candid about the fact that the new scheme was intended primarily to check the power of the United States. Leon Brittan, a member of the European Commission, lauded the fact that under the WTO, "[a] major trading power such as the United States now has *fewer levers* with which to impose its views on other countries because it has formally agreed to be more mindful of the rules of the multilateral game. This has always been an objective."[3]

Le Monde praised the Uruguay Round Agreement because it meant that "[a] great power like the United States has now *less power* to impose its views on other countries because it has agreed to the following rules of the multilateral game."[4]

As it was, the WTO dispute resolution system surpassed the most optimistic hopes of those who wanted it to undermine American power. As noted in a 2020 USTR report, the United States has found itself on the receiving end of more than a quarter of all cases filed at the WTO. Specifically, the report notes that 155 disputes have been filed against the United States, and no other member has faced even a hundred disputes.[5] As the report cited, according to some analyses, approximately 90 percent of the disputes pursued against the United States have led to a report finding that the US law or other measure was inconsistent with WTO agreements. This means that on average, over the past twenty-five years, the WTO has found a US law or measure WTO-inconsistent between five and six times per year, every year.

There is ample data suggesting, as Senator Max Baucus, a former chairman of the Senate Finance Committee, put it back in 2003, that "the WTO is a plaintiff's court." He noted:

> The decisions against the United States have had significantly more far reaching effects than those against other countries. In 30 cases brought against the United States, panels have called for the revision or removal of two U.S. laws, one regulation, three agency practices, and 21 trade measures. By contrast, in 34 cases brought against trade remedy measures imposed by countries other than the United States, no laws or regulations have been found inconsistent with WTO rules, and only one practice and 7 measures are subject to revision or removal.[6]

By contrast, what the United States has gotten out of putting up with the dispute process as currently structured is fairly meager. We have won parts of a number of cases, but the foreign practice to which we objected was seldom changed. Sometimes we won a case and the foreign government just found a way to accomplish their protectionist objective in another way. I once asked a USTR staff member to find me at least one case in which working Americans benefited from a WTO decision—that is, to find one case the result of which was more American jobs. He never found one. Many of the cases we lost, by contrast, required us to change important policy, practice, or even law to accommodate the Appellate Body's decision. In short, wins were few and hollow, while defeats were many and often very harmful to our domestic businesses and workers.

A Self-Aggrandizing Court

Our biggest single complaint, however, is not the US win-loss record per se. The larger problem is that, over time, the judges and the WTO bureaucracy came to see themselves not as those who should make a quick determination regarding whether a panel made an egregiously incorrect ruling, but rather as a group who should write the rules of trade according to their own jurisprudential understanding and vision. But there is a huge difference between deciding cases and creating rules.

Indeed, the Appellate Body became an unelected lawmaking body, creating rules that have vast implications for international trade. The initial plan was for the arbitrators to make one-off decisions on specific cases. It was not supposed to create obligations or precedents. Yet this is precisely what it did. It often referred to its own past cases in deciding new ones. This created obligations. It established laws.

US frustration with Appellate Body overreach predates the Trump administration. For the last twenty years, there have been complaints in every administration about the quality of the decisions of the Appellate Body. For example, the administration of George W. Bush objected to the assault on "zeroing" (a methodology used in determining anti-dumping duties) but did not do much about it. Under the Obama administration, the United States went so far as to prevent a judge from being reappointed. Under the Trump administration, we set out not only to document that the Appellate Body failed to abide by its own rules properly and that it was actively harmful to US interests but also to take decisive action.

The 2020 USTR report on the Appellate Body was the first comprehensive (174-page) indictment of the WTO's malfeasance.[7] It provided the negotiating history to prove the intent of the United States at the time we entered into the agreement. It showed how the Appellate Body violated its time limits on case decisions and extended members' terms beyond those set out in the text. It documented the wrongful creation of jurisprudence and detailed a number of bad decisions. Overall, it revealed that the Appellate Body is an experiment that has gone off the rails. One part of the overall body of the WTO, like some crazy monster, had begun to act independently, asserting its own authority in areas where it had none.

This was never how the WTO was supposed to work. The basic notion of its dispute settlement process was that in the wake of a country filing a complaint about a potential violation, and after consultation between the parties, a three-person panel would be appointed to decide who was right and who was wrong in the dispute. Decisions made by the panel could be appealed to an Appellate Body of seven members, which would have ninety days to approve the decision unless it found obvious mistakes in interpretation of the text of an agreement. The role of the Appellate Body was a limited one in this scheme. It was not meant to serve as a font of new obligations for member countries. Yet that is exactly what it became.

The problem may be traced back to faulty thinking that underlies the institutional design. To some extent, the flaw lies in the notion that a group of international bureaucrats could put aside its respective home countries' interests and its other biases to objectively decide a case that could have far-reaching ramifications for its own country. Stated simply, the concept assumes that, for example, a member of the Chinese Communist Party (CCP) will make decisions without considering the effect of those decisions on China. Of course, this is nonsense. To a lesser extent, the same objection could be made of bureaucrats from India, Korea, Europe, or any other country.

Aside from individual biases, there is a basic conflict between how the Appellate Body came to operate and Americans' conception of fairness and the rule of law. This reflects in large measure differences between the Anglophone and continental legal traditions. In the United States, we see trade agreements as contracts, meaning that we are entitled to what is written in contracts and our obligations are precisely those written. Texts that emerge from negotiations stipulate in precise language the substance of reciprocal concessions between countries. Indeed, in negotiations every word is weighed, and every phrase is judged.

By contrast, Europeans trained in the civil law tradition tend to see the WTO as a living agreement-in-process that can and should be interpreted by experts in ways that will lead to what they consider to be favorable outcomes. These are fundamentally different perspectives, suggestive of the difference between those who would have a Supreme Court of the United States that follows the precise wording of the Constitution (the originalists) and those who believe that the Constitution should be interpreted consistent with what people want today as intuited by judges (some progressives). The Appellate Body became the apotheosis of the latter approach.

The Appellate Body also ran roughshod over procedural rules intended to curtail its power. It figured out a way around its own term limits. The WTO rules indicate precisely what the terms are for the seven Appellate Body members. Any member can serve no more than two four-year terms. The Appellate Body itself, however, decided that its members could continue to serve on existing cases even after their term has expired. There is no authority in any of the WTO agreements for this practice. Yet many Appellate Body members served much longer than they were supposed to serve, got paid handsomely, and wrote binding opinions well after their term had expired.

In another example of usurping power, the Appellate Body made decisions by overturning the facts determined by the three-person panels, despite being specifically precluded from issuing findings of fact. Like an appellate court in the United States, it was only supposed to make decisions on legal issues. Yet the Appellate Body often reviewed the facts de novo to achieve its desired result in cases.

The Appellate Body also ignored time limits for decisions provided for in the WTO rules, which say that Appellate Body review of panel decisions was to last no longer than ninety days, period. This was not a minor, procedural nicety, the violation of which can be pooh-poohed away—it was a bulwark against the very sort of abuse that came to prevail. The time limit was also intended to stop the formation of a large bureaucracy that would be writing new rules. Yet the Appellate Body came to observe this rule only in the breach. In one of the periods studied by USTR for its 2020 report on the Appellate Body, not a single case was concluded in 90 days and the average time was 149 days. This had two pernicious effects.

One was to nullify what was supposed to have been the key benefit of dispute resolution—the ability to obtain prompt relief when a member violated the rules. Rather than crack down on cheating from countries such as China, this elongated process enabled cheating by allowing countries to continue violating the WTO rules without consequence until the conclusion of years-long litigation. In some cases, most notably those involving the solar industry, the United States found that even when it prevailed, the victory was fleeting because our domestic industry died in the interim.

Blowing past the ninety-day deadline also enabled the Appellate Body to build a larger and larger body of case law, which it would use in turn to expand and rewrite the WTO rules. With no effective deadline for the completion of its work, the Appellate Body routinely issued dictum-laden opinions exceeding a hundred pages that further expanded the scope of its authority.

The gradual shift in role of the Appellate Body was predictable, as well as very much in keeping with the trajectory of other global organizational progeny of the postwar moment. As always happens with international bureaucracies, the Appellate Body and the bureaucrats who ran it assumed more and more power over the years.

They also acquired more and more money. The judges who resolved disputes were part-time employees who worked on a few cases a year. Yet many were paid approximately $300,000 per year tax-free and given a year-round apartment for free in Geneva. Essentially, the judges were paid on a daily basis. Perhaps unsurprisingly, some claimed to work almost every day of the year, even though on average there are only about eight days of hearings per year and the entire Appellate Body issued only five or six decisions annually. This problem was exacerbated by the fact that the Appellate Body members whose terms were extended because they were finishing a case received full compensation during that period. Clearly, there is no incentive for a quick decision when one is being paid by the day.[8]

..

These complaints are not just those of an America First Republican. As noted, frustrations with the Appellate Body span multiple administrations of both parties over two decades. Indeed, some of the WTO's worst critics are those who know it best. These include the USTR career staff and a former member of the Appellate Body itself.

Thomas Graham, an American, served on the Appellate Body from 2011 to 2019. When Tom retired from the Appellate Body, he gave a farewell speech that was a blistering takedown of the institution. He described the attitudes of his former colleagues as follows:

- First, an orthodoxy of viewpoint, about the role of the Appellate Body as a self-anointed international court, with much broader authority to over-reach the rules and create judge-made law than I thought was permitted by the WTO agreements, or intended by the negotiators who created them;
- Second, a mindset that declined to re-examine the premises by which the Appellate Body expanded its role; and
- Third, a kind of group-think that de-legitimized serious systemic criticisms, and those who espoused them.[9]

Tom is a friend of mine and was for several years my partner at our law firm. Privately he told me that the Appellate Body is clearly biased against the United States in his experience and that whatever I think the size of the problem is, it is actually larger.

A Parade of Bad Cases

A few illustrative but by no means exhaustive examples underscore the Appellate Body's overreach, undermining of US sovereignty, and basic failure to fulfill its chief mission of swift and fair adjudication of trade disputes.

The Boeing v. Airbus *case.* Perhaps one of the most infamous cases that demonstrate the ineffectualness of the WTO dispute process is this one, which involved commercial aircraft. Boeing is a commercial company that grew up through the private markets in the United States. Airbus was the creation of four European countries that wanted to have a commercial aircraft industry and so took action to create one. The European nations heavily subsidized their company in order to create employment and foster technological development.

Eventually, the US government brought a case challenging these subsidies as a violation of the WTO subsidies agreement. This occurred when Airbus received below-market loans to launch two new airliners—the A350 and the A380. Europe countersued, and seventeen years of largely fruitless litigation followed. Indeed, *Jarndyce v. Jarndyce* had nothing on *Boeing v. Airbus.*

In the Trump administration, to persuade Europe to stop subsidizing, we finally took action by exercising our right under the WTO rules to impose tariffs on a commensurate amount of their imports. When the Biden administration came into office, they just rolled over and removed the tariffs. In an effort to get Europe to be more cooperative in other areas, they agreed to a five-year talk truce. Europe was (of course) not inclined to be more cooperative. There still is no resolution in sight—the great case continues.

The Appellate Body encouraged unfair trading practices. Long before the WTO was created, the United States maintained that imports that are dumped (sold at an unfairly low price) or subsidized constitute unfair trade and that our and other governments may impose tariffs to prevent such imports from hurting domestic industries. It is easy to see the unfair advantage a foreign producer would have if its production costs were subsidized by its government.

The case against dumping is less obvious but equally distorting. If a foreign manufacturer can sell at high prices at home, it can cover much of the costs of its fixed cost of production there and then sell in a foreign market (say, the United States) at a price just above the marginal cost of production. If the foreign manufacturer is competing with a domestic firm that must cover all manufacturing costs, it will have a significant advantage.

Anti-subsidy and anti-dumping rules do not undermine true market competition; they enhance it and are essential to giving American companies a fair chance to succeed in their own country. And these laws are expressly allowed under WTO rules.

Yet for decades the Appellate Body has taken the side of unfair trade. Over and over in dozens of cases, the Appellate Body twisted the rules to find that US anti-dumping and anti-subsidy rules violated our WTO obligations, even though these rules existed for decades before even the GATT was created and the United States never agreed in any negotiation to weaken them in the manner suggested by the Appellate Body. Indeed, negotiators specifically put in the agreement language that requires deference to government agency action in deciding such cases. Unfortunately, these facts have been ignored. As a result of these erroneous decisions, it is easier for foreign companies to be subsidized and to dump in our market. A separate series of cases makes it more difficult to use these laws against unfair trade against China. Indeed, China may be the biggest winner in this judicial overreach.

Reversing safeguard actions. Safeguard actions are specifically allowed under the WTO agreement. In situations where imports flood a foreign market and cause "serious" injury to an importer's market industry, the importing country can impose duties on the imports for a period of time to allow adjustment to the import surge. The Appellate Body has struck down almost every safeguard action that any country has made since its inception. For the most part, it did this by creating new obligations.

The Appellate Body interfered with US tax policy. For decades, under the GATT system, the United States and other members had an understanding that countries were not required to tax income of its domestic companies derived from sales abroad. Not taxing foreign profits makes the companies' products more competitive in export markets. Countries in Europe and elsewhere accomplished this by using a value-added tax system. Like a sales tax, a VAT is applied to the sale of all goods in the domestic market, whether the products are from domestic or foreign companies. However, when their domestic companies export products, the government rebates (refunds) the VAT. The United States does not have a VAT, but for years under our tax law, American companies had the option of structuring their operations to avoid taxes on sales outside this country. This bit of unfairness is further covered in chapter 17 as a transcending issue. Nothing in the WTO agreements should have changed these arrangements. But within a few years after the Appellate Body was created, it found that the US approach constituted an unfair subsidy—even though there was no evidence that our practice distorted trade or was more distortive than the EU's VAT system. To this day, US companies are taxed on their sales abroad, while companies in VAT countries largely avoid such taxes. These rules certainly put American companies at an unfair disadvantage and cost American jobs.

The Appellate Body interfered with US government spending. Back in the 2000s, the US Congress decided to help American companies harmed by illegal dumping and subsidization by providing those companies with funds collected as duties levied on dumped and subsidized imports. Congress plainly had the right to make this decision—no WTO provision limits how a WTO member might choose to spend anti-dumping and anti-subsidy duties. But the Appellate Body invented a new category of prohibited subsidies to rule against the US law. In order to come into compliance, Congress repealed the law and left these US companies injured and uncompensated.

The Appellate Body interfered with US social policy. For decades, Congress and state governments have regulated gambling—and the whole notion that the United States would have given this authority to the WTO is ludicrous. Nevertheless, the Appellate Body ruled that US restrictions on gambling represented a trade barrier that harmed Antigua and Barbuda. This decision was so absurd that neither the Bush administration nor the Obama administration, both of which believed in the Appellate Body, was willing to comply with it.

The WTO found against the United States on environmental safety statutes. In what were called the Tuna-Dolphin cases, the WTO repeatedly found for Mexico in its challenge to a US statute that required that tuna imported into the United States be caught using methods that adequately protect dolphins from being killed. The case went on for more than ten years, with numerous changes required in US laws. Finally, in 2018, the Trump administration won the case to end the litigation.

Back when the US government originally agreed to the current WTO dispute settlement system, we were told that the United States would be able to use that process to open markets to our exports. But as we have seen in this chapter, it just hasn't worked out that way. Instead, the United States has been the primary target of the dispute process. Why did we lose all those cases? In short, because the WTO Appellate Body never applied the agreements as they were intended. Instead, its judges engaged in extreme judicial activism, repeatedly going out of their way to find excuses to rule against us.

An Enabler of China

Even with all the above criticisms taken into account, the biggest problem with the WTO may be its inability to deal with the unfair economic practices of our biggest geopolitical adversary. The biggest problem facing the United States and most of the Western democracies is the challenge from China. It uses mercantilist practices, largely closed markets, massive subsidies, state-owned enterprises (SOEs), industrial espionage, investment controls, and the like to create huge surpluses. Most of this is not the result of economic forces but of government policies. There is very little that the WTO can do about that. Many of the most destructive Chinese practices are not covered by WTO rules. In other cases, China has been held to violate its obligations, but it simply changes the offending policy and accomplishes its governmental object in another way. To make matters even worse, the Chinese are at the table in the WTO with a veto over any new rule that might effectively challenge them.

While its own rules mean that it can't help market economies that compete with China, the WTO dispute resolution process has actually done things to make it more difficult to challenge China's unfair practices. In a series of decisions, the Appellate Body has struck down

US practices that are designed to control Chinese subsidies and illegal dumping. These cases have made it hard for the United States and other countries to counter industrial subsidies and other unfair actions.

Of course, China itself is a great defender of the current system. Not surprisingly, in June 2022, during the 12th Ministerial Conference in Geneva, the *People's Daily*, the CCP's paper of record, defended the WTO's record and attacked the United States. The article praised the benefits to China, calling its enormous growth a "win-win situation" and attacked the current US policy as "the extremely selfish 'America First' policy."[10] The "win-win" I assume referred to the CCP and a handful of oligarchs. The article went on to praise the statement of the WTO director general Ngozi Okonjo-Iweala, China's ally in Geneva. My reaction to this at the time was that it's only when you are over the target that you see the flack.

A Direct Threat to US National Security

Just when you thought things couldn't get any worse, at the end of 2022, a WTO dispute panel held that it could second-guess decisions the US government makes on sensitive national security issues. The dispute arose from the tariffs imposed by the Trump administration on steel and aluminum imports. In defending a case brought by China and others at the WTO, the United States invoked the "essential security" contained in article 22 of the GATT. This provision reads as follows: "Nothing in this Agreement shall be construed . . . to prevent any contracting party from taking any action which *it considers* necessary for the protection of its essential security interests."[11] "It considers" was plainly intended to convey that the exception is self-judging—that's how the United States has interpreted it for more than seventy years. But the WTO panel thought otherwise and sought to overrule the national security judgments of not one but two US presidents.

Now that one panel has said it can review national security actions relating to steel and aluminum, there's nothing to stop future panels from attempting to undermine the United States with export controls, sanctions, and weapons non-proliferation measures. In fact, China recently sued the United States over new export control rules on semi-conductors.

The current USTR Katherine Tai excoriated the ruling in the steel and aluminum case, saying that the WTO was skating on "very, very thin ice" by venturing into this territory and stating that the United States will not comply with this erroneous—and dangerous—opinion.[12] I couldn't have said it better myself.

A Frozen, Inequitable System

While the WTO's dispute resolution bureaucracy thrived, its negotiating function stalled. This was not a coincidence. Countries realized that they could more easily advance their trade agendas through litigation—by convincing the Appellate Body to expand or alter the WTO rules—than negotiation. As a result, many countries lost the incentive to negotiate. And, unsurprisingly, there has not been a successful round of major multilateral trade negotiations since the establishment of the WTO.

The last major attempt at negotiating, the 2001 Doha Round, ended in failure. Even smaller scale initiatives have either flopped or been major disappointments. Negotiations over e-commerce rules have dragged on for years and are hopelessly deadlocked. After twenty years of painstaking negotiations to limit harmful fisheries subsidies, WTO members threw in the towel at the 12th Ministerial Conference in 2022 and settled on a lowest-common-denominator agreement that fails to cover some of the most destructive ocean-depleting subsidies for things such as fuel and modernization of fishing fleets. This low-ambition deal seemed designed less to restore the planet's fish stocks than to provide fodder for a post-Ministerial press release and give the director general some basis for arguing that the event wasn't a complete disaster.[13]

Prior to the 1995 formation of the Appellate Body, if the contracting parties of the GATT wanted concessions, they were forced to negotiate and to make deals. Absent that pressure, it is not surprising that under the WTO, countries go straight to litigation, thereby short-circuiting the diplomatic process. Another reason for the end of successful major negotiations can be found in the composition of the current WTO. It is one thing to hold negotiations when you have 23 like-minded countries and quite another when you have 164 countries, many of which are not market economies with a rule of law and some of which are non-market autocracies. Add to that the fact that each of these countries is far more interested in looking for an edge for itself than in advancing free trade. It is extremely difficult to get consensus on any significant deal under such conditions.

While no deals are better than bad deals, I do not rejoice at the demise of serious multilateral trade negotiations. The rules-based trading system served the United States well from 1947 to 1995. And paralysis at the WTO means that inequities built into the Uruguay Round Agreement that are damaging to US interests remain. The three most serious are disparate tariff rates, the developing country loophole, and exceptions to MFN treatment that threaten to swallow the rule.

Tariff Disparities

The Uruguay Round left in place large disparities in global tariff rates. The agreement locked in high tariffs for supposedly "developing" countries such as China that have become among the dominant trading nations in the world and also left in place notable discrepancies between the United States and Europe. For example, a US automobile tariff of 2.5 percent relative to a 25 percent tariff from China and an EU tariff of 10 percent. For India the tariff rate on cars is 100 percent, and for Brazil it is 34 percent. We have an average applied tariff rate on wine of about 3.5 percent. The EU equivalent number is 32 percent. The numbers for Brazil and India are 20 percent, and duties on other products often exceed over 150 percent. There are many other examples.

Had the international trading system continued to follow the pattern set after 1947, the United States would have had an opportunity to address these disparities in future rounds of negotiations. But with the WTO's negotiating function moribund, there is no such opportunity for redress on the horizon.

The Developing Country Loophole

Another problem is its treatment of so-called developing countries. One of the oddities of trade negotiations is that while all parties profess to agree to the shared objective of creating important new rules to help open markets, to get agreement, they must create exceptions and carve-outs that essentially erase the obligation. Every trade deal that I have read has tended to follow this pattern.

One particularly pernicious example of this sleight of hand is seen in the "special and differential treatment" of developing countries. "Developing countries" have, in many cases, fewer obligations under WTO agreements than other countries do. While the actual carve-outs are specific to a particular negotiation, generally, developing countries have longer to phase in obligations and can take certain proscribed actions without penalty. They can also take certain steps to help their own companies and economies that developed countries cannot. For example, developing countries have the right to restrict imports to promote the establishment or maintenance of a particular domestic industry or assist in balance of payments difficulties. Developing countries also have access to provisions that are non-reciprocal preference treatments. The United States has a non-reciprocal preference treatment whereby these countries can get duty-free access. We call ours the Generalized System of Preferences, or GSP.

This notion of preferential treatment has some validity, but in an "only at the WTO" twist, any country can "self-designate" as a developing country. Indeed, the United States could so designate if it wished. We find, unsurprisingly, that most of the members of the WTO call themselves developing countries. In fact, of the G20 nations (a group of the twenty largest economies in the world), several self-designate as developing countries at the WTO. Those include China (the second largest economy in the world), Mexico, India, Turkey, Saudi Arabia, Indonesia, South Africa, and Argentina. It is of course ridiculous for these large and sometimes very rich economies to be treated differently than the United States is at the WTO. To counter this absurdity, the Trump administration had a policy of encouraging rich countries to redesignate themselves as developed. We persuaded both Brazil and South Korea to say they were no longer developing countries. But the problem remains.

I always point out the obvious contradiction that "developing country" status reveals. Free trade theologians say that countries are more likely to develop if they follow free trade policies such as those codified in the WTO rules. Yet 80 percent of the WTO membership call themselves developing countries precisely because they do not want to abide by rules they believe will inhibit their growth. It is a little bit like a chapter of Alcoholics Anonymous where 80 percent of the members want a pass to continue drinking. Special treatment should only apply to the very poor countries that don't have the resources to follow the rules.

MFN Treatment Is under Assault

The WTO supposedly holds the concept of Most Favored Nation treatment as its highest principle. The principle requires every country to charge the same tariff rate equally to all WTO members and to treat the goods and services of all WTO members the same. No playing favorites. But as international bureaucrats tend to do, they created an exception. If a country enters into a free trade agreement with another country or group of countries that covers "substantially all" their trade, they can give benefits to those countries that are better than MFN. In short, if you do a free trade agreement (FTA), you can get better treatment than the rest can. So, of course, many countries enter into numerous FTAs to get around the MFN principle. In reality, this is no better than the pre-GATT days of bilateral trade deals.

In some cases, such as USMCA, perhaps contiguous countries are actually moving toward a unified market, but in many others these deals are just a ruse to get preferential treatment for certain exporters. As in many of these scams, Europe is the lead offender. The European Union has entered into seventy-two such agreements. It is essentially resurrecting the "old colonial preferences" of a bygone era—something, by the way, that was harshly condemned at the time. When trading with Europe, the United States gets worse treatment than at least seventy-two other countries, even though we are their biggest market and the victim of their biggest surplus. China is another big offender. Its Regional Comprehensive Economic Partnership is a group of twelve countries that likewise ignore the MFN obligation. Thus, China also gives preferences to many other countries, even though the United States is its biggest customer. Of course, the United States has some twenty such agreements. With the exception of USMCA, they can be equally criticized.

The WTO needs to return to its roots and again be an MFN-based organization. If it won't or can't do that, then the United States should once again start the process of negotiating bilateral trade deals around the world. Clearly, in the current world of de facto qualified MFN, the United States is better off negotiating bilateral deals using the leverage of our market size to obtain favorable market access in other countries.

The Need for Change

Given the Appellate Body's inability to regulate, much less reform, itself, the Trump administration took decisive action to limit US exposure to its destructive influence. We did so by moving beyond the Obama administration's blocking of a particular judge to stopping the formation of the quorum required to conduct business as usual. We were able to do this because the judges are appointed by consensus. When, on behalf of the United States, I refused to agree to start the process of bringing new judges on board, the quorum had no way of replenishing its numbers. As a result, the Appellate Body slowly shrank from seven, to six, to five, to four, to three, to two, and finally to one, on November 30, 2020. Ironically, this last judge was Ms. Hong Zhao, a CCP member from China.

By the time that membership got down to two, the Appellate Body could no longer function. We were well rid of it. Despite some apocalyptic hand-wringing by critics, no one actually missed the Appellate Body, as I pointed out at the time.[14] Indeed, I always note that there is no correlation between actual operations of trade and the existence of this tribunal.

Killing the Appellate Body was important. But more must be done to fix the WTO. Contrary to critics of the Trump administration, absolutely no one is arguing that we should revert from a rules-based system to the so-called law of the jungle in trade relations. But sticking with the current WTO would actually entail betraying the core principles of a rules-based system, because this organization has shown itself to be chronically incapable of proceeding according to those principles.

Looking toward the future, the WTO needs to abide by its core principles and make the systematic reforms that it was designed to carry out. Mere tweaking will not be enough.

First, we need a reset on the global tariff system. This practice of countries having wildly different tariffs for the same products is unfair, inefficient, and historically anachronistic. We need a new baseline for all tariffs. There should be some small number of exceptions permitted to accommodate grave political and economic situations in some countries. The average tariffs of industrialized countries would be a good starting point for discussions on this baseline.

Second, we need to stop the FTA end run around MFN treatment. Clearly, defined custom unions of contiguous states, such as USMCA or the European Union, should be permitted, but otherwise countries should have to treat all trading partners equally.

Third, special and differential treatment has to be cut back so that only the poorest countries in the world get special treatment. The rest are either in the trading system or they are not.

Fourth, the WTO needs new rules to stop Chinese economic aggression. Clearly, compensatory tariffs should be allowed in prescribed circumstances. Further, if necessary, countries should have the ability to act unilaterally to counter predatory, mercantilist policies.

Fifth, the concept of a sunset should be incorporated into the WTO agreements. Economies change, and so should the obligations of members. No business would sign an eternal contract with its suppliers, nor should any country.

Sixth, the WTO must adopt a mechanism that assures long-term balanced trade. Commitments must be flexible when a country such as the United States runs up trillions of dollars of deficits for decades.

Finally, the dispute settlement system should be scrapped. A new one, modeled after commercial arbitration, should be put in its place. There should be a one-stage panel process with a vote of the WTO member states being able to overturn the decisions. Further, the decisions should be the basis of party negotiations and not be binding.

The strawman of the law of the jungle versus the status quo cannot obscure the fact that the current system is a massive failure on its own terms—and certainly with respect to US interests. The status quo is not an option.

Part Two

CHINA—
OUR GREATEST
CHALLENGE

Chapter 5

Our Greatest
Geopolitical Threat

In 2017, at an address to China's National Security Work Forum, President Xi Jinping declared that the time had come to leave behind the era of hiding one's capabilities and biding time.[1] Instead, he offered a narrative centered on the idea that China was assuming the role of the dominant world power. In this scenario, as a rejuvenated, aggressive China looms ever larger on the global landscape, an exhausted, confused United States flails about, on the wane. America is still powerful enough to create obstacles to China's rise but not to thwart its ultimate triumph, Xi proclaimed. The mask was off.

But in truth the mask was never all that convincing. For decades it has been evident that China was never the aspiring democratic paradise that free traders wanted to pretend it was. Now China is the greatest threat that the American nation and its system of Western liberal democratic government has faced since the American Revolution. And we helped make that happen.

One statistic puts the magnitude of the economic challenge faced by the United States into perspective. Over the entire twentieth century, no competing power was as economically powerful relative to the United States as China is today. Neither the combined economies of imperial Japan and Nazi Germany nor that of the Soviet Union at the height of its economic power came close to 60 percent of the American GDP.[2] China crossed that threshold in 2014, and its economic growth rate continues to significantly outpace that of the United States.[3] And rising economic power enables military power and global financial influence. This is the most serious challenger America has faced in more than a century.

China is a militaristic, autocratic, Communist country with an economy that is the second biggest in the world and that could soon be bigger than ours. It is dedicated to being the dominant country in the world and to spreading its anti-American, anti-democratic, Communist system.

China views us and our values as a barrier to its goal. Beyond that, it intensely dislikes the United States and our way of life. It teaches its children to dislike us. It is building up its military at a much more rapid rate than we are prepared for in any possible confrontation. While there is nothing immoral in China pursuing its national interests by growing its economy, there is much that is immoral about engaging in predatory, unfair practices, as it does routinely. It has an intensely anti-American diplomatic corps. It is the source of the most cyberattacks, the most technology theft, and the most outright spying in the world. It is the source of the most pollution and is doing nearly nothing to contain it. And it has the worst human rights practices in modern history. It spends millions of dollars every year to influence our political and academic institutions. In short, China is a very strong adversary targeted directly at us. Every American should wake up to that fact. If we lose this confrontation, the world will be a very different place. This is a life and death issue. Our very way of life—and the fate of the free world as such—is at stake.

One would never know any of this based on the rhetoric that is coming out of China and being reproduced by the compromised US leaders who are utterly in thrall to our adversary, as documented by many, including Peter Schweizer.[4] Yet it is often claimed that it is the United States that is the paranoid warmonger, while China merely seeks friendship and shared opportunities—except when someone challenges them, in which case it promises that heads will be bashed until blood flows.[5] More often than not, however, the rhetoric of its leaders, which again has an echo chamber in the United States, downplays the mortal threat that China poses to those who stand in its way. But if there is one lesson that has been amply hammered out over the long history of interactions between the United States and China on economic and geopolitical fronts, it is this: watch carefully what the Chinese government does and heavily discount what it says.

After the global backlash that followed the 1989 crackdown in Tiananmen Square, the iron hand of China was kept carefully clothed in the velvet glove. In the face of global outrage, however, China's aging leader, Deng Xiaoping, was undeterred. He did not apologize for the crackdown. Instead, he came up with a new party slogan. In a series of internal missives, Deng urged a cautious approach to Chinese foreign policy encapsulated in his famous phrase "Hide one's capabilities and bide one's time."[6]

That strategy worked. The outrage in the West that followed Tiananmen was of surprisingly short duration. China did, however, learn a lesson from Tiananmen—that a global backlash to such an egregious abuse could have harmful ramifications for its interests. The aftereffects of the incident suggested that, with care, diplomatic efforts could be used to manage the international understanding of China's actions and intent. They bet on the power of soothing rhetoric to reassure world leaders. And world leaders were in fact quite easily reassured, even in the face of serious concerns. Perhaps this was because Chinese rhetoric and money often supported the politicians' own agenda, as was the case in the United States under the Clinton administration.

Back in 1999, President Clinton had temporarily withdrawn from negotiations to let China join the WTO in the face of concerns about the scandal arising from Chinese political donations and nuclear spying. But almost immediately he restarted the process. In an April 18, 1999, op-ed in the *New York Times*, I expressed concern that the United States would be giving away economic leverage that could be used in the event of military aggression or human rights–related abuses.[7] I remarked that "using economic pressure to counteract Chinese military or diplomatic aggression is exactly what we need. . . . Unless changes are made . . . the United States may not be able, once China is in the W.T.O., to restrict Chinese imports in response to threats toward Taiwan, human rights violations in Tibet or religious persecution." This turned out to be an accurate snapshot of our current predicament. Back then I called the prospective deal one that we were likely to regret. But now the consequences go well beyond feelings of regret.

For close to thirty years, the Chinese strategy of making the most of the process of engagement with the West proved to be successful in advancing China's interests.

Most recently, however, as China has gained confidence in light of its ever-increasing economic and military clout under President Xi Jinping, the polite mask has been ripped off. In interactions with representatives of the Biden administration, the Chinese government has demonstrated overt rudeness and aggression. This is not unintentional. Little that the Chinese government states publicly is unintentional. Statements are carefully gauged to achieve specific effects, with the overall aim of enhancing Chinese control of events. The struggle for control is the primary driver of China's policy, and that did not change after Mao. What has changed is that increasingly the Chinese aren't hiding their intentions. The recent deliberate public prodding of the United States that we see reflects a sense by the Chinese that they now have the power to play a more open hand. And China fully intends to combine the leverage granted by its ramped-up military capabilities with the power inherent in its dominant role in international trade. The work report to the 20th Party Congress in October 2022 was the clearest evidence of this new approach. The tone was confident, even strident, and clearly Marxist, autocratic, and militaristic.

Today the United States is increasingly threatened by China on multiple fronts. We see China taking a more aggressive stance to grab power in its immediate surroundings in the South China Sea and vis-à-vis its neighbors. These power plays are backed up by implicit economic threats to a world that has become overly dependent on China for critical products and inputs to supply chains and for financial investment required to sustain a growing reliance on debt.

From another perspective, the new frankness of the Chinese is a welcome change. It is increasingly clear to even the more optimistic among us that the United States faces an openly hostile and powerful adversary. At least we know where we stand.

Maintaining the foolish delusion of China as a peaceful, democratic member of the international community is clearly a lost cause. We need to break down the evidence that shows the sharp discrepancy between China's words about dialogue and friendship, on the one hand, and its actions, on the other, in a range of different sectors around the world. While the primary focus of this book is on China's tactics in the trade arena, its efforts to achieve dominance are not limited to economic leverage primarily exerted through trade channels but are backed up by enhanced military, diplomatic, and financial power that extends throughout the globe. China's trade policy and practices need to be seen in the context of this broader pattern of aggressive strategic action across multiple fronts. Unsurprisingly from a country that has long recognized that, in the words of Mao, political power grows out of the barrel of a gun, military might is at the heart of its strategic plan.

The Barrel of the Gun: China's Military Is a Growing Threat

China's military is an existential threat to the United States. It is building its aggressive military capability at an unprecedented rate. It is important to remember that there are very few dictators in history who built up an army and didn't use it. The military threat of China is enabled by its economic might and by its liberal theft of technology from the West. The People's Liberation Army (PLA) is in the midst of a wholesale makeover, with China aiming to complete the first phase of its efforts by 2035 and have a world-class military equal to or exceeding that of the United States by 2049.[8] This effort has already started to bear fruit. The PLA is currently equal to or surpasses the US military in several key areas. China boasts the world's largest navy, with approximately sixty more ships than the United States has, and has more land-based conventional ballistic and cruise missiles.[9] In July 2021, China launched a hypersonic missile that circled the planet in a low-earth orbit before releasing a glide vehicle that separately fired a projectile of its own. Such a weapon could be used to evade even the most advanced missile defense systems. No other country has demonstrated a similar capability, and US military officials concede that America's hypersonic weapons-development program trails China's. Experts have suggested that an objective of the latest round of testing in China, including the completion of a supersonic missile testing wind tunnel, is to develop ways of attacking the United States from the south in a manner that avoids America's north-facing missile defense systems.[10]

The PLA is also building approximately 230 new nuclear silos, which were uncovered by the Federation of American Scientists through analysis of civilian satellite data.[11] Although it is unclear how many new nuclear missiles will actually be housed in these silos, and experts have debated whether the construction signifies a shift toward a new arms race or is simply a negotiating ploy for potential arms control negotiations, this buildup indicates a significant change in posture and is quite worrying for the United States and its allies. This aggressive positioning is matched by what the US Department of Defense has called a "robust and redundant integrated air defense system architecture" consisting of Russian- and Chinese-made advanced long-range surface-to-air systems.[12]

In parallel to its military buildup, China has become increasingly assertive in international disputes. Of particular concern is China's sharp escalation of military pressure on Taiwan, a former province that has been independent since the end of the Chinese Civil War in 1949. China has sharply increased the number and scale of military incursions into Taiwanese territory, sending 150 aircraft—including 34 J-16 fighters and 12 nuclear-capable H-6 bombers—into Taiwan's defense zone in one four-day period in October 2021.[13] Chiu Kuo-cheng, Taiwan's defense minister, emphasized in public comments that this has resulted in the worst tensions between Taiwan and China in forty years and has increased the potential for an accidental start to broader conflict.[14] The United States has, for decades, maintained a policy of "strategic ambiguity" about whether it would defend Taiwan in the event of a Chinese attack. This policy continues to this day, despite calls from some policy makers for the United States to make a clear commitment to defend the island.[15] However, the contours of such a commitment are hard to define, and it is likely that the United States would not be able to repel a Chinese assault on Taiwan without igniting a much larger and devastating war. In fact, recent war games have found that the United States and Taiwan would have enormous difficulty rolling back even a more gradual territorial aggression by China, with "few credible options" to respond if China were to seize a set of Taiwanese islands.[16]

Outside of Taiwan, China has been engaged in a set of increasingly provocative actions in the South China Sea. The South China Sea plays an important security role in the region, given that more than 80 percent of the flow of crude oil to Japan, South Korea, and Taiwan goes through its shipping lanes.[17] The strategic importance for the United States can also hardly be overstated, as the sea lines that crisscross the South China Sea carry $1.2 trillion in US trade.[18] China has made extensive claims in the area that are disputed by Brunei, the Philippines, Malaysia, and Vietnam and were found to be illegitimate by a 2016 international tribunal.[19] Nonetheless, China has piled resources into fortifying its claims by building artificial islands within the Spratly Island chain[20] and amassing fleets of civilian and military vessels in disputed territories.[21] The United States has sent navy warships on routine patrols through the sea to challenge China's asserted right to restrict military activity in the area, but China has only become more aggressive in taking de facto control over its claimed possessions.

US Indo-Pacific commander Admiral John C. Aquilino remarked, "I think over the past 20 years we've witnessed the largest military buildup since World War II by the PRC," and his comment resonates with respect to the overall dramatic increase in China's military capacity.[22]

China has also been locked in an extended face-off with India over a border dispute. In May 2020, Chinese troops crossed into territory claimed by India, a move leading to tense military buildups and standoffs between the two nations.[23] In June 2020, the tension erupted into violence that led to the deaths of twenty Indian soldiers and four Chinese soldiers.[24] Since then, the situation has been at a standstill, with China gaining effective control over hundreds of square kilometers of territory.

The Chinese army also regularly engages in espionage against the United States. Much of that spying is in the economic sphere, where the Chinese attempt to steal sophisticated technology. This is covered in the next chapter. They also aggressively practice traditional espionage. FBI director Christopher Wray called China the "greatest long-term threat" to the United States and noted that the FBI opens a new espionage case involving China every twelve hours. President Trump started a special unit at the Department of Justice to deal with this issue. The Biden Justice Department disbanded it, claiming it was unfair to the Chinese.[25]

Chinese intelligence operations in the United States have gotten more aggressive in recent years. In 2020, the Trump administration ordered the closure of China's consulate in Houston after a multi-year FBI investigation showed that it was a hub for Chinese espionage in the United States. Representative Michael McCaul, chair of the House Homeland Security Committee, said that the investigation revealed "a systematic effort by the Chinese government to get into our medical facilities, our research development facilities, academics as well."[26] In 2023, the provocative nature of Chinese intelligence gathering was made clear to the American people when a Chinese spy balloon carrying antennas and sensors for collecting intelligence and communications was identified traversing the United States and passing over highly sensitive military facilities (including nuclear sites in Montana) on the eve of what was supposed to be a major diplomatic engagement between US and Chinese officials.[27] During the episode, which a unanimous House resolution called a "brazen violation of United States sovereignty," the Biden administration allowed the balloon to cross over the entirety of the country before ultimately shooting it down off the Atlantic coast eight days later. The incident revealed weaknesses in US radar, counterintelligence, and air defense capabilities and suggested Chinese willingness to demonstrate their espionage capabilities blatantly and openly in the United States.[28]

The Chinese government also pursues its internal opponents when they flee to the United States, including through programs called Operation Fox Hunt and Operation Sky Net. Through these initiatives, secret Chinese agents operating on US soil track, kidnap, and blackmail hundreds of people, including US citizens and permanent residents, completely outside of normal extradition procedures. The programs nominally target people accused of financial crimes, but many are dissidents, whistleblowers, or people caught in provincial political conflicts.[29] The network of Chinese agents operating in the United States is systematically supported and well resourced, as was demonstrated when an FBI counterintelligence raid in the heart of New York City's Chinatown neighborhood revealed a secret Chinese police station tasked with spying on Chinese expatriates and secretly arresting and repatriating those targeted by the Chinese government.[30]

In another troubling trend, Chinese entities have recently started buying up US farmland. This is troubling both because of the often strategically significant location of the property and because of the obvious importance of our food supply to national security. Recent reports are that Chinese entities own almost 200,000 acres of prime agriculture territory.[31] In some cases China's objective may be to control production, and in others it appears that the land is located near sensitive US military facilities. A Chinese food manufacturer, the Fufeng Group, recently bought 370 acres located sixteen miles from the Grand Forks Air Force Base in North Dakota, where our highly sensitive drone program is located.[32] It is a travesty that this purchase was allowed to happen by the federal government, although the local municipal government ultimately blocked Fufeng's plans to build a corn mill operation on the site in response to political uproar (the company nonetheless continued to own the strategically located site).[33] In addition, Chinese companies have purchased major players in US food processing. In 2013, a Chinese company bought Smithfield Foods, one of America's largest meat processors.[34] Other examples of concerning Chinese investment in US food infrastructure include Chinese SOE COFCO's 2017 partnership with Growmark, a US grain logistics firm and the $127 million investment made in 2015 by China's New Hope Liuhe in the Lansing Trade Group. Other US brands with substantial Chinese ownership include American Multi-Cinema (AMC), GE Appliances, and Snapchat.[35]

China's Environmental Degradation

China's policies massively exacerbate climate change and environmental degradation. It has been the world's largest annual greenhouse-gas emitter since 2006, and emissions have continued to grow at an accelerated rate.[36] China has also taken on a role as the primary exporter of greenhouse gas emissions globally, stepping in to become the world's primary source of financing for coal-fired power plants as global lenders seek to shift away to cleaner energy supplies.[37] This problem is particularly significant in the context of the Belt and Road Initiative (BRI), which has channeled Chinese investment and expertise toward dirty energy in the developing world. At least 60 percent of total financing from the top two Chinese BRI-oriented banks has gone toward non-renewable energy.[38]

Wild animals are not safe either. China has provided cover for a thriving market in poached wildlife by allowing legal trade in exotic species such as tigers and rhinos.[39] The World Wildlife Fund found that BRI projects consistently cut through environmentally sensitive areas that are critically important for biodiversity and bird life.[40] China is also one of the world's primary consumers of illegal timber products, and despite high-profile announcements claiming China's intent to reduce illegal logging, trade analysts have found a lack of significant progress in addressing the problem.[41]

As the ocean chokes under islands of trash, China is continuing to be the primary emitter of marine plastic debris, dumping up to one million tons of plastic waste into the ocean in 2017.[42] Fish that nonetheless survive are caught up in China's massive illegal fishing operations. China has flagrantly ignored international fishing frameworks, using generous subsidies and government pressure to incentivize a large part of its fleet of more than 800,000 fishing vessels to travel into disputed and protected areas to satisfy an enormous domestic demand for fish.[43] As a result, the country is the world's largest source of illegal, unreported, and unregulated fishing, ranked as the worst of 152 surveyed coastal states in the IUU index.[44]

Human Rights Abuses and International Coercion

At home, China is the world's most significant violator of human rights. Human Rights Watch put it well when it reported: "No other government is simultaneously detaining a million members of an ethnic minority for forced indoctrination and attacking anyone who dares to challenge its repression. And while other governments commit serious human rights violations, no other government flexes its political muscles with such vigor and determination to undermine the international human rights standards and institutions that could hold it to account."[45] China's disregard for the lives of its own citizens is perhaps most brutally reflected in the demonstrated fact that it kills prisoners to extract their organs for sale.[46] Some lives matter more than others to the CCP, and certain lives do not matter at all.

The tragedy that the Chinese regime is perpetrating on its own citizens in Xinjiang is arguably surpassed only by those committed in the darkest moments of the twentieth century. In an effort to suppress expression of Muslim faith and force conformity with the regime among the Uighur population, the Chinese government is committing what the United States has formally classified as a genocide.[47] China has mobilized one million officials and CCP cadres to forcibly stay in the homes of Muslim families in Xinjiang and monitor them. These uninvited "guests" report "problems" to the regime, including prayer or signs of active adherence to Islam, contact with foreign relatives, or insufficient fealty to the CCP.[48] This human surveillance has been supplemented by a web of video cameras deployed throughout the region, which is combined with mobile phone applications and biometric technology to enable constant monitoring of activity among citizens.[49] This is occurring amid a campaign of arbitrary detention that is shocking in its scope and cruelty. At least a million Uighurs and other Turkic Muslim minorities have been arbitrarily placed in indefinite detention, where they are exposed to physical and psychological torture and exploited for labor as part of "reeducation" programs.[50]

China's actions in Xinjiang are sadly not unique or out of character for its general treatment of minorities. The Chinese government first tested the approach currently used in Xinjiang in Tibet, where it rolled out a "grid-style social system" in 2011. This included a web of surveillance and police presence, as well as "policies to control the flow of information, increase party presence in public and private spaces and encourage Chinese nationalism through re-education camps."[51] The US State Department has found that significant human rights issues continue in the region, including torture, arbitrary arrest following "cursory and closed" trials, and political imprisonment.[52]

The Chinese government's use of surveillance and arbitrary detention is not limited to minority groups. The CCP has implemented an array of surveillance technology across the country targeted at all citizens and has used its influence to clamp down on dissent domestically. The campaign of repression extends internationally, and the Chinese government often uses various techniques to pressure expatriate citizens into compliance. In Hong Kong, which had been under a "one country, two systems" model of semi-autonomy since transfer of control from the British in 1997, China asserted its complete control in mid-2020 with the passage of a draconian National Security Law.[53] The law created a broad set of offenses that covered myriad forms of supposed anti-state conduct and criminalized multiple forms of political dissent. The law also commandeered Hong Kong government institutions to serve the PRC security apparatus, broke down the traditional "firewall" between Hong Kong and PRC legal systems, and granted significant and broad-ranging powers to PRC-appointed executive authorities in Hong Kong.[54]

In mainland China the CCP has continued strengthening its control through a system of surveillance that is increasing in sophistication with every passing year. China has long censored its internet, with its "Great Firewall" wiping away even mildly anti-regime information and fostering a rabid nationalism among the nation's youth.[55] China is supplementing this censorship with a system of mass surveillance, tying together phone scanners, facial-recognition cameras, face and fingerprint databases, and an array of advanced technology to track movement and association among its citizens and provide that information for use at the discretion of police and security services.[56]

This surveillance network is combined with a progressively expanding "social credit system," which integrates data on individuals, enterprises, social organizations, and government organizations to provide a "credit score" on organizations and individuals tied to both political and financial metrics. While the system is currently fragmented across the country, and is limited to tracking compliance with and enforcement of existing laws and regulations, the Chinese government is undertaking significant efforts to standardize and integrate the system nationwide.[57] When combined with the mass surveillance systems already deployed and those in the development process, the social credit system strongly suggests that CCP control over the minutiae of life within the country will only increase in the years to come.

The campaign of political control does not end at the country's borders.

PRC authorities will often threaten the relatives of dissidents abroad to prevent them from criticizing the regime.[58] This system of control extends to Chinese students studying abroad, who report that they face constant monitoring from their peers and CCP affiliates overseas and face sanctions ranging from online harassment to retaliation against relatives in China if they veer too far from acceptable political discourse.[59]

Other countries are not safe either. The Chinese government has consistently used its economic strength to pressure other countries into doing its bidding and turning the other way in the face of human rights abuses and military buildup. For example, Australia felt the force of Chinese economic coercion after its government angered Beijing. The Australian government publicly advocated for a global investigation into China's role in potential mismanagement of the coronavirus, placed restrictions on telecom firm Huawei because of security concerns, and critiqued China's national-security law in Hong Kong. In response, China imposed 80 percent tariffs on imports of Australian barley and suspended most imports of Australian beef. It also discouraged Chinese tourism to the country, spuriously claiming a rise in racial discrimination.[60] Informally, Chinese commodities traders were ordered by government officials to stop imports of Australian coal, barley, copper ore and concentrate, sugar, timber, wine, and lobster. As Australia's most important trading partner, with agricultural shipments alone totaling $11.3 billion, China timed the restrictions to harm Australia while it was experiencing its first recession in approximately thirty years.[61] The effort did not succeed in changing Australia's position, although it did create political problems for the government.[62]

For firms, China's job is even easier. While much attention has gone to the social credit score system that China is working to roll out for individuals, its associated system for companies is at a more advanced stage. A centralized code unites previously separate data regarding company financials, regulatory compliance, and other administrative records under the aegis of the National Enterprise Credit Information Publicity System. Firms are mandated to transfer a wide range of data to the database, including information relating to investments and business operations.[63] The government increasingly uses this centralized repository to assign negative ratings to firms and place others on blacklists that are associated with restrictions on business activities, such as reduced access to loans and tax incentives, exclusion from procurement contracts, monetary fines and permit denials, and increased inspections.[64] The constitutive elements that drive a company's social credit score are vague and leave significant room for discretion by government officials. This has driven major concerns that the corporate social credit system will be used to pressure US and other foreign firms to align with Chinese economic and industrial policies and avoid antagonizing the Chinese state or those with connections to it. Furthermore, the corporate social credit score is tied to the individual social credit system and makes firms responsible for the scores of key employees and associates.[65]

Fears that the Chinese government's retribution, or threat of it, will drive companies to adopt favorable positions and follow the CCP party line are not idle speculation. There is an ample record of American and other foreign firms becoming enforcers for the Chinese government in hope of pleasing it or at least avoiding its ire. In spring 2019, Herbert Diess, then the CEO of Volkswagen, said that he was "not aware" of the Chinese government's activities regarding Uighurs in Xinjiang province.[66] While this could theoretically be attributed to an appalling level of ignorance, it more likely has something to do with Volkswagen's factory in the region and the fact that China accounts for more than 40 percent of Volkswagen's global car sales.[67] Roy Jones, a social media account manager for Marriott, was fired after he used an official company account to like a post applauding Marriott for listing Tibet as a country, instead of a Chinese province, in an online survey. This occurred after Shanghai Municipal Tourism Administration officials questioned Marriott representatives regarding the matter and the underlying survey and ordered the company to publicly apologize and "seriously deal with the people responsible."[68] The titans of American finance are not exempt either. Jamie Dimon, the CEO of JPMorgan Chase, formally apologized after making a joke that JPMorgan would likely outlast the CCP. This apology came as the China Securities Regulatory Commission reviewed JPMorgan's application to take full control of its Chinese asset-management business. The next week, Mr. Dimon said of the United States that "[the Chinese] look at us now as kind of the incompetent nation . . . America can't get out of its own underwear." He did not apologize for this statement.[69]

Abuses in the Developing World

In July 2017, the Sri Lankan government found itself between a rock and a hard place. The country was drowning in debt, and there was only one option open to it. In exchange for $1 billion, enough to delay a default but not enough to fundamentally change the country's fiscal position, the Sri Lankans gave China a ninety-nine-year lease on their port at Hambantota and threw in 15,000 acres of land around it to seal the deal. Conveniently for China, the deal barely made a dent in the amount that Sri Lanka owed Chinese state-affiliated creditors—a significant portion of Sri Lanka's $12.3 billion of international debt.

This saga began when Sri Lanka's then president, Mahinda Rajapaksa, decided that he wanted to build a massive port development project in his home district of Hambantota. Western and Indian lenders refused to finance the project, which had little commercial justification. Sri Lanka is a country of twenty-two million people well served by an existing port, which had plenty of room for further expansion. Chinese officials nonetheless stepped in to finance the project. The Sri Lankan government kept agreeing to progressively more onerous Chinese terms and explicitly directed all contracts to Chinese state-owned and -affiliated firms. Meanwhile, the Chinese funneled large payments to Mahinda Rajapaksa's campaign in the 2015 Sri Lankan elections. When Sri Lanka nonetheless eventually elected a new government that sought to cut the country's debt load and reduce dependence on China, the Chinese refused to allow an easing of terms, and instead pushed for equity in the port. Sri Lanka ultimately handed over control but has continued accumulating debt to China. This rising debt is likely to be very effective leverage in the future and will support Chinese plans to make the port a strategic military asset.[70] To service the debt, resources were funneled to Chinese enterprises. In the meantime, the Sri Lankan population found it difficult to buy necessities such as food and energy. Their frustration boiled over in July 2022. The people stormed and sacked the presidential palace. Then President Gotabaya Rajapaksa fled the country, and an interim government was set up.[71] While there are many contributing factors in this situation, the existence of the Chinese projects was clearly an important one.

The Sri Lankan case is but one example of a broader pattern of Chinese behavior in the developing world under the guise of China's Belt and Road Initiative. Since its inception as a regional trade corridor in 2013, the BRI has dramatically expanded to include more than seventy partner countries and a wide range of economic activities. It is formally intended to provide hard and digital infrastructure to a range of developing and middle-income countries at relatively low prices. The need being met is real. The World Bank estimates that lack of infrastructure has depressed trade by approximately 30 percent and foreign direct investment by approximately 70 percent among countries in the BRI corridor.[72] China is pursuing a coordinated and well-resourced strategy to take advantage of this need. The BRI has the full political backing of the CCP, and it takes advantage of support from China's state-owned banks and a huge amount of surplus productive capacity in many sectors stemming from China's aggressive industrial policies.[73] This full-court press is working. China is currently the largest source of infrastructure financing to the developing world. The loan portfolio of the Export-Import Bank of China and the China Development Bank, combined with that of the thirteen regional BRI funds, exceeds the $700 billion in outstanding loans from all six Western-backed multilateral banks combined.[74] Overall, BRI promises more than $1 trillion in new infrastructure investment and broader funding in areas ranging from health to agriculture.[75]

Unfortunately, the BRI is a wolf in sheep's clothing. The program locks developing countries into expensive loans they cannot repay, prevents the development of local expertise, and forces countries into dependency on China that it has a demonstrated history of exploiting for geopolitical advantage. The economics of BRI transactions take advantage of developing countries to push them into agreements that either are not economically viable or are exploitative. Unlike the loans provided by major Western-backed development banks, loans extended for BRI projects are typically offered on close-to-commercial, rather than concessionary, terms with no public disclosure of loan details.[76] The significant state backing provided for the Chinese firms involved in BRI encourages them to take on projects that are very costly or risky, and they pursue many projects without conducting assessments of financial viability or social and environmental impacts. The projects lack consistent governance metrics and are often made and performed with little or no transparency.[77]

Poorly assessed BRI loans have created an unsustainable debt load for developing countries. The World Bank has found that nearly one-third of countries participating in the BRI are at a high risk of debt distress as a result of underlying macroeconomic weakness. At least fifteen BRI countries saw their debt outlook downgraded to negative in 2020, amid the peak of the COVID-19 pandemic, and emerging countries have been particularly impacted as they lack the policy toolkit to stem capital flight and loss of remittance income.[78] The financial pressure raises the stakes of significant BRI debt. Countries such as Uganda are struggling to make interest payments and are entering grace periods on their BRI loans, with the possibility of losing core national economic assets if they cannot resolve their fiscal challenges.[79]

Beyond being financially exploitative, BRI projects structurally favor Chinese contractors and fail to effectively foster local development. About 90 percent of BRI-related contracts go to Chinese companies.[80] And Chinese contractors who win these contracts generally import Chinese workers for construction and development, as well as operation of the infrastructure after its completion.[81] As a result, local workers fail to gain the skills necessary to replicate such projects on their own, and the broader effects on local productivity and economic development are muted. Chinese contractors can increasingly arbitrate disputes with target countries and local contractors in China, in arbitration courts set up by the Chinese with proceedings conducted in Mandarin.[82] Making matters worse, these contractors frequently perform subpar work. In Ecuador, Uganda, and Pakistan alone, multibillion-dollar hydroelectric plants built through the BRI are currently falling apart—a mere few years after they were completed.[83] China is also actively working to rig technical standards through the BRI to ensure dependence on Chinese suppliers for maintenance or upgrading of its projects once completed.[84] This process will help lock target countries into deeper economic integration with China, as well as limit the ability of those countries to transition to local or non-Chinese multinational suppliers across critical components of their infrastructure.[85]

Losing control over ports, courts, and standards is not the only way that the BRI has threatened the sovereignty of member nations. China uses the BRI as a tool of geopolitical influence, taking advantage of its economic leverage to pressure countries to support its international positions and enable China to strengthen its military and strategic footprint. Wary of upsetting the hand that feeds them, many BRI countries have acquiesced to Chinese political priorities while accumulating Chinese investment. In Pakistan, which contains the world's second largest Muslim population and is a prime recipient of BRI funds, the government—usually eager to defend perceived abuses of Muslims abroad—has refused to criticize China's mass imprisonment of and human rights abuses toward its Muslim Uighur minority. In an interview, Prime Minister Khan responded, when asked about the Uighurs, "We don't make public statements, because that's how China is . . . China has come to help when we were right at the rock bottom . . . So I would not publicly talk about it."[86] Similarly, Malaysia publicly backed China's internationally unrecognized claims in the South China Sea while seeking to renegotiate some of its BRI projects, and Nepal reinforced its border against a wave of Tibetan refugees and repatriated refugees, sending them back to face repression in China.[87]

BRI projects also have security implications for the recipient countries. For example, the African Union discovered that the IT network of its Chinese-built headquarters in Ethiopia had siphoned confidential data on its IT network to Shanghai every night for five years. African Union officials kept the Chinese surveillance secret for a year after discovering it, and it became public knowledge only after an investigation by the French newspaper *Le Monde*. The event itself, and the African Union's reluctance to confront China over it, demonstrates the security implications and geopolitical pressures that come with BRI projects in developing countries.[88] More broadly, the US Department of Defense has warned that BRI projects "could create potential military advantages for the PRC, such as PLA access to selected foreign ports to pre-position the necessary logistics to sustain naval deployments in waters as distant as the Indian Ocean, Mediterranean Sea, and Atlantic Ocean"[89]

Part of China's expansion militarily into Africa is through arms sales, military training, and dual-use infrastructure projects. The pace of these sales has picked up in recent years. For example, nearly 70 percent of the fifty-four countries in Africa use Chinese armored military vehicles, and 50 percent of Tanzania's arms inventory is of Chinese origin. This expansion has led to a much more visible Chinese military presence. Many observers are worried about China's building a permanent Atlantic Ocean base in the small central African country of Equatorial Guinea as well as its base in Djibouti, which is very near the sensitive US Camp Lemonnier.[90]

China also routinely uses its might to bully and overpower much smaller states. On May 30, 2022, China held a video meeting with the foreign ministers of at least nine tiny island nations. It produced a draft communiqué and five-year plan seeking a sweeping regional trade and security agreement. This kind of military expansion in this area is further evidence of China's intentions.[91] Why does China need a security agreement with the likes of Micronesia, Samoa, and Tonga? The only conceivable reason is to expand its aggressive military capabilities and to intimidate Asian shipping lanes. This is the area where, after the Battle of Midway in 1942, the United States campaigned to take these islands from Japan. It is where US navy ships would have to pass to reinforce our troops in any conflict in East Asia.

China's strategy in developing countries will give it significant potential advantages if China gains military bases and infiltrates foreign intelligence apparatuses. However, in many ways, I believe history will judge China's BRI and related initiatives as a colossal failure. China will find that it spent a trillion dollars and was left, in many places, with a legacy of crumbling and often unneeded public buildings such as soccer stadiums, unused roads with grass growing through the middle, and local populations alienated by the arrogance and maltreatment of Chinese operators and endemic corruption. China may discover, as we once did, that it isn't easy to buy friends.

Fentanyl

The United States is in an opioid epidemic. In 2022 alone, more than 100,000 Americans died of overdoses. The biggest killer was opioids. The second biggest killer was synthetic opioids, and the vast majority of these are from fentanyl. Estimates are that fentanyl killed around 64,000 of our countrymen in one year, and the number is growing annually.[92] A Council of Economic Advisers report in the Obama administration found that the opioid crisis cost us more than $500 billion in 2015 alone.[93] The number is certainly much bigger now.[94] The vast majority of this fentanyl comes from China. It contributes to America's fentanyl problem both through the direct sale of fentanyl to the United States and through the sale of fentanyl chemical precursors to Mexican customers. The Mexican sales are largely produced into the synthetic drug by the infamous Sinaloa cartel. When Chinese firms directly sell fentanyl into the US market, it is transported in small mail parcels, which makes interdiction nearly impossible. Fentanyl shippers use complex tactics to further complicate this task, including multiple package transfers, false identities, and mislabeling.[95] Still, China accounted for 97 percent of fentanyl seized by mail in 2016 and 2017.[96]

China is the world's largest exporter of basic chemical ingredients and precursors for pharmaceutical products, and its industry is the world's second largest in terms of revenue after the United States. The US Department of State estimates there could be as many as 400,000 chemical manufacturers and distributors in China. It is a politically powerful "high value added" industry.

President Trump consistently raised the problem of Chinese fentanyl sales to the United States with President Xi. Finally, China put the drug on its controlled substance list, but there was limited evidence that the move made a substantial difference. It is up to readers to determine whether they believe that it is possible for such a large industry to exist in China without government awareness and connivence. Remember that illegal drug sales are a capital offense there.

China and Russia

China's hostility toward the West became even more apparent in 2022, when, in February, just before the Beijing Olympics, Presidents Xi Jinping and Vladimir Putin declared a "new era" in the global order. The "friendship between the two states has no limits," they declared.[97] The ninety-nine-paragraph statement made it clear to the world that Xi and Putin stood together against America and its allies. Of course, soon after the Olympics concluded, Russia invaded Ukraine and that deadly war began. It was difficult not to conclude that Putin went to Beijing to get approval for the attack. Many have speculated that part of the deal would be Russian support for a Chinese move on Taiwan.

After the invasion of Ukraine by Russia, there was evidence that China helped Russia evade international sanctions. Specifically, China's state-owned UnionPay system helped it avoid problems related to Mastercard and Visa stopping operations there. On a broader scale, China is developing a payment system that would be an alternative to the current global system called Swift. Russian banks reportedly have access to the process.[98] The British newspaper *The Times* reported that China launched a series of cyberattacks on Ukraine's military and nuclear facilities in February prior to the invasion.[99] Ukraine's security service further claimed that the attacks also targeted Ukraine's national bank and railway system.[100] This lends further support to the conclusion that China was aware of and a silent approver of the war on Ukraine.

••

In sum, the game is changing rapidly for the United States' relationship to China. We are facing an adversary that no longer feels the need to be conciliatory. Indeed, the rhetoric coming from China sometimes seems to stray across the line toward outright provocation. The purpose is to test us. They want to see what we will do. Will we take it? If we do, we can expect further escalations.

The first official meeting between Secretary of State Antony Blinken and Chinese diplomat Yang Jiechi in Anchorage, Alaska, in March 2021 was marked by "extraordinary rancor."[101] Yang took the opportunity to rebuke Blinken, National Security Advisor Jake Sullivan, and America in general at great length. Sullivan was quoted later as saying that "we will go back to Washington and see where we are."[102]

Where, then, are we? We are facing a problem of vast proportions that will take all our resources to address. Developing a plan of action will require that we fully take into account the newly belligerent attitude from the Chinese leadership, as well as the internal polarization within the United States that will place obstacles in the way of changing our path. In many ways the ultimate confrontation with China will be in the economic sphere—and that means trade will be central.

Chapter 6

Twenty-First-Century
Mercantilism

China's Economic System

In the early 2000s, the executives at Westinghouse Electric Company made a fateful decision. Seeking to expand their access to the newly opening Chinese market, they partnered with China's largest nuclear industry state-owned enterprise, China National Nuclear Corporation (CNNC). Together, so the agreement went, the two companies would jointly construct Westinghouse's advanced AP1000 nuclear power plants throughout China.[1] At the time, Westinghouse was one of the leading global nuclear power developers whose designs formed the "basis for approximately half of the world's currently operating nuclear power plants," according to the US Justice Department.[2] Early on, the ventures proved immensely profitable for Westinghouse.

The Chinese counterparts, however, had ulterior motives. Westinghouse was promised that its AP1000 would be at the core of China's nuclear power program.[3] As a condition of this agreement, however, Westinghouse was forced to hand over thousands of documents on nuclear power plant design. In one fell swoop, China got the details of decades of US nuclear power research.[4] What China could not get from Westinghouse through this deal, it simply stole. In 2010, hackers within the Chinese military penetrated Westinghouse's computer systems and stole confidential and proprietary technical and design specifications for Westinghouse's AP1000 plant.[5] These hacks, according to the Justice Department, "would enable a competitor to build a plant similar to the AP-1000 without incurring significant research and development costs."[6] This intrusion, moreover, was not limited to the Chinese military.

In 2014, when the Justice Department indicted the responsible military unit, they also noted that all these intrusions took place during Westinghouse's negotiations with an unnamed Chinese "SOE-1" business partner.[7] Some of the documents stolen even included confidential business negotiation strategy documents that, if given to "SOE-1," would provide immense advantage.[8]

Unsurprisingly, Westinghouse now barely operates in the Chinese market, and no new Westinghouse reactor projects have been approved in the past decade.[9] While Westinghouse executives were promised a seat at the center of China's nuclear power program, China has now replaced its reliance on Westinghouse's AP1000 technology with its own indigenous Hualong One reactor design. In 2017, after years of declining profits, Westinghouse filed for bankruptcy.[10] Though it still exists, it is far from being the leading global nuclear player it once was. China, on the other hand, is increasingly a dominant player on the global nuclear power market, led by CNNC, which was founded in the 1990s from a reorganization of the central government's Ministry of Nuclear Industry and retains its ties to People's Liberation Army programs. Like every Chinese SOE, its top executives are directly selected by the Chinese Communist Party's *nomenklatura* system. Thus, CNNC exists not just to make a profit but also to advance the CCP's goal of developing a high-tech, leading-edge industrial economy.

China's growing global assertiveness, as detailed in the previous chapter, is powered by decades of the sort of predatory Chinese economic policies that crippled Westinghouse. As Cicero once noted, "Money is the sinews of war," and China has been stunningly successful in its economic advancement relative to the United States since the 1990s. It now has very strong sinews indeed. It is not an exaggeration to say that the hundreds of billions of dollars that America sends to China every year has financed China's military expansion, its economic development, and its financial adventures in the developing world. To understand how this happened and to comprehend the economic threat that China poses, we must first start with a comprehensive understanding of how China's mercantilist, state-driven economic system operates.

China's Mercantilist History

To a non-specialist viewer—or even, sadly, to too many specialist viewers—China's economy may look fairly similar to ours. But mercantilism and a free market are dramatically different systems, with distinctions that are important to note.

Mercantilism is a school of nationalistic political economy that emphasizes the role of government intervention, trade barriers, and export promotion in building a wealthy, powerful state.[11] The term was popularized by Adam Smith, who described the policies of western European colonial powers as a "mercantile system."[12] Then and now, there are a vast array of tools available for countries seeking to go down this path. Mercantilist governments, for instance, frequently employ import substitution policies that support exports and discourage imports in order to accumulate wealth. They employ tariffs, too, of course, and they limit market access, employ licensing schemes, and use government procurement, subsidies, SOEs, and manipulation of regulation to favor domestic industries over foreign ones.

China today employs the most comprehensive suite of mercantilist policies the world has ever seen. What makes China unique is how it directly manages a state-owned sector that monopolizes upstream and strategic industries throughout the entire economy and indirectly controls all forms of private companies through the threat of its robust "anti-corruption" law-enforcement system. Directly as a government and indirectly through its companies, China engages in industrial espionage, cyber intrusion, and outright theft of intellectual property and business know-how. It uses a cadre of students in US colleges and laboratories to unlawfully obtain technology. It invests government funds in state-owned technology companies and research laboratories. It directs and manages cooperation between firms, universities, and laboratories through a complex system of government industrial policy agencies. It limits market access for foreign firms and makes any access it grants contingent on exacting technology transfer and joint venture agreements. The list goes on and on.

This Chinese mercantilist, state-driven economic model must be understood in its historical context. Chinese leaders have long believed the country should be a global superpower just as the Chinese dynastic system once was. In their view of history, the main reason China lost this status and became a "victim" of Western colonialism was the fact that Chinese industry and technology lagged behind China's Western counterparts. As a result, when the Communist Party took over China, it set its eyes toward rapid industrial and technological development as the means to restore Chinese power.

Under Mao's leadership, the party quickly adopted what the scholar Barry Naughton calls the "big push industrialization" strategy, which focused on mustering all of China's economic resources toward the development of heavy industry.[13] The CCP pushed resources into new factories, and government investment rapidly increased to over a quarter of national income.[14] A whopping 80 percent of this investment went into heavy industry.[15] As had almost always been the case in China, the economy was controlled by the state.

When the Korean War broke out in the early 1950s, the CCP's fear of conflict with the United States increased, accelerating calls for rapid industrialization through Soviet-style "five-year plans."[16] Using the war to further entrench its domestic political support, the CCP began a violent land reform campaign to dislodge local elites in the countryside.[17] Then, in 1955, the CCP began rural collectivization, ended the selling of produce on markets, and established local communes that directed and oversaw countryside agricultural production.[18] The CCP also began to launch political campaigns in the cities, taking over the remaining private businesses.[19]

By this point, Mao had come to believe that instead of focusing on changing the means of production gradually in the style of a Soviet New Economic Policy reform, China could leap ahead in modernization by changing the relations of production (i.e., making things communally owned) and relying on the revolutionary spirit of the masses to industrialize. And so in 1958, Mao launched the "Great Leap Forward." As part of this plan, rural communes were merged to form even larger "People's Communes," ambitious quotas on production were set, and communes were told to become more self-sufficient by starting their own factories.[20]

The Great Leap Forward failed miserably, and unrealistic quotas and poor management ultimately led to a catastrophic famine.[21] By 1961, the Great Leap Forward ended, and Mao accepted for a time that more technocratic, gradual economic policy was needed to modernize the country.[22] The Great Leap Forward, thus, was great only in the tragic sense, creating the largest famine in human history, with estimates as high as fifty million people dying of starvation from 1958 to 1962. Its failures, however, provided important lessons for the CCP's industrialization strategy.

But there was one policy in place during this period that worked dramatically well. At the same time as Mao's doomed Great Leap Forward, China's leaders were pursuing a separate policy program that would prove more important to China's future economic development strategy: its strategic weapons program. This program, launched in the 1950s to help China develop nuclear weapons, operated unlike other industrial policies during the Mao era. Rather than placing control in the hands of party apparatchiks, the strategic weapons program placed the Chinese aerospace and nuclear industries in the hands of technical experts insulated from the day-to-day politics of the Mao era.[23] These experts, in turn, managed to succeed in their primary mission: by 1964, China tested a nuclear bomb. This would ultimately prove to be one of the few successes of Mao-era economic development, and it provided a model that later Chinese development policies would follow.

The rocky years of Mao's leadership culminated, of course, in the Cultural Revolution—an internal battle for control of the Communist Party that sent China's economy into turmoil. When the dust of this chaos settled, China's leadership was forced to reconsider the kind of rapid, political campaign–driven economic policies that failed so greatly during the Mao years. To achieve economic and technological development, China's leadership needed a new plan.

After Mao's death, Deng Xiaoping and his allies reconsidered Mao's strategies and proposed an alternative path to economic development. Under his reform policies, Deng developed a two-track economy with heavy industry under state control and agriculture and light industry gradually going into semi-private hands.[24] In the late 1970s, the CCP slowly moved away from the commune system. Deng empowered local officials to restore family-based farming in the countryside, which gave families some independence in managing the plots of land they worked and allowed surplus production over the quota to be sold on the market.[25] Gradually, quotas were removed for agriculture as the private market showed its sustainability and efficiency. With more time to allocate to non-agricultural activities, farmers became involved in local factories in lower-end consumer industries.[26]

Around the same time, the CCP allowed "private" companies to set up stores, workshops, and factories with control over their hiring, firing, and profits.[27] However, this didn't represent a total leap into American capitalism. To appease the state-owned sector bureaucracy, the CCP also allowed SOEs to set up private firms and retain some of their profits, ensuring SOE buy-in to early economic reforms.[28] The CCP also allowed its SOEs to use excess capacity not needed to meet quotas to devote to private market activity.[29] Most of these SOEs were managed at the local level, and local governments were given control over their budget and revenues, which incentivized local officials to support industry and reform. Local bureaucrats thus became part of the system and grew wealthy as a result of the expansion. At the same time, the CCP allowed certain cities such as Shenzhen to set up "special economic zones," where foreign investors received favorable tax and customs treatment.[30] It also set up the first national SOE conglomerates in certain heavy industries to ensure that the national government retained a substantial revenue stream.

Deng also launched technology programs that sought to build on the successful model of Mao's technocratic nuclear programs.[31] These policies began with reforming China's university system. To this end, through programs such as Project 211, China began pouring billions of dollars into top-tier universities. At the same time, government industrial policy agencies began funding the construction of new, high-tech departments at these universities.[32] Alongside these policies, Deng and his allies began funding high-tech research projects through the state-run industrial programs, including Program 863, which was designed by the managers behind Mao's strategic weapons program and focused on sectors such as aerospace, automation, and information technology.[33]

This largely was the Chinese economy that entered the WTO in 2001. It contained two distinct sectors—one state-owned and the other nominally private. The state sector monopolized upstream industries such as steel production and mining, strategic sectors such as the defense and telecom industries, and certain producer's goods industries such as industrial tools and auto parts. The "private" sector, on the other hand, produced most consumer-focused goods and services. Meanwhile, behind the scenes, the Chinese government's technological policies aimed clearly at exploiting Western trading partners to restore China's once-held position at the leading edge of the global technology race.

Thus, despite China's promises of privatization, market access, and further economic reform, it was clear that China would instead continue upon a path of state-directed, mercantilist economic development. China was happy with its one-foot-in, one-foot-out mercantilist structure. Indeed, Deng's policy shifts were not changes toward a liberal market economy, as many in the West then thought. Deng was less autocratic than Mao but every bit as much of a communist, mercantilist, and economic nationalist. While he did allow some small semi-private enterprises to flourish, they were always ultimately under state control. There was no truly private industry. The swarms of American business executives and politicians who engaged with China, believing the country was on the path to open markets and economic liberalization, made a grievous mistake, and ordinary Americans paid the price.

The State Sector and Industrial Policy in China Today

Between China's 2001 WTO accession and Xi Jinping's rise to power in 2012, China continued down the path of state-centered economic development that Deng began. Though weaker than Deng and Mao, Chinese presidents Hu Jintao and Jiang Zemin both pursued industrial policies aimed at cultivating Chinese high-tech and strategic industries through a system of subsidies, government investment, industrial espionage, and forced technology transfer. Xi Jinping inherited this system, and over the course of his presidency, he has further strengthened it. As a result, Chinese firms today benefit from a complex network of overlapping mercantilist government policies that seek to advance their position in the global market.

China's state-owned sector is the largest beneficiary of these policies. Despite commitments made to the WTO and the United States specifically, China has aggressively increased the role of SOEs in its economy. Under President Xi, China has encouraged mergers between state-owned firms in an effort to create mega-SOEs that can crush global competition.[34] In 2017, SOEs were responsible for between 23 percent and 27.5 percent of China's GDP and employed 34.7 million people, or 4.5 percent of total employment.[35] Despite claims from the Chinese government that it is aiming for "competitive neutrality" between so-called private enterprises and SOEs, "private" and foreign companies in China continue to report that SOEs are favored despite significantly lower levels of productivity and innovation capacity.[36]

It is important to remember in this context, moreover, that all enterprises in China are effectively controlled by the government and benefit in some form from its mercantilist policies. There are no truly independent businesses. Every company, including US companies operating in China, must listen to the dictates of the Chinese government. Every business move and any profit exists because of state approval. While this has always been a de facto reality in China, Xi's administration has taken steps to enshrine it into law. In 2015, for instance, the Chinese government instituted a new national security law that requires all corporations to assist and cooperate with protecting "national security" as broadly defined.[37] Xi has also pressured "private" companies to establish Communist Party cells within "private" enterprises in order to organize and promote CCP ideology. As a result, as of 2018, over 73 percent of "private" companies in China have a CCP party cell within their organization, and reports from Congress indicate this percentage is only growing.[38] Xi's administration has also cultivated a climate of fear within the business community through his anti-corruption investigations and crackdowns, which encourage compliance with the CCP regime. Nowadays, when high-profile Chinese business executives step out of line with

CCP dictates or ideology, they come under government investigations and "disappear" from the public eye, as has been the case with Jack Ma and Bao Fan.[39] No business operating in a political regime like this can ever be considered truly private.

To help both state-owned and "private" Chinese companies develop and compete abroad, the Chinese state provides significant subsidies to its domestic industries, many of which blatantly violate WTO rules. The beneficiaries of China's subsidies include a web of firms across industries such as steel, solar panels, and auto parts.[40] China approximately doubled its industrial subsidies from 2013 to 2019, spending ~$22.4 billion on subsidies for companies listed on the Shanghai and Shenzhen stock exchanges in 2018 alone.[41]

In addition to direct government subsidies and SOEs, China has traditionally used a variety of mechanisms to funnel financing at below-market rates to favored firms. Before recent financial liberalization, Chinese savers had few options other than deposits in government-run banks, where interest rates were set at extremely low levels. Lending rates were also much lower than they would be in a market-based system but exceeded deposit rates enough to ensure guaranteed bank profits. The resulting cheap credit was directed to favored industries and firms, at the expense of both foreign competitors and ordinary savers and borrowers.[42] This transfer of capital from savers to favored borrowers represented approximately 5 percent of China's GDP between 2000 and the beginning of interest rate liberalization in 2013.[43]

Additionally, most credit creation in the banking system is de facto controlled by provincial and municipal governments. This means that these governments can effectively operate without a budget constraint, and banks avoid writing down bad loans in reliance on direct and implicit government guarantees.[44] Recent efforts to liberalize the Chinese financial markets and impose market discipline on the banking sector are encouraging if taken at face value, but the viability of such reforms is limited by the Chinese government's low tolerance for market instability and strong bias in favor of SOEs to maintain economic growth and limit unemployment.[45]

Throughout its government procurement regime, moreover, China implements policies that favor products, services, and technologies made or developed by Chinese companies through a combination of explicit and implicit requirements.[46] Despite assertions of reform by the Chinese government, US firms continue to report discrimination in government procurement because of concerted domestic substitution efforts by Chinese government entities and SOEs, purposefully unclear and inconsistent domestic content requirements, and broad security criteria used when evaluating bidders.[47] These issues extend beyond government contracting. Of particular concern is the Chinese government's efforts to regulate the purchase of information and communications technology products and services by information infrastructure operators.

On top of these general policies, the Chinese government also implements specific industrial policy plans that provide these benefits (subsidies, preferential financing, government procurement, etc.) to certain strategic and high-tech sectors of the economy. The most significant, and harmful, of these industrial policies is Made in China 2025. Released by China's State Council in 2015, this plan represents an increasingly sophisticated approach to building toward China's stated goal of indigenous innovation. Simply put, Made in China 2025 and other related industrial policies aim to replace foreign providers of technologies, products, and services with Chinese firms and lay the foundation for them to dominate internationally.

To achieve this goal, Made in China 2025 involves extensive support for Chinese industry in designated sectors, particularly through subcentral levels of government, and leverages more than $500 billion in financial support made available by the Chinese government.[48] After the onset of COVID-19, an additional $1.4 trillion was allocated to the programs. Strategic, high-tech industries under the programs' purview benefit from government-financed and -directed research and development, reduced taxes, direct subsidies, assistance in merger activity, and preference in regulation at all levels of government. Among the stated objectives is achieving 70 percent domestic content in targeted sectors and thus reducing reliance on foreign material. The list of key industries includes everything necessary to long-term economic dominance, such as aerospace, biotechnology, information technology, robots, and electric vehicles.

Chinese officials stopped referencing "Made in China 2025" after what seems to have been an order from the central government in June 2018, but the policy itself has not been abandoned. I have always thought that they stopped using the phrase because we in the Trump administration were so effective at using this program to show Americans and others around the world how mercantilist China was and how much of a threat it is.

In parallel to Made in China 2025, Xi Jinping also began a policy known as "Military-Civil Fusion," which aims to advance China's dual-use technological capabilities in support of its military buildup. As part of this policy, Chinese government agencies such as the State Administration for Science, Technology, and Industry for National Defense (SASTIND) provide specific subsidies, government investment, loans, and procurement contracts to nominally private companies in dual-use sectors of the economy seeking to enter the defense acquisition market.[49] Similarly, SASTIND helps to coordinate university efforts to work on defense-related research and academic disciplines with both state-owned and "private" sector dual-use companies.[50] Xi's growing focus on Military-Civil Fusion, moreover, also serves as an important domestic political signal—encouraging ambitious local CCP cadres to support and develop dual-use companies within their jurisdictions.

Labor and Environmental Abuses

Chinese companies also benefit immensely from the government's suppression of labor and lax environmental regulations. Chinese historian Qin Hui has observed that China has the "comparative advantage of lower human rights."[51] This is tragic both for Chinese workers and citizens, who face suppressed wages and an array of labor market abuses, and American workers who are forced to compete with them. It is illegal to perform labor organizing or form an adversarial union in China. Those who advocate for improved working conditions are often arrested on accusations of threatening social order.[52] Although the CCP has occasionally tolerated one-off strikes and encouraged some compromise with workers in the past, particularly when directed against American companies, President Xi has led a crackdown that has thrown independent labor organizers in prison in what the *Washington Post* termed "one of the largest campaigns to suppress civil society groups in China."[53]

China also maintains a desperate and hungry labor force through abuse of its *hukou* system, which limits the ability of Chinese citizens to move to places outside of where they were born. These laws are not actively enforced by local governments in cities and industrial centers, except to the extent that they are used as a tool for evicting and punishing workers who step out of line.[54] Furthermore, the *hukou* system blocks internal migrant workers from being able to access a wide range of public goods such as health care, unemployment insurance, and housing assistance. Perhaps most importantly, the system prevents the children of internal migrants from accessing education. As a result, as few as 24 percent of children of low-skilled temporary internal migrants in major Chinese cities attend college, as compared with 96 percent of children of high-skilled urban residents.[55] This system creates conditions under which migrant workers are willing to take extremely low wages and are terrified of protesting labor conditions. Thus, the class of abused migrants perpetuates itself.

As a result of these and other active measures to suppress labor power by the Chinese government, workers at Chinese nonfinancial corporations capture only 40 percent of the value they create—a stark contrast with the rest of the developed world, where the labor share of corporate value generally approaches 70 percent.[56] Low wages in China are manufactured by the regime—they are not an endogenous factor to be casually accepted.

At the same time, China's government also avoids implementing serious environmental protection regimes. On the global stage, China's leaders put on a show—signing agreements such as the 2015 Paris Agreement and committing to be carbon neutral by 2060.[57] Behind the scenes, however, the government remains unwilling to impose excess regulatory costs on its firms.

Today, China remains the world's largest emitter and produces over a quarter of the world's annual greenhouse gas emissions.[58] Rather than switch to cleaner fossil fuels, China has remained committed to coal—

the dirtiest form of fossil fuel—and the country represents half of annual global coal consumption.[59] When you peel back the curtain, it is not surprising why. China has abundant coal resources and its coal-producing SOEs make the nation the world's largest coal producer.[60] It supports the coal industry with billions of dollars' worth of government subsidies, which both lowers the electricity cost for Chinese producers and encourages the continued burning of coal.[61] Even though China promised that its carbon dioxide emissions will peak in 2030, it has recently gone on a coal power plant building spree—a clear sign China's reliance on coal will not end anytime soon.[62]

Though the Chinese government will frequently point to its role in solar panel production as an indicator that it is serious about moving away from coal in the long term, this is nothing more than a mirage. The raw materials that go into these panels are mined and processed using coal-powered electricity, and as a result, a single Chinese solar panel has double the carbon footprint of a Western panel.[63] On top of this, China has no policy for solar panel recycling. Solar panels contain toxic metals and are made using hazardous materials, so without adequate recycling plans, old or malfunctioning Chinese solar panels are sitting in waste sites leaking into the Chinese water supply.[64] Even when Chinese solar panels work, they struggle to generate sufficient electricity because the sunlight they need is blocked by China's air pollution.[65] If this was not bad enough, reports indicate that these panels are produced with forced labor in Xinjiang.[66] China's purported clean energy transition accordingly is powered by carbon emissions, pollution, and slave labor.

On top of this, though China has environmental regulations on the books, it rarely enforces these against Chinese companies. Enforcement is often left to local officials, who typically have ties to the firms they oversee and who need these firms to succeed in order to produce the kind of economic growth that determines CCP officials' promotions.[67] This problem is not much better at the national level. Studies have shown that when a national SOE violates an environmental regulation, it is not seriously penalized, which incentivizes continued dodging of environmental regulations.[68]

Combined, these policy decisions form the basis of China's economic system. The country's industrial policies are nothing short of twenty-first-century mercantilism, and they provide an unfair, market-distorting advantage to Chinese companies that their foreign counterparts in liberal, capitalist democracies do not enjoy. At the same time, its labor policies and lax environmental regulations keep production costs low. Even if China stopped these internal policies, American firms would stand little chance of competing with their Chinese counterparts. China's economic policies do not stop at just supporting Chinese firms and instead expand to disadvantaging and preying on foreign firms.

Chapter 7

An Economic Threat

One of my favorite stories to tell members of Congress—alongside the Westinghouse story that began the previous chapter—was that of the once US-based company Magnequench. Magnequench had a near monopoly share in the niche market of sintered magnets. These are tiny high-tech magnets made from rare earths that are an essential component in the guidance systems used in cruise missiles and smart bombs. For decades, the company was a crucial supplier for the US military in wartime. It started in 1986 as a General Motors subsidiary that developed its prized technology, in part, through a Pentagon grant. In 1995, the company was purchased by Sextant Group, a consortium of an American firm and two Chinese companies with close connections to the Chinese government and military. Soon after, the company moved part of its production facility from Indiana to China. By 2006, it had closed down its last US plant in Valparaiso, Indiana, and moved it to Tianjin. The jobs and the technology were gone.[1] To recap, US government money was used to develop a technology for the US military, the company developing that technology was bought by a group tied to China, and now the technology is abroad, and the company is controlled by China. While the Sextant deal should never have been permitted to happen, wide-eyed optimism and pure naivety in the Treasury Department led the Clinton administration to allow it to go through.

The point I was trying to make through telling these stories was simple: the modern history of American economic cooperation with China is littered with hundreds of Magnequenchs and Westinghouses, of once great American companies that we have since forgotten. Though the exact details differ, the general thrust of each story is the same. American executives seek to boost profits and shareholder value by expanding their operations and sales to China. At the Chinese government's demand, they set up a joint venture with a local Chinese partner. The Chinese partner uses this venture to co-opt, steal, or copy the American company's intellectual property. Within years, the American company finds itself out of Chinese clients; within a decade, the American company finds itself competing with its old Chinese partner on the global market. The subsidized, government-supported Chinese competitor wins, and the American company watches as its own intellectual property is weaponized to cut away at its profits and economic health. The experiences of companies with joint ventures in China such as Lucent Technologies, DuPont, General Electric, and Advanced Micro Devices (AMD) play this narrative out.[2]

Even companies that avoid partnering with Chinese companies or refuse to share technology with their Chinese partners face the threat of Chinese espionage operations. Chinese industrial spies have inserted themselves in US firms to steal their trade secrets, as was the case with Xiang Dong Yu, an employee of Ford Motors, who stole Ford's design documents to bring to his new Chinese automotive employer.[3] China has also recruited American spies, such as Noshir Gowadia, who stole cruise missile exhaust system technology in exchange for payment from the Chinese government.[4] The list of American companies whose intellectual property was stolen through attacks like this includes Apple, Boeing, Micron Technologies, Coca-Cola, DuPont, Google, Yahoo, T-Mobile, Adobe, Dow Chemical, General Electric, Monsanto, and Morgan Stanley.[5] Indeed, intellectual property theft accounts for more than $300 billion in annual losses for the United States.

China's mercantilist policies are not limited just to supporting China's own companies through industrial policies such as those detailed in the previous chapter. Rather, as the stories of Westinghouse, Magnequench, and countless other American ventures in China show, Chinese mercantilism is powered by clear economic malfeasance and predation that targets foreign firms. Although accurate data is hard to gather, available evidence suggests that China is potentially responsible for as much as 80 percent of the problem across all categories of intellectual property theft.[6] Unlike most other global firms, Chinese companies regularly receive formal and informal assistance from the government in theft of American technology and intellectual property.[7] Under the Trump administration, we took aggressive action to investigate and report upon China's trade-related practices relative to the United States and subsequently to act upon those findings. Our key determinations, as described in the *2018 Special 301 Report* issued by the USTR, included:

1. China uses foreign ownership restrictions, such as joint venture requirements and foreign equity limitations, and various administrative review and licensing processes to require or pressure technology transfer from US companies.
2. China's regime of technology regulations forces US companies seeking to license technologies to Chinese entities to do so on non-market-based terms that favor Chinese recipients.
3. China directs and unfairly facilitates the systematic investment in, and acquisition of, US companies and assets by Chinese companies to obtain cutting-edge technologies and intellectual property and generate the transfer of technology to Chinese companies.
4. China conducts and supports unauthorized intrusions into, and theft from, the computer networks of US companies to access their sensitive commercial information and trade secrets.[8]

In a later chapter, we will discuss Section 301 and how we used it. For the moment, however, it suffices to say both that we had hard evidence of "acts, policies, and practices of China that are unreasonable or discriminatory and that burden or restrict U.S. commerce" and that we took action to redress them under the Trump administration. It was about time.

Intellectual Property Violations

Broadly speaking, Chinese intellectual property theft falls into two separate—but not mutually exclusive—buckets of activity. First, Chinese hackers and spies target US companies at home to take their designs, research, and plans. It's the sort of thing you might imagine being dramatized in a film. But the second method is more subtle: China takes American intellectual property through joint ventures with stringent, coercive requirements that the American partner transfers some or all its technology and know-how to its local counterpart. Both of these activities pose a fundamental threat to the health and stability of the American economy.

Industrial and cyber espionage is a key method through which Chinese entities acquire foreign technologies.[9] The FBI has, in recent years, turned its attention to this problem. The bureau has approximately one thousand investigations into China's attempted theft of US-based technology ongoing at any one time across all fifty-six of its field offices and "spanning almost every industry and sector."[10] For example, in December 2018, the US Department of Justice indicted two Chinese nationals associated with a hacking group known as Advanced Persistent Threat 10 (APT 10) for conspiracy to commit computer intrusions, conspiracy to commit wire fraud, and aggravated identity theft. The two men were part of "a massive, years-long hacking campaign that stole personal and proprietary information from companies around the world." The team was active for more than a decade and stole hundreds of gigabytes of sensitive data "from companies in a diverse range of industries, such as health care, biotechnology, finance, manufacturing, and oil and gas."[11]

The targets of espionage also include academic institutions. State-backed programs offer significant incentives to lure Western scientists. In particular, the Thousand Talents Program was started in 2008 and has attracted more than 10,000 academic and corporate scientists with starting salaries three to four times higher than those generally offered at American universities and companies. These scientists transfer their expertise to Chinese labs and academic institutions, as well as help start companies in China, using research carried on at US universities, often with the support of the federal government.[12]

In July 2021, the United States and its allies accused the Chinese Ministry of State Security of responsibility for the massive attack on the Microsoft Exchange Bank that hacked more than 100,000 servers worldwide. The allies also condemned Beijing for working with criminal hacker groups involved in ransomware attacks. The operation "gave Chinese intelligence the ability to access and spy on or potentially disrupt tens of thousands of computer systems worldwide." Unfortunately, the Biden administration and the allies imposed no sanctions on the Chinese perpetrators. Even worse, President Biden's Department of Justice seems to be far less active in prosecuting this type of international crime.[13]

Unfortunately, Chinese efforts to acquire foreign intellectual property are not limited to cybercrime and economic espionage. China uses restrictions on foreign ownership, including joint venture requirements and foreign equity limitations, as well as various administrative review and licensing processes, to require or pressure technology transfer from US companies.[14] The Chinese government enforces strict restrictions on foreign direct investment inflows, which makes it difficult for US and other foreign companies to avoid acquiescing to joint venture requirements.

Chinese joint ventures for foreign businesses come with a catch, beyond the usual sharing of profits and losses. Foreign companies are, at least de facto, required to contribute their technology to their Chinese "partners" as part of the transaction. The foreign companies hand over their cash, technology, management expertise, and other intellectual property while the Chinese partners help secure land-use rights and financing while also providing the cover of their political connections and knowledge of the local market.[15] Eventually, the Chinese firms scale up their own production and begin to squeeze their American partners out of the Chinese and global markets.[16] Such joint ventures are required across a range of industries, including exploration and exploitation of oil and natural gas, medicine, and film, radio, and television. In certain industries the foreign share is also largely limited to a minority stake.[17]

Even where the Chinese government does not formally mandate technology transfer, the restrictions on foreign ownership provide Chinese firms with negotiating leverage to secure nominally consensual technology transfer agreements. Foreign investors are played against each other when negotiating for entry into the Chinese market. Furthermore, by observing the operations of their foreign partners, Chinese partners often gain access to important technology even where an agreement is not signed.[18]

Beyond joint ventures, the Chinese government employs a complex licensing system that is implemented via an extensive and opaque administrative process. These licenses often nominally apply to both domestic and foreign producers and concern a variety of activities, including selling products and building new manufacturing facilities.[19] Chinese regulators impose licensing requirements on more than one hundred different business activities, including food and drug production, mining, and telecom services, and have sought to extract concessions or force the transfer of intellectual property from US and other foreign firms at every stage of approval.[20] The regulators typically demand a wide array of documents, and firms tend to disclose sensitive data and information beyond what is required in other markets.[21]

China enforces an array of tech regulations that force US companies looking to license technologies to Chinese entities to do so on non-market-based terms that favor the Chinese recipients.[22] The USTR identified several key mechanisms through which China restricted the intellectual property rights of foreigners, including US firms, in its 2018 Section 301 investigation. For example, Chinese laws allowed Chinese firms to make improvements to foreign technologies and then keep the rights to any such improvements—even if the foreign owner of the underlying technology did not consent.[23] Furthermore, China imposed ten-year time limits on critical foreign patents that generally last much longer, as well as gave Chinese partners in joint ventures perpetual rights to use foreign technology after a joint venture–related technology transfer agreement.[24] These and other unfair rules were a major focus of our negotiations in the Phase One agreement reached during the Trump administration.

Beyond orchestrating hacking and espionage campaigns and pressuring companies to hand over their technology, the Chinese government has utterly failed to restrict the widespread production, domestic sale, and export of counterfeit goods.[25] In 2020, China and Hong Kong cumulatively accounted for 79 percent of intellectual property–related seizures by US Customs and Border Protection by number of seizures and 83.3 percent of seizures by MSRP value—or $1.09 billion in seized goods.[26] Owners of copyrights and trademarks have suggested that the Chinese authorities may be making more proactive efforts to address the massive problem.[27] These and other efforts to centralize enforcement may help, but significant concerns remain regarding counterfeit pharmaceutical products, unauthorized audiovisual content, and broad anti-suit injunctions issued by Chinese courts in patent disputes without notice or opportunity to participate for affected US firms.[28]

The various mechanisms to systematically weaken intellectual property rights and transfer technology were core to our negotiations in the Phase One trade deal. As a result of the agreement, China promised numerous major changes.[29] Among the structural changes, China agreed to provide effective access to Chinese markets without requiring or pressuring US persons to transfer their technology to Chinese persons. China also agreed both that any transfer or licensing of technology by US persons to Chinese persons must be based on market terms that are voluntary and mutually agreed upon and that China would not support or direct the outbound foreign direct investment activities of its persons aimed at acquiring foreign technology with respect to sectors targeted by its industrial plans that create distortion. In addition, the agreement required numerous improvements in China's protection and enforcement of intellectual property rights. For the most part, these obligations have been met. Although China has made an honest effort to follow through on these commitments, enforcement is difficult, especially at the provincial and local levels. The US government will have to monitor activity and be prepared to use the enforcement provisions in the Phase One agreement to gain compliance.

Trade Barriers and Unfair Economic Practices

Intellectual property violations and industrial policies are far from the only ways that China distorts its economic position. To support domestic firms, China maintains a wide variety of trade barriers and engages in various unfair economic practices that harm American workers and companies.

China liberally uses tariffs to suppress imports, maintaining higher levels than those of many other major economies.[30] China's average MFN applied tariff rate was 7.6 percent in 2019, and its average MFN applied tariff rate was 13.9 percent for agricultural products and 6.5 percent for non-agricultural products in 2018.

China has also abused anti-dumping (AD) and countervailing duty (CVD) measures to retaliate against US attempts to exercise WTO rights as a remedy against Chinese violations. China initiated eight domestic trade remedy investigations in 2020 alone, which resulted in dubious conclusions and failed to meet the international or WTO rules. America has won multiple recent WTO cases against China, proving its actions were inconsistent with international rules, including on chicken broiler products and automobiles. These victories confirm that China fails to abide by WTO disciplines, however limited those may be, when imposing trade remedies on US products.[31]

While many rightly focus on China's tariffs, China's abuse of value-added tax (VAT) rebates flies below the radar. China imposes a 16 percent VAT on the majority of imported US and other goods and services, aside from a few categories subject to a lower 6–10 percent rate. China also selectively refunds the full VAT upon export and manipulates the VAT rebate to incentivize firms to produce in China instead of the United States or other countries. In some cases, China games the system by opportunistically withholding refunds. Some manufacturing inputs, for example, will not get the full rebate, which makes them more expensive for foreign manufacturers to acquire and cheaper for domestic Chinese manufacturers. The downstream Chinese-manufactured products are thus cheaper than their foreign competitors are. This has created significant disruption in global markets and has contributed to severe excess capacity in industries such as steel and aluminum.[32]

More broadly, China has sometimes pursued a system of export restraints to maximize its leverage in industries where it is among the world's leading producers.[33] The latest example is a move in 2021 by China to tighten export restraints on rare earth minerals—a market that is critical for advanced energy technology and where Chinese processors are dominant globally.[34] These export restraints have the effect of advantaging domestic producers in downstream industries at the expense of foreign competitors, while putting pressure on foreign downstream producers to offshore their operations to China.[35] It is worth noting that China's dominant position in rare earths is itself largely the result of market distortionary practices. China dumped these products on the market at low prices until foreign competition was driven out of business.

China also violates WTO commitments regularly to advantage its own industries. China, for instance, made multiple commitments to the US and other trading partners regarding trade in information technology. Yet China has broken all of them. Its implementation of its cybersecurity measures seems to indicate a continued intent to suppress US and international participation in its information technology industry.[36] For example, many US firms, such as Apple, have been subject to nontransparent security reviews that they believe may be used to disrupt operations in China or extract trade secrets.[37] The selective application of nominally broadly applicable laws is a consistent practice in China.

The Chinese government has also weaponized a purported anti-monopoly effort to target US and foreign companies, in ways that fail to evince a genuine concern about restoring competition. Chinese regulators have largely avoided bringing enforcement actions against central government–level SOEs, and the law contains exceptions for SOE and government monopolies in industries identified as nationally important. However, US firms have reported that Chinese anti-monopoly regulators have used the threat of fines and other punitive action to push companies to adopt "informal" suggestions regarding how they should behave both within and outside China.

China also has a long history as a currency manipulator. From 2003 to 2014, China bought more than $300 billion annually to prevent appreciation of its currency by artificially keeping the exchange rate of the dollar strong and that of the renminbi weak. This strengthened China's competitive position by as much as 30 to 40 percent at the peak of the intervention.[38] Although China's currency manipulation has tapered off since 2014, it still actively manages its currency through a daily benchmark exchange rate for the renminbi.[39] The US Treasury Department labeled China as a currency manipulator in 2019 and retracted the label in 2020, a decision based on the disciplines on currency manipulation imposed in the Phase One agreement.[40] While it is unclear whether China is continuing to actively devalue its currency, the country's history of aggressive currency manipulation makes it a key concern.

China's Strategy Has Paid Off

All in all, China's mercantilism, industrial policy, economic manipulation, labor abuses, and expansionary activity in the developing world have paid off. The Chinese economy averaged 9.5 percent real annual GDP growth through 2018, a rate of expansion that the World Bank called "the fastest sustained expansion by a major economy in history."[41] The Chinese economy is growing fast, and that growth is translating into dominance in key industries—at the expense of the United States.

China's accession to the WTO in 2001 began a decades-long redistribution of wealth from the United States to China. In 2001, the goods and services trade deficit between the United States and China was only a little more than $80.6 billion. In 2021, that deficit was $339.2 billion. On an aggregated basis, between 2001 and 2021, the United States imported $5.39 trillion more in Chinese goods and services than it exported—feeding into China's economic rise.

China's export-driven, mercantilist growth strategy—by all measures—succeeded. In 2001, China's GDP stood at $1.3 trillion (USD). In 2021, that number was about $17.7 trillion—a growth of $16.4 trillion. Over the same period, exports' contribution to China's GDP rose from $272 billion in 2001 to about $3.5 trillion in 2021, fed in large part by weak, unbalanced US trade policies.

China is well on its way to becoming an energy powerhouse—and a dirty polluting one at that. China's coal revenue was already ~3 times larger than that of the US in 2004 but skyrocketed to ~23 times larger by 2021.[42] China is catching up to or overtaking the United States in the world of clean energy as well. China has the third largest number of nuclear reactors in the world as of 2022, fifty-four to America's ninety-two.[43] But unlike the United States, China is aggressively investing in expansion. In 2021, fourteen new nuclear reactors were under construction in China, while only two such projects were happening in the United States.[44]

The story is even darker in solar. The first photovoltaic (PV) device, made of silicon, was invented in 1954 by scientists at Bell Labs in New Jersey.[45] In 1995, the United States produced 45 percent of the world's PV cells, and the next closest player was Japan, at 21 percent.[46] China came into the game with 1 percent of global production in 2000, while the United States was still a powerful force with 27 percent of the world's PV cells.[47] That is when China turned on its state support machine. The regime pulled out all the stops—massive subsidies flowed from the central and provincial governments, a depreciated currency boosted competitiveness, provincial governments subsidized land and electricity, state-backed banks offered cheap financing, and government contracts went exclusively to Chinese firms.[48]

As a result of these industrial policies for its solar sector, China is a leading creator of non-economic excess solar capacity. Its multifaceted campaign to control the industry caused an explosion in Chinese supply that exceeded demand and caused prices to plummet. American, European, and other Asian competitors floundered and went bankrupt, bolstering Chinese plans to dominate the growing and strategic industry.[49] Today, China dominates every stage of solar panel production. In 2019, China was responsible for 66 percent of world polysilicon production, 78 percent of world solar cell production, and 72 percent of world solar module production.[50]

China's industrial policies have also positioned the country to control world renewable energy adoption through its iron-fisted control of rare earth elements. These metals are critical to the renewable energy manufacturing value chain and are essential to the production of solar panels, wind turbines, electric vehicles, efficient lighting, and phosphors.[51] It was not always this way. The United States was the leading source of rare earths from the 1960s to the 1980s, powered by the Mountain Pass Mine in California.[52] Starting in the 1990s, China turned on its industrial support juggernaut and skyrocketed to capture more than 90 percent of production capacity in the key rare earth metals.[53] Across all rare earths, China controlled 62 percent of global production in 2019, five times more than the United States' 12 percent.[54] The US government and industry are starting to wake up to the problem and are encouraging new investment in the sector, but restarting a complex industry is much harder than preserving a dominant one. The existing and growing dominance of China in traditional and next-generation energy will be a major challenge over the upcoming years and decades.[55]

How about the things we use that energy for? From the days of Henry Ford and his visionary assembly line, we Americans have proudly seen ourselves as the home of the automobile. Despite broader deindustrialization, our auto industry has survived and even thrived in the later twentieth and early twenty-first centuries. The modern American auto industry is much more than just the original Detroit heavyweights. My work on trade negotiations and the farsighted efforts to limit Japanese car sales in the United States during the Reagan administration in the 1980s played an important role in encouraging Japanese and other international actors to invest heavily in American production, and European, Japanese, and Korean automakers have invested more than $75 billion into US production since Honda opened its first US plant in 1982.[56]

US factories pumped out 8.8 million motor vehicles in 2020 and 10.9 million in 2019.[57] However, although American auto manufacturing has staved off a decline, the industry has experienced very limited growth. In the meantime, Chinese support for China's car industry has propelled it to global leadership. In 2020, the United States produced fewer than a million more vehicles than it had a decade earlier, while the Chinese made 7 million more—25 million vehicles in China to 8.8 million in the United States.[58]

The picture for the vehicles of the future is not much brighter. Let's look at electric cars. China controlled 77 percent of global lithium-ion battery manufacturing capacity in 2020, to 9 percent in the United States, and S&P forecasts that China will maintain 65 percent of capacity in 2025 while the United States falls further behind to 6 percent.[59] If current trends continue, China will be the automotive production hub of the twenty-first century, as America was for the twentieth. We in the Trump administration put 25 percent tariffs on the importation of Chinese-made cars into the United States.

The situation looks much worse in heavy industry. We have discussed cars; now let's examine ships. In the late 1970s, the United States had twenty-two large shipyards that were turning out significant numbers of cargo ships, tankers, regional containerships, drill rigs, and barges.[60] The United States now builds fewer than ten vessels for oceangoing trade in a typical year.[61] In the meantime, China is building more than a thousand ships per year, with a total capacity of fourteen million compensated gross tonnage in 2020—or 35 percent of global production capacity.[62]

The land of the free, and the home of the world's first and biggest railroads, is being lapped by China. True, it may be pointed out that the United States builds roads and bridges instead, but China is winning there, too, by a longshot. China's production capacity of cement was reported to be 1.6 billion metric tons in 2020, and some sources estimate that capacity is up to 3.5 billion metric tons per year.[63] The United States can make 133 *million* metric tons per year—or twelve times less than China can, using even the most conservative estimates of Chinese capacity.

What about those bridges? The core component of any bridge (or almost any heavy industrial good) is steel. As the global steel industry fell into recession in 2015, China provided more than $1 billion in subsidies to its thirty-three listed steel companies, which sustained the firms despite many posting operating losses that year.[64] This led to a spike in the Chinese share of global steel exports and caused prices to more than halve from a global average of $0.93 per kilogram in 2008 to $0.45–$0.50 in 2016.[65]

Now, China represents roughly one half of global capacity and boasts more than twice the combined capacity of the European Union, Japan, the United States, and Brazil. China's steel production climbed above 1 billion metric tons for the first time in 2020, reaching 1,053 million metric tons, a 5.3 percent increase from 2019, despite a significant contraction in global steel demand caused by the COVID-19 pandemic.[66] As a result of these actions, global excess capacity is almost six times the productive capacity of the entire US steel industry.

Finally, China is outpacing the United States at the cutting edge of advanced industry. Silicon Valley is often considered the hub of American innovation. It got its name because it was an early center of the semiconductor industry. Through the 1960s and 1970s, US semiconductor fabs were responsible for approximately 60 percent of global production.[67] The United States has now lost that dominance, with only 12 percent of global semiconductor manufacturing in 2021.[68] And China is working very hard to claim the mantle of chipmaking leader for itself.

China is even outspending the United States on research and development—traditionally America's core strength. China spent $621 billion on research and development in 2021, compared with $599 billion spent by the United States and $182 billion spent by Japan.[69] To complement these efforts, it is also poaching American R&D expertise. In 2021 alone, more than 1,400 Chinese-born US-trained scientists left US institutions to move back to China. This R&D strategy appears to be paying off. In a 2023 report, the Australian Strategic Policy Institute determined that China led the United States in thirty-seven of forty-four areas of key technology research across sectors ranging from defense to space to artificial intelligence.[70] Here, as elsewhere, the overall takeaway is that America is falling behind, and China is rising as the world's technological leader. Its policies are succeeding, while the United States struggles to follow through on the course correction that we undertook in the Trump administration.

Chapter 8

Changing the Direction

On November 9, 2017, the American state car, known as "the Beast," bearing President Trump rolled through Beijing into Tiananmen Square. It was the first official visit of his administration to China. In front of the Great Hall of the People, the red carpet had been literally rolled out for President Trump and the American delegation to which I, as the United States trade representative, belonged. Ranks of soldiers marched in formation, flashing bayonets. A military band played "Stars and Stripes Forever" as Presidents Trump and Xi walked side by side. A crowd of children waved a forest of small American and Chinese flags.

This was the third stop in a five-stop Asian swing near the beginning of the Trump presidency. We had spent a few days in Tokyo and then gone on to Seoul, South Korea, for talks. By far, however, the most important part of the trip was the visit to China. Prior to his election, President Trump had campaigned hard on the issue of the imbalance in our trade relationship with China and had strongly critiqued China's unfair practices. Chinese officials were very much aware of this and had set about to charm our new president by engineering a visit to Mar-a-Lago in Palm Beach in April, right after the president's inauguration. That visit—with its memorable images of the president's granddaughter singing a song in Mandarin to the smiling Chinese president and his wife—had succeeded in getting the two leaders off on the right foot. Indeed, President Trump went on to develop a good personal relationship with President Xi Jinping. Nevertheless, President Trump still maintained his position on the significant issue of China trade. He was capable of having a good personal relationship with world leaders while still being able to take hard decisions against them.

China's early charm offensive at Mar-a-Lago continued in full force when we arrived in Beijing in November 2017. In an unprecedented move, President Xi and his wife had given President Trump and Melania a personal tour of the Forbidden City—the vast palace complex in the center of Beijing that is the ancient seat of Chinese emperors. The tour was followed by an ancient dance routine in the opera house in the imperial city and then a private dinner.

The next day, the official meetings between the two delegations began. After the formal welcome for the state visit outside the Great Hall of the People, there was a small meeting of just a handful of senior Chinese and American officials in preparation for a larger meeting later that day. There were only five people attending on our side, and I'm sure that the Chinese wanted to set the tone without any trade minister present. But Chief of Staff John Kelly had told me to go in and take his place so that I could follow what was going on. I was later told that the Chinese were not happy about the substitution, but John Kelly was a tough, Italian-Irish four-star marine from Boston, and he tended to get his way. The meeting featured the normal chitchat and pleasantries, with serious issues dealt with at a top-line level.

A few minutes after the small meeting concluded, I found myself sitting in a cavernous room in the Great Hall of the People under a crystal chandelier that was perhaps ten feet in diameter. The American and Chinese delegations faced each other in two parallel lines across a gleaming conference table of heroic proportions. At the center of one side was President Xi. On the other side, facing him, sat President Trump with his twelve senior officials. President Trump was flanked by Secretary of State Rex Tillerson and our ambassador to China, former Iowa governor Terry Branstad. I sat next to Tillerson, the former longtime CEO of Exxon. He looked the part of secretary of state. He was very much at home at big ceremonies such as this, if rather less so in the day-to-day back-and-forth of working as a member of a team behind the scenes.

Despite the warmth of the welcoming ceremonies, this was essentially a meeting between the leading ranks of two armies facing off against each other. As with all such occasions, the opening comments were highly scripted, with the wording having been hammered out in conference with staff and the implications of each phrase carefully weighed in advance.

President Xi read his formal statement, followed by President Trump.

Both statements were cordial, raising issues only in the most diplomatic of terms. After that, President Xi called on his foreign minister to make a statement on foreign policy issues. Following protocol, President Trump did the same thing and called on Secretary Tillerson, the only other cabinet officer in the meeting besides myself. The statements had been thoroughly vetted down to exact details. All proceeded according to plan.

Then came the curve ball. Following a short statement on economic issues, President Trump looked briefly in my direction. Then he called on me and asked me to speak to the Chinese about our position on trade. I had no carefully scripted statement with each word curated for content. What followed was very much my spontaneous thoughts on trade, on its effects on the American economy over the years, and on American workers. Oddly, the impromptu nature of the speech made it easier to find the words.

For the next several minutes, in a very respectful but direct way, I explained to the Chinese leadership our thoughts on the current trade situation. I talked about the theft of technology, the failure to protect intellectual property, cyber theft, the lack of progress in the multitude of talks held over the course of the previous two administrations, and the stream of gigantic trade deficits. I tried to explain all of this from our perspective, how the American people viewed our economic relationship as an uneven, unfair relationship that wasn't sustainable and how it had affected people's lives in many communities.

The Chinese appeared surprised by my statement. There was a pause. The group grappled with an appropriate response to an outbreak of candor in the midst of a highly choreographed meeting. It was not exactly a setting known for open, critical speech directed at the highest authorities of the CCP. After I spoke, as if by some silent consensus, the Chinese delegation continued to read the rest of their formal statements prepared by their officials. There was no straightforward response to my argument, although I can imagine that it inspired considerable debate and reaction behind the scenes. When the meeting ended a few minutes later and we began to leave, President Trump came up to me and said he would like to read my statement. I told him that I didn't have any written statement prepared.

At the big state banquet that night, I had been told that I would sit between the fifth and the seventh members of the seven-member standing committee of the politburo. These are the seven people who run China. As we approached the dinner table, my staff told me that I was now sitting between the fifth and the third members of the politburo in rank. It occurred to me that the Chinese finally realized that I may have some role in making Chinese trade policy. My relevance had been reevaluated and recalibrated up a couple of notches.

Turning the Boat Around

Without the means to ensure a level playing field, the decision to let China join the WTO in 2001 was a fundamental error. It followed from a miscalculation about the way China's economy and political system function and about the dynamic function of strategic leverage held by the United States. The annual review of China's trading status—which we gave up when we granted it Permanent Normal Trade Relations (PNTR) status in 2000—had been a vital bargaining chip. More importantly, the annual review had created a level of business uncertainty. What US company would shift a plant to China if it might face high tariffs the next year when exporting its products back to America? Yes, in practice, the favorable trade status for China had been extended every year. But the potential for withholding this status existed. Granting PNTR removed much of the leverage that the United States exercised in attempting to maintain a level playing field for trade with China. Meanwhile, the WTO's enforcement actions turned out to be time-consuming and ineffectual. Predictions made in the 1990s and early 2000s regarding the future of trade between the United States and China proved to be far off base. By the time I assumed the role of USTR under the Trump administration, then, our hands were tied.

Efforts to work through official channels of the WTO brought frustration to a fine art. The WTO's arcane rules meant that any complaint must be structured in very specific terms that precluded addressing problems at the level of their root causes. Even when the WTO chose to act in our favor, there was no effective means to enforce compliance. If we wanted to see real and sizable enforcement actions, the United States had no choice but to act on its own. But how could we find room to move within the strictures of US law?

My solution to this problem lay in the revitalization of a legal tool called Section 301. Section 301 of the Trade Act of 1974 states that if there is an "act, policy or practice" of a foreign government that is "unreasonable or discriminatory" and "burdens or restricts U.S. commerce," the president, acting through the USTR, can take "all appropriate and feasible action" to counteract that policy—and this includes placing tariffs and restrictions on imported products coming into the United States.

Section 301 has been used in one way or another several times over the years, mostly as an enforcement mechanism that gave some teeth to our trade negotiations. I constantly had it on my desk during my time as deputy USTR in the Reagan administration. For example, in 1984, President Reagan instructed me to negotiate VRAs on carbon steel with several countries around the world. The objective was to slow the flood of foreign steel into our market that was devastating our industry. South Korea initially refused to cooperate in the effort. I threatened to go to the president and ask for authority to bring a Section 301 case, potentially leading to a loss of access to the US market. This move was effective—we ended up making a deal with South Korea and with all the other target countries. Later, the Clinton administration used Section 301 in a similar way, as leverage in negotiations with Japan on auto trade.

Because we used this statute so effectively as a threat during the 1980s, free trade advocates and our trading partners were determined to defang it. During the long and tortuous course of the Uruguay Round trade negotiations (1986–93), numerous countries (led by Japan and Europe) had pushed hard for rules at the WTO that would stop the United States from taking unilateral action on trade. The primary channel for that action was Section 301.

In the final text of the agreement, severe limitations were put on Section 301 and on unilateral US action. The implementing bill as enacted by our Congress in 1994 stated that if a trade agreement violation was found using Section 301, the only remedy was to bring an enforcement action at the WTO. At the time, everyone expected this to be a workable channel for enforcement. Few anticipated that any action through the WTO would develop into a laborious effort that would rarely lead to effective remedies. A few years later, this downside became abundantly evident.

There was, however, still one opening left in the former Section 301. That opening said that if the USTR determines that the unfair or discriminatory foreign practice against the United States is not a violation of a trade agreement, then the prior authority still pertained. That meant that the president (acting through the United States trade representative) could still legally use all appropriate and feasible authority to force the foreign country to stop the practice—including through raising tariffs and restricting access to our market.

I had long believed that putting appropriate tariffs on Chinese exports to the United States was the only feasible way to address China's systemic mercantilist practices. I publicly called for such tariffs in my testimony before the US-China Commission in June 2010. There were few ways to impose such broad tariffs. There was Section 301, and there was an act of Congress. Unfortunately, going to Congress and getting it to pass a sanction against China for unfair trade was not a realistic option in 2017. The combination of big business, the Chamber of Commerce, and Chinese lobbying would stop any action in its tracks. Free trade absolutists in the Senate and House of Representatives were pleased that we had so many imports from China (meaning cheaper goods for all). They would have worked against any action to stem the flow. Anyone concerned about the threat from China had to find an existing statute that would authorize action by the president.

My proposal was to revitalize Section 301 for this purpose, as well as to make maximum use of the powers that it gave the president to act on China's unfair trade practices. No president had ever attempted to use this authority to fight systemic mercantilism. No one had ever used it to impose large tariffs on a trading partner. No one had ever used the law to broadly attack such massive and damaging unfair practices. This powerful tool was left sitting on the shelf. As USTR, I was determined to make full use of it to serve the needs of American workers and communities and, in effect, to reorient our trade policy toward the common good.

We decided to single out the most egregious of China's actions that were clearly within the parameters of Section 301. We would focus on technology theft, cyber intrusions, and failure to protect intellectual property. We launched an investigation to determine whether these prac-tices were unreasonable or discriminatory and whether they burdened or restricted US commerce. That is the course that President Trump laid out in the summer of 2017.

We would have a full and thorough investigation over the course of several months. We would exhaustively document our findings. Then we would take action within the context of the WTO for any practices that we found to be in violation of a trade agreement as required by the Section 301 statute. With respect to those items that were not found to be a violation of a trade agreement, we would use the other part of the statute—the remaining opening that allowed for unilateral action in such cases.

We would take all appropriate and feasible actions necessary to force China to stop these unfair practices. That was our plan from the begin-ning, and we followed that plan to the end.

"The Era of Economic Surrender Is Over"

That process of reorienting our trade relationships was launched at the White House on August 14, 2017. President Trump stood behind the podium in the White House diplomatic reception room that had once hosted Franklin Roosevelt's fireside chats. There the president signed the order that authorized me to begin an investigation of China's prac-tices on forced technology transfers, intellectual property protection, and cyber theft.

"The theft of intellectual property by foreign countries costs our na-tion millions of jobs and billions of dollars each and every year," the president stated. "For too long, this wealth has been drained from our country while Washington has done nothing . . . But Washington will turn a blind eye no longer." At long last, we were taking action.

"The reality is that the U.S. government has long known about these aggressive Chinese efforts but until today has been reticent to consider serious trade measures," commented Jamil Jaffer of George Mason University Law School in the *Washington Post*, concluding that the action was an important step forward to counter cyber theft and forced technology transfer.[1] That authorization of the investigation was the first official step on a journey that would ultimately lead to a series of forceful and effective actions to remedy multiple serious infringements of fair-trade practices centered on the appropriation of intellectual property.

The seven-month investigation was conducted by USTR staff and supported by staff from the Council of Economic Advisers, the Commerce Department, the Treasury Department, the Justice Department, the State Department, the Small Business Administration, and other parts of the US government. The USTR's office reviewed over ten thousand pages of relevant Chinese-language documents. We spent more than four thousand man-hours reviewing and analyzing the documents. We held a public hearing on October 10, 2017, where we heard from fifteen witnesses and received seventy-three written submissions. China had a full opportunity to participate.

When the investigation was complete, on March 22, 2018, the Office of the USTR released its 200-page-long historic report. The result was a critically important document concerning economic relations between the United States and China. The report carefully demonstrated the many abuses of the Chinese system in four key areas. The first was China's technology transfer regime. The second was Chinese licensing restrictions for US businesses. The third was Chinese state-sponsored investments to acquire US technologies. Finally, it addressed the ongoing problem with China's repeated attacks on commercial computer networks in the United States.

For the occasion of the release of the report, we gathered in the same historic diplomatic reception room where we had started out some seven months earlier—but with a lot of water under the bridge having passed since that day. Our report, embodying the work of all those months, found that China's actions resulted in harm to US business and the economy through multiple channels and that the impacts had imposed costs in the billions of dollars per year. In response to the findings of unfair trade practices, a presidential memorandum laid out the actions that the

United States planned to carry out. Tariffs would be imposed on a selected range of Chinese goods. In addition, restrictions would be placed on Chinese investment in US technologies considered to be sensitive in nature.

Standing behind the podium, President Trump signed the memorandum with a flourish. "We're doing things for this country that should have been done for many, many years," he concluded. "We've had this abuse by many other countries. . . . We're not going to let that happen." He looked in my direction. "Ambassador Lighthizer, thank you." As Vice President Mike Pence memorably declared that afternoon, "The era of economic surrender is over." And indeed it was, but the fight was just beginning.

The Battle Begins

With the release of the Section 301 report, the president directed that the actions to address China's harmful acts, policies, and practices would take three forms—tariffs, dispute settlement to address violations of the WTO agreements, and investment restrictions. We at the Office of the USTR were responsible for the first two efforts, and the president instructed Secretary Steve Mnuchin and the Treasury Department to pursue the third. In our original discussions of a remedy, I wanted to use the broad powers in the International Emergency Economic Powers Act to construct a new regime to limit Chinese investment in US technology. Of course, institutional Treasury Department forces opposed that. Losing the battle for control of Chinese investment in the US was my one regret.

We wasted no time in getting started. A day after the issuance of the Section 301 report, we launched a dispute at the WTO challenging the discriminatory technology licensing requirements used by China to transfer technologies from US companies to Chinese companies. Stephen Vaughn, the USTR general counsel, had worked with career staff to prepare the complaint at the WTO. He called the staff in Geneva, and they filed it that same day.

Our complaint was that the discriminatory requirements broke WTO rules in the Agreement on Trade-Related Aspects of Intellectual Property Rights (the so-called TRIPS Agreement) by denying foreign patent holders, including US companies, basic patent rights to stop a Chinese entity from using patented technology after a licensing contract ends and by imposing mandatory adverse contract terms against imported foreign technology. Thus, despite the criticism that we were "going it alone" in unilaterally taking action against China, we pursued WTO dispute settlement where China's conduct was covered by and ran afoul of WTO rules. However, the WTO agreements did not address many of China's unfair trade practices, including much of what we had detailed in our Section 301 report. These practices could only be addressed only through the remedies provided under US law.

Less than two weeks later, on April 3, 2018, we announced the list of products under consideration for the $50 billion worth of Chinese imports that would be subject to 25 percent tariffs pursuant to the Section 301 action. The $50 billion number was what administration economists came up with as the amount of damage done to our economy as a result of the unfair Chinese practices. The proposed list of products was based on extensive interagency economic analysis and targeted products benefiting from China's industrial plans such as the Made in China 2025 plan. We wanted to have those goods that benefited from the unfair practice pay the price. The sectors subject to the proposed tariffs included aerospace, information and communication technology, robotics, and machinery. Within a day of our announcement, China retaliated with a list of $50 billion of US imports that would be subject to 25 percent tariffs. In other words, instead of taking constructive action to address the harmful acts, policies, and practices identified in the Section 301 report, China doubled down. This started the pattern of retaliation and counterretaliation.

Although Secretary Mnuchin wanted to find a negotiated solution to avoid having the 25 percent tariffs go into effect on Chinese imports, I firmly believed that the tariffs were a necessary, appropriate, and measured step to take to address China's harmful conduct identified in the Section 301 report. The president was on my side and constantly resolute. The secretary and I sent a letter to Chinese vice premier Liu He on April 20, 2018, setting forth the broad outlines of an agreement to resolve outstanding issues between our two countries. We also agreed to travel to Beijing for talks. Vice Premier Liu He would be my counterpart for the remainder of the Trump administration. He had earned a bachelor's and master's in economics from Renmin University of China, a government-affiliated university and the most prestigious in the country in his field. He also had a master's of public policy from Harvard University, so he had spent some time in the United States in his youth. He was a lifelong member of the CCP. He was a trusted adviser of Xi's predecessor Hu Jintao. Liu's views on economics were very much affected by the great 2008 global recession. Many in Xi's circle interpreted the developments in 2008 as an indication that the Western economic model was fatally flawed—some believed that it was doomed. Liu had a reputation for being more interested in the development of what passes for "private" industry in China than some of the hard-liners were. He proved to be a tough and very smart negotiator but always an honorable man. I came to admire him.

Shortly before leaving for Beijing, on May 1, 2018, we delivered a "draft framework" and appendices that were intended to serve as discussion documents. These conveyed the changes we needed to see in China's trade, investment, and intellectual property rights regimes. Among other things, the framework addressed the policies and practices identified in our Section 301 report on forced technology transfer and intellectual property as well as issues relating to investment restrictions, tariff and non-tariff barriers imposed by China, and market access for US service providers and US agricultural products. It also outlined the need for strong enforcement and implementation provisions, which I pushed for given China's track record of repeatedly failing to comply with its agreements.

We met with Vice Premier Liu. While he was close to Xi, he was not thought to be one of the hard-liners who mostly wanted confrontation. He handled difficult situations very well, and he could argue his position without relying on talking points. He and his immediate team understood the issues. They spoke English and were familiar with Western history and philosophy. His delegation met ours at the Diaoyutai State

Guesthouse in Beijing from May 3 to May 4, 2018. The primary members of our delegation consisted of myself, Secretary Mnuchin, Secretary Wilbur Ross, Larry Kudlow, and Peter Navarro, with Mnuchin as the designated lead of our delegation.

During the course of the meetings, China attempted to test the mettle of our group and how unified we were by proposing an "early harvest agreement"—that is, a partial agreement that would relieve pressure on the Chinese and lift some of the tariffs. This would be like the dialogues of the past where they strung us along. I'm sure they knew that as with most groups of government leaders, there was a diversity of opinion among members of the Trump administration on how to deal with China. For example, Peter Navarro and I strongly opposed any early harvest. We thought it would reduce our leverage and make it much harder to make any real progress. When Secretary Mnuchin showed some openness to an early harvest concept, Peter was livid. He erupted at Mnuchin in front of members of the Chinese delegation. I knew that I would have to navigate the clear divisions in our group to ensure that we resisted China's repeated efforts to have us accept a quick and easy deal. The president wanted to make an agreement with the Chinese only if it was the strongest possible, one that would make a difference, and we were light-years away from reaching that point.

Later that month, the vice premier and his delegation came to Washington for three days of meetings at the Treasury Building. The plan was for these meetings to focus on rebalancing the relationship between the United States and China. Secretary Mnuchin continued ostensibly to serve as the lead for our side, but he was less concerned with structural issues causing the distortions and unsustainable imbalance in our trade relationship with China. Secretary Ross and I also participated extensively in the discussions.

Once again, the Chinese wanted to home in on an early harvest deal addressing purchases and issues on which China had previously made commitments on multiple occasions but failed to fulfill. The Chinese provided a lengthy non-paper addressing the numerous items included in the draft framework and appendices that we had sent to them as well as a limited list of issues to which China "could positively respond." I had to fight to keep the focus on the major structural issues and not have our side settle on an agreement covering purchases together with some "old wine in new bottles." Along those lines, I had our USTR team prepare a list of more than 125 Chinese measures relating to forced technology transfer that needed to be repealed or modified, and we presented that list to the Chinese side.

On one of the evenings after our meetings in Washington, the two delegations had dinner at Café Milano in Georgetown in an upstairs private room, with about ten people on each side of the table, including Ambassador Cui of China and Jared Kushner. At dinner, as they had in the meetings, the Chinese continued to put on the full-court press for a mini-deal. This event and other dinners offered the opportunity to build relationships and rapport that could help in achieving agreement. However, these get-togethers also posed a risk in that the Chinese side could probe soft spots if anyone in our delegation let their guard down.

At the conclusion of the meetings in Washington, the two sides issued a joint statement on May 19, 2018. The joint statement was short on specific commitments and focused far more than I would have preferred on purchases. It provided that "China will significantly increase purchases of United States goods and services," that the two sides "agreed on meaningful increases in United States agriculture and energy exports," and that the United States would send a team to China "to work out the details." It also went on to vaguely indicate that the two sides had agreed to create favorable conditions to increase trade in manufactured goods and services, to strengthen cooperation on intellectual property protection, and to strive to create a fair, level playing field for competition. The fact that we had not reached any type of real agreement was fine with me. In fact, I was thrilled that there was no deal that would prevent us from moving forward with the tariffs. They had been announced, but the law required a process to select and actually implement them.

Secretary Mnuchin had a different take. Considering the meetings in Washington, Mnuchin went on one of the Sunday talk shows on May 20, 2018, and claimed that the tariffs were "on hold." But there was never any agreement or understanding that the tariffs would be on hold. I knew that I needed to talk to the president as soon as possible to make sure that we stayed on track with the imposition of the tariffs. Imposing the tariffs was the only way to effectively counteract China's unfair trade practices and gain the necessary leverage to get a good deal with the Chinese in which they would agree to make changes to those practices. Otherwise, we would be right back where we were before in the endless dialogues that took place under prior administrations, where China made commitment after commitment that it never fulfilled. I spoke to the president, who was in his White House residence, over the phone, and he was completely supportive.

I released a statement indicating that while the two sides had agreed on a framework to address the issues raised in our investigation, "the United States may use all of its legal tools to protect our technology through tariffs, investment restrictions and export regulations." I added, "Real structural change is necessary. Nothing less than the future of tens of millions of American jobs is at stake." And on May 29, the White House released a statement saying that we would impose tariffs on $50 billion in goods from China shortly after announcing the final list of covered imports on June 15.

Following up on the May 19, 2018, joint statement's language about sending a team to China "to work out the details" on China's increased purchases of US goods and services, Secretary Ross traveled to Beijing for meetings beginning on June 2, 2018. We sent a few people from USTR, including my chief agricultural negotiator, Gregg Doud, and the assistant USTR for China affairs, Terry McCartin. However, neither I nor my deputy on the China negotiations, Jeff Gerrish, made the trip. From the start, I wanted to minimize the importance of the purchases and keep the focus on structural issues, including those related to forced technology transfer and intellectual property that were identified in our Section 301 report and on keeping the tariffs. During this trip, China made proposals to purchase more US agricultural products, but its proposals were contingent on our terminating the Section 301 investigation and tariffs—a total non-starter.

Throughout this time, we continued to move forward with the legal process for the imposition of the Section 301 tariffs. Considering the public comments that we received, we decided to modify the group of products that would be subject to the tariffs by eliminating some from the list. We wanted to minimize the pain felt by US companies and consumers while ensuring that we hit the products and industries targeted by the Made in China 2025 industrial policy. As a result of this process, we wound up with multiple lists of products that would be subject to the tariffs beginning at different times. The original $50 billion list of Chinese products was split into two—the first covered $34 billion of Chinese products and the second covered $16 billion of Chinese products.

Immediately after we announced, on June 15, 2018, that we would proceed with the two lists, China decided against taking any steps to address our concerns, and instead published its own two-phased list of retaliatory tariffs. We had shown restraint in imposing tariffs on only $50 billion of Chinese imports, but no administration had ever stood up to them before, and I'm sure they were confident that they would get us to back down and that the old, failed policy would be followed once again. I always assumed that all the lobbyists and former government officials opposing our actions believed this. They had not faced Trump and this new team, so they didn't fully know who they were dealing with. It was one of many serious miscalculations the Chinese would make in our trade dispute.

On June 18, 2018, the president directed USTR to identify another $200 billion worth of Chinese goods for additional 10 percent tariffs in order to address China's failure to change its unfair trade practices and instead pursue unlawful retaliation that could result in additional harm to and burden on the US economy. We had a valid reason for the $200 billion number. We took the position that the $50 billion that we had put on Chinese goods was compensation for the cost to our economy from China's unfair practices. The $50 billion in retaliatory tariffs the Chinese put on was 40 percent of our total exports to them. Our $200 billion in new tariffs would get us back to even on a percent-of-trade basis (approximately 40 percent of their $500 billion in exports). Essentially, we used against the Chinese the fact that they don't buy from us—which means they have fewer things to tariff than we do.

Our first 25 percent tariffs went into effect on July 6, 2018, for the first list of $34 billion of Chinese goods and then on August 23, 2018, for the second list of $16 billion of Chinese goods. Each time, China's retaliation of 25 percent tariffs on the same value of US goods became effective the same day.

Thus far, the Chinese had been matching us dollar for dollar with their retaliatory tariffs. But they had a problem with the tariffs on the $200 billion of additional Chinese goods. China only had about $60 billion in imports left to hit. In response to our proposed tariffs on $200 billion of additional Chinese goods, China announced its intent to impose tariffs on the remaining $60 billion of US goods exported to China. China had overplayed its hand. The Chinese now were proposing to tariff all our sales to them. They were out of ammunition.

China's failure to change its harmful behavior and its ongoing illegal retaliation led us to continue with our process to impose the tariffs on the additional $200 billion of Chinese goods. It also prompted the president to direct USTR to consider increasing the proposed level of the tariffs from 10 percent to 25 percent. Ultimately, we decided to move forward with 10 percent tariffs on the third list of $200 billion in Chinese goods starting on September 24, 2018, and then increase those tariffs to 25 percent on January 1, 2019. The January 1 deadline would give us additional leverage in our negotiations with China.

Not much had been happening in the talks leading up to that point. There had been meetings in Washington at the level of the vice minister and deputy USTR in August, and Secretary Mnuchin had sent a letter to Vice Premier Liu inviting him to Washington for further discussions. But there had not been any real progress.

The Emergence of China's 40-40-20 Framework

The dynamic started to change with the approach of the January 1 deadline for the increase in tariffs to 25 percent on the $200 billion. China began peppering us with a number of non-papers responding to the structural issues that we had been raising regarding forced technology transfer, intellectual property, non-tariff barriers, services market access, and agricultural market access.

By its calculations, China determined that we had raised 142 separate issues. In early November 2018, China provided us with a non-paper (an unofficial diplomatic note) describing its methodology for placing the 142 issues into three categories and then another non-paper placing each issue into one of these three categories. China even color-coded the three categories with the colors of a traffic light. Category One covered the "green light" issues on which China believed we could reach agreement if we "met each other halfway." The "yellow light" issues in Category Two were ones on which China believed we could have "in-depth discussions" and potentially reach agreement if the US side were to negotiate in good faith. And finally, China declared the "red light" issues in Category Three as off limits. According to China, no agreement would be possible on those issues. It claimed that 40 percent of our issues fell into Category One, 40 percent were in Category Two, and 20 percent belonged in Category Three. The Chinese began referring to this as the 40-40-20 framework, and it represented one of several numerical designations or frameworks that China used in the negotiations.

As China provided us with additional non-papers explaining the basis for its classification of each issue in one of the three categories, it became clear that even with China's renewed level of activity, it continued to misjudge our side and overplay its hand. China had become accustomed over decades of experience under several US administrations to the Americans caving in to them in negotiations and agreeing to watered-down, sometimes rehashed, commitments that the Chinese never planned to fulfill anyway. It was apparent from their non-papers that the Chinese believed we could reach agreement on the "green light" issues in Category One only because they thought that actions China had already taken or was planning to take would be sufficient to resolve the issues—essentially by doing nothing new or real. We had to explain to the Chinese repeatedly and clearly that if the actions China had taken or was planning to take were sufficient, we would not be raising the issues with them in the first place. In addition, China classified the most important issues as "red light" issues in Category Three. By trying to pull these issues off the table, China ensured that no progress could be made.

China also continued to raise its own "major concerns" in its non-papers. Each of China's asks was highly problematic and easily dismissed.

The Chinese apparently believed that a good offense is the best defense. They had a $400 billion surplus with us but claimed they had a list of barriers or unfair practices to complain about. In some communities, that would be called chutzpah. For example, China sought to have the United States substantially reduce export controls on products, software, and technology going to China. They were essentially asking us to weaken our own national security procedures. This was unacceptable. In fact, we were trying to make our export controls even stronger for exports to China, particularly for sensitive technologies and items that were essential to national security. I thought we needed to have a broader definition of national security to encompass more products, software, and technology as yet another step to ensure that we did not lose our technological edge. The Export Control Reform Act passed by Congress in 2018 provided for more stringent controls on strategic and emerging technologies, and the Department of Commerce started the process of implementing these requirements in November 2018. Secretary Ross was a great leader in this area.

China also sought a more favorable environment for Chinese investment in the United States. Once again, this flew in the face of what I and others in the administration were trying to do. After the Section 301 report was issued, I had worked closely with Secretary Mnuchin, Peter Navarro, and others in the administration to roll out new restrictions on Chinese investment in the United States. While Mnuchin favored a more conservative approach, I wanted to be aggressive. Like the tariffs, the new investment restrictions and export controls would pressure China to stop its unfair trade practices from threatening the United States' technological leadership in areas such as information technology, robotics, aerospace and aviation equipment, and new energy vehicles.

Ultimately, these efforts became subsumed under the Foreign Investment Risk Review Modernization Act passed by Congress in 2018 and the implementation of FIRRMA by the Treasury Department. I thought we should go even further in imposing restrictions on Chinese investments, but the Treasury Department believed that FIRRMA went far enough. One thing was clear—China's request for us to loosen investment restrictions certainly was not going anywhere.

Meeting at the Buenos Aires G-20 Summit

Looming in the background of these events was the upcoming meeting between President Trump and President Xi at the G20 meeting in Buenos Aires, Argentina. It was announced in late October 2018 that the two leaders would meet on the sidelines of the G20 meeting taking place on November 30 and December 1. The two had last met the year before in November 2017, and the meeting in Buenos Aires was a highly anticipated development given the rising trade tensions between our two countries.

Throughout this process, the president was heavily involved. I and others spoke to him daily. When there was a decision on escalating, we usually had a long meeting in the Oval Office. The key players would attend—me, Mnuchin, Ross, and Navarro and later Kudlow, National Security Council representatives, and often the vice president. Some wanted a quick deal. I and others wanted real change. We thought China was "tapping" us along. They wanted to delay the tariffs and engage in inconsequential talk for months. After a while I took to bringing a telegraph key with me. I would place it on the president's desk and tap it. The point was clear enough. After a while, I figured that the boss was getting tired of my gesture. Unlike the Chinese, I did not want to overplay my hand or my telegraph key.

I traveled to Buenos Aires for the G20 meeting, which served as one of several monumental meetings for trade during our administration. On Friday, November 30, 2018, in a historic event, President Trump, Prime Minister Trudeau, and outgoing Mexican president Peña Nieto signed the USMCA. After a long, hard-fought negotiation on it, the signing of this agreement—the largest trade deal ever—allowed us to focus even more on our efforts with China (the USMCA negotiations are described in detail in chapters 12, 13, and 14). Soon after the signing, people around the world were focused on the meeting between President Trump and President Xi that would take place the following day.

Before that meeting, Secretary Mnuchin and I met with Vice Premier Liu. The Chinese still wanted our deal to be one that focused on their agreeing to increase their purchases of some more US goods. Their proposal seemed unrealistic, unenforceable, and insufficient. After going over their latest numbers, we discussed a framework and agenda for the meeting between Presidents Trump and Xi and potential outcomes for that meeting.

Our team—including the hawks and the others—had a premeeting with the boss in which we rehashed our positions. We sat around a conference table in the presidential suite of the Palacio Duhau–Park Hyatt Buenos Aires Hotel. Peter and I were on the "hawk" side, along with John Bolton, while those from the Treasury Department and some others were more cautious.

On Saturday evening, December 1, 2018, President Trump met with President Xi for a working dinner. In addition to the president, the US delegation for the meeting included Secretary Mnuchin, Secretary of State Mike Pompeo, National Security Advisor John Bolton, Peter Navarro, Jared Kushner, Larry Kudlow, and me.

The dinner lasted about two and a half hours. It began with President Xi making a long, prepared intervention in which he covered a variety of issues mostly focused on trade. He also covered such things as the Chinese government's not letting certain dual Chinese-US citizens leave China, fentanyl, and North Korea. After the Chinese president made his intervention, President Trump made his. It was cordial but business-like. There were comments made back and forth. When it came to trade, President Trump provided an overview of our concerns and then turned it over to me.

While respectful in addressing President Xi and his senior delegation, I provided a blunt and frank assessment of where we were in our dispute. I mentioned the massive distortions in the trade relationship caused by China's unfair trade practices and the egregious harm that our workers, farmers, manufacturers, and other businesses had suffered as a result of those unfair trade practices. I explained why the United States viewed itself as the aggrieved party in our trade relationship with China, a theme I would return to time and time again in our trade talks. I explained why no progress had been made on these matters over the years of our talks. As the dinner concluded, the two presidents agreed that there would be a pause before we would increase the tariffs. It would last ninety days, and during that period, we would have to make progress in a substantial way. Coming into the dinner, we had all known that China would seek a removal of the tariffs we had imposed, or at least the tariffs on the third list of $200 billion of Chinese goods, so it was no surprise when China made this request. To address our concern about the enormous trade imbalance between our two countries, President Xi offered to have China increase purchases of US goods and services by $1.2 trillion over six years. I had met previously with the president to explain why I believed we needed to hold firm with the tariffs already in place. I also continued to emphasize to him the importance of the structural issues in our negotiations.

As he so often did during these times, the president held firm, and the two leaders agreed on a path forward for the trade negotiations. We would keep the current tariffs in place but agreed not to raise the 10 percent tariffs on the third list of $200 billion to 25 percent as was then scheduled to occur on January 1, 2019. China committed to purchase a substantial amount of additional US goods and services of all types in order to reduce the trade deficit and to start purchasing US agricultural products immediately through SOEs or other businesses directed by the government. And most importantly, China agreed to immediately begin negotiations on the structural issues relating to forced technology transfer, intellectual property, non-tariff barriers, cyber intrusions and cyber theft, services market access, and agricultural market access. If no agreement was reached on these issues within ninety days, we would raise the 10 percent tariffs on the $200 billion of Chinese goods to 25 percent. In other words, we had a tight deadline of March 1, 2019, to complete these high-stakes, difficult negotiations.

Unbeknownst to the president and to me during the dinner, on that same night, Meng Wanzhou, the chief financial officer of Chinese tech giant Huawei and daughter of the company's founder, was arrested in Canada at the request of the United States. Ms. Meng and Huawei were alleged to have violated US sanctions against Iran. Had it been known, Ms. Meng's arrest could have completely scuttled the agreement reached by the two presidents. The treatment of Huawei would become a regular source of discussion and, at times, complication in our talks with China.

For the time being, we were focused on the path ahead. Immediately after the dinner ended, we all raced to the airport in a motorcade. I returned to Washington on Air Force One with President Trump. The real negotiations with China were about to start, and the president made it very clear that I would lead them. We had our work cut out for us.

Chapter 9

Beginning to Negotiate

After the meeting in Buenos Aires between President Trump and President Xi, we immediately began work on the negotiations with China. Given the ninety-day time frame and the enormity of the issues to cover, we had no time to spare. These negotiations presented a historic opportunity to reverse the failed policies of the past and change the course of our trade relationship with China for generations to come.

In the first days of our negotiations, we saw that movement was possible, but it would be painstaking. Our counterparts in the negotiation were acting in good faith, but we saw backsliding when our agreements were reviewed by officials in Beijing. I knew the only way to make these deals concrete was to convince the Chinese that we were serious in a way Americans hadn't been before. We had to let them know that their trademark tactics—"tapping" us along, reneging on commitments, making vague and unenforceable promises—were no longer going to cut it. We needed serious proof of good faith.

Our first contact with China after Buenos Aires was a phone call with Vice Premier Liu on December 10, 2018. After noting the short time frame leading up to the March 1, 2019, deadline, the vice premier made a proposal as a show of good faith. Under the proposal, China would make major purchases of US products consisting of 5 million tons of soybeans, 150,000 tons of rice, and 15 million tons of coal. It would also suspend its high 25 percent retaliatory tariff on US autos, bringing it back down to 15 percent, and approve certain import licenses for agricultural biotechnology products that had been denied or delayed for years in the Chinese system. The vice premier also came back to China's 40-40-20 framework for the issues we had raised and outlined a plan for addressing those issues. One specific matter that I emphasized and asked him to think about was the monitoring and enforcement of any trade agreement we might reach. China had a long track record of failing to fulfill its commitments in trade agreements, and this agreement had to be different in including a mechanism to ensure effective and meaningful enforcement of China's commitments. The issue of enforcement was so important to me that I wanted to flag it on this initial call before we even started talking about other issues.

The next meetings in Beijing were being held at the deputy level, but we received word that Vice Premier Liu would attend and deliver a statement at the plenary session to open the meetings. I had Ambassador Gerrish read a statement on my behalf. This statement emphasized several key themes. First, it expressed that we were trying to achieve a bilateral trade relationship with China based on the principles of fairness, reciprocity, and most importantly balance. To this end, the statement explained that we believed that the issues we were discussing should be viewed not as demands the United States was making of China but rather as reciprocal economic conditions that we required with all our trading partners. To achieve this kind of relationship, we would need to address structural issues, market access issues, and purchasing commitments of US goods and services. In addition, the statement made clear that any agreement we reached on these things had to be binding, verifiable, and enforceable. Mere promises would not be enough given the long history of China's committing to make significant changes to important policies and practices and then not following through.

On January 30, 2019, the first formal principal-level meeting started with an opening plenary in the Diplomatic Reception Room located in the Eisenhower Executive Office Building. I personally selected the Diplomatic Reception Room to ensure that the setting for this opening plenary was grand enough to match the momentousness of the occasion. The oldest part of the Eisenhower Executive Office Building is the southern section. It was completed in 1875, and the State Department moved in. This was the beginning of the Gilded Age, and America wanted an ornate home for its diplomats that projected the new power that we felt as a nation on the world stage.

The US delegation for the opening plenary included me, Secretary Mnuchin, Secretary Ross, Peter Navarro, and Larry Kudlow as well as key staff. In my opening statement, I once again highlighted certain key themes and offered a quote from Confucius that I thought was particularly apt for our talks. As I recounted, Confucius said, "In the past, when I evaluated a person, I believed what they said. Now, when I evaluate a person, I listen to them and then I see what they do." I went on to state that for us, this was critical and that we had to have a strong and clear path for enforcement in any agreement we reached.

After the opening plenary, the two delegations began the principal-level meetings at USTR's Winder Building. They were small group meetings consisting of me, Secretary Mnuchin, Ambassador Gerrish, and Assistant USTR Terry McCartin for the US side and Vice Premier Liu He, Vice Minister Wang Shouwen of the Ministry of Commerce, Vice Minister Liao Min of the Ministry of Finance, and the vice premier's chief of staff for the Chinese side. Over the course of our negotiations with China, Secretary Mnuchin, to his credit, would spend far more time in USTR's Winder Building than any secretary of treasury had before. He was fully engaged while still directing the Treasury Department's other responsibilities.

Vice Premier Liu and I kicked off our principal-level meetings with brief overviews of our positions before moving into discussions of forced technology transfer, intellectual property, and enforcement that took up much of our two days of meetings. On forced technology transfer, I raised China's joint venture requirements and ownership restrictions and its administrative licensing and approval processes that resulted in both formal requirements and informal pressure on our companies to transfer their technology to Chinese companies. I also addressed China's discriminatory intellectual property licensing regulations and its state-led investment in high-tech sectors. While we made some progress in these areas, issues such as state-sponsored cyber intrusions and cyber theft proved more difficult.

The intellectual property issues that I raised included both systemic issues and procedural issues that were important because they determined whether intellectual property cases could be brought in China and fairly adjudicated and whether appropriate remedies could be provided for breaches of our companies' intellectual property rights. In other words, would China truly prosecute and remedy these offenses against

American companies? We discussed a host of such issues, including requirements to ensure stronger civil and criminal enforcement of intellectual property rights, expansion of the scope of trade secret protection, the need for deterrent-level penalties and greater enforceability of judgments for breaches of intellectual property rights, cracking down on bad-faith trademarks, rules to allow greater use of expert witnesses, enhanced protection of pharmaceutical intellectual property, and patent term extensions for delays in the patent process. As I explained and as Vice Premier Liu acknowledged, greater intellectual property protection and enforcement were important not only to the United States but to China as well. Our negotiations were very technical. Every detail of the laws and practices was covered.

On enforcement, Vice Premier Liu seemed to understand our concerns, but his first suggestion was unsatisfactory. He provided a rough outline for an enforcement process that relied heavily on discussions between the parties. In response, I told him that while process and discussions were important, the two keys to any mechanism would be who determines whether there is a breach of the agreement and what the consequences are when there is a breach. When the vice premier suggested the use of a dispute settlement panel process such as that provided for under the United States–Mexico–Canada Agreement (USMCA), I was quick to note that the United States would want, at least in certain cases, to make its own decision on compliance and remedies, rather than have those decisions made by a panel. It seemed impossible that truly neutral Chinese arbitrators could be found, and the idea of using third-country judges was out of the question for both the United States and China.

Toward the end of our meetings on January 31, we submitted a list of actions that could and, we believed, should be taken immediately by China. It was important for us that we see some evidence of China's good-faith intent to actually implement suggested changes, given their history of reneging on commitments. We were giving them an opportunity to prove it. These immediate actions ranged from lifting China's foreign investment restrictions to eliminating China's discriminatory intellectual property licensing regulations to granting approvals for US companies' seeking to provide credit rating, electronic payment, and insurance services in China. Vice Premier Liu responded favorably to certain of these items but said China would respond formally at a later date. We also agreed with the vice premier that we would draft agreement text to reflect our discussions in the form of memorandums of understanding (MOUs) that we would provide to them when ready. MOUs represent the end goal of our negotiations, the customary form for agreements between nations.

My USTR team continued work on the draft MOUs to cover each of the subject areas in the negotiations. On February 8, 2019, we delivered three MOUs to the Chinese side—the MOUs on forced technology transfer, intellectual property, and agricultural barriers and market access.

There was now less than a month before the tariffs would escalate, and we were about to find out that the MOUs we thought we had settled were not seen the same way by China. Our next meetings took place in Beijing on February 11 and 12, 2019, at the deputy level and on February 14 and 15, 2019, at the principal level. In the deputy meetings, which were led by Ambassador Gerrish, the two sides began discussing the draft MOUs that we had sent to China. Based on those discussions, it became clear that there was backsliding by China in a number of areas from where we had been in our meetings in Washington. This was a major problem that needed to be addressed at the principal level. And that is exactly where I started in our principal-level meetings.

I expressed that we had great confidence in Vice Premier Liu but that we were discouraged by China's backsliding on intellectual property issues such as the scope of trade secret protection, the availability of preliminary injunctions to prevent the use of trade secrets, and various aspects of pharmaceutical patent protection. I also identified backsliding on China's commitments relating to forced technology transfer. Noting China's history of unkept promises, I emphasized the great risk if we reverted to prior failed efforts. The vice premier assured us that this time was different and that the Chinese would do everything that he promised without any changes. Unfortunately, issues with backsliding by China would be a recurring theme.

Although I could not definitively know what was going on behind the scenes in China, I was sure that Vice Premier Liu was dealing with multiple, interrelated tensions within the Chinese political system as he syndicated our proposed agreements. Beyond pushback from CCP hardliners, who opposed market-oriented reforms or concessions to American demands instinctively, he also faced tensions from China's entrenched administrative bureaucracy—which feared losing control and discretion over important policy areas. He also had to navigate long-standing divisions between the provincial and national governments in China, as many provincial leaders staunchly opposed concessions by the national government that would limit their ability to control local economic policy. Finally, he faced difficulties when agreeing to changes to policy areas outside of his direct portfolio of responsibilities separate from his (temporary) role as the chief negotiator—we often saw that the negotiations were most productive when discussing matters that the vice premier could implement himself. The vice premier surely kept President Xi continuously apprised of our discussions, but negotiated concessions continually disappeared or reemerged in watered-down form as the details spread to different interest groups within the Chinese government and Chinese leaders responded to consequent internal pressures. We were vigilant to track, and forcefully reject, such behavior from the Chinese side throughout our negotiations.

Our discussions then moved to areas that we had not reached in our meetings in Washington, such as barriers to services and agriculture trade and, importantly, China's massive subsidies that provide an unfair advantage to its companies in countless industries, their enormous excess capacity in industries such as steel and aluminum, their needed disciplines on SOEs, their "secure and controllable" policies for information and communication technology, and the use of their anti-monopoly law. Vice Premier Liu recognized the importance of eliminating subsidies and excess capacity and sought only to carve out subsidies for laid-off employees. He also expressed openness to strong disciplines on SOEs and to SOE reform, which was another area within his portfolio. In addition, I argued to the vice premier that China's "secure and controllable" policies, which provide for the government to require companies to maintain backdoors in their encryption to preserve government access to data, represented pure protectionism, dismissing the claim that it served national security interests. I told him how I heard repeatedly about China's misuse of its anti-monopoly law to target our most successful high-tech companies.

Our discussions on services covered barriers and market access restrictions in numerous service sectors, ranging from financial services to telecommunications to express delivery. China continued to treat our companies unfairly in these sectors, and our companies were treated much differently than Chinese companies were in the United States. For example, while US companies such as Visa, Mastercard, and American Express could not get the necessary approvals to provide their electronic payment services in China, China UnionPay had full access to the US market. This was an example of the lack of reciprocity in our economic relationship. We made progress in certain of these areas. However, it became apparent that other areas, such as allowing our companies to provide the full range of cloud computing services in China and allowing for greater ability to transfer data across borders, were highly sensitive for China. Any issue that in the opinion of the Chinese party officials might restrict ultimate control by the Communist Party was off limits.

On agriculture, China maintained regulatory processes and restrictions that unfairly prevented our farmers and ranchers from selling a number of products in the vast Chinese market. One of the key issues was China's failure to approve our agricultural biotechnology products for sale in China. China had a regulatory process for the approval of agricultural biotechnology that clearly was not science-based, required US farmers to transfer sensitive technology, and dragged on interminably without any approvals being granted. This was one of the issues where China had repeatedly made commitments to take action in the past but never followed through. China also administered tariff rate quotas on wheat, rice, and corn in a slow bureaucratic way that prevented our farmers from being able to fully utilize them. TRQs permit a lower tariff on a specified quantity of an import and then a higher tariff on additional imports. China was permitted to have this restriction as part of its accession to the WTO, but it had to administer the TRQs fairly. In addition, the Chinese government used a variety of restrictions to keep our beef, poultry, and other meat out of China, including unreasonable age and traceability requirements for beef. These were just a few of the areas we covered. The Chinese position seemed to be an odd combination of entrenched bureaucrats wanting to maintain control and real concern about health issues. On the latter it was hard not to be sympathetic, given China's history of catastrophic pandemics and natural calamities. Just in the past one hundred years, China has been the source of flu epidemics in 1918 and 1957 and coronavirus outbreaks in 2002 and of course 2019.

Another area we addressed was imposing disciplines on currency manipulation. China had a track record of manipulating the value of its currency, the yuan or renminbi, to enable its companies to have an unfair advantage over US and other foreign companies. A country with a weak currency can sell its goods more cheaply in export markets and effectively deters imports from strong-currency countries. We also started to converge on a structure for an enforcement mechanism for our ultimate agreement. However, I made it clear that any agreement had to provide for the United States to take enforcement action to address violations without China's being able to retaliate or bring a case at the WTO. After a great deal of discussion, Vice Premier Liu appeared to understand our idea. We also discussed China's commitments to increase its purchases of US goods and services. In every one of our meetings, including this one, I made it a point to discuss purchases only briefly and toward the end of the meeting. Although the purchases were important and helpful, the structural issues would have far more long-term impact. I did not want these talks to deteriorate into a mere sales list.

On the evening of February 14, we had dinner at the Beijing Hotel with the Chinese delegation. The Beijing Hotel had great symbolic significance for relations between the United States and China because it served as one of the locations where Henry Kissinger and Zhou Enlai met in 1971 before President Nixon's visit to China the following year. The hotel overlooks the Forbidden City and has views of Tiananmen Square.

At the conclusion of this trip to Beijing, Secretary Mnuchin and I and a few other members of our delegation were invited to meet with President Xi in the Great Hall of the People. The gathering took place in a cavernous meeting room. The delegations sat at conference tables facing each other. President Xi sat at a table at the head. Behind him was a wall-size painting of a ragged mountainous scene. The president and I both made statements reflecting the importance of our trade talks, not only for our two countries but for the world. The grandeur of this event and of our work was not lost on me.

Continuing the Negotiations from Washington

Once we got back to Washington, we realized the results of the Beijing talks hadn't been as concrete as they had seemed. We hosted the next set of meetings in Washington on February 21. During deputy meetings at the Winder Building, Ambassador Gerrish reported that the Chinese side was attempting to change language in the MOUs that represented commitments made by Vice Premier Liu in Beijing. This backtracking necessitated that I go through each of the MOUs with the vice premier provision by provision to nail down the language. In doing so, I had to explain the basis and justification for each of the provisions and the language used. It was again clear what was happening. The vice premier would act in good faith in our talks, but when word got back to other power sources in Beijing, there would be blowback.

Although the process of going through each provision line by line required much time and painstaking effort, it was essential and resulted in our making a great deal of headway. To take advantage of the momentum, we extended the two-day talks throughout the weekend for two more days. Key progress was made on issues across the MOUs on forced technology transfer, intellectual property, non-tariff measures, services, agriculture, and currency. Even on seemingly intractable problems such as industrial subsidies, excess capacity, and SOEs, China was willing to agree to critical disciplines. In fact, the two sides reached full agreement on the text of the currency MOU. The text was largely based on the USMCA currency chapter but was stronger in that it included a mandatory obligation not to engage in competitive devaluations or target exchange rates for competitive purposes.

We still faced major obstacles to reaching an agreement in the form of gaps on critically important issues. For example, protections against cyber intrusions, key provisions on trade secret theft and pharmaceutical patent protection, access to the Chinese cloud computing market, and approvals of agricultural biotechnology products were among the issues that proved particularly challenging. However, for the most part, things seemed to be moving in the right direction.

The issue of enforcement was, once again, a key topic of discussion. As I told the vice premier, the section on enforcement would be one of the key sections that would determine whether President Trump had the necessary support for an agreement in the United States. We agreed to exchange drafts of text on this issue, which we did shortly after our meetings. In addition, we had a lengthy discussion on what would happen with the tariffs if we were to reach an agreement. I explained that the 25 percent tariffs on the $50 billion of Chinese goods would remain in effect for the long term and that the 10 percent tariffs on the $200 billion of Chinese goods would remain in effect initially but could be reduced over time as China implemented its commitments under the agreement. It was clear that the removal of the tariffs represented a core issue for China.

We also arranged for the vice premier to meet with President Trump on February 22 in the Oval Office. After the press had been called into the Oval Office, Secretary Mnuchin mentioned that we were documenting multiple MOUs that would be binding and enforceable. When the president was later asked by a reporter whether the MOUs would be long-term and how long they would stay in place, he made clear that he was not a fan of MOUs, that he thought they did not mean anything, and that the MOUs would still have to be put into a final, binding contract. The president was, of course, thinking of an MOU like a term sheet in the context of a commercial real estate deal. I tried to explain that in the international trade context, an MOU is not a term sheet. It is a binding agreement, and it is the way international agreements and trade deals such as this are generally done. Indeed, the State Department has hundreds of MOUs on the books, as does the Defense Department. However, the president disagreed, and there was no convincing him. With that, I announced that we would never use the term "memorandum of understanding" again and that instead we would call it a trade agreement between the United States and China. The president liked that better, and the vice premier agreed. All of this played out in front of the assembled press and on national television. It, of course, was completely understandable that President Trump did not want us to have an MOU as that term is used in his former business world. Because of the way this exchange unfolded on national television, people asked me about it for months.

After the conclusion of our meetings on Sunday, February 24, Secretary Mnuchin and I briefed the president in detail on the status of the talks. President Trump was a hands-on boss. He was constantly involved in the details of our negotiations. For me that was a great way to work. I always knew I was precisely representing his position and that he would back me up. Given the progress we had made, the president decided to postpone the tariff rate increase on the $200 billion of Chinese goods that was scheduled to go into effect on March 1, which he announced by tweet. We would have more time to talk. The tariffs on the $200 billion of Chinese goods would remain at 10 percent—at least for now.

At this point in the negotiations, there were regular, ongoing exchanges of text between the parties. So as not to use the term "memorandum of understanding" or "MOU," each of the various subject areas covered in the negotiations would have its own chapter as part of the trade agreement. Despite the substantial progress in our meetings in Washington, the consensus we reached on a number of key issues was not reflected in the text we received from China. For issues on which we thought we had reached agreement, it started to appear as though we had not. For example, China changed the agreed text on industrial subsidies, excess capacity, and SOE disciplines. And although Vice Premier Liu agreed to key intellectual property protections relating to patent terms and the use of supplemental data to support patent applications, China's text rejected those provisions. China also watered down commitments made by the vice premier on forced technology transfer. Further, China tried to bilateralize commitments to make them applicable to both the United States and China where it was not possible or appropriate to do so, including for China-specific issues. In some cases, as in the intellectual property and agriculture chapters, China sent us entirely new, US-only commitments. Once again, I suspected the Chinese hawks and bureaucrats were undercutting their negotiator.

On March 6, 2019, we had the first of a series of conference calls with Vice Premier Liu and his team. At one point, he suggested that we could follow the approach of the Shanghai Communiqué, the famous document issued by the United States and China during President Nixon's visit to China in 1972 to normalize relations. The Shanghai Communiqué reviewed the differences between the two countries and then expressed their mutual interests. It was what is called "constructive ambiguity." This was not the first—and would not be the last—time that the Chinese mentioned following this approach. I rejected this idea. I had no interest in any kind of ambiguity—constructive or otherwise. We had to have binding commitments that were clearly expressed and agreed to by both parties. The vice premier acquiesced, and we appeared to be back on track. I was not surprised that the powers back in China thought they could get us to agree to a soft non-binding solution. This strategy on their part had worked with successive US administrations for two decades. I had to convince them that this time the situation was different. Four more conference calls followed this one in March 2019. Over the course of these calls, the negotiations had progressed sufficiently that we talked at various times about a potential meeting or telephone call between President Trump and President Xi to conclude an agreement. In our calls we continued to discuss the language of the agreement line by line—back and forth. My negotiation binders were beginning to have more lines and written notes in multicolor than print on the pages. They looked a little bit like a Jackson Pollock painting.

During this time, as we did throughout the negotiations, we continued to consult with US company officials and other interested parties about issues in the negotiations. I was also in regular, close communication with members of Congress from both parties to brief them on the status of the negotiations and to elicit their feedback and ideas. I had long since learned that surprising senior senators and representatives was not a good idea. Years before, Senator Dole had impressed upon me the importance of consultations. He used to say, "If you want me on the plane when it lands, you better put me on it when it takes off."

Our next meeting took place in Beijing beginning on March 28, 2019. Shortly after arriving, we toured the Forbidden City with Vice Premier Liu and his team. During our tour, we were allowed to enter a building that typically only foreign national leaders were permitted to enter. In fact, Vice Premier Liu told us that he had not previously been in that building himself. After our tour, we had a working dinner in another building located in the Forbidden City and then met all day on March 29. As a general matter, we were further along in our negotiations on forced technology transfer and intellectual property, and we decided to focus our discussions in these meetings on non-tariff barriers, services, enforcement, and purchases.

Our discussions on non-tariff barriers covered industrial subsidies, SOEs, standards setting, and technology localization. For services, we had extensive discussions on commitments to ensure that our companies could provide the full range of credit rating, electronic payment, cloud computing, and express delivery services and that US film studios were fairly compensated with an adequate revenue share for movies distributed and shown in China. Progress continued on enforcement, and the issues appeared to become more focused. I made clear that we had to be able to enforce all obligations under any agreement, including for a single violation of an obligation. Moreover, if we took enforcement action, China would not be able to take a counteraction. Vice Premier Liu raised a few other issues for our consideration. One was how to deal with force majeure situations. Clearly, it was in the United States' interests to limit the applicability of force majeure as much as possible so that China could not avoid its obligations by merely claiming unforeseen circumstances. Another question he posed was how we should treat the actions of a party taken before the agreement entered into force but that are maintained or continue to have effect after that date. On this latter issue, I knew that the enforcement mechanism had to apply to those situations, but we would deal with it later.

Vice Premier Liu and his team returned to Washington the following week for meetings from April 3 to 5, 2019. Going through the text of the different chapters provision by provision and often line by line, we continued to make steady progress. On the issue of enforcement, Vice Premier Liu indicated that the Chinese were thinking of creating a new office that would have responsibility for implementation of the agreement not only at the central government level but also at the provincial and local levels. Offices would be set up in the different provinces in China, and they would designate an extensive group of officials to address issues that arose. This is particularly important since many of the unfair practices in China are conducted by provincial and local officials often without central government knowledge. The national government would therefore need to intervene actively to ensure the terms they agreed to would be realized at the provincial level.

While we made headway on a number of issues, others proved more difficult, including on services barriers in areas such as cloud computing. In response, I raised the prospect of imposing fees on Chinese service providers in the United States where we provided greater market access to Chinese companies than our companies had in China. If it was fair for China to deny access to our companies, it seemed we should at least charge them to operate in the United States. Not surprisingly, the Chinese didn't like the idea. Certain issues also remained a struggle in our agriculture discussions, including our push for systemic changes in China's process for approving agricultural biotechnology products and the administration and allocation of China's TRQs.

Following our meetings in Washington, which represented the ninth round of negotiations, we had another series of conference calls throughout the month of April. In these calls, we continued to nail down the text for the substantive elements of each chapter of the agreement. We also discussed broader issues regarding the negotiations. Vice Premier Liu was conducting domestic political consultations with the top leadership in China, and those officials had raised certain fundamental concerns. One was that the removal of all tariffs had to be the foundation of any deal, and another was the need for more balance in the agreement. I countered that I, too, had been consulting with our top political leadership in the form of the president and key members of both the Senate and the House of Representatives about the status of the negotiations and the commitments to which China had agreed. It was critical that we not revisit language that was already closed. On the topic of balance, I had to make clear that while China's leadership wanted the agreement to be balanced and fair, we wanted balance and fairness across the entire trading relationship. We had a mammoth trade deficit in goods with China of more than $400 billion that was the result of China's unfair trade practices, not market forces. To achieve more balance and fairness in the relationship, we needed the substantial structural changes targeted to address China's unfair trade practices in the agreement. Where appropriate, we agreed to make certain technical changes to the text, including by moving language into annexes, and to bilateralize certain provisions. This was our way of making the language look more balanced without changing the substance of the agreement and the commitments being made by China.

We next traveled to Beijing for meetings on April 30 and May 1, 2019. At the outset of our meetings, I conveyed that we had this round and the next round to complete the agreement and that we needed to decide whether or not we would have a deal. If not, President Trump would move forward with additional tariffs on Chinese goods. What we heard from Vice Premier Liu was highly discouraging. He explained that the Chinese needed the complete removal of all tariffs and additional changes to the structure of the text to make it more balanced. But even more significantly and troublingly, the political leadership in China had strong objections to specific structural changes provided for in the agreed text. They contended that it would look as if China's sovereignty and dignity were being undermined and as if the United States were imposing another unfair treaty on China.

In response, I explained that we were very much aware of the history of unfair agreements for China, including those from the Opium Wars through the Japanese occupation of China. We understood the "Century of Humiliation" and its effect on Chinese thinking. But this situation, I argued, was the exact opposite of that one. Here, we had the world's two largest economies, and the United States viewed itself as the aggrieved party because of our unsustainable trade deficit with China and China's unfair trade practices that had, among other things, preyed upon our technology and intellectual property. I asked how China could feel aggrieved when it had accumulated over a trillion dollars in trade surpluses with us? We had already made changes where we could in order to make the text look more balanced. I stressed the importance of having an agreement with enough specificity to be enforced. We needed specific and enforceable commitments by China to make structural changes to ensure that the agreement had support and sustainability. That was the only way the president would ever agree or that I could convince people in the United States that this agreement was different than the agreements China had failed to fulfill in the past. The language we were discussing had been agreed upon for weeks or months. We were devolving rather than evolving. I huddled with Secretary Mnuchin and Ambassador Gerrish to confirm that they shared my views of the significance of China's proposed changes and its movement backward from agreed upon commitments. We made clear to the vice premier that we were dismayed and discouraged by what we had heard. In a private session with the vice premier, Secretary Mnuchin and I asked that the Chinese side send us their revisions to one of the chapters of the agreement, which we believed would be the intellectual property chapter, to show us an example of the changes they sought. We left Beijing disappointed.

When we received the revised text of the intellectual property chapter later that week, it confirmed our worst fears. The document was a sea of redlines. China struck out major portions of agreed-upon text covering important specific commitments. In seeking to make these substantial changes to the agreed-upon text, China had unquestionably reneged on its commitments. Over the weekend, Secretary Mnuchin and I briefed the president on China's actions. Considering this backtracking by China, the president issued a tweet on Sunday, May 5, 2019, indicating that the tariffs on the $200 billion of Chinese goods would increase from 10 percent to 25 percent and that the remaining amount of Chinese imports not already covered by tariffs could face the possibility of 25 percent tariffs. Showing the unity of the diverse viewpoints within the administration, Secretary Mnuchin and I briefed the press the following day about China's backtracking together with Larry Kudlow and Peter Navarro. At the press meeting, I clearly stated that China had "reneged" on prior agreed-upon commitments and that at 12:01 a.m. the following Friday, we were raising the tariffs on the $200 billion in Chinese goods from 10 percent to 25 percent.

We had a previously scheduled negotiating session set for Washington a few days later. Despite apparently weighing the possibility of canceling the trip, Vice Premier Liu and his team returned to Washington on May 9, 2019, to continue our talks. The meetings primarily consisted of private sessions in my office with Secretary Mnuchin, the vice premier, and me to see if we could make any progress. It was apparent we could not, and the negotiations stalled.

The United States and China soon embarked on a series of actions as tensions grew. On May 10, 2019, I announced that at the direction of the president, we were increasing the tariffs from 10 percent to 25 percent on the $200 billion worth of Chinese imports on List 3 and that we would begin the process of raising tariffs on essentially all remaining imports from China, which were valued at approximately $300 billion. China followed by announcing that it would increase tariff rates on roughly $60 billion of US goods. Less than a week later, the US Department of Commerce placed Chinese tech giant Huawei and sixty-eight of its affiliates on its Entity List, effectively cutting those companies off from exports of US goods, software, and technology. Not to be outdone, China reported that it was working to establish an "Unreliable Entities List" of banned US companies on May 31, 2019.

We were now two years into this effort to balance our relationship with China, and it was apparent that China's leadership had no intentions of changing. The tariffs were in place, and they would have the effect of counteracting China's unfair trading practices, putting economic pressure on the Chinese government to make a deal, and in the meantime discouraging US corporate investment in and supply chain integration with China. However, we had learned some things through the process. We'd confirmed that China is distrustful of the United States, and while individual officials may be acting in good faith, the hard-liners hold more power back home. Painstaking work through details may be the way to get initial commitments, but would they be worth anything? What we'd need to find was a way to make those commitments enforceable. As the tariffs went into effect, it was time to have another serious meeting, one where the president would step in personally.

Chapter 10

Making a Deal Concrete

In mid-June 2019, it was announced that President Trump would meet President Xi at the end of the month on the sidelines of yet another G20 meeting, this one in Osaka, Japan. Once again, I made the trip with President Trump and attended the meeting with President Xi on June 29. The summit was held at the International Exhibition Center, and our meeting took place in one of the side rooms set aside for bilateral consultations. Considering all that had happened, I thought the meeting was friendly and productive. While the current tariffs remained in place, the two sides agreed to not escalate, to hold off on imposing additional tariffs on each other, and to resume the negotiations on a possible deal. In addition, President Xi agreed that China would immediately begin making significant purchases of US agricultural products. He also raised issues not related to the trade talks. In response to President Xi's inquiries regarding both the treatment of Chinese students in the United States and Huawei, President Trump indicated that the United States would treat Chinese students fairly and would look at allowing exports to Huawei that did not present a national security threat.

While the meeting was encouraging, it did not change the fundamental Chinese tactics of reneging on commitments, rewriting the history of the talks, and raising unrelated issues that only muddied the waters. Further, China's tactics reinforced our view that everything had to be in writing and that an effective enforcement mechanism was essential. It was again apparent to me why so little progress had been made in past US administrations' talks with China. The difference this time was that the tariffs would stay in place and that they were having an effect on our economic entanglement with China.

Wasting no time after the meeting in Osaka, we had conference calls with Vice Premier Liu on July 9 and July 18, 2019. Joining him for the first time on these calls was the Chinese minister of commerce, Zhong

Shan. Minister Zhong was viewed as a hard-liner—rather than an economic reformer like Vice Premier Liu—whose participation in the discussions could impede progress. On several occasions in these two calls, Vice Premier Liu emphasized the need to conduct the talks on the basis of cooperation, equality, and mutual benefit. In response, I stated that our talks should follow the principles of cooperation, mutual respect, equality, and *balance*. Balance was critical. As I explained, the United States approached the talks from the point of view that our relationship with China was unbalanced and that the United States had not been treated as well by China as China had been treated by the United States on issues relating to forced technology transfer, intellectual property, market access, and the other structural issues we were discussing.

In our conference calls, the vice premier raised two issues unrelated to our trade talks. One was arms sales that the United States had made to Taiwan. The other was the treatment of Huawei by the United States. The vice premier asserted that President Trump had agreed in Osaka to remove Huawei from the Entity List. While I explained that the Huawei situation represented a law enforcement and national security issue, not a trade issue, I also made clear that the president had never agreed to remove Huawei from the Entity List and had only committed to consider allowing sales of US products, software, and technology through the issuance of export control licenses where it did not raise national security issues. The Commerce Department had already started a process to consider granting such licenses. The vice premier and his team regularly raised issues unconnected to our trade negotiations that their officials viewed as affecting the "atmosphere" for the talks.

In contrast, an issue that clearly was related to our trade talks and that was essential to keeping them on track was President Xi's agreement at Osaka to make immediate and significant purchases of US agricultural products. When I raised that commitment in our conference calls, the vice premier surprisingly indicated that President Xi had only agreed that the two sides could have talks on possible agricultural purchases. He also offered several reasons why additional agricultural purchases may not be possible, including the continuation of the tariffs on Chinese goods. To avoid any possible confusion, I stressed in the strongest possible terms the urgency of the situation and that we understood President Xi to have agreed to proceed immediately with increased agricultural purchases. If the agricultural purchases were tied to other issues, such as the removal of tariffs, it would not be conducive to a productive outcome. In our call on July 18, the vice premier stated that China would make agricultural purchases starting the next day, July 19.

We agreed to conduct our next face-to-face meetings in Shanghai on July 30 and 31, 2019. These talks were held at the Xijiao Conference Center, another state guesthouse.

In discussing what had happened in the past, Vice Premier Liu laid the blame for the previous breakdown of the negotiations squarely at the feet of the United States. He contended that China had to go through its domestic procedures, that the Chinese had shared China's core concerns with us, and that the United States failed to recognize these core concerns. Additionally, he indicated that we needed to have a keener and deeper appreciation for political and cultural considerations and suggested that we were unfairly accusing China of forced technology transfer and intellectual property theft. Minister Zhong even accused us of moving the goalposts in continuing to increase our purchases figures and in starting with no demands on the structural issues and then asking China to address numerous issues. Not surprisingly, we had a dramatically different understanding of what happened in the past. I explained that we had agreed upon precise text and that, after making a commitment, the Chinese side regarded the text as unsustainable for its internal political reasons and backed off of major commitments it had made. In short, it had reneged. On several occasions, we had agreed to make changes to the text to make it seem fairer and more balanced to the Chinese side. I also made clear that any effort by China to deny problems with unfair trade practices such as forced technology transfer, inadequate protection of intellectual property, and industrial subsidies was not helpful and would only slow progress in the trade talks. I took issue with any suggestion that the United States had increased its asks in the negotiations. Our positions had remained consistent, and we had sought structural changes from the outset of the negotiations. If China was not willing to make structural changes, it was not clear why we were having talks on a trade agreement, because trade agreements require structural changes.

More Chinese Stalling, More American Tariffs

To create some momentum, the vice premier proposed that we clarify the positions where we had agreement on the text and that we have discussions at the deputy level in August and early September and a meeting of the principals later in September. Although these proposals appeared constructive and generally made sense, we had another problem confronting us. We needed to see progress on President Xi's commitment in Osaka to buy more US agricultural products in order to create the conditions necessary for us to succeed. Not only had China failed to follow through on making immediate and substantial agricultural purchases following the meeting in Osaka, but it had failed to meet its commitments for such purchases throughout the negotiations, including the promises made by the vice premier to President Trump in his meetings in the Oval Office. Despite our efforts to convey the urgency of the situation to the vice premier, we received a lukewarm response. I worried that it would not be enough to satisfy the president.

After we briefed the president upon our return from Shanghai, he directed me to move forward with imposing 10 percent tariffs on the remaining Chinese imports not already subject to tariffs starting on September 1, 2019. These were the so-called List 4 tariffs and would be in addition to the 25 percent tariffs then in place on $250 billion (the original $50 billion and the $200 billion in escalation) worth of Chinese imports. A few days later, on August 6, the Treasury Department designated China as a currency manipulator based on steps it had recently taken to devalue its currency. Not long after our announcement of what products would be tariffed on List 4, we started receiving requests from US companies to delay at least part of the tariffs because of the impact they would have on those companies and American consumers during the holiday season. List 4 included more consumer goods, such as clothing, footwear, laptop computers, and video-game consoles. Considering our goal throughout this process of minimizing the pain on US parties, we decided to delay the tariffs on $160 billion of the $280 billion in remaining Chinese imports until December 15. In other words, the new tariffs would go into effect on September 1 for $120 billion in Chinese imports (List 4A) and on December 15 for the other $160 billion in Chinese imports (List 4B).

We had a conference call with Vice Premier Liu and his team on August 13, 2019, to advise him of the latest developments on the tariffs. After briefly explaining the president's decision to impose the additional tariffs, I informed the vice premier of the postponement of a major portion of the tariffs from September 1 to December 15. While somewhat encouraged by this postponement, the vice premier expressed his disappointment and surprise at the decision to impose new tariffs. Both he and Minister Zhong indicated that China would retaliate.

China announced its retaliation in the form of additional tariffs on $75 billion of US goods on August 23, 2019. Its list included some auto parts, agricultural products (pork, beef, chicken, and soybeans), chemicals, and crude oil. Once more, China had miscalculated. They had never been up against a president as tough as President Trump. He followed the negotiations. He knew the issues, and he was determined to correct the relationship. China still had not addressed the unfair trade practices identified in the Section 301 report and instead chose yet again to retaliate against the United States to protect and defend those practices. In the process, it tried to inflict more harm on the US economy. As a result, the president directed me to again increase the tariffs—this time on the Chinese goods in Lists 4A and 4B from 10 percent to 15 percent and to increase the tariffs on the $250 billion of Chinese goods already subject to tariffs (i.e., Lists 1, 2, and 3) from 25 percent to 30 percent starting on October 1. On September 1, the 15 percent tariffs on the $120 billion of Chinese goods in List 4A went into effect.

Our next steps would be highly important in deciding whether or not we would be able to reach a deal with China. We scheduled a conference call with Vice Premier Liu and his team on September 4, 2019. In that call, I proposed that there be meetings at the deputy level during the week of September 16, that there be exchanges of text before and after that meeting, and that the principals then meet in early October. While the vice premier agreed with that proposal, he raised an issue of grave importance. The date on which the tariffs on the $250 billion in Chinese goods on Lists 1, 2, and 3 were scheduled to increase from 25 percent to 30 percent was October 1, the seventieth anniversary of the founding of the People's Republic of China. He cautioned that if the United States were to proceed with the tariff increase on that date, it risked derailing the whole process again. After assuring the vice premier that we had not selected the date to send a message of any kind, I told him that Secretary Mnuchin and I would ask President Trump to postpone the date. The president agreed to delay the tariff increase until October 15.

Based on deputy level discussions in September, it was becoming increasingly clear that certain subject areas might have greater prospects for agreement than others, including forced technology transfer, intellectual property, financial services barriers and market access, agricultural barriers and market access, and purchases. Even for these areas, we still had important gaps that would need to be closed, and we would need to ensure that the enforcement provisions were as strong as possible. Areas that would be difficult to address in the near term included industrial subsidies, China's "secure and controllable" policies for information and communication technology, and other elements of the non-tariff measures chapter, as well as services beyond financial services.

As we entered October 2019, it appeared that we were building momentum. However, we had been in this situation before, only to see things break down. The two sides met again in Washington in early October 2019, with meetings at the deputy level beginning on October 7 and principal level meetings on October 10 and 11. These meetings would prove to be crucial.

Reaching a Deal

On the first day of the principal level meetings, we started with a discussion of enforcement. We revisited the fundamental issue of who decides whether there has been a violation of the agreement and what action may be taken in response to that violation. Once again, I asserted our position that it should be the aggrieved or complaining party who decides those issues. We did not want to have panels of arbitrators from other countries make those decisions. To prevent abuse, any action taken by the complaining party would have to be proportionate to the breach. I also made clear that the enforcement mechanism needed to allow for action to be taken for any individual violation, that it should apply not only to actions that postdate the agreement but also to actions that predate the agreement but continue to have effect, and that the force majeure clause had to be narrow and limited to natural disasters and similar events. As I explained, this was the chapter that everyone would read more than any other, and the enforcement mechanism had to be comprehensive in its coverage and not subject to potential loopholes.

We next moved to the intellectual property chapter, where it was clear we had made substantial progress. Vice Premier Liu realized that better protection of intellectual property was in China's interest. China was now a creator of intellectual property, not just a user. Its own creative sector needed protection to encourage innovation. China sought greater balance in the text and wanted to bilateralize the obligations. While I indicated some willingness to bilateralize provisions, it did not make sense in a number of areas because the obligations were directed to the specifics of China's system, including on the parties subject to liability for trade secret theft, the provisions for authenticating evidence in judicial proceedings, and protections against intellectual property infringement in the online environment and on e-commerce platforms. In addition, it did not make sense for us to take on obligations for things that we already did and where the problem was exclusively with China's lack of protection and enforcement of intellectual property rights. When Minister Zhong objected and tried to defend China's record, I quickly pointed out China's long and well-documented history of violating intellectual property rights, that China was by far the largest source of counterfeit goods seized by US Customs and Border Protection, and that China was consistently cited and placed on the Priority Watch List in USTR's annual *Special 301 Report* for China's failure to protect and enforce intellectual property rights.

Another issue that we discussed was China's request to carve certain items out of the intellectual property chapter. These included provisions addressing unauthorized camcording, protections for broadcasts of sporting events, streamlining China's process for reviewing and approving television shows, and cracking down on apps used with illicit streaming devices. According to China, these issues raised ideological or cultural concerns. I interpreted this to mean that China needed to control what its citizens saw and how they saw it. Once again, it was about control. I resisted this effort at the time, but I expected that we eventually would agree.

We also made significant headway on forced technology transfer. Specifically, we agreed to cover general obligations addressing several key issues in this area. Although we would not be able to address cyber intrusions or commitments targeted at China's industrial policies, I made clear that we would have to address those items at some point.

Similar progress was made in our meetings with respect to agricultural barriers and market access, financial services barriers and market access, currency, and purchases. In particular, for the first time in our discussions on agricultural barriers and market access, we made meaningful progress on commitments to establish a science-based, fact-based, and efficient process for the approval of our agricultural biotechnology products with reasonable time frames and limits on the information that would have to be turned over to Chinese officials. Moreover, we had fruitful discussions on other key agriculture issues, including the administration and allocation of China's TRQs, its massive domestic support programs and policies, and its unreasonable and unjustified restrictions on the use of certain hormones and feed additives in our beef and other meat products. All these issues severely limited the ability of our farmers and ranchers to export their products to China.

China continued to raise its own issues, some of which were new and some of which related to areas outside of our trade discussions. The vice premier also continued to insist on the removal of all tariffs as a bottom-line position. We did not engage on these issues.

Although President Trump and I previously had not wanted to do a phased agreement, it had become apparent that a comprehensive agreement covering the breadth and depth of all the issues we had been discussing with China would not be possible in the near term. We briefed the president and decided to do the agreement in phases, with the first phase covering the areas on which we had made substantial progress in our meetings and a second and possibly third phase to cover the other areas. Because we would keep the tariffs in place throughout the talks on the later parts, the United States maintained its leverage.

On October 11, 2019, the president met with the vice premier in the Oval Office and announced that we had reached an agreement in principle on a Phase One trade deal with China that would require China to make important structural changes in the areas of intellectual property, forced technology transfer, agriculture, services, and currency. The deal also would require China to significantly increase its purchases of US manufactured goods, agricultural goods, energy, and services, with China committing to increase its purchases of agricultural goods from current levels to $40 billion or $50 billion per year over the next two years. We agreed not to proceed with the increase in tariffs from 25 percent to 30 percent on the $250 billion in Chinese goods on Lists 1, 2, and 3 that was scheduled to go into effect on October 15. But we kept all the remaining tariffs in place.

Soon after the announcement, we began talking about the possible timing and venue for President Trump to sign the Phase One agreement with President Xi. The next meeting between the two leaders would take place in Santiago, Chile, at the Asia-Pacific Economic Cooperation (APEC) forum on November 16 and 17, 2019, and we decided to target that meeting for the agreement to be signed.

That allowed little time to finish the deal. We had almost daily video conferences at the deputy level. Our next conference call at the principal level was held on October 25, 2019. As was often the case, I started with the issue of enforcement because I believed it was the most important issue and we continued to be stuck on certain key elements. First, on the issue of who decides whether there is a violation of the agreement, China proposed that both parties would have to agree. As I pointed out, if both sides had to agree, there would essentially be no enforcement at all because in every case, the party accused of a breach would disagree. We had to go back to our original language that the complaining party decides whether there has been a breach. Second, China had struck our language providing that after the complaining party takes remedial action for a breach, the party that breached the agreement could not retaliate or bring a WTO case. I explained that this was the way it worked in any other trade agreement. A complaining country had to choose its venue. And third, we needed to have appropriate language to address the continuing effects of actions taken before the agreement and make them subject to dispute settlement. I tried to reassure the vice premier that we were not looking to take enforcement action for China's not opening up certain sectors ten or twenty years ago. However, if we had a theft of trade secrets a year before the agreement entered into force and the person responsible was still benefiting from it, China would have an obligation to stop it. We seemed to be gaining some traction on these issues.

On intellectual property, the vice premier again sought the removal of provisions addressing unauthorized camcording, protections for sporting event broadcasts, streamlining the television review process in China, and cracking down on apps used with illicit streaming devices. These issues were not under the vice premier's purview, and he wanted to move them to the US-China Social and Cultural Dialogue. Although I could agree to remove the provisions from the Phase One agreement, I was not willing to accept moving them into another dialogue. As with cyber intrusions, they would have to be addressed in a future phase of the trade deal.

The vice premier repeatedly raised the removal of all tariffs as a core issue for China. He indicated that without a satisfactory resolution of this issue, we would not be able to make headway on other issues or move forward with the Phase One deal. Additionally, he noted the heated debate in the United States on legislation relating to Hong Kong and expressed his concern that it could have an effect on the trade agreement and the atmosphere for the talks. I quickly responded that the Hong Kong issue was not related to our discussions and that we needed to stay in our own lane.

Unexpectedly, on October 30, 2019, Chile decided to cancel the upcoming APEC summit because of ongoing anti-government protests in Santiago. President Trump and President Xi would no longer be meeting in mid-November to sign the Phase One agreement. Given the work still required, the cancellation of the APEC summit served as a blessing. We simply needed more time to finalize the agreement and resolve issues such as the question of what we were going to do about the tariffs.

That question was the focus of another conference call with Vice Premier Liu on November 1, 2019. In that call, the vice premier started out by expressing, as he had before, that the removal of all tariffs was China's core concern and that without the tariffs' removal, we could not move forward. In response, I recounted the history of the tariffs and our negotiations because it was important to recall that the Phase One agreement would only deal with a portion of the United States' core concerns. As I explained, it was curious that China was asking us to address all of what it wanted on its core concern in return for a portion of what we wanted on our core concerns. Because we had decided to proceed in phases, any tariff removal had to be done in phases and reflect what was covered in that phase. The vice premier ultimately relented and agreed to my approach. But the next question became how we would determine the portion covered by the Phase One agreement. Clearly, this would be our next battle, and we agreed to have discussions on it at the deputy level.

Following the November 1 conference call, we saw some progress on the agreement text, and both sides made important good-faith gestures. Specifically, we agreed to proceed with regulatory action by the US Department of Agriculture to allow imports of Chinese catfish and cooked poultry, and China lifted its unwarranted ban on US poultry and poultry products, which would open a market worth more than $1 billion annually for our poultry farmers. However, much of the work on the substance of the agreement stalled while we tried to resolve the question of how much of the total deal was covered by Phase One and how much of the tariffs should therefore be affected. In several videoconferences, the Chinese articulated their position that we were addressing well over 70 percent of the total deal. It soon became clear that this position was based purely on a straight arithmetic calculation of the number of provisions we were addressing in the various chapters. In contrast, our position was that different provisions had different levels of importance and that the calculation had to be done based not only on the number of provisions completed but also on the relative importance of the provisions.

Discussions at the deputy level bogged down, and we had a conference call with Vice Premier Liu on November 15, 2019. In that call, I laid out our methodology for determining a reduction of tariffs that was approximately equal to the percentage of issues resolved in Phase One. As I explained, we attributed different levels of importance to the different chapters and then calculated a percentage based on how important the chapter was and the amount of the chapter that was covered. We next compiled that into one overall percentage representing the portion of the total deal addressed in Phase One. Based on our methodology, we determined that Phase One covered roughly 40 percent of the total deal. Our position was that the amount of the tariffs that would be collected should be reduced by approximately the same percentage.

The total amount of the tariffs that would be collected equaled $117 billion. This amount included the following: the 25 percent tariffs on $250 billion in Chinese goods on Lists 1, 2, and 3; the 15 percent tariffs on $120 billion in Chinese goods on List 4A that went into effect on September 1, 2019; the 5 percent increase in the 25 percent tariffs on the $250 billion in Chinese goods that had been scheduled to go into effect on October 15, 2019; and the 15 percent tariffs on $160 billion in Chinese goods that were scheduled to be imposed on December 15, 2019. Our proposal to reduce approximately 40 percent of the tariffs that would be imposed was to indefinitely postpone the List 4B tariffs that were going into effect on December 15, continue the postponement of the October 15 increase indefinitely, and reduce the September 1 tariffs on List 4A from 15 percent to 10 percent. In addition, we would proceed with exclusions from the tariffs worth about $6 billion that we had decided to grant based on the merits of the exclusion petition. Vice Premier Liu wanted a reduction in the List 3 tariffs from 25 percent to 15 percent, but I did not want to touch the 25 percent tariffs on Lists 1, 2, or 3. We agreed to have further discussions on the issue.

After additional deliberation and discussion, the two sides ultimately settled on a resolution close to our original proposal. We would indefinitely postpone the December 15 tariffs and the October 15 increase in tariffs, reduce the September 1 tariffs from 15 percent to 7.5 percent, and proceed with granting the $6 billion in planned exclusions. The 25 percent tariffs on $250 billion in Chinese goods on Lists 1, 2, and 3 were left completely intact. However, a number of important open issues remained in the text.

To address China's insistence on greater balance in the intellectual property chapter, we tried simply inserting language stating that the United States "affirms that existing U.S. measures" did what was provided for in a particular provision without taking on any obligation. It worked. The two sides also were able to resolve other difficult issues in the intellectual property chapter, including the ability to obtain preliminary injunctions in China to prevent the use of stolen trade secrets and the threshold for initiation of a criminal investigation for trade secret theft. On intellectual property protections for pharmaceutical products, China was willing to agree to certain periods of time for which small-molecule drugs and biologics could be on the market before generic drugs could be approved. China did not provide any period of protection for biologics and would now grant eight years of protection. However, our pharmaceutical companies did not want to agree to eight years because they feared undermining the ten years of protection for biologics then under active consideration in Congress as part of the USMCA. As a result, we decided to address the provisions on the periods of protection for small-molecule drugs and biologics in future negotiations in return for China's commitment to implement a strong patent linkage system where our pharmaceutical patent holders could obtain the early resolution of infringement disputes as well as other significant commitments on patents.

As our negotiations on the English text of the agreement wrapped up, we had a conference call with Vice Premier Liu on December 12, 2019. We decided to announce the agreement the following day and began making plans for next steps. On the morning of December 13, 2019, a few issues remained to be resolved in the purchases chapter of the agreement. After we received word that the Chinese side was about to hold a press conference announcing the agreement, we had to quickly call them and tell them to hold off. Once everything was resolved, both sides announced on December 13. We could not yet release the text publicly, and many in the press quickly jumped to the conclusion without reading the agreement that it was merely a purchases deal that did not address significant issues. They could not have been more wrong.

In fact, the Phase One agreement we reached requires significant structural reforms and other changes to China's economic and trade regime in the areas of intellectual property, technology transfer, agriculture, financial services, and currency and foreign exchange practices. In addition, China committed to make substantial additional purchases of US goods and services in the coming years to help address the imbalance in our trade relationship. Everything in the agreement is fully enforceable pursuant to a strong and effective dispute resolution mechanism. A review of some of the key provisions of the agreement shows that it contains real, significant, substantive commitments by China covering a wide range of areas and issues. Importantly, the tariffs stayed in place.

The intellectual property chapter of the agreement is comprehensive in scope and addresses numerous long-standing concerns of US companies in the areas of trade secrets, patents, pharmaceutical-related intellectual property, geographical indications, trademarks, and enforcement against pirated and counterfeit goods. Among other things, the intellectual property chapter requires China to:

- Have substantial civil penalties on companies that steal trade secrets from US companies.
- Enable trade secret owners to obtain preliminary injunctions to prevent the use of a stolen trade secret before that trade secret has lost its value.
- Ensure that US companies can obtain criminal investigations and penalties for the theft of trade secrets by Chinese companies.
- Establish a mechanism for the early resolution of pharmaceutical patent disputes to ensure that the parties' rights are determined quickly and to prevent the marketing and sale of patented pharmaceutical products in China while the dispute is pending.
- Provide patent term extensions to compensate for patent office and marketing approval delays that would otherwise reduce the effective patent term.

- Provide adequate and effective protection and enforcement of trademark rights, particularly against bad-faith trademark registrations. This, among other things, addressed the practice of some Chinese companies' filing bogus trademark registrations to undercut legitimate foreign trademarks.
- Provide effective and expeditious enforcement against pirated and counterfeit goods, including: (1) requiring the government to act against counterfeit products in the online environment and in physical markets; (2) enhancing government action against e-commerce platforms that fail to take necessary steps to address infringement; and (3) mandating similar government action against counterfeit pharmaceuticals and other counterfeit products with significant health or safety risks.
- Implement significant improvements to its judicial system to enable US companies to effectively enforce their intellectual property rights, including by providing deterrent-level civil remedies and criminal penalties for intellectual property theft, ensuring expeditious enforcement of judgments for violations of intellectual property rights, and providing a reasonable opportunity to present witnesses and cross-examine opposing witnesses in judicial proceedings.

The technology transfer chapter prohibits China from employing a range of formal and informal acts, policies, and practices to force or pressure US companies to turn over their technology and intellectual property. These obligations apply not only to the central government in China but also to provincial and local governments where problems have frequently arisen in the past. Specifically, the chapter includes commitments by China not to:

- Impose technology transfer requirements as a condition for obtaining market access, administrative approvals, licenses, or any benefits or advantages such as tax credits or subsidies.
- Require or pressure US companies to transfer technology to Chinese companies or individuals in connection with acquisitions, joint ventures, or other investment transactions.

- Require or pressure US companies to use or favor Chinese technology as a condition for granting market access, licenses, administrative approvals, or any other advantage, because these practices had led to US companies' transferring their technology to Chinese joint venture partners so that the technology could qualify as local or indigenous.
- Force or pressure US companies to accept adverse, non-market terms for the licensing of their technology.
- Support or direct Chinese companies or individuals in making investments to acquire foreign technology in support of China's industrial plans.
- Require or pressure US companies to disclose sensitive technical information, including trade secrets and other confidential business information, if the information is not necessary to show conformity with administrative or regulatory requirements.

China's commitments in the agriculture chapter of the agreement will further open China's market and lead to a dramatic expansion of US food, agriculture, and seafood product exports to China. This chapter addresses structural barriers in China to a wide variety of US products, including meat, poultry, seafood, rice, dairy, infant formula, horticultural products, animal feed and feed additives, and pet food. For example, it includes commitments for China to:

- Grant greater market access for US beef by expanding the scope of beef products allowed to be imported into China, eliminating age restrictions on cattle slaughtered for export to China, eliminating unnecessary cattle traceability requirements, and adopting maximum residue limits for certain key hormones used in American beef.
- Broaden the list of pork products eligible for importation into China.
- Authorize the importation of US rice from any USDA-approved facility.
- Approve the importation of dozens of aquatic species and streamline the timelines and procedures for registering US seafood facilities and products.

- Immediately resume imports of pet food that had previously been banned and streamline the timelines and procedures for registering US pet food facilities.
- Make a number of critical improvements in the approval process for agricultural biotechnology products, including requiring the implementation of a transparent, predictable, efficient, and science- and risk-based regulatory process for approval of agricultural biotechnology products and substantially reducing the time frame for review and approval of new products.
- Make specific, important improvements to the administration of its wheat, corn, and rice import restraints so that more US products can be imported into China.

In the financial services chapter, China made commitments to address a wide range of trade and investment barriers impeding the ability of US companies to supply financial services in the Chinese market. The chapter includes obligations for China to:

- Eliminate the foreign equity cap for companies in the securities, fund management, and futures sectors and ensure that US suppliers of these services are able to access China's market on a non-discriminatory basis.
- Eliminate the foreign equity caps for US suppliers of life-, health-, and pension-insurance services, remove all discriminatory and overly burdensome regulatory requirements in all insurance sectors, and expeditiously review and approve applications from US companies to supply insurance services.
- Make improvements to its licensing process for US suppliers of electronic payment services, such as Visa, Mastercard, and American Express, to enable them to have access to China's market.
- Expand opportunities for US financial institutions, including bank branches, to supply securities investment fund custody services in China and expeditiously review and approve applications from US financial institutions to operate in China.
- Remove barriers to US suppliers of credit rating services and approve

any pending license applications of US companies to provide these services.

The chapter on currency and exchange rate practices contains the strongest provisions of any trade agreement on these issues and is designed to ensure that China cannot manipulate its currency to compete unfairly against US companies. In particular, it contains binding and enforceable commitments barring China from engaging in competitive devaluations and targeting of exchange rates. It also significantly enhances transparency into China's currency and exchange rate practices.

In addition to the extensive and meaningful structural changes required by the agreement, China agreed in the purchases chapter to increase the purchase and import of US goods and services in 2020 and 2021 by no less than $200 billion over 2017 levels. China's commitments covered a wide range of US manufactured goods, agricultural products, energy products, and services. In fact, the agreement included specific commitments by China to significantly increase the purchase and import of twenty-three subcategories of US products and services falling under the four broad categories. And although the agreement provides specific commitments for 2020 and 2021, it expressly states that the parties project that the trajectory of increases in the amounts of manufactured goods, agricultural goods, energy products, and services purchased and imported into China from the United States will continue through 2025.

While all the structural and purchase commitments in the Phase One agreement are unprecedented, the chapter on dispute resolution represents yet another crucial departure from the past by making all the commitments fully enforceable. We have never before had an enforcement mechanism such as this with China. The agreement establishes a roughly ninety-day process for the resolution of disputes regarding breaches of the agreement. At the end of that roughly ninety-day period, if there is no resolution, the complaining party alone decides whether there has been a breach and what is a proportionate remedy for the breach. In addition, as long as the action taken by the complaining party is in good faith, the other party cannot retaliate or challenge the action at the WTO. If the party that breached the agreement considers that the action taken by the complaining party is in bad faith, its only remedy is to withdraw from the agreement. The enforcement system set forth in the agreement is the strongest possible system we could have hoped for and works exactly as we had wanted.

The final part of the agreement related to tariff reduction. The agreement on tariff reduction remained what we had decided previously. We would not move forward with the 15 percent tariffs on the $160 billion in Chinese goods on List 4B or with the 5 percent increase in the tariffs on Lists 1, 2, and 3. Additionally, we would reduce the tariffs on the $120 billion in Chinese goods on List 4A to 7.5 percent and would proceed with the $6 billion in tariff exclusions that we had already planned to grant.

Finalizing the Deal

Most observers thought that the announcement of the agreement meant we were done and all that was left was for the agreement to be signed. However, an entirely new negotiation was about to start—the negotiation over the translation of the English text into the Chinese text. At times, this negotiation would prove nearly as intense and challenging as the negotiation over the original text, and it lasted until the early morning hours of the day the agreement was to be signed. China had a history of obtaining favorable translations of agreements that introduced ambiguity into otherwise clear commitments or watered down the strength of the commitments they had made. We had anticipated for months that the translation of the agreement into Chinese would be difficult and were fully prepared for the effort that would be required. Although the State Department provided translators to assist with this process, we were fortunate in that we had numerous officials at USTR who were fluent in Chinese and understood the importance of particular forms of phrasing in the trade agreement context and for specialized and often technical issues such as intellectual property protection. We relied primarily on these USTR officials in the Office of China Affairs, the Office of Innovation and Intellectual Property, the Interagency Center on Trade Implementation, Monitoring, and Enforcement, and the Office of the

General Counsel, and their work was invaluable in ensuring that there were no gaps between the English text and the Chinese text.

Although there were extensive battles over the translations of various terms, the most difficult fight was over whether the term "ying" or "jiang" should be used as the Chinese translation for "shall" in numerous instances throughout the agreement. Our Chinese-language experts at USTR insisted that "ying" was the appropriate Chinese term to use for "shall" because it represented an obligation, whereas "jiang" represented the future tense relating to something a party merely planned to do in the future. However, the Chinese side vehemently disagreed, arguing that the use of "ying" was inappropriate and even insulting. We even decided to consult outside Chinese-language experts on this issue, including one who had worked on important agreements with China over several decades while serving with the US embassy in Beijing. They all confirmed that if we wanted the term to convey an obligation, we should continue to insist on using "ying." That is exactly what we did. After several conference calls between Ambassador Gerrish and Vice Minister Liao on this issue, the Chinese finally relented and agreed to use "ying." As we went through this "ying versus jiang" discussion internally at USTR, I asked my staff to bring me the famous cyber-intrusion agreement that President Obama had made with President Xi. I wanted to see which Chinese word that agreement had used. After some delay and checking around the government, my staff discovered that neither word had been used in Obama's agreement. That was because the agreement had never been written down. There had not even been a joint press release agreed to. This vaunted "agreement" was nothing but a US press release. I realized again why the Chinese side was so surprised by our approach. They were used to dealing with Americans who were more interested in a show than actual enforceable agreements.

Making the arrangements for the signing of the agreement also took on a life of its own. We had to decide where and when the agreement would be signed and by whom. Eventually, the two sides agreed to have the signing in Washington. We would return to Beijing if and when we launched Phase Two. Although China decided to have Vice Premier Liu sign the agreement in lieu of President Xi, President Trump wanted to sign this historic agreement for the United States. As for the timing, we were targeting January 14 or 15, 2020. However, the Chinese side immediately balked at January 14 given that the date included the number 4, which is considered unlucky in China because it sounds like the word for death. The signing would thus occur on the following day.

The signing for the Phase One agreement occurred on January 15, 2020, in the East Room of the White House in a grand ceremony matching the importance of the occasion. After remarks by President Trump, Vice President Pence, and me as well as by the Chinese side, the president and Vice Premier Liu signed the agreement in front of several distinguished guests, ranging from members of Congress to significant business leaders to Dr. Henry Kissinger. After the signing, the key members of the US and Chinese delegations had a celebratory lunch in the State Dining Room with President Trump. During the lunch, the president wasted no time in trying to get a start on China's purchases of US goods. He arranged to get West Virginia governor Jim Justice on the phone to talk to Minister Ning Jizhe, the vice chairman of China's National Development and Reform Commission, about purchases of coal from West Virginia. I think the Chinese officials had never seen anything like that, and they did not know what to expect next.

The Phase One agreement entered into force one month later, on February 14, 2020. Efforts were already underway to implement the agreement and to assess whether Phase Two would be possible. However, the world, and our relationship with China, would soon change dramatically. Within a few days, we began to hear about a virus, one that would change everything.

The Impact of the Phase One Agreement and Section 301 Tariffs

In the end, China implemented most of the structural reforms to which it had agreed in the Phase One agreement. But the trade deficit has continued to go up since the start of the COVID-19 pandemic. And as is well known, China did not meet its purchasing commitments. Critics of the Trump administration gleefully pounce on this as evidence that the Section 301 tariffs were a failure. I disagree.

The trading relationship between the United States and China was profoundly changed by the Section 301 tariffs in ways that have made the United States less dependent on its most dangerous global adversary. Although overall trade with China rose during the pandemic and has remained at record highs, the mix of trade has changed considerably. Imports of the most sensitive, technology-heavy products on Section 301 tariff lists 1, 2, and 3, which are subject to a 25 percent tariff, are down considerably—60–70 percent in some cases.[1] China's overall share of US imports is also down.[2] And, more importantly, US companies have woken up to the dangers of having all of one's eggs in the China basket. Surveys show that US companies' optimism about the business outlook in China is at an all-time low.[3] In board rooms across America, talk of reshoring and friend-shoring have replaced knee-jerk offshoring. The investments companies are making today in more diversified, resilient supply chains will help to eliminate our dangerous dependency on China, create US jobs, and, over time, create new manufacturing capacity outside of China, which will put downward pressure on the trade deficit. China's own actions, including its disastrous "zero COVID" policy, as well as tighter US export controls have contributed to this trend. But the Section 301 tariffs started the process and remain an essential part of the strategy of reducing US dependence on China.

Remarkably, all of this has been achieved without any meaningful inflationary effect and while US exports to China have increased to record levels. For a brief period of time in 2022, globalists such as China's favorite former secretary of the treasury Lawrence Summers hoped to take advantage of inflationary pressure caused by the Biden administration's reckless spending to convince the administration to ditch the tariffs, but even free traders such as Janet Yellen were forced to admit that a complete abandonment of the tariffs would have only a negligible effect on consumer prices. US exports to China have increased considerably in recent years. After dipping to $106 billion when China's retaliatory tariffs were in full effect, US exports to China reached $151 billion in 2021 and surpassed that record in 2022 with $154 billion.[4] US agriculture has been a major beneficiary of this trend. Indeed, I always viewed China's admittedly ambitious purchasing commitments as a face-saving way for China to effectively reduce its retaliatory tariffs—and thereby reduce hardship for US exporters—while allowing the United States to maintain significant tariffs on Chinese imports that, over time, would help to reorient supply chains and reduce US dependence on China.

It is also important to note that the Phase One deal was a product of the pre-COVID-19 era. If, after the signing of the deal in January 2020, China had not lied about the plague that came from its lab, it had ceased rather than escalated its harassment of Taiwan, it had not continued a genocidal crackdown in Xinjiang, it had not eliminated the "one country, two systems" regime in Hong Kong, it had not doubled down on state capitalism, and it had not anointed Xi president for life, it's possible the Phase One agreement could have formed the foundation for a more balanced, sustainable, and less contentious relationship between the United States and China. Indeed, during the deal's implementation phase before the change of administrations, USTR staff worked quite productively with their Chinese counterparts to ensure that the new laws, regulations, and other measures China had agreed to adopt were consistent with the agreement and that China was taking actions necessary to implement the agreed-upon structural changes.

The change in administrations also had an effect on the deal. Although I have been pleasantly surprised by President Biden's China policy on the whole, the fact that the Democrats had trashed the deal for political purposes during the 2020 campaign meant they were not in a strong position to enforce it once Biden took office. Personally, I suspect that the Chinese held back on meeting their purchasing commitments in the hope that the Biden administration would agree to further tariff reductions, thereby allowing China to get paid twice with the same concessions. Fortunately, the Biden administration so far hasn't taken the bait. In any event, the structural commitments made by China in the Phase One agreement on intellectual property, technology transfer, agriculture, financial services, and currency remain and can be fully enforced by any administration that chooses to do so.

Beyond the specifics of the Phase One agreement, the Trump administration also deserves credit for changing forever the way Americans think and talk about China. After the 2016 election, it became increasingly untenable to openly take the pro-China line, as so many US business and political elites had done for decades. Talk of turning China into a "responsible stakeholder" is no longer credible.

The establishment's grudging concession that it had gotten China wrong was, however, typically paired with criticism that tariffs were the wrong solution. It bears noting that many of these dissenting voices were among the loudest in favor of PNTR back in the day and have been proven wrong on all things China ever since. But setting that aside, none of these critics ever identified a plausible alternative path for confronting China. Bilateral dialogue with the Chinese had been tried by the Clinton, Bush, and Obama administrations for two decades to no avail. Many asserted that rather than act unilaterally, the Trump administration instead should have linked arms with allies and confronted China together. I agree that if the European Union and Japan had imposed their own tariffs on China simultaneously with ours, such joint action would have been helpful. But this was a kumbaya fantasy. Especially in 2018 with Angela Merkel, Beijing's chief promoter in the European Union, firmly ensconced in the Chancery, there was no chance whatsoever that Europe would have agreed to meaningful joint actions to confront China. The same was true of Japan, given its own economic entanglement with China and generally non-confrontational approach to foreign affairs. Waiting to confront China until we had the allies on board would have meant waiting forever. Indeed, despite considerable effort over the last two years, the Biden administration's attempts to enlist allies' support on China has yielded virtually no tangible results.

Some WTO devotees argue that we should have filed something called a "non-violation" case at the WTO, a rarely used form of action in which the United States would have argued that it did not receive the benefits it expected when China was allowed to join the WTO. Such cases, which turn on wholly subjective criteria, are hard to bring under the best of circumstances. And nothing in our long, troubled history in WTO litigation (as recounted in chapter 4) suggests this effort would have ended well for the United States. Moreover, confining ourselves to the WTO process would have meant waiting years while the litigation played out before taking any meaningful action to confront China. All the while, China would have continued to steal our technology, the trade deficit would have continued to grow out of control, and the United States would have become ever more dependent on its chief adversary. The WTO had nearly twenty years to discipline China; it failed. President Trump was right to use every tool available to him to address this problem, even if it meant offending bureaucrats in Geneva and their supplicants in the United States.

Having endured more than four years of mostly uninformed armchair quarterbacking on this subject, I remain unimpressed with arguments from the "Trump identified the problem but not the solution" crowd. By my surmise, opposition breaks down for the most part into four camps: those who really don't believe China is a threat but are too afraid to admit that openly; those who have never seriously examined the problem or potential solutions; those who, for political reasons, can't bring themselves to give President Trump due credit; and those who value the WTO and the international trading system more than the US national interest. To use less charitable shorthand: anyone who concedes that China is a problem but insists that there is some magical, disruption-free solution to the problem China presents is quite likely a liar, a fool, a knave, an irredeemable globalist, or some combination thereof.

..

In the end, the Section 301 action began the process of strategic decoupling of our economy from China's. It was the right policy at the right time, and it has achieved its intended objectives. Today, US high-tech imports from China are on the decline, and businesses across the country are questioning the long-term wisdom of producing their products in China. That alone makes the Section 301 action a historic success.

Chapter 11

The Way Forward

Anyone who had doubts about the direction that China was going or how it would be governed in the future had those doubts resolved in October 2022. China has a way of telling its citizens and the world what it is up to. The report to the 20th National Congress of the Communist Party was a time for the telling. Xi Jinping was, to no one's surprise, given another five-year term as president. Surely that means he is there for life. The real revelation was what was contained in his work report to the National Congress and his selection of the most senior people in his circle. First, the report makes it clear that China will increasingly be a Marxist-Leninist country. The foolishness of all those who thought trade would change China was exposed. Second, the report states that increasingly there will be "a decisive role being played by the state."[1] The CCP will assert even more control over business. The era of Deng Xiaoping's using capitalism to advance socialism is over. Finally, and perhaps most disturbing, the report adopts a distinctly militaristic tone. Here it is important to note that there is often a major difference between what China says in Chinese to its people and the way it officially translates those words into English for Western audiences. Routinely, the harsh, combative language is watered down. It thus is important to look to an unofficial and candid translation to determine what is being conveyed. One such source is Kevin Rudd. He is a Mandarin speaker, a China expert, and a former prime minister of Australia. According to his translation, the report deemphasized words such as "peace" and "development" and added phrases such as "preparing for the storm" and "the spirit of struggle."

The announcement of the all-important seven standing committee members and the rest of the politburo was also revealing. Usually, in Chinese governments, there is some effort to have representatives at the senior level from various points of view. There is none of that in this group. All were strong and longtime supporters of Xi. There will be no dissension or alternative voices—no balancing. They as a group are also less expert in foreign policy, and notably absent are any economic reformers. On the diplomatic side, Xi promoted all hard-liners. The reenforcing of "wolf warrior" diplomacy is evident.

I have tried to make the case here that the Chinese government is a lethal adversary. This conclusion then requires an economic and international trade policy of what I call "strategic decoupling." We need to continue our economic relationship to the extent that it is beneficial to America and its workers, farmers, and businesses and stop it to the extent that it is harmful to us. We must achieve balance and fairness, eliminate important dependencies, reduce investment in each direction, and stop technology interdependence. Over the course of four years, the Trump administration began this policy. History will view this as the start of something of global historical importance. In its 2017 National Security Strategy, the Trump administration for the first time labeled China a "strategic competitor" and decried its military, diplomatic, and economic aggression. In this context, the president said, "For the first time, American strategy recognizes that economic security is national security." So what specifically should this strategic decoupling look like?

The first objective of our economic policy must be a rebalancing. We have transferred $6 trillion of our wealth to China in goods trade deficits. Of course, part of rebalancing will involve doing the things that make our economy strong. We need lower taxes, the elimination of unnecessary regulation, and sensible subsidies and industrial policy. An important step in this direction was the enactment of the bipartisan CHIPS and Science Act of 2022. This law, which among other things provides subsidies and tax credits for the manufacture of chips and for research, will help America regain its leadership as the essential semiconductor sector. These steps alone, however, will not suffice to bring balanced trade. Even with all the right domestic economic policies, we will still face an overvalued currency and unfair Chinese practices. We need a strong trade policy to force balance.

An important step to force balance is for the United States to repeal the granting of Most Favored Nation (MFN) status, which is also called "Normal Trade Relations," to China. This would correct the mistake that was made in 2000. Essentially, China would be required to pay the higher "Column Two" duties on imports. Under the law, that could be waived, and Congress could review Chinese behavior annually to see if a waiver should continue.

The withdrawal of MFN status would not bring about balance by itself. Another mechanism would be needed. I propose putting additional tariffs on all imports from China and escalating and de-escalating those tariffs to achieve balanced trade. Tariffs are a simple flexible tool. They are simple to impose, the structure is well established, they are relatively easy to police, and we generally know what the results will be. Further, tariffs will help with our fiscal deficit by enabling the US government to collect billions of dollars in additional revenue. Of course, China would object, as would US businesses operating there as well as other businesses that are reliant on their imports, but the overall benefit to our workers and country should outweigh their concerns. The Chinese presumably would find a way to retaliate, but to the extent that they do, that would also contribute to the strategic decoupling. Additionally, our relationship is so unbalanced that China's options are limited. We showed that with our Section 301 process, in 2018, where China's retaliation was bounded because it imports so little from us. I propose doing this clearly and phasing it in over time to minimize disruptions and allow for businesses to change their current practices. These tariffs would eventually return much of our manufacturing, including computer and cell phone production, to America and in some case to our allies.

As with all the policy changes recommended here, we need to be clear about our goals and tell the Chinese side and our businesses what our objective is and what we intend to do. We are not trying to hold back fair Chinese development, but rather to promote our own. It is important that there be no misunderstandings about our objectives.

Second, we need to make it easier for US manufacturers and service providers to bring unfair trade cases against competition from China. Currently, there are a number of unnecessary hurdles in the way of initiating anti-dumping, countervailing duty, and similar cases. Other barriers prevent cases that are ultimately brought from providing effective relief. Many of these problems are technical and can be corrected. The point is that in addition to the balancing tariffs, our companies must be able to take specific actions to counteract unfair advantage by China's producers in our market and to take those actions quickly and efficiently.

Third, we must reduce strategic dependencies. Right now, we import critical medicines, protective equipment, essential technology, many materials needed for production, and more from China. It makes no sense to have this reliance on an adversary. In times of crisis, we are at their disposal. We need a policy of domestic production of all this material, and where that is not possible, we need to find trusted alternative sources for our strategic needs.

Fourth, we need a policy of reducing investment between the two countries. The US capital markets are an essential source of new investment in China, and Chinese investment here is only made if it helps China's strategic objectives of gaining technology, data, or other advantages. Further, China only allows inbound investment that it determines is in its interest. We must do the same. The Committee on Foreign Investment in the United States (CFIUS) is an interagency committee authorized to review certain transactions involving foreign investment in the United States in order to determine the effect of the investments on national security. The secretary of treasury is the chairman of the committee, and the bureaucracy that administers it is at the Department of Treasury. CFIUS is designed to deal with all foreign investment national security threats, not just those from China. In fact, the essential power of the committee to reject deals comes from the Exon-Florio Amendment that was enacted in 1988 because of the fear of Japanese investment. In recent years, the committee's most important work has been related to dealing with China, directly and indirectly. Here again, CFIUS under Secretary Mnuchin's leadership was much more actively used to reject deals and to mitigate threatening effects where deals were permitted to go forward. Any China policy going forward must intensify and enlarge the review. There must be much more rejection of proposed investments and less approval for investments to go forward through so-called mitigation agreements designed to reduce the damage to the United States. Further, the CFIUS statute should be expanded to allow for the denial of Chinese investment in the United States for reasons other than a traditional national security threat. The likelihood of the investment causing long-term economic harm should be enough to block.

Traditionally, the United States has had no real regulation of outward-bound investment. In general, allowing free investment by Americans in foreign economies is in our national interest, but in the case of China, we need such authority. High-tech US firms working on sensitive technology such as artificial intelligence frequently invest in China not just for their production needs but also for their research and development requirements.[2] This, in turn, supports the development of dual-use advanced technologies in China, something that feeds directly into China's military strength. In its 2021 annual report to Congress, the US-China Economic and Security Review Commission recommended that the United States pass legislation setting up an interagency review screening program similar to CFIUS for outbound investment to China. Senators Bob Casey, Democrat of Pennsylvania, and John Cornyn, Republican of Texas, introduced legislation to this effect. They also offered an amendment to the National Critical Capabilities Defense Act that would establish a process at USTR to review all outward investment to China (as well as Russia). The House's Competes Act contained a much stronger provision that would not only require government review of outbound investment to adversaries but also authorize the executive to stop it, much like CFIUS does for inward investment. We need to use existing laws, such as CFIUS and the new outward-investment restriction in the CHIPS legislation, and to pass new authority to give the government the power to stop US entities from investing in China except where it is in our interest. These new powers must include prohibiting any Chinese investment in critical infrastructure or technology serving that infrastructure. Businesses will never do this on their own.

Fifth, we need a policy of strong export controls. The Trump administration started a new policy toward China, and we now need to follow that blueprint and to strengthen it using the knowledge we gained. Controlling the export of our technology is essential. The export control regime in the United States is complicated. Several statutes—including the Arms Export Control Act, the International Emergency Economic Powers Act, and the Export Control Reform Act—convey jurisdiction over the export of defense articles and services, dual-use materials, nuclear materials, and biological weapons. The principal agencies involved are the Department of Commerce, which controls sensitive dual-use goods, software, and technology, and the Department of State, which controls defense articles and services. In addition, the Department of Defense plays a key role in evaluating license requests, and the Department of Treasury administers US sanctions in this area. Commerce secretary Wilbur Ross took a personal interest in expanding his department's role. Under Ross, the US government both expanded the scope of items covered and raised the standard for licenses to be granted. He added many more companies, particularly Chinese companies, to the Entity List of foreign persons or businesses that are subject to greater scrutiny, more stringent restrictions on export, and additional export license requirements. As an April 2022 Carnegie Endowment study concluded, "The Trump administration then went much further, elevating techno-nationalist thought within US strategy and rhetoric and greatly expanding the number and scope of measures targeting Chinese tech threats."[3] Our strategy going forward must continue this policy and, where necessary, create new tools. There should be limited entanglement of our economies in the sensitive technologies sectors.

Sixth, we need to stop technology interdependence. America must stop any cooperation in the technology areas of security and dual-use technologies (those that have both civilian and military applications) and, where necessary, stop the importation of these products. Products and services that are controlled because of their technology value should be made in America or imported from an ally with no Chinese input. Important dual-use products with security implications, such as drones, should be in this category—made in America or imported from allies with no Chinese content in material, software, or technology. There must be a very carefully crafted break between our tech sectors and those of the Chinese. We also need to carefully review any US company's involvement with Chinese companies in any of the Made in China 2025 sectors. These sectors are all critical to economic security, and China has told us that its plan is to become superior and independent in these areas. These industries include aerospace, biotechnology, information technology, smart manufacturing, advanced rail, electric vehicles, new materials, robotics, artificial intelligence, and others.

Seventh, we must insist on reciprocity of market access across the board. The combination of tariffs and other measures discussed above may lead to balanced trade in goods and protect technology, but there are still large issues remaining regarding market access in services. There are many Chinese services companies, such as Alibaba, TikTok, and WeChat, that have access to our market, while companies such as Amazon and Google do not have access to theirs, and companies such as Microsoft and IBM have only limited access. We should deny a Chinese company the right to operate in the United States if our companies don't have an equivalent right there. It is extremely unlikely that China will ever grant this right so US companies will again dominate in their own market. Independently, the United States must ban social media platforms such as TikTok from operating here. This app is used by the Chinese Communist Party to gather data on American citizens. It is also used to spread Chinese propaganda and otherwise disrupt our national discourse.

Eighth, the United States should enact laws to combat China's efforts to influence American politics and society. The Chinese government and its affiliates regularly attempt to influence debates within US civil society and shape how Americans view China and US-China relations. Chinese state-owned newspapers take out full-page advertisements in local US newspapers.[4] Parts of the Chinese government partner with American universities to establish "Confucius Institutes" that teach American college students Chinese language and culture through Chinese government–funded teachers who avoid "sensitive" topics such as the Tiananmen Square massacre.[5] Chinese donors contribute to major American nonprofits that shape American political discourse, including the Clinton Foundation.[6] There have also been credible reports that Chinese sources gave millions to the University of Pennsylvania around the same time that the Biden Center for Diplomacy and Global Engagement was established, and the same may be true of the University of Delaware and its Biden Institute.[7] Additionally, the nominally "private" Chinese social media app TikTok manages algorithms that determine what its overwhelmingly young, impressionable American audience sees. Americans should not allow our primary adversary to pervasively influence our society. The United States must act to put a stop to this. We should ban Chinese state actors from purchasing advertisements in American newspapers, prohibit Chinese social media companies from operating in the US market, and strengthen US foreign donation laws to require all nonprofits to publicly disclose the foreign money they receive. We also should expand our Foreign Agent Registration Act to require all individuals involved in political lobbying who have coordinated with Chinese entities to register themselves as foreign agents and report these activities to the US government.

In short, strategic decoupling means balancing trade, limiting imports to needed items, limiting exports that contain sensitive technology, controlling inward Chinese investment and our outward investment in China, and developing a smart technology regime that completely decouples in security technology and only engages in other technology when it is in our interest and never in sensitive sectors.

The strategic decoupling that I propose here is really no different from that followed by the Chinese right now. This is what Kevin Rudd calls "decoupling with Chinese characteristics." Essentially, the Chinese are moving away from interdependence and toward a relationship where they supply to us as they want and develop and produce on their own in important sectors. The first sign of this strategy was China's indigenous innovation policy, which goes back to at least 2006 when the State Council issued "The Guiding Principles of Program for Mid-to-Long Term Scientific and Technological Development." This plan was a combination of regulations, strategies, and practices designed to create independent innovation so that China could advance without outside dependencies. Continuing this policy, China's Made in China 2025 program was published in 2015. In recent years under President Xi, the explicit need for decoupling has become clearer. Another way to think about the strategic decoupling is that it is merely enforcing reciprocity with China—that is, reciprocity of trade, reciprocity of investment, and reciprocity of technology.

..

The Trump administration, for the first time in our history, took on the China challenge. As discussed in previous chapters, we used Section 301 to raise tariffs on Chinese imports. Ultimately, we negotiated a Phase One agreement that kept the tariffs, obtained structural changes to correct China's unfair and discriminatory practices, required massive new purchases, and was enforceable. While the Chinese failed to meet the purchases elements of the agreement, they did implement important structural changes. The Trump administration also used CFIUS to prevent harmful inward investment more than had any of its predecessors and exercised its power over export controls more effectively. The process of strategic decoupling has already begun.

Those who predict that America will lose this great competition should consider that Japan engaged in some of the same industrial policy practices used by China. Although we should never forget the fundamental difference that Japan was an ally and a friend, Japan engaged in forced technology transfer from US companies (but not theft), maintained a closed domestic market, manipulated its currency, and utilized cheap credit and massive debt to grow impressively in the 1970s and 1980s. Its GDP was 73 percent of the size of ours by 1995. Predictions were that Japan could surpass us. However, nearly forty years later, after Japan's debt bubble burst, inefficient policies caught up with the Japanese, and the Reagan administration adopted policies to help our industry, Japan's economy is now 25 percent of ours. China's GDP is currently 73 percent of ours. With a sensible policy of strategic decoupling combined with pro-growth tax cuts, regulatory reform, and industrial policy, America can and will prevail.

Part Three

MANAGING GLOBALIZATION— NORTH AMERICA

Chapter 12

From NAFTA to USMCA

The Great Issues

In November 1993, CNN talk show host Larry King hosted a televised debate between Vice President Al Gore and former presidential candidate Ross Perot. The subject was the North American Free Trade Agreement, which had been negotiated by the George H. W. Bush administration but by that time was being pushed by the Clinton administration. During the 1992 presidential campaign, the Clinton-Gore ticket criticized NAFTA and vowed to renegotiate it. When the Clinton administration took power, however, it negotiated what at best could be described as "fig leaf" agreements on labor and environment, pronounced the deal "fixed," and proceeded to advocate strongly for its congressional passage.

Gore's showdown with Perot came on the eve of the congressional debate. Pundits at the time said that Gore had bested Perot and ridiculed the pugnacious Texan for his prediction that NAFTA would create a "giant sucking sound" as US jobs moved south across the border. Gore may have won the debate, but history vindicated Perot.

NAFTA benefited certain businesses and communities in the United States. The agricultural sector, which gained access to Mexico's large market for grain and pork products, is often cited as the prime example—though to this day the United States maintains a *deficit* with Mexico in agricultural goods, and cheap (sometimes subsidized) imports of fruits and vegetables from Mexico have devastated farmers in the southeastern United States.

The chief victims of NAFTA were US manufacturing workers. The United States lost at least 700,000 manufacturing jobs to Mexico as a result of NAFTA, and, perhaps more importantly, workers lost considerable leverage in contract negotiations with employers, who used the threat of relocation to Mexico as a cudgel to force workers to accept lower wages and fewer benefits.[1] When factories did move, in some instances American workers had to suffer the indignity of having to train their company's new Mexican employees to take their jobs.[2]

At the same time, NAFTA's effects on Mexico were not uniformly positive. Imports of US grain products devastated Mexico's inefficient, but highly labor-intensive, subsistence agricultural sector. Some of those workers found factory jobs. But others turned to the informal economy—and in some instances to the drug trade. Hopes that NAFTA would cause Mexico to import US political values in addition to goods also turned out to be misplaced. Although Mexico's judiciary system gained some measure of independence (at least for a time), widespread corruption and violence continue and, indeed, have escalated in recent years.

And while NAFTA arguably helped stem the tide of illegal immigration from Mexico, the persistent weakness of Mexican institutions means that Mexico has done very little to prevent a new wave of migrants from Central America, who use Mexico-based trafficking networks to make their way to the United States illegally.

The situation was made far worse by the fact that this experiment in North American economic integration overlapped with China's entry into the World Trade Organization. This meant that American—and Mexican—workers had to compete not only with each other but with hundreds of millions of Chinese workers, backed up by massive state subsidies. Proponents of NAFTA such as Al Gore predicted that, in time, NAFTA would cause wage rates in the United States and Mexico to converge, which would not only level the playing field for American workers but also create a thriving Mexican middle class that would become a major customer for US goods and services. NAFTA certainly brought new wealth to Mexico. But much of it was concentrated in the hands of elites. And to the extent that ordinary Mexicans benefited, they used higher wages primarily to purchase goods made in China and elsewhere in Southeast Asia, not in the United States. Indeed, as much as I believed at the time that NAFTA was a mistake, even I would concede that the story might have turned out differently if NAFTA and PNTR had not overlapped. And if Congress had defeated NAFTA but nonetheless acquiesced in China's accession to the WTO, the likely outcome would have been not more auto jobs in the United States but more in China.

For his part, Donald Trump had been a vocal critic of NAFTA from the very beginning, well before his foray into the political arena. He routinely referred to it as the "worst agreement ever negotiated." (With all respect to my former boss, I'd give that distinction to China's WTO accession protocol, recounted in chapter 7.) And he pledged to renegotiate or terminate the agreement if elected. After the inauguration, there were some in the administration who wanted to simply tear up the agreement—before my own confirmation, a story circulated that Peter Navarro and Steve Bannon had gone so far as to draft a notice of termination.

Although a critic of NAFTA, I was not in the termination camp. Regardless of whether Congress should have passed NAFTA in 1993, by 2017 there were substantial reliance interests, investments, and supply chains caught up in the agreement. Upending thirty years of economic integration in North America would have sent shock waves through the economy. It would have hurt Trump voters in Texas and throughout the farm belt. And it would have caused Republican senators to be in open revolt against the White House. In short, a precipitous withdrawal would have been an economic and political catastrophe for the new administration. Yet President Trump was willing to take that step if it was the only way to keep his campaign promise. It thus became the job of myself and my team to figure out how to overhaul NAFTA in a way that would satisfy President Trump, Trump voters, and Congress and yet still be acceptable to Canada and Mexico—a difficult puzzle to say the least.

I'll tell this story first by explaining what we were trying to achieve and then recounting the key milestones in the negotiations that led to NAFTA's ultimate termination and replacement with the United States–Mexico–Canada Agreement (USMCA).

Setting the Agenda

We started by identifying the problems with NAFTA, which fell broadly into three categories—autos, labor, and a grab bag of trade irritants and structural flaws in the agreement—and then set about testing and identifying solutions.

The auto sector—the fulcrum of North American trade. Trade in autos accounts for 20 percent of total North American trade in goods and is the key source of the trade imbalance that resulted from NAFTA.[3] Although the United States has run large trade deficits with Mexico for most of the last twenty-five years, if auto trade is taken out of the equation, the relationship is much more balanced.

NAFTA's impact on the auto industry in the United States—and on US autoworkers—was profound. The post-NAFTA evolution of the industry came in two phases. It started with the "Big Three" American auto companies' moving assembly of economy cars and low-end sedans to Mexico. That was painful for workers in Michigan and other places who lost their jobs as a result. But the companies kept their manufacturing of trucks and higher-end models in the United States, and their Mexican factories sourced high-value-added parts such as engines and transmissions from US factories. While cold consolation to American auto workers who lost their jobs, there's an argument that the US auto companies needed a low-cost manufacturing platform such as Mexico in order to remain competitive during this period with Asian and European car companies who had their own low-cost assembly venues in Southeast Asia and Eastern Europe.

The second phase of automotive drift was much more troubling, however. The Mexican government deployed an aggressive industrial policy—driven by rock-bottom wages and pliant company-controlled labor unions—in order to attract even more investment. General Motors started assembling trucks in Mexico. Manufacturing activity moved beyond assembly to the production of engines and transmissions. And perhaps most disturbingly, car companies from outside North America realized that they could use Mexico as a backdoor to the US market.

Ordinarily, the benefits of trade agreements are supposed to accrue to the nations that are parties to the agreement. But as time went on, that increasingly wasn't the case with NAFTA. The chief culprit were the so-called rules of origin for the automotive sector.

Rules of origin are features of every trade agreement. They require that a certain percentage of the content of goods originate in the territory of countries that are parties to the agreement. While NAFTA had rules of origin that, in theory, required that a car have 65 percent North American content in order to qualify for duty-free treatment, these rules became more and more permissive over time because of a concept called "deemed originating." Essentially, if a part wasn't on a list of auto components that was created in the early 1990s, that part was "deemed" to have originated in North America—regardless of whether it was produced in Germany, Korea, Japan, or China. At first this wasn't a major problem. But as cars evolved over twenty-five years, they came to be composed of more and more components—such as electronics, onboard navigation systems, and, now, increasingly, high-capacity batteries—that simply did not exist at the time the NAFTA parts list was formulated. By the 2010s, that meant a car could qualify for duty-free treatment under NAFTA even if over half of its content originated outside the region.

In order to facilitate free riding, Mexico went on a free trade agreement negotiating spree, doing deals with Japan, the European Union, and numerous other countries after 1994. These deals enabled Asian and European auto companies to ship the automotive equivalent of IKEA assembly kits to Mexico, assemble cars there, and ship them north to the United States duty-free. Mexico was becoming a way station that allowed Europe, Japan, Korea, and, increasingly, China to have duty-free access to the US market without offering the United States reciprocal access to their own markets.

The result was disastrous for US autoworkers. Nine of the last eleven auto plants that had been built in North America as of 2017 were built in Mexico. Nearly all the cars manufactured there were sold in the United States. Employment in the US automotive sector declined by 200,000 jobs from 1997 to 2014, with particularly large declines in the parts sub-sector.[4] And once more, the prospect of further outsourcing to Mexico and other low-wage jurisdictions eroded workers' bargaining power in those jobs that stayed in the United States.

As bad as these trends were, they stood to get even worse in the coming years. As new energy and autonomous vehicles come online, laden with more and more parts and components that were not on the early 1990s parts list, it would have been possible—had the Trump administration not acted—for cars to qualify for duty-free treatment under NAFTA even if 70 or 80 percent of the content originated in China. It's hard to believe the United States would have maintained any meaningful auto manufacturing capabilities in that scenario.

We started with what should have been a non-controversial position: the benefits of NAFTA's successor agreement should go to the countries that are parties to that agreement, and not to others. In other words, no free riding. We proposed raising the regional content requirement from 65 percent to 85 percent. We ultimately settled on 75 percent, but we also made sure that the 75 percent would be a real 75 percent by eliminating "deemed originating." We also added a separate requirement that 70 percent of steel and aluminum purchases had to be sourced in North America.

But we didn't stop there. In order to stop the race to the bottom in wages, we included a new requirement that 40 percent of a car and 45 percent of a truck must be made by workers who make at least sixteen dollars per hour—the prevailing wage for parts manufacturers in the United States. This was a revolutionary provision. It is the first time that a trade agreement contained a wage requirement—the first time the dignity of work, rather than efficiency, was the motivating principle behind a trade compliance rule.

The reaction to what we did was mixed at best. Free traders howled that the new rules would raise costs for consumers. Republican Senator Pat Toomey of Pennsylvania, a high priest in the cult of free trade, lamented that we were trying to destroy Mexico's "comparative advantage" in low wages. (One wonders whether the citizens of Altoona and Johnstown shared their now former senator's profound enthusiasm for cheap Mexican labor.) In fact, however, Mexico's advantages in the auto sector had virtually nothing to do with Adam Smith's invisible

hand. Mexico became an attractive automotive manufacturing platform not because Mexican workers are unusually skilled, productive,
or thrifty. Instead, Mexican industrial policy, free riding, weak rules of
origin, and corrupt labor unions conspired to create a massive market
distortion—and a massively unfair trade advantage for Mexico. Yes,
Americans had cheaper cars. But we lost untold numbers of jobs and
billions of dollars in investment in a critical industry. In any event, the
Trump administration saw this as a problem to be fixed, rather than an
achievement to celebrate. Rebalancing the auto trade in North America thus became one of the most important parts of our agenda in the
USMCA negotiations.

The reaction from labor unions representing autoworkers was surprisingly tepid. At one point, I flew to Detroit to meet with about 400
autoworkers at a United Automobile Workers meeting hall. The union's
president, Gary Jones, introduced me at the meeting. I was a Republican
Trump official in the heart of Democratic union country. I explained
what we were trying to do and was met with a mostly polite but highly
skeptical response from the rank and file. Their response was partly attributable to the fact that unions had been burned time and again by
trade agreements. The UAW itself had major buyer's remorse from having endorsed the Korea FTA during the Obama administration. I'm
sorry to say, however, that it was also partly attributable to the fact that
union leadership had never invested the time and effort needed to understand the rules changes. They were largely disengaged—and perhaps
distracted by a pending Justice Department investigation that ultimately
led to the imprisonment of the same UAW president. There was also the
fact that we insisted on a policy that would support *American* auto jobs,
regardless of whether they were union jobs in Michigan or non-union
jobs in Alabama. Many in the union seemed to dislike the non-union
auto companies as much as the imports.

Perhaps most interesting, however, was the reaction from the auto
companies themselves. Their first, reflexive reaction was to oppose tighter
rules of origin, and their lobbyists—supported by ideological free trade
think tanks—acted as if even marginal tightening would be apocalyptic.
At a certain point, however, we essentially kicked the lobbyists out of the

room and started dealing directly with the CEOs and senior management at the companies.

What we found was a surprising amount of understanding, pragmatism, and flexibility from the C-suites. The give-and-take continued. But as we explained our objectives and built trust, we were able to make real progress with the companies. As it turned out, most were willing to source more from North America and in particular the United States, and most completely disavowed the free trade puritans' predictions of higher consumer prices and harm to the companies. The main thing they wanted was more time so that the new sourcing plans would overlap with the launch of new model cycles, a demand we viewed as quite reasonable. Of course, their first bids on transition times would have been more than generous—I recall the word "decades" being mentioned. But in the end, we agreed on an aggressive but reasonable timeline under which the new rules would be mostly phased in over three years and fully phased in at the end of five.

But it wasn't just weak rules of origin that threatened US autoworkers but also rock-bottom wages. As noted, NAFTA proponents had claimed that, over time, NAFTA would cause wages between the United States and Mexico to converge. That never happened—in fact, wages in Mexico today are *lower* in real terms than they were in 1994. Some of this had to do with increased competition from China and other low-wage countries. But corruption in the Mexican labor system played a major role as well. Unlike in the United States and Western Europe, Mexico historically has not had independent, representative labor unions. Mexico's most powerful unions have been part of an unholy alliance with the government and business. To maintain their power and largess, these unions did not allow free and fair elections. All labor disputes were handled by employer-dominated conciliation and arbitration boards.

Nor did these unions allow workers to vote on collective bargaining agreements. In fact, it was not uncommon for unions to negotiate contracts with the owner of a large manufacturing facility *before* any workers were hired. And these contracts of adhesion—known as "protection contracts"—had no ending point. They went on and on. The workers had no vote and no say in the contract's terms and options permanently. So while the union bosses looked out for themselves by ensuring the employers would deduct hefty dues from workers' paychecks, the workers were stuck with low wages that did not keep up with inflation. The severe devaluation of the Mexican peso in the mid-1990s made the problem even worse.

The Obama administration had taken steps to improve the labor situation in Mexico with its Trans-Pacific Partnership trade deal. But the key disciplines the administration negotiated were vague and would have been difficult to enforce. Mexico had passed a labor law getting rid of the conciliation and arbitration boards. But there was no requirement for secret ballot elections or other foundational aspects of the right to organize. In short, TPP left protection contracts intact, which was one of the many reasons why organized labor was (rightfully) hostile to TPP—and, as it turned out, one of the reasons why onetime TPP-champion Hillary Clinton lost blue-collar voters in the 2016 election.

While I felt it absolutely critical that we get rid of protection contracts and require that Mexico adopt basic union democracy, we had to be sensitive to Mexico's sovereignty interests as well. Labor provisions in trade agreements are essential to ensuring a level playing field for workers and eliminating unfair regulatory arbitrage. And given the size and attractiveness of the US market—and in the case of Mexico, its huge trade imbalance with the United States—it was reasonable for the United States to make these demands. Still, it was difficult even for the United States to dictate to Mexico in chapter and verse what its domestic laws must contain.

Our first suggestion was for the Mexicans to simply pass a new labor law requiring secret ballot votes on its own. Mexico would then acknowledge that this procedure was fundamental to the right to freely organize and take on a high-level obligation to guarantee this right to its workers in the agreement. But as the term of Mexico's then president Enrique Peña Nieto drew to a close, there was little appetite for that on the Mexican side. This gave us the opportunity to insist that we specify the contours of the needed reforms in the text of the agreement itself.

The result was the so-called Labor Annex, containing the most sweeping and detailed labor provisions ever included in a trade agreement. The

Annex set forth in exquisite detail everything that Mexico needed to do in order to reform its labor system: hold secret ballot votes to recognize a union, throw out a union, elect union leadership, and approve collective bargaining agreements. Although facially reciprocal, a footnote in the agreement clarified that it applies to the United States only in situations in which an employer is openly defying a court order enforcing decisions of the National Labor Relations Board.

This was an area where organized labor played it straight. When we showed the draft text to cleared labor advisers, they were stunned at what we were on the verge of achieving. There was some inevitable back-and-forth—both with the Mexicans and with the US labor unions. One critical issue was how fast the Mexicans would be required to implement the reforms—which would require, among other things, holding new votes on thousands of preexisting collective bargaining agreements. The US labor unions initially demanded two years; Mexico wanted ten to fifteen. We settled on four—a reasonable but not unduly long period. And the agreement provided that any new collective bargaining agreements or union elections had to be consistent with the Labor Annex on day one.

Autos and labor were the major issues in the negotiations, as well as the areas that were most critical to rebalancing the North American trading relationship in ways that will benefit working people. But there were also other important issues.

Oh . . . Canada. Although most of the structural problems with NAFTA involved Mexico, a number of trade irritants had piled up between the United States and its northern neighbor since NAFTA's entry into force. Although outwardly supportive of free trade and internationalist in orientation, Canada is in reality a quite parochial—and at times quite protectionist—country. For years Canada has operated a dairy supply chain management program that would make a Soviet commissar blush. To placate quite well-heeled dairy farmers in the politically important province of Quebec, Canada not only excludes US importers but also facilitates the dumping of artificially low-priced dairy products in third-party markets, which further harms US dairy farmers around the world. Ensuring greater market access for US dairy farmers in Canada became our top priority, especially after President Trump heard firsthand the complaints of dairy farmers in Wisconsin and Michigan about this issue.

There were other northerly trade irritants as well. Many stemmed from the so-called cultural exemption that was a relic of the original United States–Canada trade agreement negotiated by the Reagan administration. Canada has a number of laws and programs designed to promote and protect its bilingual character and placate separatists in Quebec, some of whom claimed that the original agreements, and later NAFTA, could be a threat to those policies. The Mulroney administration was successful in convincing the Reagan administration and later the Bush administration to agree to what was intended to be a narrow carve-out from its trade obligations to the United States for policies designed to protect French Canadian culture. Over time, however, this provision was used by Canada not to deal with genuine cultural sensitivities but to give unfair advantages to Canadian companies and shake down US investors in Canada. Among other things, Canada invoked the cultural exception to exclude the Home Shopping Network, shortchange US recording artists on royalties, and even refuse to allow the NFL to fully monetize broadcasting rights for the Super Bowl. Ensuring fair treatment for US entertainment companies operating in Canada seemed like a reasonable demand to make in exchange for giving Canadians duty-free access to the largest economy in the world. And while we ultimately were unsuccessful in killing the cultural exception altogether, we worked out one-off solutions for particular investors and gave the United States the right to unilaterally impose punitive measures against Canada any time it invokes the exception.

Investor-state dispute settlement (ISDS) has been a feature of US trade and investment agreements for decades. These agreements provide that when a party to the agreement violates investor protections, the investor can file a claim against the government and have that claim litigated before a panel of private arbitrators, many of whom are members of the international arbitration bar who hear cases as arbitrator one day and then shift to an advocate role in the next. The idea behind ISDS is that it gives investors an outlet to resolve claims against foreign governments and therefore alleviates pressure on the United States and other governments to engage in gunboat diplomacy of the kind often practiced in the first half of the twentieth century. But in the era of offshoring that took hold later in the century, ISDS became something else—free political risk insurance for companies who wished to offshore American jobs to countries with weak rule of law. In this sense ISDS effectively nullifies what should be a core US comparative advantage— our independent, fair, and relatively efficient legal system. In making a decision on where to invest, one should give preference to a country with a dependable legal system. In deciding whether, for example, to put a factory in the United States or Mexico, this factor should strongly favor staying at home. Yet ISDS put a thumb on the scale in favor of Mexico.

For these reasons, ISDS became a lightning rod for labor unions, progressives, and some nationalist-leaning Republicans who feared that it erodes US sovereignty. And ISDS was another issue that led to the demise of TPP. Having studied the TPP autopsy report very carefully— and finding the whole notion of effective subsidization of offshoring offensive—I was all in on killing ISDS in NAFTA. I always thought ISDS encouraged moving plants abroad and subsidized those who want to invest overseas instead of here in America. But I can't exaggerate how controversial eliminating this provision was.

The Chamber of Commerce and the other usual suspects once more cried bloody murder. And they sicced their supporters in Congress on me. I remember one particularly testy long conversation with former Speaker of the House Paul Ryan, who insisted breathlessly that the agreement would attract zero Republican votes unless ISDS protections were maintained. When House members were unable to persuade me to relent, many went to the president directly. At one point, the president called me into the Oval Office to discuss the matter and said, "Bob, nobody agrees with you on this!" But I explained that ISDS was really subsidizing businesses to invest out of America, and the president backed me up.

I suspected that at the end of the day, the hysterical reaction of Washington lobbyists and ill-informed members of Congress was out of proportion to the actual economic consequences of eliminating ISDS. And when we talked to individual companies, what we learned was that the only investors in North America who really depended on ISDS were American oil and gas companies who had invested in Mexico after the Peña Nieto administration opened up the country's energy markets to foreign investors. But for the availability of ISDS under NAFTA, these companies very well may not have invested in Mexico, or they would have sought other guarantees from the Mexican government before doing so. And these companies likely would have included arbitration provisions in their deals. Given the political sensitivity of energy issues in Mexico and, as we shall see, the prospect that the next Mexican government would roll back the Peña Nieto energy reforms, the risk of expropriation to these companies was non-trivial. Even to an ardent ISDS critic such as myself, it seemed unfair to pull the rug out from under American companies under these circumstances. Moreover, these companies were just going where the oil was—they weren't outsourcing US jobs.

Once more, in order to solve the problem, we started by kicking the professional lobbyists and the trade associations out of the room and engaged directly with senior management for the major oil companies, whom we found to be far more constructive and less ideologically motivated. We also maintained a back channel to progressive anti-ISDS activists to ensure that the concessions we made to the oil and gas industry would not undermine support among congressional Democrats for the eventual deal. In the end, we crafted a narrow solution that would allow for continued ISDS protections for energy companies and a handful of similarly situated investors in Mexico. But we eliminated ISDS with Canada and, more importantly, ended the thirty-year-long US policy of effective government subsidies for offshoring. Once we arrived at this solution, the oil and gas companies stopped funding the pro-ISDS lobbying campaign, and it collapsed overnight. The ideological warriors in favor of ISDS were left with their ideology but no ammunition. It turned out that being wrong was not enough for them. They wanted to be paid too.

Another important area of focus was the digital economy. NAFTA was negotiated in the early 1990s, before even the dial-up internet era. Cloud computing, streaming platforms, digital payments, and massive cross-border data flows were all in the future and not in the minds of the original negotiators. USTR had done good work during the TPP negotiations in developing and advancing digital trade disciplines. But in order to get such a diverse group of countries to sign on to those disciplines, the United States ultimately had to agree to sweeping exceptions to the core digital trade obligations. To give just one example, the requirement that TPP countries not require companies to localize data centers as a condition of doing business in that country did not apply if the policy measure in question was intended to advance a "legitimate public policy objective." That's code for "I'll agree not to require data localization, unless I don't want to." In fairness, this incident fits a well-worn pattern in trade negotiations. The United States often gets other countries to sign up for what seem to be meaningful top-line obligations but then agrees to exceptions that effectively swallow the rule. This makes for upbeat press releases and good news stories if lazy reporters don't dig into the details but does little to advance American interests.

We wanted a meaningful digital trade chapter that eliminated, or greatly narrowed, the exceptions. We also wanted to take on tech transfer of the kind that has long plagued American businesses operating in China. Although not a significant problem in North America at present, including strong provisions that prevent forced disclosure of proprietary source code and other tech-related intellectual property would set a strong precedent that the United States could use in future digital trade negotiations.

The renegotiation of NAFTA also offered an opportunity for the United States and its closest trading partners to make a statement about China. Again, this is an area where we built on the foundation that had been laid in TPP. TPP contained disciplines on SOEs and a side letter on currency manipulation. But as with digital trade, the need to corral a diverse and unwieldy group of countries—which includes Vietnam, a non-market economy with a history of currency manipulation—meant that the rules were watered down. We insisted on tighter provisions on subsidies and, for the first time, an anti-currency-manipulation provision that was in the text of the agreement and subject to dispute settlement.

But we also went a step further by proposing language that would make it more difficult for our trading partners to enter into new trade agreements with non-market economies such as China. The idea of a Canada-China free trade agreement seems fanciful now in the aftermath of China having held hostage two Canadian citizens—Michael Spavor and Michael Kovrig—for a period of nearly three years in order to pressure Canada to release a Huawei executive detained in Vancouver while she awaited possible extradition to face US criminal charges. But early in the Trump administration, Canada's prime minister, Justin Trudeau, cozied up to Beijing and openly flirted with the notion of an FTA with China. This would have completely changed the relationship between the United States and Canada, by both squeezing out US market share in Canada and allowing China to piggyback off Canada's duty-free access to the United States. The same would be true of Mexico. Should either country ever decide to enter into such an agreement with America's chief global adversary, that should, at the very least, lead to a fundamental rethinking of the North American trade relationship.

What we ultimately settled on was short of an absolute prohibition on any of the USMCA countries doing an FTA with China. But we made that result more difficult to achieve by requiring that if one of the three parties wishes to engage in FTA negotiations with China, it must first notify the other USMCA countries and be transparent about its negotiating objectives. The provision also allows the other two countries then to effectively kick the country negotiating with China out of USMCA—at a minimum that's a strong disincentive for Canada or Mexico to play footsie with China in ways that would undermine US interests.

Perhaps none of our proposals for the new agreement attracted as much attention—or ire—as the sunset. The idea was that the new agreement—like nearly every commercial contract and many international treaties—would have a fixed term. If at the end of the term, the parties decided to re-up, the agreement would continue. If not, it would terminate.

This was a radical proposal in the international trade world. Every trade agreement the United States had entered into up to this point—from the GATT to the WTO agreements to our bilateral and plurilateral FTAs—had been intended to endure forever. And that's how many—including large corporations—wanted it. An indefinite term, so the argument goes, allows for stability and predictability.

That may be good for investors. But it's not necessarily good for the United States—or even for the overall health of trading relationships. If the default is that an agreement lasts forever, there's no decision point at which policy makers must reevaluate whether the agreement is working and make tough decisions. Moreover, it's typically the case that trade relationships evolve in unpredictable ways, and the distribution of benefits over time rarely matches the parties' pre-agreement expectations. Without a fixed term to the agreement, there is no natural point at which the parties can come together to discuss ways to update, rebalance, or otherwise improve the agreement—and no forcing mechanism that would cause policy makers to devote the attention and political capital necessary to address such issues.

Our solution to this problem was the sunset. The original idea was that the new agreement would have a fixed term of four years, at which point it would expire. This admittedly was an aggressive opening bid. But it allowed us to communicate to Mexico and Canada—and to the US business community—that we wanted a paradigm-changing agreement that would not only address current trade irritants but prevent the United States from ever again finding itself saddled with an unbalanced, outdated agreement and with no leverage to change it other than the costly and disruptive threat of outright withdrawal. As the proposal evolved, the term lengthened to sixteen years, and the decision about whether to extend the agreement was brought forward to year six. That means that every six years, the political leadership in each of the USMCA countries must make a decision of consequence—whether to extend the agreement for another sixteen years. And if they decide not to extend, a ten-year clock starts ticking, during which time the parties can work out any disagreements that led one or more parties to decide not to extend. That's a generous amount of time that will prevent market disruptions but still force politicians to make difficult decisions and resist the temptation to defer maintenance on the agreement indefinitely. If the United States had insisted on a sunset provision in prior trade agreements, including NAFTA and China's WTO-accession protocol, both the United States and the global trading system would be much stronger today.

Chapter 13

USMCA

Mexico and Canada

NAFTA had been a failure for America. Renegotiating to a better deal was therefore high on my list of priorities. Deciding what kind of agreement we wanted was only the first step; actually negotiating it was quite another. And we didn't have just one party to negotiate with but multiple—Mexico and Canada, of course, but also the US Congress, the private sector, organized labor, and other interested constituencies. All this would play out with the ongoing daily dramas of the Trump administration in the background—tax reform, the failed effort to repeal the Affordable Care Act, a contentious immigration policy, Charlottesville, the Mueller investigation, the United States–China trade war, and, ultimately, the first impeachment trial. The consequences of failure would have been devastating for the administration, the Republican Party, and the country. It was a fascinating challenge—but also a harrowing ordeal.

The first formal round of negotiations over what would become USMCA started in August 2017. In the public session launching the talks, I was joined by my counterparts from Mexico and Canada, Ildefonso Guajardo Villarreal, the Mexican secretary of the economy, and Chrystia Freeland, then Canada's minister of international trade. Guajardo is a veteran trade negotiator, impeccable dresser, and man of the world. Freeland—now the deputy prime minister and finance minister and quite likely a future prime minister of Canada—is a plucky Rhodes scholar and former journalist who once found her way onto a KGB watch list when reporting in the former Soviet Union. Much would later be written about the personal dynamics between the three of us, which, contrary to press accounts and the expectations of some, were always professional and at times quite friendly. But our first formal meeting didn't augur well for the future of free trade in North America.

We began the first formal session of the negotiations on August 16 in a large ballroom of a major Washington hotel. Each of the ministers laid out their positions in an opening statement and then some 1,000 total government officials (about 330 per country) broke into subject groups to talk. Guajardo and Freeland each gave upbeat remarks, focusing on the strength of the relationship between the three countries, extolling the virtues of NAFTA, and suggesting with little subtlety that there wasn't much that needed to be changed. I struck a different—and intentionally dour—tone. I said that NAFTA was an extremely flawed agreement that had led to the loss of good-paying US jobs. I said, "For countless Americans this agreement had failed."

To address this problem, the Trump administration was not looking simply for a few new chapters and tweaks here and there. We would insist on a fundamental overhaul of NAFTA and a rebalancing of the North American trade relationship in favor of US workers. Up to that point, there had been speculation that the Trump administration was simply after window dressing that would allow it to declare victory, host a nice signing ceremony complete with a "Mission Accomplished" banner, and move on to other issues. I told the audience: "I want to be clear that [President Trump] is not interested in a mere tweaking of a few provisions and a couple of update chapters. We feel that NAFTA has fundamentally failed many, many Americans and needs major improvement." When my remarks concluded, everyone was disabused of any notion that these talks would be easy. They were going to be tough, and the results were going to help US workers, farmers, and businesses.

One of the difficulties in any trade negotiation is that, typically, there is no deadline for completion. That makes it hard for the parties to know when it is the right time to reveal their true bottom line. Uncertainty about the timeline for the negotiation also accommodates the natural instinct, particularly among politicians, to defer hard choices and confrontations with domestic stakeholders. The trick is to find—or construct—a deadline to sharpen minds and break logjams. The political calendar can be one such disciplining force. Initially our strategy was to tie the renegotiation timeline to the 2018 midterm elections in the United States. To have the agreement passed by the 115th Congress, in which the president's party controlled both the House and the Senate, the negotiations had to be wrapped up at the latest by late spring 2018. Delay past that point meant that we faced the possibility of not only Democratic control of the House of Representatives at the very least but also a new administration in Mexico, given that Mexico's presidential election was scheduled for July 1, 2018, and President Peña Nieto's term was set to expire on December 1.

In the formal negotiating rounds that followed the August launch, however, it quickly became clear that Canada and Mexico did not share our sense of urgency—nor did they fully comprehend the limits of President Trump's own patience and his resolve to withdraw from NAFTA should the negotiations reach an impasse. In fact, it seemed that Canada—and to a lesser degree Mexico—thought that the best strategy was not to negotiate with me or anyone in the administration at all but instead to lobby members of Congress in the hope that they would pressure us to drop demands Canada and Mexico didn't like, take the threat of withdrawal off the table, and perhaps abandon the whole exercise entirely.

Indeed, when representatives from both countries went to Capitol Hill, they received a great deal of encouragement from NAFTA enthusiasts, which included leading establishment Republicans on the Senate Finance and House Ways and Means Committees. What they failed to grasp, however, is that the Republican base had shifted considerably on trade issues, and many of these members were out of step with the new Republican Party. The working-class voters President Trump brought into the party in 2016 had very different views about trade in general and NAFTA in particular than Pat Toomey and the Cato Institute did. President Trump, needless to say, was all in with the former, not the latter.

While the personal relationship between Guajardo, Freeland, and myself was quite cordial, I can't recall a single meaningful concession that Canada or Mexico made during the first nine months of the negotiations. They clearly were coordinating all their moves. I guess they simply hoped to wear us down or hoped that Congress would roll us in the end.

As the June deadline approached, the outlook for the future of NAFTA was grim. At that point a series of events started to unfold that, though tense, in the end were critical to changing the dynamics and paving the way for a successful conclusion to the negotiations.

One was President Trump's decision to impose tariffs on steel and aluminum imports using Section 232 of our trade laws, which allows the president to impose duties in the interests of national security. This was—and remains—the single most controversial trade decision President Trump made. Initially, Canada and Mexico were exempted. But in order for the steel and aluminum program to function effectively, it was necessary for Canada and Mexico to agree to some limitation on steel and aluminum shipments to the United States—otherwise, Canada and Mexico could ramp up steel production for export to the United States, flood the US market to take advantage of higher prices, and import cheap Chinese or Russian steel for their own domestic consumption. But when Canada and Mexico made clear that they were not amenable to any kind of restraint, President Trump responded by taking the unprecedented step of imposing tariffs on steel and aluminum imports from both countries. Although the tariffs were allowed under the national security exception to both our NAFTA and WTO obligations, the fact that President Trump was willing to impose tariffs on two of America's closest trading partners—one of whom, Canada, is also one of our closest allies—sent an unmistakable signal that business as usual was over. The Trump administration was willing to ruffle diplomatic feathers to advance its trade agenda.

Second, the president followed up the imposition of steel and aluminum tariffs under Section 232 with the announcement of a new 232 investigation into auto imports. If a 232 on steel and aluminum exports was inconvenient and irksome for Canada and Mexico, an auto 232 would be nothing short of catastrophic, even more so than a withdrawal from NAFTA. The US's MFN tariffs on passenger vehicles, which would apply in the absence of NAFTA, are only 2.5 percent. But under Section 232, the president has authority to raise those tariffs as high as he determines necessary to address the national security risk at issue. A Section 232 action on autos would have been extreme—and could have been struck down by the courts. But the damage to the auto sectors in Canada and Mexico, which exist to service the US market, would have been crippling if not lethal. It was a much bigger threat than imposing tariffs on steel and aluminum. In fairness, given the high degree of integration between the three countries in this sector, the US auto industry would have suffered substantially as well. But especially after the steel and aluminum 232, the auto 232 seemed not like an errant Trumpian bluff but rather like a genuine threat to the Canadian and Mexican economies.

Finally, the frustration that was building in all three countries due to these policy moves erupted during a tense G7 meeting held in Charlevoix, Quebec, in early June. In the weeks leading up to the summit, Prime Minister Trudeau had hoped to convince President Trump to close out the negotiations in Charlevoix with a so-called cars and cows deal—the idea being that Canada would agree to give some additional dairy access, Mexico would relent some on autos, and the United States would drop all its other demands. It was the sort of anemic offer you make when you're taking a positive answer for granted. Canada and Mexico still hadn't realized those days were over.

In order to build momentum for this cars-and-cows stampede, the Canadian government leaked to the press in advance of the summit that the negotiations were in their final stage and that an agreement could be announced soon. Annoyed by this ploy to go around me and sell the president on what would have been a bad deal for the United States, I responded by issuing a rather harsh press release that stated the truth: the parties were "nowhere close" to a deal, and "gaping differences" on a host of issues remained.

The summit that began on June 8 was less a G7 meeting than G6 versus 1, with the United States being the odd man out. Pitched disputes over the 232 tariffs and the US withdrawals from the Iran deal and the Paris climate accord cast a pall over the entire event. And the already uneasy relationship between President Trump and Prime Minister Trudeau reached its lowest point in its immediate aftermath. Irked by Trudeau's criticism of US tariff actions to the press at the conclusion of the summit, President Trump launched a signature tweet storm against his Canadian counterpart from Air Force One while he was en route to his unprecedented first meeting with Kim Jong-un. This was followed by an intemperate quip made by White House staffer Peter Navarro to a reporter that there was a "special place in hell" for Trudeau. US-Canadian relations arguably were at their lowest ebb since the failed American invasion of Upper Canada during the War of 1812.

At that point, there was no hope of having the agreement done in time for ratification by the 115th Congress, and polls and historic trends predicted strong Democratic gains in the fall elections. We effectively were at an impasse on every major issue, and the United States and Canada weren't speaking. We decided to suspend the negotiations until after the Mexican elections on July 1. NAFTA was hanging on by a thread.

What happened next was the arrival on the scene of a new and ultimately hugely important new character in this drama, Andrés Manuel López Obrador—better known by his initials, AMLO. A leftist, populist rabble-rouser, AMLO had twice failed in his quest for the Mexican presidency. After his first unsuccessful run in 2006, he claimed widespread voter fraud, proclaimed himself the "legitimate president" of Mexico, and even staged a mock inauguration in the Zócalo, Mexico City's main square. By the third time around, there was no controversy: AMLO had won a stunning victory in the July 1 presidential elections, beating his nearest rival by over thirty percentage points.

This was another hold-your-breath moment in the negotiations. Like Trump, AMLO was a die-hard nationalist and no fan of NAFTA. He was also a vociferous critic of Peña Nieto and his PRI party, which he believed had come to represent the worst of the "neoliberal" consensus that had dominated Mexican politics for the last several decades. He had also seen firsthand the economic devastation that NAFTA had wrought on Mexico's subsistence farmers. Would AMLO want to scrap all our work and start the negotiations from the beginning?

The answer came shortly after the election when AMLO appointed an old friend of mine, Ambassador Jesús Seade, as his personal representative in the negotiations. Seade, a well-connected academic who had spent years in Hong Kong, had been Mexico's representative to the GATT in Geneva when I was deputy USTR in the 1980s. When Seade arrived in Washington, we had lunch at one of my favorite Washington haunts, the Metropolitan Club. I wasn't sure what to expect, but was quickly encouraged when he announced that while the incoming administration wanted visibility into the negotiations and wanted some areas of sensitivity addressed, AMLO was prepared to support the new agreement. But there was one caveat: AMLO would support an agreement hammered out by the Peña Nieto administration, but if negotiations were not completed before Peña Nieto's term was up at the end of November, AMLO would insist on starting over. I felt a mix of relief that we still had a chance—but also deep anxiety knowing that we had only a few weeks to complete the negotiations. It also meant that we would be negotiating with the Mexicans alone. Tripartite talks could never move that quickly.

When we assembled for our first negotiating session after the election, there wasn't enough room on the Mexican side of the negotiating table in the main conference room of the Winder Building to fit the entire Mexican delegation. As a gesture of goodwill, I invited Seade to sit next to me on the US side of the table. I said the representatives of workers should sit together. He did so with a smile, and the atmosphere in the room lightened for the first time in several months.

While AMLO's desire for a swift conclusion to the negotiations was a positive development, there was no time to spare. The agreement had to be done and executed prior to AMLO's swearing in on December 1, 2018. But given the deadlines required under the Trade Promotion Authority statute in the United States—which requires that the president give ninety days' notice to Congress prior to signing a trade agreement—that meant we had less than two months to wrap up the negotiations, or until August 28, 2019, ninety days before the expiry of Peña Nieto's term.

At that point we launched into a furious six weeks of negotiations, with sleeves rolled up and minds focused. We quickly reached convergence on the auto rules of origin, an issue that had been stuck for months. Mexico agreed to both a 75 percent "regional value content" requirement and a 40 percent (for cars) and 45 percent (for trucks) "labor value content" requirement (sixteen dollars per hour for workers). Mexico also agreed to extend its period of exclusivity for protection of clinical data for biologic drugs and to protect internet platforms from liability for user-posted content—the trade equivalent of the controversial Section 230 law in the United States, a key demand of Senator Wyden.

In the end, the most contentious issue was labor. The negotiation of the labor chapter was atypical to say the least. My direct counterpart, Minister Guajardo, was under great pressure by powerful Mexican private sector lobbyists, who were dead set against going further than the labor reforms the Obama administration had forced Mexico to accept during the TPP negotiations. While he showed flexibility on other issues, Guajardo wouldn't budge on labor and didn't seem to appreciate the political significance of this issue in the United States.

It became clear that we needed another interlocutor. We found him in Mexico's foreign minister, Luis Videgaray. Videgaray, a brilliant, MIT-educated economist and sophisticated political operator, understood better than anyone else on the Mexican or Canadian side the existential threat both countries faced if President Trump made good on his threat to terminate the agreement. And unlike others, Videgaray didn't think Trump was bluffing. Videgaray was not about to let the negotiations flounder because Mexico was insisting on clinging to an outdated and wholly indefensible labor system.

At that point, the labor negotiations took place mostly in secret and wholly outside the regular channels between my deputy, C. J. Mahoney, and Minister Videgaray's chief of staff, Narciso Campos Cuevas. When other members of the Mexican delegation found out about the draft text that was circulating, they started referring to it derisively as "Narciso's Annex." Like everything else in this ordeal, the negotiations over the labor chapter presented a difficult puzzle. We needed to push the Mexicans, but there were limits to how far we could push them. Especially given that we were anticipating the need for the agreement to pass a Democratic House after the November midterm elections in the United States, we had to have the full buy-in of the US labor unions upfront. Moreover, we had to make sure that the obligations were at least facially reciprocal so that it wouldn't look like the United States was dictating labor policy to Mexico—yet we couldn't go so far that we would threaten right-to-work laws and other labor practices on the US side, which would have chased Republicans away.

In the end, the Mexicans agreed to phase out protection contracts and commit to free, fair, secret ballot elections to recognize a union, elect union leadership, and approve collective bargaining agreements. Guajardo and Mexican business made a last stand to try to water down the reforms that culminated in Guajardo's threatening to resign his position in a phone call with President Peña Nieto. But Peña Nieto stood firm, and Narciso's Annex became one of the most important parts of the agreement.

But as always seemed to be the case in these fraught negotiations, there was one more curveball. This time, it was energy. The energy sector has been a major source of political sensitivity in Mexico and in its relationship with the United States for decades. In 1938, President Lázaro Cárdenas declared all hydrocarbon resources in Mexico the property of "the Nation," kicked out all the foreign oil companies, and consolidated the nation's petroleum reserves in a state-owned entity, Pemex. While Mexico had agreed to a number of market reforms as the price for entering NAFTA in the early 1990s, it refused to take on any obligations in the energy sector. The one exception was something called the "ratchet clause," which said that while Mexico had no obligations to open up its energy sector to US and Canadian investors, if it voluntarily chose to do so in the future, it could not later reverse course—that is, market opening would be a one-way ratchet. One of Peña Nieto's signature achievements (an initiative designed by Luis Videgaray) was an opening up of the Mexican energy sector that unleashed a flood of new foreign investment, including from leading US companies, and triggered the ratchet clause.

We had negotiated a chapter on energy regulation that was mostly symbolic. But the new agreement made clear that the obligations in the agreement's investment chapter would now apply to the Mexican energy sector. And when AMLO learned about this, his light-touch approach to the negotiations changed. At first, AMLO insisted that *all* energy obligations be scrapped entirely. This would mean that American investors who had put capital in Mexico in reliance on the ratchet clause would be at risk of expropriation. In addition to hurting American companies and their employees, this would have ensured that the entire Texas, Oklahoma, New Mexico, and Louisiana delegations in Congress would have voted in bloc against the new agreement.

So, what to do? I made clear to Seade that there was no path forward in the negotiations if AMLO was really insisting on stripping out all energy commitments from the agreement. That said, if what he needed was a reaffirmation that Mexico's energy resources ultimately belonged "to the Nation" and wanted to ditch the largely symbolic energy chapter, without diluting Mexico's substantive obligations to US energy investors in the investment chapter, we could talk. The result of the ensuing discussions was one of the most unusual chapters in USMCA or any other US trade agreement, chapter 8, "Recognition of the United Mexican States' Direct, Inalienable, and Imprescriptible Ownership of Hydrocarbons." This brief, two-paragraph chapter is laden with nationalist rhetoric about Mexican sovereignty, but the whole thing is caveated with a recognition that everything in the chapter is "without prejudice to [the United States' and Canada's] rights and remedies available under the Agreement"—that is, Mexico still has to accord US and Canadian energy companies all the rights they are owed under USMCA's investment chapter and other relevant provisions.

The precise wording of this chapter was hammered out over a tense twenty-four-hour period with AMLO himself making line edits. At one point, my team and I retreated to the Metropolitan Club—which, as the reader will surmise, became an important redoubt for USTR during the Lighthizer years. C. J., in flagrant violation of club rules, had been checking his email throughout the evening, waiting for a reaction from Mexico City on the latest draft. When he received it, he and I scurried downstairs to the club's correspondence lounge and called Seade, who announced that AMLO had signed off on the compromise language. USMCA had survived yet another—but far from the last—near-death experience.

As the clock ticked down to our September 1 deadline, the American and Mexican teams camped out in the Winder Building, sometimes overnight. After some final jockeying, we reached an agreement late in the evening of August 27, with only a few hours to spare.

Of course, at this stage, an important part of the cast was absent—

the entire Canadian delegation. This is because the deep freeze in US-Canadian trade relations continued well beyond the June showdown in Charlevoix. What had been agreed to on August 27 was a new "United States Mexico Agreement"—Canada hadn't yet agreed to join. When we announced the deal on August 28, we said that Canada was welcome to join if it wanted but made clear that we were prepared to move forward bilaterally if it did not.

Again the clock was ticking. Under TPA we had only thirty days from the delivery of the notice that an agreement was to be signed to provide Congress with the full text of that agreement—or until midnight on September 30. If Canada was going to get on board, it needed to act fast. Yet nearly three weeks went by with no meaningful contact between USTR and its Canadian counterparts. It wasn't until the UN General Assembly in New York on September 18 that the lines of communication were reopened. Prime Minister Trudeau's chief of staff, Katie Telford, reached out to Jared Kushner and proposed, for the first time, a meaningful offer on the dairy issue. The Canadians returned to Washington shortly thereafter to join us and the Mexicans. Another furious round of negotiations commenced. There were ups and downs. I remember a late Sunday evening when the Canadians made us wait for several hours for a response to one of several "close out" offers only to arrive at the Winder Building at 11:00 p.m. to tell us they needed more time.

One of the problems we had—which isn't unusual in trade negotiations—is that while the politicians in Canada clearly had decided it was time to make a deal, the professional bureaucrats were continuing to fight for every inch of turf—or, in this case, every liter of milk. Every time we thought we were close to finalizing the text, the Canadian negotiators would come back with some cleverly worded caveat designed to undermine the spirit of what had been agreed to at the political level. I give great credit to my good friend Jared Kushner and Gerry Butts, Trudeau's political consigliere, for keeping the negotiations on track in this stressful final stretch.

With the midnight September 30 deadline only hours away, I called Jared, Gerry, Katie, and Minister Freeland into my office and made one final plea: "No more sneaky shit." They agreed and instructed their professional staff to put pencils down.

At precisely 11:59 p.m. on the evening of September 30, 2018, the text of what was now the US-Mexico-Canada Agreement was posted on the USTR website. In announcing the final agreement on October 1, the president said: "I want to congratulate the US Trade Representative Bob Lighthizer who has worked—nobody understands how hard he has worked. No matter when you called him, he was in the office or he was in someone else's office doing the same thing. Bob Lighthizer is great; I've heard it for years. I said, 'If I ever do this, I want to get Lighthizer to represent us' because he felt the way I did."[1] Through all the headwinds, President Trump always backed me up.

The heads of state met two months later on the sidelines of the G20 summit in Buenos Aires to sign the deal. But by this point there was another key player with the power to sink the agreement: Speaker Designate Nancy D'Alesandro Pelosi.

Chapter 14

Round Two of USMCA

On to Congress

Whatever one thinks of her politics, the Speaker—and that's always how I referred to her—is a formidable woman and a historic figure in American politics. The daughter of a former mayor of Baltimore, she raised five children before entering politics and ultimately attaining the Speaker's gavel, not once but twice. That feat put her in a select club of only five other Americans including Henry Clay and Sam Rayburn. While her views—indeed her entire worldview—were quite different from President Trump's, one area where they were quite simpatico was trade. Speaker Pelosi was one of the holdouts during the 1993 debate over NAFTA and was ultimately convinced by the Clinton administration to vote in favor based on its promise that the labor side agreement would be meaningful. When it became clear that the side agreement was largely a joke, the Speaker felt betrayed and deeply regretted her vote. The Speaker had also been a China hawk well before that was mainstream. She was a vociferous opponent of PNTR and predicted, accurately, that the Chinese would never abide by the letter or the spirit of its WTO commitments.

Thus, while the atmosphere in Washington was quite divisive when Democrats reclaimed control of the House in January 2019—and would only deteriorate as the year went on—we started the negotiations with the Speaker from a point of common ground. It also helped that I genuinely liked the Speaker—and, I believe, she liked me. Both of us were the products of the Catholic school system of the 1950s and 1960s. We'd both attended college in the District of Columbia around the same time. And both of us loved politics and showed respect for each other.

We wanted a big bipartisan vote on USMCA, so gaining the House Democrats' support was key. While the bill would proceed under a statutory process called Trade Promotion Authority (TPA), little in TPA actually helped. In exchange for imposing a variety of congressional consultation requirements, time limits, and paperwork, TPA was supposed to make passage simpler. The idea was that a so-designated trade bill could come before the House with a specific limited timeline for votes and then, if passed, would proceed to the Senate, where a similar timeline would apply. Importantly, the bill could not be filibustered in the Senate. In theory, once a negotiation and its implementing bill was finished, a trade deal would get its vote in fairly short order.

As with most things in Washington, the reality was much different. The process requirements of TPA merely acted to slow down the negotiations and made getting a deal more difficult. Not allowing a filibuster in the Senate was usually beneficial, but our USMCA bill passed by enough votes so that even that didn't really matter. The House timetable that began the legislative march was meaningless because the Speaker had the ability to stop the clock whenever she wanted. With that power, the calendar and all those time constraints were irrelevant. The success of our USMCA approval process hinged solely on the Speaker and her House Democratic Caucus.

During my years negotiating USMCA and getting it passed through Congress, I constantly met with members, and I appeared before just about every major congressional caucus. I met with the New Dems, the Progressives, the Blue Dog Coalition, and, on our side, the Freedom Caucus, the Republican Study Committee, and the Main Street Caucus. I also met with the Problem Solvers, a group in between. Because of the nature of TPA, however, the most important constituency was the House Democratic Caucus. On two occasions I met with the entire House Democratic Caucus—all 235 Democrat members were invited. The Speaker presided over the meetings. Both times, I was generously introduced by Chairman Neal and one time appeared jointly with AFL-CIO president Rich Trumka. These meetings consisted of about an hour of examination from every House Democrat who had a question. I found the encounters to be intense but always respectful and professional. I'm sure I was the only Trump cabinet official who appeared at any of these weekly meetings. This exposure made a big difference in garnering support.

One of our first meetings with the Democratic House leadership was quite a scene. All the key leaders, mostly men, were seated on one side of the table in one of the Speaker's grand conference rooms, with the Speaker in the middle—firmly in charge. She made clear that Democrats would insist on changes to the agreement to strengthen labor enforcement, improve the environment chapter, and water down intellectual property provisions they believed would hamper Congress's ability to lower prescription drug prices. She was clear, forceful, and articulate. I had one demand: please appoint a member—or a group of members—who can sit down with me to negotiate the details. She agreed.

The whole time, my staff (which was sitting behind me in chairs lining the wall) looked rather pensive, knowing that a single nod from the Speaker during this meeting might blow up the entire enterprise. The Speaker must have taken notice, because at the end of the meeting she walked over to the USTR staff, tapped my deputy C. J. on the arm, and said, "Don't worry, we'll get this done." While the negotiations with House Democrats would prove difficult and last for months, I felt the Speaker was not just a force to be reckoned with but someone with whom we could do business.

In April 2019, the Speaker gave me what I had asked for. She appointed a USMCA working group that would be charged with negotiating with me on behalf of the Democratic caucus. It was a somewhat motley crew of members reflecting the diverse nature of the caucus: Richie Neal, an old-school Irish Catholic Democrat from Massachusetts, the powerful chairman of the House Ways and Means Committee, a good friend and the leader of the group; Rosa DeLauro, now the chairwoman of the House Appropriations Committee, a fiery liberal from Connecticut with a signature shock of dyed purple hair; Earl Blumenauer, a cycling enthusiast and cannabis supporter from Portland; Jimmy Gomez, a former labor leader from Los Angeles; Terri Sewell, a Harvard-educated moderate from Birmingham, Alabama; Suzanne Bonamici, a low-key Oregonian and ally of Blumenauer; Jane Schakowksy, a hard-edged liberal from Chicago's Gold Coast; Mike Thompson, a decorated Vietnam veteran from Napa Valley and close ally of the

Speaker; and John Larson, a jovial Connecticut pol and close friend of fellow New Englander Neal.

Several of these members were well known to me before their appointment to the working group. Neal and I had maintained a very constructive relationship throughout my nearly two-year tenure as USTR. Rosa DeLauro and I had been in close touch throughout the negotiations and bonded over our mutual disdain for ISDS. Blumenauer, Sewell, and Gomez were members of the Ways and Means Committee, where I had frequently testified. The fact that these members knew me and had worked with me in the past—including on USMCA—was enormously helpful. I was also helped by the fact that I had worked closely with organized labor in my career as a trade lawyer, and the nation's key labor leaders, Rich Trumka of the AFL-CIO and James Hoffa of the Teamsters Union, had vouched for me. That was critical in helping me build trust with members who represented districts where, in some cases, Donald Trump barely cracked double digits in 2016. None of this is to say the negotiations were easy. They were not. It had taken four months simply to get the group established.

Of the issues on the table, labor was the most difficult and consequential. Under NAFTA the labor provisions, such as they were, were unenforceable. The new labor rules we had negotiated were enforceable under a dispute settlement system that had been carried over from NAFTA into the new agreement. But that system had a fatal flaw. A few years into NAFTA, the parties discovered that once one country initiated a dispute, the opposite party could block the formation of a dispute settlement panel by refusing to appoint its arbitrators. Throughout the negotiations, I had resisted the idea of binding dispute settlement and initially had proposed that decisions of dispute resolution panels could be set aside by the losing party. This reflected the troubling experience I had had with the WTO's Appellate Body, which, as discussed, had time and again interpreted the WTO rules in ways the parties never intended. I nonetheless told the Democrats I was willing to solve the panel-blocking problem, which meant the United States would have the ability to bring labor cases over Mexico's objection. But the Democrats—and organized labor—wanted more: an entirely new enforcement mechanism that would allow the United States to block imports of Mexican goods at the border if they were manufactured in facilities operating in violation of the USMCA labor commitments.

In concept, I wholeheartedly endorsed this idea and, in fact, had made a late run in the negotiation at including something similar, though less ambitious, that had been developed by my staff and Ohio Democratic senator Sherrod Brown's team. At the same time, however, I realized there was a limit to what we could demand of Mexico. A proud Mexican patriot such as AMLO was never going to accept a unilateral enforcement mechanism that allowed the United States to block trade with Mexico whenever it damn well pleased.

There had to be due process, adjudication by a neutral decision maker, and an opportunity for the Mexicans to cure the violation before remedies could be imposed. It took several months to convince the Democrats and labor to accept that the Mexicans would never accept the justice of the Queen of Hearts—execution first and trial later. But after several weeks of staff-level negotiations led by C. J. and the estimable Katherine Tai, the lead House Democrat staffer for the negotiations and my ultimate successor as USTR in the Biden administration, we hashed out a groundbreaking facility-specific "Rapid Response Mechanism." This mechanism gives the United States the ability to bring enforcement actions targeting labor violations at individual worksites and, ultimately, impose severe penalties on those facilities, up to the outright blocking of goods at our border.

By the end of October, I thought we had worked through all the difficult issues. Then another tedious waiting game ensued as the Speaker went about trying to sell the deal to organized labor. For several weeks we heard very little from the working group or the Speaker's office. Then, as Thanksgiving approached, negotiations heated up again.

In addition to the Rapid Response Mechanism, some marginal improvements to the text of the labor chapter, and mostly cosmetic changes to the environment chapter, the one final concession I was forced to make was to drop the hard-won provision on data exclusivity for biologic drugs. Data exclusivity is extremely important to America's innovative biopharmaceutical companies, who typically cannot obtain meaningful patent protections in the United States for the life-saving drugs they spend billions to develop. In lieu of patents, Congress passed legislation that prevents generic companies from relying on the clinical trial data the innovator submits to the FDA for a period of twelve years, effectively barring the generics from marketing their own versions of the drug during that time.

One of the reasons that even some ardent free traders in Congress had opposed TPP was because the Obama administration had negotiated a weak provision on data exclusivity. The fact that we had succeeded where the Obama administration had failed was a point of great pride for me as a negotiator. Moreover, my sympathies on this issue were with the innovator companies—not because I particularly cared about filling their coffers but because the disparity in exclusivity periods in North America allows Canada and Mexico to free-ride off US innovation. Remarkably, the Democrats wouldn't even accept a compromise proposal we made that would peg the data exclusivity period in all three countries to that of the United States—their hatred of the pharmaceutical companies was so intense that they were willing to let the free riding continue. Although I thought the Democrats' position was unreasonable and misguided, in the end I wasn't willing to sacrifice the agreement to satisfy the drug companies, and neither was President Trump.

One of the most remarkable things about the working-group process—which incidentally took place while the House was holding impeachment proceedings—is that it all took place behind closed doors, with no leaks. I credit the Speaker, Chairman Neal, and their key staff leads, Katherine Monge and Katherine Tai, with running a disciplined, aboveboard process that allowed us to build trust and ultimately achieve something quite significant.

Of course, this lack of transparency meant that key players were left in the dark about what was being negotiated, most notably the Mexicans. I knew Mexico's first reaction to the Rapid Response Mechanism would be negative. But I believed the Mexicans would accept it in the end if I could present it alongside a commitment from the Speaker to support the agreement. And I felt that if we tried to engage in parallel negotiations with the Democrats and the Mexicans at the same time, the process would have been too unwieldy to complete. Seade and I had high-level discussions about where the talks with the Democrats were going, but we didn't present him with the text of the proposal until right before Thanksgiving.

As predicted, the initial reaction was quite heated. Seade fired off an uncharacteristically inflammatory email on Thanksgiving morning rejecting the Rapid Response Mechanism. After he arrived in Washington the following week, I was perturbed when Seade held an impromptu press conference on the steps of the Winder Building recounting the details of a meeting we had just finished. I responded by canceling our next meeting to give him twenty-four hours to cool off. When we reconvened at the end of the week, the two of us met in my office for over an hour and agreed to some minor adjustments to the Rapid Response process, which, of course, then needed to be sold to the Democrats.

By the end of the first week of December, I was confident enough we were nearly finished that I asked Jared to look into securing a government plane to fly us to Mexico City to sign the amendments to the agreement the following Monday. On the morning of Sunday, December 8, the Speaker and I talked and worked out a few remaining details regarding implementation funding. At that point I thought we were done and told the Speaker of my travel plans. She instructed me to hold off: there was one more, rather important box to check. Labor leader Rich Trumka of the AFL-CIO still needed to give final a sign-off on the deal—and he had decamped to a remote area of central Pennsylvania with spotty cell phone reception for an annual deer hunt. The trip was delayed for twenty-four hours. Finally, the Speaker and Trumka were able to connect, and labor gave a thumbs-up to the agreement.

Here I must give credit to President Trumka, who in the course of the negotiations became a very good friend. Rich was a rare combination of toughness, political savvy, and raw partisanship but also impeccable integrity, patriotism, and courage. I can personally attest to each of these attributes. When we had started the negotiations two years earlier, most of Washington—and nearly all Republicans—thought I was hopelessly naive for attempting to fashion a deal that Democrats, Republicans, business, and organized labor could all support. "Lighthizer's fantasy," they called it. After all, organized labor and many of its Democratic allies in Congress fiercely opposed the original NAFTA and nearly every trade agreement that followed.

What they didn't understand was that Rich saw the renegotiation as an opportunity to clean up the Mexican labor system in a way that would level the playing field for American workers and set a new worker-friendly template for future trade deals. He also realized that the reforms we were advocating (not just labor provisions but also stronger rules of origin for autos to eliminate free riding, a sunset clause to allow for continued updates, and stronger environmental obligations) would be insulated to some extent from criticism by the Right precisely because the renegotiation was being conducted by a Republican administration—the trade equivalent of Nixon goes to China.

"I won't be a cheap date," he told me one evening during the negotiations as we enjoyed cigars on the magnificent roof of the AFL-CIO's headquarters. But he also gave us his word he would work with us in good faith and publicly support a deal that met his objectives—even if that meant giving Donald Trump a major political victory in a reelection year. Rich didn't disappoint on either front. Sadly, Rich passed away unexpectedly less than a year after USMCA was signed into law. I miss my friend but take great pride in having played a role in the capstone achievement to his illustrious career.

The day after the white smoke billowed from Trumka's cabin in the Alleghenies, Jared, key members of my staff, and I embarked for Mexico City. C. J. and I spent the plane ride briefing over the phone Republican members of Congress and the business community on the contours of the deal. We had kept key Republican members up to speed on the negotiations with the Democrats throughout. Chuck Grassley and my predecessor at USTR, Rob Portman, in the Senate, and Kevin Brady in the House were invaluable partners who helped us determine exactly how far we could go to accommodate the Democrats without alienating Republicans (or at least not too many Republicans). But this was the first time we had revealed all the details of what we had been negotiating with down-dais Republican members and staffers on the Finance and Ways and Means Committees. There was some carping from the dwindling number of theological free traders—and an ultimately futile attempt from the vindictive junior senator from Pennsylvania to concoct a procedural maneuver to slow us down. But for the most part, Republicans and the business community were just happy we'd reached a successful conclusion.

The Mexicans put on quite a show. The signing ceremony took place in the baroque Sala de Tesorería in the Palacio Nacional. AMLO was a gracious and warm host. In my remarks, I surprised many by reflecting on the importance of the US-Mexican relationship, noting that the United States has a deep stake in the success of Mexico. We share a border, a long history, and, increasingly, a common heritage as more and more Americans are of Mexican descent. It wasn't what many expected from a representative of an America First administration.

There was one more dramatic and somewhat amusing episode in store for us. At the signing ceremony, Seade, Minister Freeland, and I had signed instruments amending the actual agreement. The full closing package also included an environmental side letter between the United States and Mexico on cooperation on illegal trafficking of wildlife and plants. It was a non-controversial, and frankly not altogether substantive measure we had agreed to in order to give the Democrats something else to take back to their supporters in the environmental movement. But the Mexican cabinet member who was supposed to sign, Graciela Márquez, Guajardo's successor, refused to do so, we always thought out of pique because she had been excluded from the negotiations up to that point.

A standoff ensued between the Mexican and American delegations in one of the grand courtyards of the palace, with Seade shuttling nervously between us. He ultimately suggested we return to DC and work the issue out later. But after telling the Speaker that this side agreement would be part of the final package, I was not about to return to Washington without a Mexican signature on that document. Finally, Mexico's chief legal adviser on foreign affairs, who had joined the melee by this point, opined that the foreign secretary, Marcelo Ebrard, could sign in lieu of

Marquez. The only problem was that Ebrard, who had been at the signing ceremony, had already departed the palace for his Ministry. So Jared, C. J., a retinue of Secret Service agents, and I jumped in a Suburban and scurried across town to get Ebrard's signature.

The House of Representatives voted on USMCA a few days later. The most special memory of that day for me was sitting in the gallery and listening to the great John Lewis of Georgia announce his support for the agreement. Lewis had long been a hero of mine, and my staff and I had spent a memorable evening with him a few months before in which he recounted his life and history in the civil rights movement. When speaking of NAFTA in his signature baritone voice, Lewis said the following:

> Twenty-six years ago, I opposed NAFTA with every bone in my body. I never thought that the day would come when we would have the opportunity to right some of the wrongs in that agreement. NAFTA failed our workers. It failed our Mexican brothers and sisters. It failed mother earth. NAFTA destroyed the hopes and dreams of a generation. . . . It started a race to the bottom. With this vote we have a chance to reset the clock, to chart a new path, and to create a new trade model. We can always do more. But today we build a new foundation for trade policy, a floor that reflects our values as a people and as a nation.

I felt the same way. And with that one glorious floor speech from a great man, all the toil—at times agony—we had experienced over the preceding two years to get to this point seemed to dissipate. Lewis would also die a few months later and would become one of only thirty-eight people in American history to have the honor of lying in state beneath the Capitol dome.

The House of Representatives passed USMCA by a vote of 385 to 41 and the Senate by a vote of 89 to 10. NAFTA, a hugely controversial agreement that passed by only a handful of votes in 1993 and was much reviled in many parts of the country ever since, had been replaced with a new gold standard agreement, passed with overwhelming bipartisan support, that prioritized the interests of workers, not just corporations. The North American trading relationship, which seemed on the verge of collapse so many times over the past two years, now rested on a foundation stronger than ever.

Lessons learned. Washington's foreign policy establishment was aghast that the Trump administration had the temerity to press America's interests in these negotiations and with the lack of diplomatic niceties in the president's speeches and tweets. But it turned out these elites were far more offended than were the Mexicans or the Canadians (well, most of the Canadians).

In addition to ignoring advice from the foreign policy blob, our decision to kick the professional lobbyists out of the room at key points in the negotiation also was critically important. At least when it comes to trade—if not other areas of public policy as well—issues that lobbyists and trade associations claim to be existential to the business community sometimes matter very little to actual businesses. Perhaps this should be unsurprising, as lobbyists have an incentive to overdramatize the impact of various public policy decisions; doing so only increases the demand for lobbyists. But these efforts to turn up the temperature often narrow the space for compromise. When we went directly to the CEOs and general counsels of large corporations—be they the auto companies when we were negotiating rules of origin or the oil companies on ISDS—we found them to be far more reasonable than were their uncompromising and generally less impressive retainers in Washington.

Another lesson of these negotiations was the importance of compartmentalization in politics. Some of the rabid partisans in the White House never understood how I could be negotiating with the Speaker at a time when she was overseeing impeachment proceedings against the president and otherwise doing everything she could to undermine the Trump agenda. But I had grown up in a Washington where politicians such as Bob Dole, Russell Long, Danny Rostenkowski, and Pat Moynihan worked easily across the aisle and readily understood that today's enemy can be tomorrow's ally. As much as I disagreed with the Speaker on taxes, health care, immigration, and a host of other issues, I had no problem working with her on an issue where our values and policy preferences overlapped. The country would be better governed if more people in Washington—on the right and left—abandoned tribalism and took a similar approach.

Part Four

MANAGING GLOBALIZATION— THE REST OF THE WORLD

Chapter 15

Europe and Japan

Among the most important geopolitical relationships in the world are those between the United States and Europe and Japan. While recognizing their importance to us, we should address inequities and imbalances in these two relationships. We must reduce our trade deficits and stop transferring our wealth to them as well as others. Countries can be friends and still constructively deal with economic friction and seek balanced relationships.

Europe and America: The Need for Balance

The United States and Europe are bound socially, culturally, economically, and historically. We are military allies with most of the countries of the European Union through NATO, and we share an enormous amount of both cross-border investment and trade. Our relationships vary greatly within the group, but all are significant.

The creation of a European Common Market really began in 1951 with the signing of the Treaty of Paris and the founding of the European Coal and Steel Community. In 1957, this coal and steel agreement—spurred by a desire for further economic integration—evolved into the European Economic Community with the signing of the Treaty of Rome.

In 1992, the final step was taken when the Maastricht Treaty was signed and the European Union was created. It is a political and economic union consisting of twenty-seven member states (twenty-eight before the United Kingdom withdrew). All are bound by the founding treaties and subject to common legislation and a common judicial system. It is a market of some 450 million people with a GDP in 2021 of around $17 trillion. While the joint economy of the European Union is smaller than that of the United States, its population is larger. The total GDP of the United States and Europe collectively comprises more than

40 percent of global GDP. Europe therefore serves as a major consumer within the global trading system, and the European Union notably imports more from China than it does from the United States.

This relationship, while critical geopolitically, is becoming wildly unbalanced economically. The US goods trade deficit with the European Union has more than doubled in recent years. In 1997, soon after the WTO was created, the United States had a $17 billion trade deficit in goods with the European Union. By 2001, it had grown to $65 billion. Ten years later (2011) it was $100 billion. Ten years after that (2021) it was $220 billion. If one wants a policy that leads to balanced trade overall, one must examine the European trading relationship. President Trump, while mindful of the importance of these countries as allies, was always concerned with this growing imbalance.

At the EU-wide level this surplus with the United States has several causes. First, certain significant tariff differences exist because of poor negotiating by prior US administrations. For example, a very large part of the trade between the United States and the European Union is in automobiles and auto parts. The United States has a 2.5 percent tariff on these products and Europe has a 10 percent tariff. That is a $3,700 difference on a $50,000 car. Autos and auto parts contribute more than $24 billion to the deficit and are largely sourced from German-owned companies. There are other significant tariff inequities as well. For example, the European Union has tariffs of up to 26 percent on wine, while ours are often less than 1 percent. Likewise, the EU's tariffs on processed wood products are 10 percent, while ours are less than 1 percent. The same pattern can be seen across a wide range of products, including nitrogen fertilizers and plastics. In addition to high tariffs, the European Union uses product standards as a way to keep US products out or to encourage manufacturing in Europe. In the United States, standards on products (think standards on, say, electric fans, auto brakes, or food) are made in a uniquely American way. Most are determined through one of a couple hundred different, independent standard-setting bodies. These are greatly influenced by US industry, and the objective is a cost-benefit analysis on safety versus affordability. Industry experts meet and discuss the science and current data. They then establish what is a reasonable standard considering risks and costs associated with the product. Sometimes these requirements are made official through adoption by government agencies, but often they are voluntarily adopted by industry without formal government involvement.

In Europe, standards are largely set by the government, although also with industry input. These standards tend to prioritize product safety above all else and are less concerned about associated costs. The Europeans have standards on things such as cars and consumer goods that are often much higher than ours and, we would say, higher than necessary. Some in the United States assert that the Europeans' standards are not based on science. These higher standards encourage people to manufacture in Europe.

There were negotiations in the Obama administration on something called Transatlantic Trade and Investment Partnership. The idea was to have a further integration of the US and EU economies. These negotiations lasted from 2013 to 2016. Little real progress was ever made. In theory the talks continued into the start of the Trump administration, but in reality they had been long since abandoned by Obama's USTR. The talks ultimately broke down over a series of differences. High on the list among them was the fact that Europe wanted to maintain its own ability to have standards on products that would help promote European manufacturing.

In addition, European industry is helped by the reliance of their countries on VATs. As discussed in greater length in chapter 17, VATs tend to protect domestic industries by discouraging imports and encouraging exports. Unlike income taxes, which cannot be reimbursed on export because of WTO rules, these VATs are assessed on all imports and are deducted from products that are exported. The average EU VAT is 21 percent, which is a significant contributor to their trade surplus.[1] An American product that cost $100 in New York would cost $121 in Europe (excluding transportation and other costs). On the same basis, a European product that costs $100 in Paris could be exported for $79 with all else held equal. Economists argue about the effect of VATs, but businesspeople understand the impact. They must pay their own countries' taxes at home and then additionally pay the VAT when exporting to

Europe (or any other market with significant VATs). Likewise, the European importer has an advantage when competing with the fully taxed US producer in our market. There is no logical reason why a VAT is border adjusted but federal and state income tax is not allowed to be. State sales taxes are border adjusted, however, but they are almost universally much lower than the European VAT—which is a primary source of revenue for European governments.

Europe also has a very protected agriculture sector. The EU's member countries use safety, health, and other similar food and agricultural standards to keep many US products out. The result is that we have an approximately $20 billion deficit in agricultural goods and foods. This in spite of the fact that we have a very efficient agricultural sector.

Finally, Europe is a much larger user of industrial subsidies than the United States is. One big contributor to the US-EU goods trade deficit is commercial aircraft. The European competitor, of course, is Airbus. We annually import about $4 billion worth of aircraft and parts from Airbus and its suppliers, and Airbus would not exist were it not for extensive and long-standing government subsidies.

Another way to analyze the huge and growing US-EU trade deficit is to look at the different EU countries individually. While Europe is a common market, it is still a group of individual countries with unique domestic industrial policies and economic advantages and disadvantages. Only four bilateral deficits are significant among the twenty-seven EU member states. If we could move toward more balanced trade with Germany, Ireland, Italy, and France, the problem would be solved.

Germany

While in theory all European Union countries are equal, the reality is that Germany is the most important. It has the biggest economy, and it has the most influence in EU matters. Germany's GDP is more than $4 trillion. By contrast, France's is around $3 trillion, and Italy's is less than $2 trillion (as of 2021). The German goods surplus with the United States in 2021 was about $70 billion. This is the biggest piece of the overall problem.

Germany, of course, has a world-class manufacturing sector. Its firms are leaders in auto technology, machinery, and pharmaceuticals. But other countries also make great products, and they don't run persistent trade surpluses. Germany has run large trade surpluses for decades. Its industrial policy has always encouraged exports and generally discouraged domestic consumption. The biggest reason, however, for the German trade dominance since 1999 is the euro. I believe that the basic compromise that cements Europe together is that Germany gets the benefit of a relatively weak currency, and in return it makes cash payments to many of the other countries in the European Union. If Germany were still using the deutsche mark, its currency would appreciate after years of trade surpluses, which would make it harder for Germany to export and easier to import. The large surpluses would then disappear. By using the euro, the value of which is determined in part by the trade performance of all the EU members, Germany can continue to run surpluses with the United States and much of the rest of the world while maintaining a relatively undervalued currency that boosts its export industry. In many years, Germany has had the biggest current account surplus (incoming payments exceeding outgoing payments at the economy level) of any country. Some economists might say this is because the Germans are diligent savers. The reality is that the Germans are running large trade surpluses because they have a weak currency that does not adjust to their surpluses. So instead of believing the Germans are somehow supersavers, I believe they have a mercantilist industrial policy premised on their use of the euro. That policy creates an enormous surplus and that makes Germany richer and richer.

Germany's habitual trade surplus has been the subject of much discussion over the years. In a 2015 piece for Brookings, Ben Bernanke (the noted American economist and former chairman of the Federal Reserve) identified two major reasons for the perennial German trade surpluses.[2] First, he noted the effects of the undervaluation of the euro for the German economy. He noted that the International Monetary Fund (IMF) in 2014 estimated Germany's inflation-adjusted exchange rate was undervalued by 5 percent to 15 percent and that the euro had fallen substantially even from that time. Second, he found that the surplus is buoyed by Germany's tight fiscal policy that suppresses domestic spending—including on imports. He concluded that these surpluses, particularly with other EU countries, were a destabilizing element within the European Union.

Germany heavily supports its manufacturing industries through government industrial policy. The German government openly says that "strengthening the country's industrial base is . . . a task of national importance" that government policy must support.[3] It specifically targets key sectors, including steel, metals, chemicals, automobiles, medical devices, and aerospace.[4] To support this objective, the German government has developed an industrial policy that involves subsidies and encourages company mergers where size is needed for success.[5]

In addition, in 2003–4, Berlin passed several labor reforms called the Hartz reforms.[6] As part of these reforms, the German government lowered restrictions on firing workers and reformed the unemployment insurance system to lower benefits for the "long-term unemployed" and increase job search requirements.[7] These changes weakened German workers' bargaining power and reduced wage growth to a level below GDP growth. To quote Professor Michael Pettis, "In a globalized world, the way to gain competitiveness is to reduce the real value of wages (as Germany did), or by undervaluing the currency (as many Asian countries did)."[8] The German policy, accordingly, was a trifecta: weak currency, artificially low labor costs, and a government-run industrial policy.

Germany, particularly by the end of Merkel's sixteen years in power, also developed closer relationships with Russia and China. Merkel visited China thirteen times while in office, far more than had any other Western leader. She resisted US requests to keep China's telecom company Huawei out of German telecom networks to prevent spying.[9] Partially as a result of these efforts, Germany has regularly run sizable trade surpluses with both countries (this has changed recently, at least temporarily, because of sanctions associated with the Ukraine war and the effects of COVID-19). The Germans wanted Russian gas as a low-cost energy source, and they wanted to secure any advantage possible in their Chinese businesses. Near the end of her term as chancellor (and when Germany held the rotating presidency of the EU Committee of

Ministers of the Council of Europe), Merkel pushed through, over the objections of several countries, a long-delayed China–European Union investment treaty. The treaty has not been ratified and is not likely to be, but it was viewed as an economic win for China. During our negotiations with Europe, I always believed that many of the German officials I engaged with were sympathetic to China. Unfortunately, the new chancellor, Olaf Scholz, seems to be following the same shortsighted China-friendly policy over the objections of his security experts and some coalition partners.

On one occasion early in my time at USTR, I had a senior German economic delegation come to my conference room. I told them of my concerns about China. These officials told me they were not worried about China. They had a good trade relationship (read that as a surplus) and were not troubled by Chinese policies. They thought China was no real threat because they (arrogantly) believed that Germany would always be more technologically advanced than the Chinese. I disagreed with this view during the meeting, and finally when they walked out the door I said, "Good luck with your ideas about China." I've known a lot of Germans and a lot of Chinese, and I don't believe one group is smarter than the other. Some in the new German government, informed by the new China-Russia partnership, seem to have a better understanding of the threat. There is also a growing awareness that German as well as American industry is being hollowed out by Chinese industrial policy.[10] Germany's automobile and auto parts manufacturers are under stress from Chinese imports, and Germany's solar power industry has been wiped out.

Ireland

People are always surprised to hear that Ireland poses a trade problem for the United States. The fact is that Ireland, with five million people and a GDP of just more than $400 billion, has the second largest (and perhaps fastest-growing) goods trade deficit with us in Europe. The tiny island nation had an $11 billion goods surplus with us in 2001. This surplus grew to $32 billion in ten years, and by 2022 (another ten years later), it was an astonishing $60 billion. The drivers of Ireland's surplus are pharmaceuticals (which contribute $25 billion to the surplus), chemicals, and optical equipment.

The Irish economy is not more efficient than ours is. Not even close. The Irish don't have abundant natural resources or Asia-style cheap labor. Their competitive advantage is simply low corporate taxes. Their industrial policy is clear—a 12.5 percent business income-tax rate. This means that companies can circumvent US (and other countries') taxes by shifting their profits to Ireland by either manufacturing or basing their intellectual property there. It is largely a tax avoidance scheme. In fact, hundreds of billions of dollars in annual profit from US companies is booked in Ireland. The benefit to Ireland is substantial employment and revenue. For the United States, it means a loss of both.

The biggest users of Ireland for tax avoidance are American pharmaceutical companies. The value of their products can be thought of as having two parts: the actual cost of production and the value of the intellectual property in the product. Typically, pharmaceutical companies set up an Irish subsidiary. They place the intellectual property right to their products in that company and complete their manufacturing process in Ireland through that subsidiary. Say they are making a pill. The actual cost of making the pill might be, say, $0.50. They then export the pill to the United States (by having the Irish subsidiary sell to the same company's US subsidiary) with an export price of, say, $10. If they sell the pill in America for $11, they would have only a dollar of taxable profit in the United States. The $9.50 in profit (the difference between the $0.50 and the $10 export price) would be taken in Ireland and subjected to the low Irish tax rate. The companies justify the high Irish export price that they set on their internal transactions because they hold the intellectual property for the pill in the Irish subsidiary. The Irish subsidiary then pays a small license fee back to the American parent. That royalty is subject to US tax, but it is quite small compared to the actual profit on the pill. So, they are shifting profits that were actually made in the United States back to Ireland and avoiding our taxes. Under this completely legal scheme, Ireland gets a substantial part of the tax revenue that would normally be due to the US government, and the pharmaceutical company employs tens of thousands of Irish workers. These warped incentives feed our increasing trade deficit with Ireland. As we have seen, this is cumulatively another transfer of wealth from us to them. For many years some companies enhanced this scheme. They did what was called a "double Irish" tax arrangement. In this they followed the process above but then put the profits of the Irish subsidiary in another tax haven subsidiary and avoided the Irish taxes too. The European Union objected, and this device was phased out between 2015 and 2020.

There are several ways to stop this profit shift. We could reduce our own corporate taxes so that the tax advantage to companies of setting up shop in Ireland would be too small to make a significant difference. The Tax Cuts and Jobs Act signed into law by President Trump in December 2017 reduced our corporate income tax rate from 35 percent to 21 percent. This was an important step in the right direction. Another approach would be that proposed by the Republican House in 2016.[11] The bill would have denied importers the deduction for the cost of imports when calculating their income. If it had become law, there would have been no advantage to the low Irish rate. All importers would have paid our full tax rate on all their imports. This would have been good for American manufacturers and for our workers. However, retailers and other importers successfully lobbied to stop this from becoming law. This significant issue is discussed in detail in chapter 17.

Italy and France

The remaining two European Union countries that have significant trade surpluses with the United States are Italy and France, and their combined surplus totaled about $60 billion in 2021. Both these countries have unique products that are difficult for us to compete with. In the fashion, food, and wine sectors, France and Italy lead the world. In addition, Italy has a unique auto industry. The Italians also have the advantage of the EU industrial policy. They benefit from the bloc's agricultural protectionism, a significant VAT advantage (20 percent for France and 22 percent for Italy), and the EU's highly subsidized aerospace sector.

In 2021, Italy had an almost $40 billion surplus in goods with us. The drivers of their export number were nuclear equipment and machinery, vehicles, pharmaceutical products, and beverages. Italy also regularly runs a significant trade surplus with the world. Recently, this surplus has been responsible for about 3.5 percent of Italy's GDP. Perhaps surprisingly to some readers, Italy is the second most important industrial country in the European Union behind Germany.[12]

Our trade deficit in goods with France is less significant. At about $20 billion, this deficit is driven by beverages, some machinery, and, of course, perfume and cosmetics. France has traditionally run a small global trade deficit. It tends to have surpluses with much of the world and a deficit in trade within the European Union.

Still, French trade policies pose significant challenges to the United States. For example, France's tax and reimbursement policies for pharmaceuticals and its abnormally long approval process pose challenges for US pharmaceutical firms. The French government has also been highly protective of its defense industry, maintaining ownership shares in several major defense contractors and making it difficult for non-EU firms to participate in French defense procurement. Such defensive practices also extend to media through France's implementation of the EU-wide Audiovisual Media Services Directive. In addition, French exports benefit from the subsidies to Airbus. I discussed this in chapter 4 (on the WTO), but this is a major European company that would not exist but for the industrial policy of four countries—Germany, France, Britain, and Spain.

There is another aspect of our relationship with Europe that always bothered President Trump, and that is that the United States pays a disproportionate amount through NATO to defend its members. In 2014, NATO members agreed that all the countries in the alliance would spend at least 2 percent of their GDP on defense. Remember that NATO defense is largely oriented against Russia, but it is also a bulwark against China. Nineteen of NATO's thirty member countries have not met their commitment. Germany is a particularly egregious offender. Eight years after the agreement, Germany pays about 1.5 percent of its GDP for defense. The United States, in contrast, pays about 3.5 percent. In a sense, Germany is keeping its own government spending down in part by having us pay for part of their defense while running an enormous trade surplus with us. Interestingly the United Kingdom and France have met their obligation. Italy has not, and Ireland does not belong to NATO. In a way, Ireland is a big beneficiary of the stability the alliance has brought and has not contributed financially to NATO or needed to spend heavily for its own defense.

Despite the remaining problems with European underinvestment in Europe's own defense, one of Trump's great achievements was that he nonetheless got many NATO members to significantly increase their payments. By one calculation, our NATO allies now pay $50 billion more for their defense than they did in 2016.[13]

United Kingdom

The trade and investment relationship between the United States and the United Kingdom may be the healthiest one in the world. We have more than $280 billion in two-way trade. We are each other's largest source of foreign investment, and we each employ about one million citizens of the other country. In the years between 2010 and 2021, the United States had seven years of goods surpluses with the United Kingdom, and it had five with us. That is how trade is supposed to work. Further, the two countries have the most two-way services trade globally. Economically, we really do have a "special relationship."

In June 2016, the citizens of the United Kingdom voted to withdraw from the European Union. The vote was close. It was interpreted in the United States as a populist uprising. Domestically the issues were very complicated, but it seemed to be a battle between conservative nationalists and London globalists. I know that many Trump supporters sympathized with Brexit. After much negotiation and an equal amount of hand-wringing, on January 31, 2020, the United Kingdom was officially out. As is usually the case in great dramas such as this, the world went on.

The conservative party in the United Kingdom is composed of many people who were for withdrawal but also for free trade. That never made much sense to me. To be in favor of national control of your institutions and government while being unconcerned about maintaining some level of self-sufficient economy seemed contradictory. While the country has a strong but specialized manufacturing sector, it runs a chronic goods trade deficit with the world every year. Its trade surplus in services has mitigated the problem until recently, but now the total goods and services deficit is itself getting large.

After Brexit, the conservative government doubled down on free trade. The government seemed to tell its people that while it was withdrawing from the European Union, it was engaging more with the rest of the world. The government entered into several FTAs and explored joining other trade pacts. Of course, the big one on leaders' wish list was with the United States. Prime Minister Johnson and President Trump announced that talks would begin on a "massive" trade deal, and so, on May 5, 2020, I sat in the former office of Secretary of State Cordell Hull in front of a portrait of the great man and began the talks, remotely. My counterpart was UK trade minister Liz Truss. She sat in an equally ornate office somewhere in the bowels of White Hall. I always enjoyed talking to her. She went on to briefly become prime minister.

Since we have such a healthy trade relationship with the United Kingdom, I was a little skeptical about how much we were going to be helped by a new deal. Clearly, the British wanted tariffs reduced. In particular, they sought a reduction in auto tariffs that would increase UK exports of British-made vehicles to the United States. We already had a large deficit in this sector, and I didn't want to add to that and risk more US jobs. As we began to prepare our strategy, I called the CEOs of a few large US manufacturing companies. I asked them what I could do in a trade deal that would help them sell more products to the United Kingdom. The answer was not surprising. With the exception of Ford, which thought it could probably sell a couple of thousand more Mustangs (remember, with left-hand drive in a right-hand-drive country), none of the company bosses could find anything that would move the needle. The existing UK tariffs were mostly small, and the businesses already had established patterns. The truck manufacturing companies, for example, said that they make their trucks for the United Kingdom in Europe and would continue to do so. They were not going to make changes to their US plants for no significant benefit. The same was true for chemical companies and others.

Still, I began the talks in good faith. We exchanged tariff offers and talked about myriad issues: financial services, UK agricultural protections, industrial standards, the purchasing regime of the British National Health Service, and the like. Many of the issues were extremely sensitive over there, but the one that seemed most delicate was chlorinated chicken. I'm not kidding. I had first come across this bombshell issue when Liz's predecessor, Liam Fox, and I were negotiating on US-UK trade irritants a couple of years before. It seems that Britain keeps our chicken products out of its country by claiming that our process for assuring high health standards was not safe. The notion is preposterous, of course, but the issue is at the intersection of farmer protectionism and European standards extremism. That is a dangerous intersection. Whenever I was eating with my British colleagues in the United States, I always made it a point to order chicken. The UK talks never finished—and, of course, our chicken is still kept out.

Finally, no discussion of US and European trade could be complete without mentioning the steel and aluminum tariffs. In 2018, after an investigation at the Department of Commerce and a corresponding report, President Trump determined that tariffs were needed to protect our steel and aluminum industries. He elected to use his authority under Section 232 of the Trade Expansion Act of 1962. He reasoned that these industries were in danger of collapse in the United States, threatening the country's ability to ramp up military production in the event of a conflict, and that a 25 percent tariff was needed on certain steel imports and a 10 percent tariff was called for on aluminum. The problem in steel was clear. Massive uneconomic oversupply, largely from heavily subsidized Chinese steel and aluminum mills, was flooding the world market with cheap steel and threatening the viability of the US metals industry. Only a global remedy would help. Taking action against only one country would just lead to more steel coming in from others. Tariffs that targeted only the most egregious overproducers, such as China, would not work at adjusting steel and aluminum prices because other countries (such as those in the European Union) would export their output to the

United States while importing cheap Chinese metal—keeping global and US steel prices artificially low. This action enraged the Europeans. They had a healthy trade surplus in these products and wanted to keep it. They viewed it as an assault on the trading system, but mostly they were offended by the national security justification.

While I was not particularly moved by what I considered to be essentially faux outrage from countries that practice protectionism with the best of them when it suits their interests, I knew the Section 232 tariffs would cause political problems for the White House once the Europeans imposed retaliatory tariffs on US exports. This problem was compounded by the fact that the Section 232 investigation coincided with the Section 301 investigation, which likewise would spark retaliation from the Chinese. My preference, therefore, was to move forward first with the Section 301 tariffs. It would be harder for globalists to criticize the Section 301 tariffs if the focus was on combating unfair Chinese trade practices. But if we first imposed the Section 232 tariffs, the debate would be about the efficacy of tariffs in general, an area where it would be harder for the administration to rally support, particularly among Republicans in Congress.

I would have also tried harder to get Europe to agree to voluntary quotas before imposing Section 232 tariffs, and the resolve demonstrated by the Section 301 tariffs would have given us some leverage to achieve that result. In the end, I'm not sure this gambit would have succeeded. Although the European Union ultimately agreed to accept steel and aluminum quotas proposed by the Biden administration, I imagine the Europeans' supposed piety about the WTO rules would have prevented the Europeans from making the same concession to the Trump administration. Still, delaying the imposition of Section 232 tariffs at least on the European Union would have blunted criticism that the Trump administration was "going it alone" when it came to China. All this said, I continue to admire the fact that whenever it came down to a choice between American workers and foreign interests, President Trump always chose the former.

And as it was, the Europeans' overwrought reaction to the Section 232 tariffs was a master class in hypocrisy: while reaching for the vapors to calm themselves over our supposed violation of the WTO rules, they immediately imposed retaliatory tariffs without first availing themselves of the WTO's supposedly sacrosanct dispute resolution process, in blatant violation of the rules. It turns out that Europe's religious devotion to that international body had its limits.

Japan

In my early days in trade, I was very concerned about Japan. It was an ally and a friend of the United States, but we had a very unbalanced relationship. Its economic development plan for decades had been to grow by maintaining a closed domestic market and to do everything possible to increase exports. This was pure mercantilism. The Japanese ran large surpluses with several countries, but none as big as their surplus with us. They used large subsidies to build up the traditional industries of steel, automobile, and general manufacturing. Their businesses were intertwined through so-called keiretsu, business conglomerates, which served to prevent external competition. The government gave its industries 0 percent interest rates on loans. The Japanese had a seriously undervalued yen. And they used coercion to obtain technology, particularly from US companies. The results of this policy were astounding. Japan grew from a poor, ravaged country in 1946 to a nation whose economy rivaled that of the United States by the early 1990s. The "Japan Miracle" was the watchword of the world. Over time, Japan's non-market methods and unfair practices were being analyzed and criticized by the likes of Karel van Wolferen, Eamonn Fingleton, and my old friend Clyde Prestowitz.[14] Another critic was a young New York real estate mogul named Donald Trump.

During my time as deputy in the Reagan administration, I did a lot of negotiating with Japan. Our ultimate objective was to stop their unfair practices, but our short-term strategy was to limit their exports to the United States and help our domestic industry. We negotiated export restraint agreements on steel, autos, and semiconductors, just to name a few. As we've discussed, Reagan was an America-first president before "America First."

The Japanese industrial policy did damage to our economy, and it cost us jobs, but it was never truly an existential threat in the way China is. In the final analysis, Japan was a friend, and while it wanted to grow by whatever means, it did not want to harm us. Its leaders talked sincerely, I believe, about a "big brother–younger brother" relationship. By the 1990s, Japan's bubble burst. Many debate the cause, but it is some combination of excessive debts, failed tax policy, flawed industrial policy, and demographics. Japan's economic growth slowed and has never really come close to ours since. The extent of Japan's success, and subsequent fall, can be seen in this comparison: starting from near zero in 1946, by 1995, Japan's GDP was $5.5 trillion (that year, by comparison, the US GDP was $7.6 trillion). That is about 72 percent of ours. Since the bubble burst, the Japanese economy has barely grown. Today, Japan's economy is still about $5.5 trillion and ours is $23 trillion. It is less than a quarter our size.

There is a story about one of my Reagan-era negotiations with Japan that was widely reported at the time. To this day I am asked whether it is true, and I say it is. In 1984, in response to a crisis in the US steel industry, President Reagan announced a steel program. He would limit imports from all major suppliers. His views were very much like Trump's a generation later. Essentially, we threatened to use Section 301 and to enforce other trade laws to get countries to agree to limit their steel exports. The Japanese were particularly tough negotiators. They always had excellent government officials in their trade ministry, and they weren't used to making concessions. The talks finally came down to how much steel they could send and the precise categories of that steel. The final round of the negotiations was in Washington.

One evening, the Japanese indicated that they wanted to come by my office and present their final offer. Three negotiators came in and sat on my couch with me and my principal assistant. They made their presentation. I didn't talk except to welcome everyone at the beginning of the meeting. When they concluded, my counterpart handed me their piece of paper with their "final" offer. It was totally unacceptable, not even close to what would be needed. Without saying anything, I folded the piece of paper into the form of a paper airplane and flew it back to the leader of their delegation. I then sat there silently. They got the point. The next day they came by again, and we had a deal that was satisfactory to everyone. My objective was not to be disrespectful but to dramatically show that their position was unacceptable. I was not going to cave like some other prior negotiators.

From the late 1970s to 1980, the US auto industry was really hurting. Losses were in the billions, and a million workers were laid off. One of the principal causes was Japanese imports. Japan's companies had increased Japanese exports to us from a few hundred thousand to two million cars per year. President Reagan again insisted on a "voluntary" restraint agreement to deal with the surge. My boss, Ambassador Brock, negotiated a deal that lasted for a number of years. The Reagan demand for car quotas is one of the major reasons why the Japanese auto companies began to shift production to the United States. Now Japanese companies such as Toyota and Honda are a major source of US employment and a significant part of our industry. As always, Reagan's pragmatic nationalism paid off.

When I took over as the USTR in 2017, my views on Japan were very different than they had been during the Reagan years. The Japanese still had an unacceptable trade surplus, and they continued to keep many US products out of their market, particularly in agriculture, but they also were major US employers and our most dependable ally in the confrontation with China.

In April 2018, we had a pivotal meeting in Palm Beach at Mar-a-Lago. By this time President Trump and Prime Minister Shinzo Abe had developed a very close working relationship. Clearly, Japan was our closest ally in Asia and one of our closest allies in the world. Abe was a historic figure. He was head of government of Japan longer than any other person since the Meiji Restoration in 1868. The close personal relationship, however, did not keep the president from pushing US interests. The most sensitive import from Japan was still autos, and Trump had threatened to put 25 percent tariffs on those imports if the Japanese did not do something to balance the trade.

On Wednesday, April 18, we had a crucial meeting in the small ballroom at Mar-a-Lago. It is an ornate room in the French Louis XV–Trump style. There was a long conference table set up in the middle of the room. On one side were ten Japanese officials with the prime minister in the middle, and on our side was the same number with President Trump in the center. As we began to talk about trade, Prime Minister Abe gave a spirited presentation of Japan's position—the trade was not unfair, and we benefited as much as them. It was clear he had spent a great deal of time preparing his remarks, and they were quite impressive. When he was finished, President Trump asked me to respond. I pointed out the way the trade pattern looked from our perspective. I said that we had more than a trillion dollars in cumulative deficits in the last two decades, that we had lost employment, and that many of our products (particularly farm products) were unfairly excluded from Japan's market. Underlying all these discussions was Trump's threat of tariffs on cars if an adequate deal was not reached. The president and the prime minister concluded that trade talks would begin immediately. I would represent the United States and Minister Toshimitsu Motegi would represent Japan. He was not the trade minister. As minister of state for economic and fiscal policy, Motegi was senior to the trade minister in Japan's cabinet. Motegi was a very smart, very shrewd political figure in Japan. He knew America and spoke some English.

The principal benefit to the United States in the defunct Trans-Pacific Partnership agreement would have been additional access to Japan's agriculture market. The president and I wanted to obtain that same advantage without joining TPP and making new large concessions on foreign access to the United States. This negotiation was a classic example of our negotiating philosophy. We have the largest market in the world, and Japan has a significant persistent surplus with us. The Japanese should make concessions not to get more from us but to maintain their current access. After several rounds and many calls, we reached agreement. The United States would gain 95 percent of the market access that had been negotiated with Japan in the TPP, with minimal concessions. Japan obtained some tariff reductions but, more importantly, it was assured of its current access—there would be no new 25 percent car tariffs. In addition, we concluded a second agreement on digital trade and e-commerce. This agreement was modeled after the USMCA provisions and will be a model for future digital trade agreements. The final agreements were signed by Trump and Abe during the UN General Assembly meeting in New York in 2019.

On December 12, 2017, Japan's minister of economy, trade, and industry, Hiroshige Seko, and Cecilia Malmström, European commissioner for trade, and I met for the first time as a trilateral group. We pledged to work together at the WTO and in other forums to counter the unfair practices of China. China wasn't mentioned in the joint statement that we released in Buenos Aires, but everyone knew what we were about. The group met several more times during my tenure and has continued with my successor. The Trump administration was criticized for not working enough with our friends on trade problems, but this was clearly unfair. We tried not only to work with willing allies but also to pursue our American objectives at the same time.

Chapter 16

Other Major Trading Partners

Addressing the existential threat that we faced in China could have occupied the whole of the Trump administration. Likewise, renegotiating NAFTA would normally be an all-encompassing effort in a typical administration. Making headway on the difficulties in our economic relationship with Europe and Japan were also major efforts, but the fact of the matter was that the United States had trade problems all over the world that needed to be dealt with immediately.

My first overseas trip as USTR was in May 2017. I went to Vietnam for the ministerial meeting on trade for the Asia-Pacific Economic Cooperation. The meeting was held in a vast convention center in Hanoi for two days. All twenty-one ministers of the Asia Pacific Economic Cooperation forum attended. President Trump had pulled the United States out of the Trans-Pacific Partnership on his first day in office, rightly concluding that it was a very bad deal for our workers. This was the first trade ministers' confab since that event, and the other ministers were curious about the Trump administration's plans and priorities. My objectives in going to the meeting were twofold. First, I wanted to show that the world was not coming to an end—the administration understood that the United States is also a Pacific nation and that economically and geopolitically we all needed to work together. When asked by the media upon my arrival what I hoped to convey to my fellow ministers, I said simply, "I'm here." I essentially meant that we understand the importance of these meetings. My formal statement said, "It was important to me to come to APEC first and foremost to reaffirm the President's strong commitment to promoting bilateral free and fair trade throughout the Asia-Pacific region."

There was a second objective, however. I needed to convey that things would be different. The United States was not going to continue to sacrifice its industry for illusory geopolitical consistency. There is a normal pattern for these meetings in which the delegates take the joint statements and declarations from past years, add a little fluff to them, then redate and release them to the world in a press conference. There are bilateral side meetings on the margins of the conference where ministers can get to know one another on a superficial level and exchange trade talking points.

In Vietnam, I did not follow the normal pattern. I directed USTR staff to reject any declaration language that was inconsistent with what we were planning to do with US trade policy. The US position was to avoid making any sweeping promises about maintaining an open economy at all costs and pursuing a policy centered on the WTO. This approach shocked the sensibilities of establishment American trade professionals and some of my foreign counterparts.

On top of that, I used each of my bilateral meetings with Asian trade ministers to point out the extensive and persistent trade surpluses they enjoyed with the United States. This was the core theme of my first visits with my counterparts, and I dispensed with the usual talking points about "regional economic integration" and an aspirational "free trade area of the Asia-Pacific." I wanted to make our point that we would seek balanced trade and would not stand for unfair trade practices, even if it meant taking strong unilateral enforcement actions. This was the policy we pursued with many of these countries. At the end of the meeting, when the staffs of the various officials drafted the usual statement (much of which would be read as condemning our policy), I refused to go along. There was no consensus statement. The chairperson summed up the meeting realizing that I didn't agree. Everyone knew that things were going to be different.

It is important that the United States' trade policy focus on Asia. It not only is the most vulnerable area to Chinese influence, but it is a region with some of the most vibrant economies on the planet. It also contains countries with large and growing trade surpluses with us. In some ways, we are rebuilding Asia, and we can't afford that anymore. I've picked a few Asian countries to focus on.

India

India and the United States should be natural friends. We are both democracies. We both have many similar Anglo-Saxon institutions, and there are more than four million Americans of Indian heritage. Perhaps most importantly, the rise and growing militarism of China is the greatest geopolitical concern for both our nations. India and China both claim territory in the mountains that separate them. India feels as threatened as we do by the aggressive surge of China. There is truth in the old saying (modified for obvious reasons) that the adversary of my adversary is my friend.

India has a long, more than two-thousand-mile border with China. There has been conflict on this border for more than a century. In 1962, China attacked India in a dispute over territory on the Himalayan border. Bitter fighting lasted about a month. The Soviet Union, which was in a time of tension with China, heavily supplied India. The United States would not intervene. The war was largely a success for China, which took the territory it claimed. India regrouped and attempted to modernize its army. Another brief war was fought on its border again in 1967, when the People's Liberation Army of China attacked the Indian border post at Nathu La. This conflict ended more favorably for the Indians. Over the ensuing years, there has been armed conflict between the two countries on a smaller scale along that mountainous border numerous times. Perhaps this explains why India became the fourth member of the Indo-Pacific Security Dialogue that became the "Quad."

Prime Minister Narendra Modi is a particularly interesting figure. He came up through the ranks of right-wing political organizations and clearly considers himself a nationalist. His political party, the Bharatiya Janata Party, is a right-wing Hindu party. He also came up through the Rashtriya Swayamsevak Sangh, a right-wing paramilitary volunteer organization. He is an extremely gifted politician and the first leader of India who was born after its independence in 1947. He is from Gujarat in northwest India and from a modest background. Of course, Modi is dedicated to raising India out of poverty. He believes in doing it through state control of innovation, high tariffs, mercantilism, and protectionism.

There are lots of hangovers from the time of British rule, but free trade is not one of them.

India has a reasonably large economy—well more than $2 trillion—and it has grown at a healthy rate, on average almost 6 percent a year for two decades, although its per capita GDP is small. It is poor and needs rapid economic development to maintain stability. In 2020, the US trade deficit in goods and services with India was $33.7 billion.[1] The largest goods driver of this deficit was an $8.1 billion deficit in pharmaceutical products, followed by a $5 billion deficit in jewelry and silverware.[2] India also exports large quantities of auto parts, travel goods, and steel pipe.

Indian trade policies have long caused tensions with the United States. India uses many of the tools of modern mercantilism. It has high tariffs, a bureaucracy focused on keeping imports out, and a system of industrial policy and protectionism. Its average MFN applied tariff rate of 17.6 percent is the highest of any major world economy.[3] It maintains particularly steep tariffs on some goods including motorcycles (50 percent), automobiles (60 percent), and walnuts and raisins (100 percent).[4] Further, India remains on the US government's watch list for intellectual-property-rights violations, and the Indian legal system provides limited patent protections and poor copyright enforcement.[5] India also limits foreign investment in sectors such as insurance and banking.[6] In addition, India has applied price controls to certain US imports in the medical device sector, forcing US companies that want to continue to have access to the Indian market to sell these price-controlled products often at a loss.[7] India is particularly protectionist in the agricultural sector, where it uses tariffs and safety standards to help politically potent farmers groups.

India is increasingly developing its own industrial policy through programs such as "Made in India" and "Self-Reliant India."[8] To this end, it has aimed to increase foreign investment, lower some regulatory burdens, increase exports, and protect products in targeted sectors including electronics and communication devices.[9] It also subsidizes exports through tax and customs exemptions for companies in industries such as textiles, steel, and wood products.[10] These programs are relatively new, so the exact details remain murky, but it is clear that India is embarking on the path toward developing an industrial policy like that of East Asian nations including China.

India was one of the twenty-three founding contracting parties to the GATT, the predecessor of the WTO. (The talks were concluded in October 1947, and India became a member in July 1948.) In those original negotiations, India managed to maintain very high tariffs, and more than a third of its tariff lines are not bound and can be raised to any level. In the subsequent rounds of trade negotiations, it continued to avoid taking on commitments that would limit its industrial policy.

India suffers from an extremely strong professional bureaucracy in all areas of government. It is also unusual in the extent to which oligarchs influence government policy. When I was in negotiations with Indian officials, I kept a copy of the biography of each of the country's fifteen or so billionaires on my desk. In predicting Indian government positions, I would look to the interests of these men. I can remember at one point telling an Indian friend of mine who had made a fortune in business that I thought there were fifteen oligarchs who basically ran the country. He corrected me. "Bob you're wrong. Only about seven of them actually run the country. The others just try to influence the seven."

The Trump administration's strategy with India was to maintain good relations but to use what leverage we had to increase our access to their market, to obtain fairness and reciprocity in trade, and to achieve balance. We tried to leverage India's use of our duty-free program, the Generalized System of Preferences, to obtain more market access. GSP is a program in which developing countries can sell their products in our market without paying the normal tariffs. India is by far the biggest user of the program. A large percent of all its imports come into the United States under this preference duty-free. While India uses GSP and runs large trade surpluses with us, it denies us equal access to its market and charges our producers high tariffs.

After an investigation, and following all the requirements of US law, we removed India from GSP in June 2019. We then negotiated to restore it in exchange for more market access concessions. Our objective was fairness and balance. After several sessions, it was obvious that these talks would not succeed. India was not in the habit of opening its market, and many of the concessions we needed were in the agriculture area, and at that time, India's farmers were in a state of agitation for a variety of reasons.

During the G7 meeting in Biarritz, France, in August 2019, President Trump had a bilateral meeting with Prime Minister Modi. They had an excellent relationship. India is not in the G7 but was invited by France as a special guest. The two leaders sat in the customary way next to each other in the middle of the room with senior aides sitting at their sides facing their counterparts. After they discussed foreign policy issues, Prime Minister Modi switched to trade. He clearly wanted to get GSP back. He told Trump that it had been unfairly taken away and further that it had been done during his reelection campaign, that the US was being very difficult, and that I was refusing to deal with his minister. It was odd but not unprecedented for me to be the subject of discussion between Trump and another leader. After briefly responding, President Trump asked me to speak. I had had enough. I thought Modi's entire story was lopsided. He had clearly been misinformed by his staff.

I told him that India was removed from the program after his election (not before it) precisely so that it would not be an election issue for him. Then I stated our case that it was "the most protectionist country in the world" and that it was causing a large and growing trade deficit. Americans were losing their jobs because of their practices. They were hurting our farmers. I said that I had been negotiating with their trade minister, Suresh Prabhu, for two years and had made absolutely no progress. At times, I said, he had not even returned my call for weeks. I went through the specifics of their unfair practices. I told Prime Minister Modi that we could do a deal with India, but it would have to make concessions. The effect of my intervention was palpable, but, of course, the two leaders ended on a positive note. When the meeting was over, Prime Minister Modi came up to me to shake hands. He asked me to come to India and to see him at his house. Unfortunately, COVID-19 made that impossible. Several members of our delegation congratulated me for the respectful but forceful presentation. Jared Kushner told me it was worth the price of admission by itself.

Soon after that meeting, negotiations began in earnest. This time they were with a new trade minister named Piyush Goyal, a smart, gifted politician from Mumbai. We raised our issues: tariffs, agriculture access, medical device impediments, barriers to e-commerce and insurance, discrimination in the electronic payment sector, fish subsidies, and the list goes on. We made headway but could never quite close a deal. I always felt that Goyal wanted one but had to contend with the bureaucracy and the farmers as well as with me. I really concluded that India was just protectionist. That was part of its political DNA, and the best way to deal with that was through unilateral action.

It would be ideal if the United States could have a closer economic relationship with India. We clearly have the geopolitical reason to do it. India is a natural adversary of China. It also has a population that contains an enormous number of very educated and smart people as well as a large inexpensive labor force.

South Korea

South Korea is an important ally of the United States. As with some countries in Europe, however, the economic relationship has gotten out of balance. It used to upset President Trump that we would pay billions of dollars to defend Korea and that it would maintain obstacles to US exports and have a large trade surplus with us every year.

Korea's GDP was about $1.7 trillion in 2021, about the size of Canada's. That is quite an accomplishment for a country whose whole economy was less than $4 billion in 1960. From 2001 to 2020, Korea's GDP has grown $1.09 trillion (USD) at an average annual growth rate of 3.62 percent.[11] Between 2001 and 2021, the US trade deficit in goods and services with South Korea added up to a cumulative $216.4 billion.[12]

In 2020, the total United States–Korea trade deficit in goods and services was $17.2 billion.[13] The largest contributor to this deficit was transportation equipment, where there was an $18.47 billion deficit (which included a $13.7 billion deficit in motor vehicles and a $5.4 billion deficit in motor vehicle parts).[14] The second largest contributor was a $10.46 billion deficit in computer and electronic products, which included a $5.5 billion deficit in semiconductors and electronic components and a $4.1 billion deficit in magnetic and optical media.[15] We sell the Koreans mineral fuels, machinery, some vehicles, and a large quantity of agricultural products.

Historically, South Korea's economic development, like Japan's, has been driven by targeted industrial policies that cultivate high-value-added industries. In the 1970s and 1980s, the Korean government targeted Korea's heavy and chemical industries with cheap credit, government investment, and protection from imports.[16] This, coupled with currency manipulation and government oversight of firms in favored industries, enabled Korea's rapid industrialization.[17] Today, Korea maintains this policy scheme through the Korea Development Bank's financial support for Korean companies in targeted sectors.[18]

Korea also has some aspects of an oligopoly. It has several large conglomerates that operate to enrich themselves as a group and often to fight imports. These are called chaebol (which literally means "rich family"). This chaebol system clearly led to accelerated economic growth and an increased Korean presence abroad, but it has also led to monopolistic practices as well as governance and political corruption charges. The chaebol use their size and political influence to maintain control of the economy in a way similar to the keiretsu in Japan.

Korea and the United States have a generally favorable trade relationship. In 2012, the United States–Korea Free Trade Agreement (KORUS) went into effect. The agreement had a bit of a tortured history. It was negotiated in 2006 and 2007 in the George W. Bush administration. There was not enough political support in Congress to pass the needed implementing legislation. In the 2008 presidential election campaign, candidate Obama opposed the agreement as "badly flawed." He largely echoed the position of the automobile unions. After the election, however, just as he did in the case of NAFTA, Obama did an about-face. His administration renegotiated some minor changes until December 2011 and then submitted those to Congress. They passed with a large Republican majority.

As many expected, KORUS greatly increased the size of the US deficit with Korea. The biggest single sector, of course, was automobiles. Korea imported very few additional US cars, but it significantly increased exports to us. Candidate Trump campaigned against the deal as a job killer. Unlike his predecessor, though, President Trump meant what he said. He threatened to withdraw from the agreement and to put 25 percent tariffs on all cars—including those from Korea. The national security policy makers in the administration were concerned. He instructed me to renegotiate the deal, or he would cancel it. We prepared the legal groundwork for US withdrawal, and the president said he was prepared to sign absent a successful new deal.

As with other trade agreements, a little bit of research showed that President Trump's instinct on our trade with Korea was correct. The terms of trade between our countries were unbalanced and destined to continue deteriorating because of certain provisions in KORUS. Absent a change, our trade deficit with Korea would get much worse. For example, in the first four years after the entry into force of KORUS in 2012, the value of Korean auto exports to the United States had increased from about $400 million to almost $1.3 billion.[19] The 2016 number that we were looking at continued the same troubling increase.

The situation was soon going from bad to worse. KORUS provided that the United States would begin to phase out its protective 25 percent tariff on pickup trucks in 2019. And the Korean automakers were ready for this opening, developing pickup trucks solely for sale in the US market. These manufacturers had success marketing to American customers, and with a phased-out truck tariff they could move Korean-produced vehicles into a sector of the market that had heretofore been dominated by manufacturers in America and in the USMCA region. This posed a challenge for American workers because a truck imported from Korea likely would have no US content at all.

With the start of the phaseout of the truck tariff on the horizon, there was some urgency to our negotiations. So in July 2017—just two months after announcing our intent to renegotiate NAFTA—we notified Korea of our request to modify KORUS through a consultation mechanism provided for in the agreement. This was a necessary procedural step, and it clearly demonstrated our seriousness.

Once we sent this notification, the Koreans knew they were facing a crisis. As a first step, they recalled Kim Hyun-chong from his post in

Geneva as a WTO Appellate Body member to reprise his role as trade minister. Minister Kim had been the trade minister during the original KORUS negotiations and was viewed as someone who could provide experience and leadership in dealing with a challenge from the Americans on trade issues.

Negotiations did not begin on a friendly note. At this time I did not have my deputies confirmed, so a delegation led by my chief of staff, Jamieson Greer, and the assistant USTR for Korea went to Seoul in August 2017. My Korean counterpart and I were scheduled to appear by video at the start of the session. However, the meeting started with the Koreans disagreeing about when we were supposed to show up on screen, and the day's negotiations were almost scratched. Once that issue of protocol was resolved, the Koreans had their say first. They aggressively told the US delegation that our concerns about the unbalanced trade were unimportant. Our team nearly walked out, but eventually was able to raise several issues related to the terms of KORUS and its incomplete implementation by Korea. This included issues related to automotive safety standards, pharmaceutical procurement, customs procedures at the border, and other matters. No progress was made during these initial talks.

Over the next few months, we had additional talks as the Koreans attempted to buy time and garner support in Congress and in the US national security apparatus. But every day that the Koreans delayed making concessions, they risked the president's withdrawing from the agreement.

Negotiations accelerated once additional leverage was introduced into the equation. In February 2018, President Trump imposed national security tariffs on nearly all imports of steel and aluminum. These had a particular impact on Korea, a major exporter of steel to the United States. As a result, the Koreans sought to find a settlement on steel as part of the ongoing KORUS talks.

Now that the Koreans were facing significant pressure on one of their key exports, they finally came to the table in earnest. By this time, Jeff Gerrish had been confirmed as deputy USTR with responsibility for Korea as part of his portfolio. Minister Kim and his delegation came to the United States for talks in March 2018, and they ended up staying for the next several weeks in order to arrive at a final resolution to the dispute. The Koreans told us stories about eating instant noodles and bouncing around hotel rooms in downtown Washington, DC, during this grueling stretch of negotiations.[20] Minister Kim was a taskmaster and expected his team to work around the clock.

I had had several meetings throughout this process with Minister Kim, who was eager to showcase his familiarity with US culture and negotiating styles. He usually knew more about US sports than anyone in the room. I liked him. His American persona was that of a New Yorker. Eventually he recognized that politically he was in a position to work out a deal. Our teams toiled together for weeks to grind out modifications to KORUS in line with our requests, focused primarily on making it easier to export US cars to Korea and putting off the phaseout of the truck tariffs.

The renegotiated deal contained several concessions to lead to balance. Korea agreed to remove certain agricultural barriers. It agreed to major changes in its importation restrictions on up to 50,000 US cars. It agreed to a limitation on its steel exports to the United States and several other technical changes to ease frictions faced by US businesses in Korea. Most significantly, however, it agreed to postpone the elimination of the small truck tariffs that had been included in the original deal. The vast majority of the profits of US automobile companies are derived from the sale of American-made small trucks to American drivers. Simply stated, if it weren't for this segment of the market, many would not survive. The reason for this is also simple. There are essentially no imports in the small truck market. This is because, for historic reasons, the United States has a 25 percent tariff on these trucks. The United States, in the original KORUS deal, had agreed to the elimination of those tariffs beginning in 2019. Korean auto companies that had never made a truck before were in the late planning stages of an all-out assault on the American small truck market. If this had been allowed, our industry and its workers would have paid a heavy price. In the new agreement, Korea agreed to push that off another twenty years. I figured that I'd let my successor deal with the problem in 2038.

Korea also agreed to make changes to certain customs- and pharmaceutical-reimbursement procedures. For our part, we agreed to authorize a quota of steel to enter the United States free of additional duties under Section 232 (although anything above the quota would be subject to the duties). We also agreed to find an acceptable path forward on two outstanding WTO cases that the United States felt were wrongly decided. The agreement modifications were formally signed by the two presidents a few months later, in September 2018, in a side meeting during the UN General Assembly in New York City. We had done our first big deal correcting a bad agreement, helped our autoworkers and many others, and had avoided doing any serious damage. For Korea, it still had a free trade agreement with the United States.

As with other agreements, we at USTR found a way to complete the deal without the need for significant congressional action. We kept House and Senate leaders informed and consulted regularly, but we did not need a new implementing bill passed. This enabled us to move decisively and avoid a drawn-out political fight in the United States. Of course, had Congress been opposed to anything we did as part of these modifications, it could have passed legislation limiting our ability to make or seek concessions.

Moreover, we felt confident that our approach moved the needle on our trade relationship with Korea. The US deficit in goods trade shrank from $27.6 billion in 2016 to $21 billion in 2019.[21] Much of this was attributable to significantly increased US exports and a relatively flat level of imports. Even in 2020, where trade figures were distorted by COVID-19, the goods deficit was $2.5 billion less than it was in 2016. Had the Koreans enjoyed reduced US tariffs on steel and pickup trucks and had we not made our point on various non-tariff barriers in Korea, there is no question that the goods deficit would have continued to increase.

President Moon Jae-in and his team were smart to settle the trade issues with the United States early. They had to make important concessions, but if they had delayed negotiations, the concessions would still have been made eventually. By putting trade behind them, they moved on to more important security issues with us. For our part, we got an important first deal. We helped US industry and reduced the trade deficit. We acted unilaterally, and the world did not blow up as all the free traders had predicted. We showed that an America First trade policy could work.

Vietnam

Vietnam is a small country with a reasonably small economy that has become a big trade problem for the United States. In 2001, we had essentially balanced trade with this former war foe, and they had a $33 billion economy. By 2021, their goods surplus with us had grown to $90 billion, more than doubling in the previous three years. Vietnam's GDP also skyrocketed to $300 billion. Astonishingly, more than 30 percent of the whole economy of Vietnam is exports to the United States. It's almost as if we had created a modern-day Marshall Plan for the Viet Cong. Some of this increase is likely Chinese products illegally being called Vietnamese in order to avoid US tariffs on China. While being highly dependent on our market, Vietnam maintains significant barriers to our exports, particularly in agriculture. Vietnam also has free trade agreements with Europe, Korea, and other countries. This means that Vietnam gives them preference over the United States on tariffs and other regulations. This imbalanced economic relationship and the unfair treatment of our producers must be corrected.

In 2020, the largest contributors to this deficit came from the computer and electronic products category, which included a $13.5 billion deficit in communications equipment, a $4.2 billion deficit in semiconductors and other electronic components, and a $3.2 billion deficit in audio and video equipment.[22] US trade disputes with Vietnam largely center around its currency manipulation. Vietnam has historically devalued its currency to support its export-oriented industries. The Trump administration labeled Vietnam a currency manipulator, but the Biden administration removed this label after obtaining promises from Vietnam to avoid devaluing its currency further.[23] In October 2020, I initiated a Section 301 investigation into Vietnam's currency valuations. After a hearing, much study, and a report, the USTR, on January 22, 2021, issued a Federal Register notice that the USTR had determined that "Vietnam's acts, policies and practices related to currency valuation, including to excessive exchange market interventions and other related actions, taken in their totality, are unreasonable and burden or restrict US commerce and thus actionable under Section 301." The table was set to take action against Vietnam for its unfair practice and to bring about balanced trade. On July 23, 2021, the USTR announced that no action was to be taken on this 301. Essentially, Vietnam said it wouldn't cheat and the United States said, Deal. Sadly, this was an early indicator that this new crowd was not going to fight for American jobs.

Chapter 17

Transcending Issues That Affect the Economy

There are a number of issues that seem to be unusually important for our economic future. These matters affect many sectors in our economy or have immense societal or political importance. I call these "transcending issues," and I believe that some deserve special exposition.

Currency, Income Tax, and Value Added Tax

The effects of a floating currency, our current income tax laws, and the existence of value-added taxes in other countries around the world all combine to very negatively affect manufacturing in the United States. Each one of these factors makes it hard for our companies to compete in foreign markets, but they also burden our producers in our market. The combination of the three is overwhelming.

The US dollar is a floating currency. Essentially its value is set by supply and demand. Generally, the dollar's value is measured by how much of other currencies it can buy (although the demand for treasury notes and how many dollars are held in foreign exchange reserves are other common measurements). In classical economic theory, a country that runs a trade deficit will see its currency weaken over time. A country that runs a surplus will see its currency strengthen. For the surplus country, its customers in importing countries will need the exporter's currency to buy its goods or services and will thus increase demand for that currency and bid up its price. The opposite will happen in the deficit country. There will be less demand for its currency because its consumers are buying other currencies to import, and its price will fall. The effect of this is that as a country's trade surplus grows and its currency becomes stronger, the country becomes less competitive. The stronger currency makes its exports more expensive and its imports cheaper. There is a self-correcting mechanism. Likewise, countries in deficit become more competitive because their exports get cheaper and their imports are more expensive. Floating exchange rates thus tend to move countries toward balanced trade over a period of time. They facilitate production when a country runs a deficit and consumption when the country has a surplus.

As we've discussed in other places in this book, this phenomenon does not work well for the United States. For the last twenty-five years, we have run up hundreds of billions of dollars in trade deficits, and we have not seen our currency weaken sufficiently to move us toward balanced trade. The International Monetary Fund (IMF) found in 2020 that the dollar was as much as 11.8 percent overvalued, and the midpoint of its analysis was 8.8 percent.[1] Effectively, every export we sell costs as much as 11.8 percent more than it should. Of course, imports are cheaper by the same percent. This is a major contributor to our trade deficit. It encourages consumption and hinders production.

There are a variety of theories for why this is true. Clearly, there is a large demand for dollars unrelated to trade. International capital flows are in the trillions of dollars a year, including private cross-border financial investment and public sector investment by central banks and sovereign wealth funds. People and investment funds around the world buy dollars in times of economic crisis as a hedge. This is the so-called safe haven effect. We saw the dollar strengthen to parity with the euro, for example, during the Russian-Ukrainian war. During that period the yen also fell to 137 to the dollar. The dollar also tends to not adequately adjust because it is the world's reserve currency. Other governments hold foreign exchange reserves much as they used to hold gold. There is a lot of buying dollars for trade between non-dollar economies. This creates demand for dollars and pushes up their price. Also, some countries manipulate their currency to gain economic advantage. This makes it easier for them to run a trade surplus, and it builds their manufacturing sector. Many countries do this. Japan and China have both used this technique from time to time. Whatever the verdict on the ultimate causes, what is clear is that the United States has a currency that is well overvalued. This makes it difficult for us to compete both in our domestic market and in export markets. It directly hurts our farmers and manufacturers and by extension all of their employees.

American manufacturers and their workers are also disadvantaged because, by international agreement (and as a result of myriad odd cases at the GATT and WTO), some taxes are border adjusted and some are not (this was briefly discussed in chapter 15). The effect of this seemingly tiny distinction is enormous. Border adjustment means that some taxes on exports are rebated (returned) to the exporting companies, and these same taxes are also imposed on imports as they enter a country. Governments fund themselves through direct taxes and indirect taxes. An example of a direct tax is the income tax, one that is paid directly to the government. An example of an indirect tax is a value added tax or sales tax. They are generally collected by a business and then paid to the government. Economists draw distinctions about who actually pays the various taxes and then justify different treatment. Thanks to such metaphysical analysis by economists, and by historical precedent, indirect taxes are border adjusted and direct ones are not. Although most of the world funds a large portion of its government through a combination of both direct and indirect taxes, most countries rely far more on VATs than the US does. The US federal government relies almost entirely on income tax and Social Security/Medicare taxes, although there are a few small excise taxes, and some states rely on a sales tax. The fact that the United States relies almost entirely on a tax that is not border-adjusted has immense implications for business.

Let's look at how this works in the real world and why it is so bad for America. Say you have a French company and an American company who both make a machine. The French company would pay a 25 percent VAT on its products sold in France. When the machine is exported, however, say, to the United States, that 25 percent tax it had paid on value added in its manufacture is rebated to the company, effectively making its product cheaper to sell and more profitable to the producer and effectively incentivizing export sales. That's the border adjustment. So in the export market (our market in this example), the French company can sell without that tax burden. It is more competitive.

Meanwhile, the American company making the same machine pays all its taxes when it sells in the United States, but when it wants to export the machine, say, to France, its American tax burden (including corporate income tax and the employer's share of Social Security/Medicare taxes) is not rebated, and it must also pay the French an additional 25 percent VAT when the machine enters French territory. Income taxes are not rebated or border adjusted, but the VAT is. It is easy to see from a business point of view the enormous economic impact. Importantly, if the French machine is sold in another country with a VAT instead of to the United States, there is little effect. Each customs regime rebates its VAT, and each charges the import its VAT. This arbitrary distinction almost uniquely hurts US competitiveness. Thus, a machine that an American company could sell at home for $100 would sell for $125 in France. A machine that a French company could sell at home for $100 could sell in the United States for $75. I am of course simplifying to make the point. There are other factors that would affect the price, including shipping and other related export costs.

Economists would argue that there is no substantial difference because both manufacturers are paying the tax in France, and neither is paying the VAT in the United States. But businesspeople see it quite differently. To them the VAT functions very much like a tariff. Now in fairness the state sales tax would operate the same way as the VAT (applied to imports and rebated on exports), but the sizes are quite different. A sales tax might be 6 percent, while the average VAT in the European Union is 21 percent. Economists also minimize the effect, claiming that if there was a substantial impact, the value of our currency would weaken to offset the tax advantage the foreign companies have. The problem with this argument is that, as we've seen, our currency really doesn't adjust adequately. Given the obvious advantage from a manufacturing point of view of a VAT, many countries tend to reduce their income taxes and raise their VATs. To the extent this happens, it of course further disadvantages countries such as the United States that don't have a VAT. I always wonder, if the economists are right and this disequilibrium doesn't matter, why do the Europeans fight so hard to keep it?

Some have suggested that the answer to this dilemma is that the United States should put in place its own VAT. But this is really a public policy issue. There are obvious issues of regressivity about this tax. Sales taxes are not popular in America. There would be disruptions of commerce and other effects. But more fundamentally, why should we have to change our tax system to overcome an unjustified inequity? Furthermore, there is no logical reason to have a difference between border adjustments for various taxes.

Attempts have been made to deal with this unfairness over the years. In the 1970s and 1980s, the US tax code provided for a so-called domestic international sales corporation (DISC). An exporter in the United States could set up a subsidiary that was not taxed on a certain percentage of export sales. This would offset some of the disadvantage. This was the state of our law for many years, until the WTO (as a result of a case brought by Europe) decided it was inconsistent with the agreement. Our choices were to get rid of it or face retaliation. Later in the Reagan administration, we modified the DISC rules so as to make them WTO compliant. The new entity was called a foreign international sales corporation. Within certain parameters, profits on exports were not taxed. This also was struck down by the WTO. Everyone saw the unfairness, but those with the advantage were unwilling to give it up, and the WTO was not a particularly friendly forum for our grievances.

In 2016, Speaker Paul Ryan, Ways and Means Chairman Kevin Brady, and their Republican colleagues in the House proposed tax legislation (referred to as the "House Blueprint" proposal) that would have solved most of the problems that arise from the US not having a VAT. They proposed: 1) converting our current business income tax to a 20 percent tax on cash flow, which allows for expensing of capital expenditures for plant and equipment and a deduction for labor; and 2) making the tax "border-adjusted" by disallowing as a deduction the cost of imported products, intangible property, and services and exempting from the tax all revenues from the export of products, intangible property, and services. Essentially the proposal would tax cash flow instead of domestic corporate profits but only allow a deduction for domestic inputs and not allow one for foreign ones. To simplify, this proposal would mean that (1) cash flows from American-produced goods and services that are exported are not taxed, (2) cash flows from American-produced goods and services consumed domestically are taxed at 20 percent with essentially full deductibility of costs, and (3) cash flows from imported goods and services are taxed at 20 percent with no deduction for foreign production costs.

This proposal would have largely nullified our disadvantage, and given the current trade and services deficits, it would have raised sufficient revenues to allow a substantial reduction in corporate tax rates (for example, the 20 percent corporate rate proposed in the House Blueprint was estimated to raise as much revenue as the then 35 percent rate on corporate income). The proposal would have converted the tax on domestic corporate profits into a tax on cash flows attributable to domestic consumption. Because of the deduction for wages, it would be different than a VAT; the tax would only apply to domestic business profits as measured by net cash flows including the cost of labor.

While many economists have for years praised this type of tax for its potential to stimulate domestic manufacturing, intellectual property development, and services activities, in the political arena it was a bold proposal. It attracted the support of many of our largest exporters: Boeing, General Electric, and Intel, to name a few. But like any tax that focuses on domestic consumption and not on domestic income, it risked a one-time increase in consumer prices and the potential strengthening of the US dollar in response to the increased after-tax costs of imports and the reduced after-tax costs of exports (because the United States would be reducing its trade deficit, and according to the economic theory, the increase in exports and reduction in imports should increase relative demand for the dollar and strengthen the currency).

In particular, the profits of retail companies that make money off selling imported goods—led by Walmart and others that sell goods made in China and elsewhere—would be at risk during the transition (the time before the dollar appreciates to offset the new costs). That fear and these retailers' desire to maintain the status quo led companies such as Walmart to undertake a sophisticated multimillion-dollar marketing campaign that blasted the proposal as costly to consumers and inflationary for our economy. Because congressional action on tax legislation was delayed by debate over Obamacare repeal, the retailers' campaign had plenty of time to take hold. While many economists pointed out that the strengthening of the US dollar (which results from increasing the cost of imports and reducing the cost of exports) could mitigate much of the pain from a one-time price increase, in the political arena, those arguments were not given credence.

Arguments about the long-run benefits of the proposal for US manufacturing, research, and services jobs were also lost in the outcry. Moreover, in the final analysis, the administration did not support the proposal. I was not yet confirmed as USTR when this debate took place in government, so I can't say for certain the reasons for this choice. I feel, though, that most of the president's economic advisers were very eager to get the corporate tax cut through to stimulate growth. The retailers and other importers made this part of the House Blueprint look as if it might lead to the defeat of the whole tax bill. We have to remember that the outcome of that much-needed legislation was quite uncertain until the end. In fact, it passed the Senate on December 20, 2017, by a vote of 51 to 48. There was never enough strong support for the idea among some Senate Republicans, and Democrats were going to vote against the tax bill solely because it was a Trump initiative. Also, several of the president's key economic advisers had backgrounds in trading on Wall Street rather than manufacturing. They were of course on board with the president's agenda, but they were susceptible to arguments about market disruption, et cetera, and less focused on the long-term effect on manufacturing and the trade deficit. Also, although Speaker Ryan was committed to his tax border adjustment proposal, he argued that the overall rate reduction and other provisions were crucial. In the final analysis, he went along with the conventional wisdom.

The House Blueprint failed in part because it was too revolutionary to be taken seriously without strong backing from some of the key advisers and Senate Republicans. But the proposal could easily have been modified to ameliorate the concerns about inflation, a strengthening dollar, and the profits of companies' selling imported products. Most importantly, Congress could have adopted a partial border adjustment as part of the overall business cash flow tax. If the corporate tax rate were, for example, 20 percent, and the border adjustment applied to disallow as a deduction only 40 percent of the cost of imports and with 40 percent of export revenues being exempt from the tax, the transitional impact on prices, the US dollar exchange rate, and retailer profits would be much more manageable. But the incentives for US manufacturing and services activities would still be substantial. Under this compromise, (1) the tax on cash flows from American-produced goods and services that are exported would be reduced, but not as much as the original proposal, (2) cash flows from American-produced goods and services consumed domestically would be taxed the same, and (3) the tax on the cash flows from imported goods and services would be increased, but less than in the original proposal. In effect, the United States would have had a 12 percent income tax on US-based manufacturing, services, and other activities that are exported (a 20 percent tax on 60 percent of income from US-based activities as measured by cash flow). This would have made the United States competitive with Ireland and most other tax havens that now host substantial manufacturing and services activities of US multinational companies. In hindsight, perhaps if the Speaker and the administration's economic advisers had coalesced around this compromise, it might have been adopted. Still the ultimate question of whether this proposal would have sunk the whole tax bill will never be known. We do know it passed without it.

Technology and Digital Trade

For more than one hundred years, America has been the world's technological leader. In no small part, our economic and political success is reliant on our technological superiority. I think it is also no exaggeration to say that we will win our great competition with China if we maintain our edge in this sector. The Chinese certainly believe that. As we have shown, no country is as obsessed with technology as China is.

America's tech companies are the best in the world. Giants such as Microsoft, Apple, and Oracle are examples. We have in several places in our country great ecosystems of infrastructure, skilled workers, and capital that foster these companies and spur innovation. Big tech is big business. The ten biggest US tech companies have a combined $8.5 trillion dollars in market capital. They employ hundreds of thousands of people and lead in exports and innovation and productivity improvement. But therein lies the problem. We say our companies are the envy of the world, and the world acts on their desires. We have written a great deal here about China's plan to create tech megacompanies. They force technology transfer as a condition of market access. They buy small tech companies. And they steal what they cannot buy. They force US companies to take on joint venture partners and then those partners become enormous competitors. The Chinese efforts have been very successful. Look to Baidu, Tencent, and Alibaba as examples. These companies combined have a market capitalization of almost half a trillion dollars.

Europe is relatively lacking in large successful tech companies. True, Europe leads in some telecom companies, such as Ericsson and Nokia, but that is relatively low tech, and Europe lags in other tech sectors. Unfortunately, it looks as if in its desire to build world-class tech companies, Europe is going to follow the Chinese model. First, the Europeans used the digital services tax (DST) as a way to disproportionately tax our tech companies. This is a complicated issue, and I don't want to oversimplify it, but the digital services tax is designed to tax our companies doing business over there while generally not taxing theirs. We in the Trump administration took on this unfairness. We threatened to put tariffs on French and other products if France discriminated against our companies. The Biden administration has basically surrendered to Europe. In exchange for smiles and a promise to discuss the problem, the Europeans were permitted to continue taxing for five years.

Far more pernicious, however, is the recent European effort to closely follow China's model. It is a sort of "China-light" strategy. Coerce but don't exactly steal. France is putting in place a regime that says that cloud service providers can sell to the French government only if they have a French company operating them. France is claiming this is due to privacy and security concerns, but it is really just protectionism. This joint venture requirement is exactly how China started. Once a company has a forced joint venture partner, the partner learns how to do the business. It learns the technology and the business know-how. Ultimately, the joint venture partner takes all its acquired expertise, goes out on its own, and competes with the US company. The joint venture requirement also of course directly cuts into profits and makes our companies less successful. For now, the proposal is just to implement this for government cloud services but surely as their companies grow, the French will expand the requirement to "critical infrastructure" and then the whole economy. Germany is also looking at this model, and it will spread across the world if unchecked. Of course, this is the opposite of the free trade that these European countries preach—but that does not seem to deter them. Do as I say, not as I do.

Scale is obviously critical to the successful deployment of technology, and our tech companies therefore need access to the markets of our US allies, but we must stand up to this forced technology transfer because it will cut the ground out from under our feet in the long term once Europe has copied our infrastructure.

The next thing to think about in the tech sector is data. Data in and of itself is extremely valuable. Some call it the new oil. For example, data is essential to the creation of artificial intelligence. The more data, the better the artificial intelligence. For this reason, China has been hacking and buying its way into data all over the world—and particularly so in the United States. In the CFIUS review process, we often see Chinese companies attempt to buy small US companies at a great premium in order to obtain their customer or patient data.

US policy in this area must protect the privacy of data, protect our companies from unfair and predatory treatment, and defend against Chinese access to our data. First, America and Europe need to come to some agreement on the rules both will follow regarding when their respective law enforcement and security agencies will have access to the data of citizens and foreign nations stored in their respective territories. There is much work to be done in this area. Clearly, we all understand that the Chinese and, say, Vietnamese governments easily access data of all companies operating in China and Vietnam. But it is possible to agree on ground rules for us and our allies. This is made more difficult by the Europeans' distrust of our companies and Europe's protectionist desires to build its own tech sector.

Second, the US government needs to do what is necessary to stop foreign governments from coercing our companies to give up intellectual property and business know-how as a condition for doing business in their countries. This will require vigilance and unilateral action to retaliate for discriminatory policy.

Third, we need to take steps such as those recommended by Senator Ron Wyden of Oregon to prevent sensitive data's being exported to China. His bill would establish minimum privacy and cybersecurity standards for all companies that deal with data. The bill also establishes enforcement resources at the Federal Trade Commission and provides for hefty fines for violators. Finally, the bill prohibits the transfer of any sensitive data to China and similar unfriendly countries.

In the Trump administration, we negotiated the first comprehensive, high-standard trade agreement in digital trade. The USMCA was the state of the art in digital trade rules. These same provisions were later included in the United States–Japan Digital Trade Agreement, and they are the model for the Indo-Pacific talks the Biden administration engaged in. I'm in favor of more digital trade agreements, within reason. But as business practices and technologies evolve, we need to constantly reevaluate the template. US trade negotiators should be mindful of our sorry history of path dependency in trade policy and ensure that digital trade agreements continue to serve the national interest, rather than facilitate regulatory arbitrage or offshoring.

Automobiles and Auto Parts

The automobile industry is extremely important to US manufacturing. It accounts for $1.1 trillion (or 5.5 percent) of total US GDP and about 11.4 percent of our manufacturing output. Every car job spins off several other jobs in the community. Further, this industry is one of the biggest consumers of our steel and aluminum, and it disproportionately contributes to research and development. In many ways it also drives our trade deficits. The largest contributors to our deficit with Europe, Japan, Mexico, Canada, and Korea are all cars and car parts. The United States is by far the largest importer of both. The total for the two is about $250 billion. In 2021, we imported over 6 million ($164 billion) light vehicles and exported just 1.6 million ($55 billion).[2]

The industry trend has not been good in recent decades. The United States went from being the largest producing nation to now making fewer than half as many vehicles as China does and only about a million more than Japan does. Imports have skyrocketed. The number of workers in the industry declined 17 percent from 1994 to 2018, and real average hourly earnings were down a similar amount.[3] Between 2000 and 2017, the vast majority of new North American car plants were built in Mexico, not the United States.

There are several reasons for this poor trade performance. First, the United States has lower tariffs than those of most other countries. Our MFN tariff is 2.5 percent and has been low since the 1950s. The auto tariff in Europe is 10 percent. In Brazil, for example, it is at least 14 percent, and in China it is usually about 15 percent. In contrast, the US tariff on small trucks is 25 percent, and that segment of our industry is very strong. Second, some other auto-producing countries have over the years used subsidies, closed domestic markets, and industrial policy to promote their industry. Many used currency manipulation as well. In the 1980s and 1990s, US auto companies complained that the Japanese yen was as much as 10 percent undervalued. And, of course, the poorly negotiated NAFTA agreement contributed to the loss of auto jobs in America. Finally, from time to time, US costs of both labor and material have gotten high and uncompetitive.

In the Trump administration, we took a number of steps to address these problems. We put a 25 percent tariff on automobiles coming from China. This prevented what would surely have been an import surge and a serious blow to US workers. Chinese imports had grown from 1,000 in 2015 to 45,000 two years later. That number would have gone to hundreds of thousands quickly. Europe, which did not take a similar step, saw its car imports from China grow from around 60,000 units in 2016 to over 400,000 five years later. European car imports from China are projected to be 800,000 in another three years.[4] When Trump announced our tariffs, the giant Chinese automaker SAIC abandoned its plans to enter the American market;[5] Ford decided not to import into the United States from China;[6] Volvo stopped importing from China and switched to Europe; and General Motors was forced to alter its plans and not import from China. A future crisis was averted.

As is described in the USMCA chapters, we also radically changed the NAFTA "rules of origin" to force more manufacturing in the United States and in North America generally. We required that cars qualifying for the tariff elimination have at least 75 percent regional content and that 40 percent of the value be made with sixteen dollars per hour of labor, largely American. We also required that much of the steel used in the cars be from North American mills and that key parts be made here. Once again, the results have been significant, with new plants now being built here.

Finally, we renegotiated our trade agreement with Korea. Under the old agreement, Korean companies could have begun selling small trucks in the United States without paying the 25 percent duty very soon. We pushed that date off decades.

The net of these three Trump actions surely saved tens of thousands of high-paying US manufacturing jobs and stopped what would have been a huge increase in our trade deficit.

De Minimis

There is a provision of US trade law that does not get proper attention. Most Americans realize that when they come home from an overseas trip, they fill out a customs form in which they declare that they had less than $800 in goods from their vacation. They then do not have to pay any duties on the things they bought, and no other import forms are needed. This is the so-called de minimis provision in operation. The application to individual American travelers is quite benign.

The use by American and foreign businesses, however, is different and has become very pernicious. It has cost us jobs and revenue and diminished our national security. Essentially what the de minimis provision does is allow US citizens or legal residents to import one package each day valued under $800 without paying import duties or taxes and without using the normal import forms that trace contents and origin of products. This has become an enormous loophole in American trade.

This law was initially enacted in 1938, and the idea was that citizens who wanted to import, say, a small gift should be able to do so with a minimum burden. *De minimis* is a Latin term meaning "too trivial to merit consideration." The initial threshold was $5 for a gift and $1 for everything else. No harm was done. After several interim steps, the amount was raised to $200 in 1994. Still, shipments were under control.

In the Trade Facilitation and Trade Enforcement Act of 2015, Congress increased the threshold of duty-free access from $200 to $800. The intentions of legislators and President Obama were innocent enough. They want to streamline lower duties and paperwork to help consumers. What they unintentionally did was create an enormous loophole.[7] The businesses that lobbied for the change had very different intentions. They were massive importers such as Amazon and shipping companies such as UPS and FedEx. They built their entire business plan around this tax dodge.

Of course, this increase in the de minimis threshold came at the same time that the already large e-commerce market began its exponential growth. As a result of this change, billions of dollars of imports now come into our country duty-free and largely uncontrolled. We went from importing a few thousand packages a year to bringing in more than two million a day. Official estimates of the cost of this loophole don't exist. It has been reported that de minimis imports soared from $40 million in 2012 to $67 billion in 2020.[8] Considering company reports from Amazon and other large importers, the Washington think tank Coalition for a Prosperous America estimated de minimis imports in 2021 at $128 billion, adding about 4.5 percent to our annual total goods imports.[9]

Companies such as Amazon and Alibaba worked with businesses in countries around the world (but mostly in China) to avoid our duties and import a massive amount of goods under the de minimis threshold (by breaking out the shipments from abroad into direct mail to individual consumers under $800 each). This threatens our manufacturers. Almost all the Chinese products ordered from these online sources use this loophole. They are each set up as individual sales to a single customer, although in reality the importer is moving a massive amount of products across the border each day. Every one of us participates in this hustle every week.

The effects of this for our economy are serious. If one buys a sweater from a store, for example, that store must pay applicable duties and fill out necessary customs forms. If the same sweater is bought online, all this is avoided. We have essentially given every country an FTA and done it without demanding any reciprocity—a free giveaway of our jobs and wealth. And, of course, by far the biggest beneficiary has been China.

First, this provision costs American manufacturing jobs. Duties that are intended to protect our producers and their workers are easily avoided. The competitive advantage swings overseas. Our domestic manufacturers now must compete directly with foreign producers—even unfair traders.

Second, our government cannot effectively determine what is coming into the country because there is no real paperwork associated with these transactions. This makes much of our import data inaccurate. This loophole is so large that it affects the accuracy of nearly all trade data.

Third, brick-and-mortar stores are put at a disadvantage to online retailers. We lose employment and billions of dollars in profits in the sector.[10] The dodge is putting stores across our country out of business. This is particularly true of small businesses that cannot easily jump into the import-and-manufacture-overseas business model. This was never intended or foreseen by policy makers.

Fourth, we are putting a tremendous burden on the customs officials who are trying to police our borders. The de minimis provision also makes it much harder to keep illegal drugs out of our country and nearly impossible to stop counterfeits and other contraband.

Further, there is no reciprocity in this area. We permit packages valued at up to $800 to come into America, while our trading partners only allow packages to come into their countries valued at much lower amounts. China can use this technicality to ship us billions of dollars' worth of products, and we have no equivalent way to attack the Chinese market. And the problem is not just China. For example, Canada has a de minimis threshold of 150 Canadian dollars. Mexico has a $50 (USD) amount. For the European Union, the amount is 150 euros and for China it is 50 yuan.[11] Clearly, the United States is way out of line. We are not protecting our brick-and-mortar retailers or our manufacturing workers.

Not surprisingly, enormous foreign companies have made taking advantage of this loophole a key part of their business plans. The giant Chinese company Shein has grown from nothing to controlling 30 percent of the US fast fashion market in just a few years, without selling through any US stores or brands. Shein's entire business model is exploiting this technicality by shipping from China to individual American consumers. It has used this customs loophole to create a $100 billion business in just a few years. There are dozens of other multibillion-dollar companies that do the same, and this is just the beginning if no action is taken.

In another take on this problem, the Mexican company Baja Fulfillment imports millions of dollars in Chinese imports, loads them in bonded trucks in Los Angeles, and brings them duty-free to Mexico. They technically never enter the US customs area. The products are stored in Mexico until they are sold directly to US consumers duty-free and with limited formalities. According to one article, using this dodge, on $75,000 in women's tops, Mexico can avoid paying $29,000 in duties.[12]

Some in Congress are trying to at least partially stop the hemorrhage. Congress proposes not allowing the use of de minimis by non-market countries such as China. Further, Congress would end the use of de minimis to avoid duties that are imposed on products that are dumped or subsidized.

Clearly, this is a policy that has been shown to be detrimental, and it must be changed. It is also an example of how big business uses its lobbying and political force to obtain laws that make big business rich but are not in the public interest. No one should be allowed to avoid our customs laws in this way.

Part Five

MOVING
FORWARD

Chapter 18

A Prescription for the Future

For decades, American leaders followed a trade policy that failed the American people. Despite promises of job growth and rising wages, the radical free trade theology of the 1990s and early 2000s delivered only decimation for the American industrial base and the workers, families, and communities who relied on it to make a living. Vital products ranging from rare earth minerals to semiconductors are now sourced abroad. The barriers to entry into the American middle class have never been higher. And millions of American families now live in the hollowed-out ruins of our once great manufacturing heartland—where rampant drug abuse and unemployment have taken the place of fast-moving factories and bustling streets.

It is no exaggeration to say that the future of this country hinges on a continued shift in our trade policy. It is no longer possible for Americans to continue to think of ourselves just as consumers and not as producers. It is no longer possible for us to outsource jobs and give up on communities and the working people and families who live in them. We must have a trade policy in which every decision is made with the goal of helping working people. Economic efficiency, low prices, and corporate profits are important goals—but they should be secondary to improving the lives of and opportunities available to regular working people in this country. To prevail in the great competition with China and to have the world's most successful country in the years ahead, it is important that we use trade policy, just like every other economic tool in our policy arsenal, to achieve our ultimate goal. We must have a trade policy that contributes to the common good.

In the four years of the Trump administration, we began this process. To use an overworn metaphor, we began to turn the aircraft carrier of bad policy and poor results around. It takes time to change supply chains, business attitudes, and consumer preferences—but we energetically began this process. As I've tried to detail in this book, we dramatically and urgently used every tool available to begin the tough work of bringing good jobs back to America, keeping the ones we have, preparing for the jobs of the future, and increasing family income. We took on China, raising tariffs exponentially to combat its unfair trade practices, and we greatly expanded the concept of what was unfair in the process. Overall, we put additional duties on more than $400 billion dollars in imports, infinitely more duties than our predecessors imposed. We acted not just against China but against every trading partner that had an improper advantage. We challenged all the unfair advantages that our trading partners have, from tax policy to currency manipulation to domestic standards and subsidies.

We renegotiated NAFTA and for the first time used the rules of origin to bring manufacturing back to our region and more importantly back to America itself. We wrote rules that will force advanced battery and much other manufacturing of the future to be based here. We incorporated, for the first time, binding environmental and labor rules to remove foreign unfair advantages. We got rid of the system of corporate arbitration that had done so much to encourage investment away from America and to lower standards abroad. We incorporated new concepts, such as sunset clauses that require periodic reevaluation, into our trade agreements. Why should trade agreements last forever? Nothing else does. Why should some American workers lose their livelihood because of a deal that made sense fifty years ago but now is hopelessly outdated? We obtained concessions from our trading partners not by granting more access to our market but by threatening to take away existing access. Clearly, the biggest economy in the world—and one that runs huge deficits that power the world's exporters—has leverage.

We negotiated new rules for e-commerce and technology. We rewrote the rules on more than 50 percent of our agricultural sales. We helped our farmers in their largest markets—Mexico, Canada, China, and Japan—and saw record American farm sales. The results of this new worker- and farmer-oriented policy were good for the country. The trade deficit was down in four of the five quarters year over year before the onset of COVID-19 in March 2020. Millions of jobs were created, and hundreds of thousands of manufacturing jobs returned. Real wages were up. The stock market soared. Most importantly, median real family income was up by 6.8 percent—a historic high point.

The Trump administration laid the foundation for this fundamental shift in American trade policy: a shift that was long overdue and in the interest of all working Americans. In the ensuing years, the Biden administration—with a few important exceptions—has continued along the path President Trump and I laid out. Over the first two years of his presidency, Biden's team has continued to buck WTO rulings against America, refused to draw down the Section 301 tariffs on China, and enacted the beginnings of an industrial policy. The tides have changed in this country's trade policy.

There is more work, however, that must be done. China remains the largest geopolitical threat the United States has faced, perhaps since the American Revolution. It is an adversary not only for America but also to the liberal democratic system of governance and economics as a whole. China's leaders view themselves as an enemy of our country and of the system that we lead and champion globally. Despite this, we transfer hundreds of billions of dollars to China year after year. The Chinese government, in turn, uses this money to build up its military, challenge America around the world, and develop China's economy in a manner designed to challenge us at every step. It is no exaggeration to say that the biggest navy and the biggest army in the world has been built with US dollars and it is not in America. If we do not find a practical way to respond to this challenge, and defend our interests, the United States is headed for disaster. Here are a few suggestions.

Before all else, of course, the United States must maintain the biggest and best military so that we can challenge Chinese aggression. We must also be prepared to counter China diplomatically. In the economic trade sphere, the most important single part of any prescription for the US policy toward China is to begin a strategic decoupling of our economies.

As I laid out in chapter 11, strategic decoupling means limiting US economic ties with China across high-tech and strategic sectors. A policy of strategic decoupling must start with repealing the mistaken granting of PNTR to China. But it must not end there. It also means imposing tariffs and other measures on Chinese imports sufficient to bring about balanced two-way trade very quickly. It means limiting both incoming investment from China into the United States and our outbound investment into China to those things that will clearly benefit the American economy. Finally, it means refusing to share technology in the national security and dual-use areas and in other sectors that will affect critical infrastructure or have a significant effect on our future ability to compete. Products such as drones, for example, should be made in America or imported into our country from an ally—and the drones should contain no Chinese content or software. Products such as laptop computers, which are in the lower range of high technology, should be heavily tariffed to bring the manufacturing and the technical know-how back to the United States or, perhaps, allied countries.

China is not the only bad actor in the trade policy space. Many of our closest allies and partners across the world also treat American producers unfairly. We must remember that engaging free democratic countries in negotiations to obtain fair and balanced trade is in our interest. We should continue trying to achieve agreements that set appropriate rules on e-commerce, create product standards based on science not national advantage, and limit market-distorting subsidies and other unfair practices. The WTO can facilitate those talks. These goals are very important, but at best they would achieve only incremental progress for most Americans. Because WTO negotiations require unanimous agreement—even among countries such as China and Russia—nothing we do at the WTO will fix the major problems we face or change the trajectory of our trade. Rather than wait for developments at the WTO, we must be prepared to act either unilaterally or together with a handful of like-minded countries.

With those points in mind, I would like to suggest several specific changes to US trade policy.

First, we've talked in previous chapters about the political argument for free trade versus protectionism and how that became a debate of free trade versus fair trade. Clearly, it is important that we continue to demand fair trade within our own market and to require reciprocity from our trade partners. We also need to take the existing basic tools of trade policy—including anti-dumping laws, countervailing duty laws, Section 301, and other US trade remedy laws—and enforce them vigorously. This approach, however, will always be inherently limited. When we stop one unfair practice, countries will start two more. The foundation of these laws is strong, but the implementation is not always consistent, and the laws themselves need to be updated and strengthened for a world where China's industrial base may become larger than ours. No matter what we do with enforcement, however, "whack a mole" is not a long-term winning strategy.

Second, the United States has the biggest market in the world. If it is being treated unfairly in export markets anywhere in the world, it must demand fairness. Countries should not deny us their true MFN benefits and still have access to our market. They shouldn't be allowed to defend basic unfairness by using agreements negotiated many years ago or improperly decided dispute resolution decisions from the WTO. To persuade other countries to take us seriously, we must be prepared to take unilateral action. We must firmly and consistently use Section 301 to force other countries to give us fair access. Where they do not, then we must deny them access. If a country has free trade agreements granting access to its market to others on terms more beneficial than those it grants to the United States, we should respond by limiting that country's access to our market. Such a policy combines the traditional idea of reciprocity with the updated notion of unilateral enforcement of our rights.

Third, we need a substantial change in our import laws. We must take our domestic social compact and apply it to imports. When we, as a civilized country, make an agreement with our citizens that we will demand that our employers meet certain minimum standards in socially advantageous areas such as labor rights, environmental protections, and health and safety concerns, we are essentially saying that these goals are more important than pure economic efficiency. We are showing that we are willing to pay a higher price at the store because of the importance of certain societal outcomes, such as clean drinking water or fair labor practices. Now we must apply the same principle to those companies that are importers into our market. Why should any company be allowed to import into the United States any product that is manufactured more cheaply in its country solely because that country violates basic environmental standards? Likewise, why should any company get an advantage from not meeting minimum labor standards in its country of production and then selling that product into the United States? We need to agree upon the list of socially necessary policies and then set minimum standards that all products, whether domestically produced or imported, must meet. Ideally, we would agree on this list with like-minded countries. Clearly, environment and labor are areas where this would be possible, but so are worker safety, food safety, and the like. Imports that aren't produced meeting those minimum standards should have a duty applied to their import price that offsets the unfair and artificial advantage that they currently have.

One example of this idea is working its way through Congress right now. Many members would like us to have a carbon border adjustment fee put on imports. I agree. If a product is produced in another country by using much more carbon than we would tolerate here, why should that import have a price advantage in our market over a US product that is made producing much less carbon? Such a fee would help clean the global environment and create jobs in America.

Fourth, the United States needs to continue to improve its policy of subsidizing specific crucial industries. As a general matter, industrial subsidies are not a good idea. They add to inefficiency in the market and often lead to the misallocation of resources because of political considerations that are not always consistent with what is best for the people. But in some areas, we cannot compete without subsidizing. There are some economic competitions that the United States cannot afford to lose. We have already addressed the Made in China 2025 program. Every one of the ten areas covered by that program is crucial for the future of any global economy. The United States cannot afford, for example, to lose the competition for artificial intelligence, robotics, advanced materials, and other industries of the future.

Unfortunately, manufacturers in the United States cannot prevail when competing against foreign firms that are buoyed by a trillion dollars of subsidies flowing not just from Communist China but also from Europe, Korea, and Japan. Clearly, we have to be careful and do it the right way. Caution should be the byword. But we have to carefully subsidize. For example, our advanced semiconductors industry is critically important both for our ability to make highly sensitive military technology and as an input into a variety of civilian technologies that will form the foundation of the twenty-first-century economy. The United States invented this technology, and we are in danger of losing it to subsidized foreign production. Even now we are at least two generations behind in the highest-technology logic chips, and we import more than 80 percent of our total semiconductor needs. Indeed, we can't make an F-35 fighter without imported chips. We must manufacture most of them in the United States. This goal cannot be achieved without government support. The bipartisan CHIPS and Science Act, which directs tens of billions of dollars toward semiconductor manufacturing in the United States, passed in 2022 and is a good first step in this process.

Fifth, and critically, the United States needs to achieve balanced trade. We cannot continue to transfer, year after year, hundreds of billions of dollars and even at times $1 trillion of our wealth overseas in the form of trade deficits. Everyone knows that if you are consuming more than you produce, you are getting poorer. We have been doing this for thirty years and have transferred more than $18 trillion of our wealth to foreign countries. As we have shown, this money comes back to the United States in the form of foreign interests' owning US assets and the future profit and productive value of those assets forever. We are transferring our wealth, the ownership of our equity, real estate, and debt to other countries and getting poorer as a result.

There are three ways that we have discussed to achieve this needed balance. One was recommended by Warren Buffett almost twenty years ago. He would require that anyone who imports a product into the United States have a certificate showing that there was a product of equal value exported from the United States. Clearly, this policy would lead to balanced trade. Another possible approach is to put an adjustable fee on investment funds coming into the United States. Essentially this would be a market access charge on foreign capital coming here. The notion is that in periods of high demand for dollars, the fee would kick in and moderate the foreign demand for dollars by reducing the yield on foreign capital here. The effect of this would be to reduce the value of our currency. When foreign interests bring their trade surplus dollars back to America, they would be able to buy fewer of our assets than they would without the fee. Over time this market access charge would also work to create a more balanced global trading system. Those espousing this approach, such as the bipartisan group of senators who proposed such a system in the 2019 Competitive Dollar for Jobs and Prosperity Act, would give the Federal Reserve the power to regulate the size and duration of this fee in order to achieve balance.[1]

Finally, we could achieve balanced trade by imposing tariffs on imports. We could put tariffs on all imports at a progressively higher rate year after year until we achieve balance. Once we have balance, we could lower the tariffs down to the lowest level that maintains that balance. This approach would effectively offset the overvaluation of the dollar and other systemic unfairness abroad. Personally, I would accept any of these three options, but I have a preference for tariffs because they're simple to implement, it's easier to predict what will happen, and the mechanism is already in place to collect the duties. Tariffs also would help reduce our chronic fiscal deficit by raising government customs revenue.

The policy agenda I have set forth above is, admittedly, quite ambitious. And I do not propose that Congress implement it immediately. It will have to be done carefully over a period of time. The most urgent priority should be strategic decoupling from China. I also believe that the United States should phase in a mechanism to ensure balanced trade and ideally do it in conjunction with our allies if that is possible. The historic Plaza Accords of the 1980s, which resulted in France, Germany, Japan, and the United Kingdom's agreeing to devalue the US dollar relative to their currencies (among other measures) to address trade imbalances, set a precedent for this kind of significant negotiation among American allies to address unfair global practices' making America's participation in the previous regime untenable.

Reversing decades-long trade imbalances will also take time, and the mechanisms for achieving this result should be carefully phased in to minimize increases in consumer prices and market disruptions. But persistent trade deficits are not a problem that can be kicked to the future indefinitely, and delaying needed actions won't make them any easier. The sooner the administration and Congress begin serious discussions about how best to address this problem, the easier it will be to do so.

On a hopeful note, we are beginning to see this happen. The views in this book on China and trade generally are becoming mainstream in our country. They have long been considered common sense by Americans sitting around their kitchen tables. A recent poll verified this and found that 61 percent of Americans support placing new tariffs on foreign goods, while only 16 percent oppose such a move. Even more agree on strong trade action to counter China, which 72 percent of Americans support and only 12 percent oppose.[2]

Now our political class is catching up. We hear tough-on-China, tough-on-trade statements from a growing number of senators, governors, and representatives. For example, many of the members of the new House Select Committee on China, both Republicans and Democrats, believe that some form of strategic decoupling from China is necessary. Likewise, in February 2023, former president Trump called for a four-year plan of decoupling from China, using tariffs and other restrictions. He also said that he favored the use of tariffs to bring about trade balance for the United States.

..

Americans need international trade. There are efficiencies that come from deploying our resources in the most productive way and having other countries do the same thing. We need trade, however, much less than other countries do. We have an enormous economy, and we can produce most of what we need. Trade is good. More trade is better. Fair trade is essential. But balanced trade is imperative. And going forward we really need smart trade. We owe as much to our workers, farmers, and businesses.

Trade, like all other economic policies, involves trade-offs. A country gives something up to get something else. Cheaper consumer goods result in fewer US jobs and lower wages. More imports mean less manufacturing. Trade deficits result in less national wealth. Just as with the rest of our lives, everything is paid for. No trade is free.

Donald Trump, in four years, changed the way we think about trade and the way we think about our competition with China. His consistent policy was not bound by outdated notions and failed trade deals. He focused on jobs and wages, and he instructed all of us in his administration to consider the impacts on workers of every decision we made and then pushed us to consistently pursue those actions that would do the most to help working people. The transformation of our trade policy was not completed in those four years—but there sure was a darn good beginning.

ACKNOWLEDGMENTS

My objective with this book was to write the most accurate record of what happened on international trade in the Trump administration and during those four years. I try to present the facts as we understood them and provide the philosophy that drove us. Others, particularly journalists, have written about these things. This account is the one from the inside, and I have tried to make it as devoid of partisan politics as possible while working in a town consumed by it. In this acknowledgment I will try to give credit to many of those who made it possible.

As documented in this book, we accomplished great things during the Trump administration in international trade and China policy. None of it would have been possible without the superb team that we had at USTR. This team was invaluable to me in getting the negotiations and policy changes done and in advising and encouraging me along the way. They also were essential to writing this book. They recalled events and helped with drafting and editing. I am greatly indebted to them for all they have done for me personally, and I am proud for all they have done for our country. Importantly, they are keeping up the fight for the things we believe in.

Stephen Vaughn worked with me for decades at my law firm, Skadden, Arps. He was a superb trade lawyer but, more importantly, he was a consigliere during that time and for the years at USTR. Stephen was my general counsel and served the acting USTR while I went through confirmation. Jeff Gerrish was my partner at Skadden for twenty years and was a deputy during my USTR years. He is an excellent anti-dumping and countervailing duty litigator. Jeff was central to much of what we accomplished and notably was the key person for our China talks. C. J. Mahoney was the other initial deputy in Washington. I had not worked with him before he joined my team, as I had with Jeff and Stephen. He was highly recommended by a close friend and proved to be even better than advertised. He was also involved in all aspects of our work and was the key person on the USMCA negotiations. Interestingly, C. J. was born in tiny Russell, Kansas, the hometown of Bob Dole. The final member of our initial core group was Jamieson Greer. Jamieson, an air force veteran, also worked with me for a few years at my law firm. He was an excellent chief of staff. He was organized, patient, and always at the office.

I also want to thank Dennis Shea, who was my deputy to the WTO. I had known Dennis for years, and we shared the experience of working for Senator Dole. He also is a trade expert and was early to China skepticism. I appreciate his knowledge and advice on all things coming out of Geneva. Greg Doud was my deputy for agriculture. He is a Kansas man, raised on a farm, and had worked on the Hill and in other agriculture-related groups for years. All these associates were smart, hardworking, and sacrificed much to serve.

Over time, people leave and a new group comes into government. I am deeply indebted to them, too. Joseph Barloon was my second general counsel. He also had been a partner of mine at the firm for years. He was an excellent, seasoned litigator and stayed with me to turn off the lights. My second chief of staff was Kevin Garvey. He continued Jamieson's good work and kept the trains moving. Mike Nemelka was deputy after Jeff left. He also served our country well. Mike, like everyone on this list, sacrificed financially and personally in service to our country.

I would like to thank my colleagues in the career staff at USTR both in the 1980s and under President Trump. They were professionals and taught me a lot.

Thanks as well to the other senior members of the Trump administration economic team. Here again lists risk unintentionally offending those who have not been listed, but I am particularly grateful to Jared Kushner and Ivanka Trump. They became very close friends. They always espoused the right policy for the right reasons. Thanks to Wilbur Ross, Steven Mnuchin, Peter Navarro, H. R. McMaster, Robert O'Brien, Kevin Hassett, Larry Kudlow, and many other top-quality senior officials. Trump's economic team was excellent to a person. Kevin and Larry have commented on how their free trade economist views changed over the course of the administration. We always welcome converts, and they were the best. Peter's views never needed to change. He was dogged and prescient throughout. He gets a lot of the credit for everything we did on trade. Wilbur moved the Department of Commerce to America First policy and was an ally in almost every battle. He was the first secretary to aggressively use our export control laws. Steven also became a good friend. We bonded over fights about tariffs and on flights to Beijing. He was another partner in our policy, although sometimes a reluctant one. He gets a lot of the credit for the great Trump economy. H. R., a true scholar and soldier, helped develop the China policy early on. Like the others, Robert is a patriot. He supported every effort vigorously. I often sought his advice. Another NSC friend was Matt Pottinger. Matt is a Mandarin speaker and a real China expert.

In the course of writing this book I came to know two young Harvard law students. Michael Starr and Trevor Jones were my researchers. They were diligent, knowledgeable, and very hardworking. I cannot overstate how important they were to this effort. I expect great things from them in the years ahead. I'll be able to say I knew them when they were just in school. Thank you.

I would also like to acknowledge a host of private advisers, many of whom I have worked with for decades. Particularly, I would like to single out Lori Wallach, a longtime friend and co-conspirator who was a constant adviser and liaison with many on the Hill. John Thornton played an important role as a back channel during our China negotiations. Dan DiMicco and I were allies for decades of trade battles. I always appreciated his energy.

Thank you to my agent, David Vigliano, and Thomas Flannery, his colleague, as well as Eric Nelson, my editor at Harper Collins. All three provided invaluable advice, encouragement, and help along the way. Their belief in the importance of this policy book made it possible.

I want to acknowledge the essential contribution to this work of Brooke Rollins and her colleagues at the America First Policy Institute. After the end of the Trump administration, Brooke set about creating a grand, Washington, populist, conservative, anti-swamp think tank—an almost impossible task. She went from 0 to 100 mph in just a few months.

It was a land speed record. The fruits of her efforts will be harvested for decades to come in conservative policy.

Thank you to Senator Robert Dole. He found me in a law firm and mentored me for decades. I'm proud to say he was a friend for forty-five years. Ambassador William Brock should also be acknowledged. He was a super USTR and a wonderful boss. Both of these gentlemen have died in recent years and are now enjoying a just reward. And what would the world be like without my boss from the eighties, Ronald Reagan? Thank you for making me part of your revolution.

The first version of many of the thoughts in this book were laid out in a *Foreign Affairs* article published in the July–August 2020. This was an early attempt to articulate the philosophy underlying our actions. I recommend the article. I also recommend an October 5, 2021, "by invitation" essay that I did for the *Economist*. It drafts an insight of Warren Buffett and shows how pernicious trade deficits are for America. For those who want to read my first warning about the threat that is China, I recommend a *New York Times* article from February 25, 1997, titled "What Did Asian Donors Want?"

I once told President Trump that when his great-grandkids read the history of his presidency, it will be a story of how he recognized and took on the challenge of China, and the rest would be a lot of footnotes. He obviously accomplished an enormous amount in many areas, but my objective in making the statement was to emphasize how crucial the China threat is. It will in many ways define our history in this century. Among major American politicians, he was the first to recognize the enormity of the threat and to create a policy to challenge it. His policy developed over time and was an across-government approach, but at its core was trade and economics. His critics cannot take away this historic achievement.

Over my years in Washington, I often heard that the times were the worst ever, that partisanship had overtaken policy to an unprecedented extent. Having read a lot of American history, I always resisted this thought. I read about the 1820s, the 1850s, and the 1930s, and remember the late 1960s and the early 1970s. I lived the division in the Reagan years. But I have to confess that the current discord and partisanship really rival the worst in our history. In spite of that, I worked with a number of great Republicans and Democrats in Washington during my tenure. I'll list a few and probably annoy many more not listed. Speaker Pelosi, in spite of her dislike for the president, treated me fairly and helped at some political cost getting much of my program through Congress because she thought it was right. The chairmen of the Ways and Means Committee Kevin Brady and later Richard Neal were both true professionals and a delight to work with. I developed friendship and close working relations with a number of other representative of both parties. Thank you for your support and for often putting national interest above party and for believing me when I told you all we wanted to do was help working people.

On the Senate side, I want to remember with great admiration the two chairmen of the Finance Committee, Orrin Hatch, a truly great American, and the iron man Chuck Grassley. I met Senator Grassley on his first day in the US Senate, January 1981. He's been a friend ever since. The ranking member of the Finance Committee was Ron Wyden. I did not know him well before my confirmation. We became friends and spoke almost every Monday morning at ten, so there would be "no surprises." Rob Portman was another friend and inspiration on trade. He is from Ohio, was USTR, and worried about our workers.

I also worked closely with a number of American labor leaders. Richard Trumka, the president of the AFL-CIO, became a friend and was key to getting USMCA passed and to my maintaining polical support in Washington. I truly miss him. Likewise, James Hoffa was a friend and was essential to accomplishing a worker-centered trade policy. I would also like to acknowledge Leo Gerard of the United Steelworkers, with whom I worked for years.

Vice President Pence deserves a lot of the credit for everything we did. He was devoted, loyal, and, frankly, good. In my area, he was always supportive and provided vital counsel on key policy and political issues.

Finally, I want to thank President Donald J. Trump for entrusting me with his trade portfolio. He was a delight to work for and always supported me. He worked around the clock, and I can honestly say that I never had a bad meeting with him. He was a great president, truly one of the greatest, and I am proud to have made a contribution to his list of achievements. Anyone who reads this book will know of my affection.

NOTES

Introduction

1. John Mullin, "The Rise and Sudden Decline of North Carolina Furniture Making," *Econ Focus: Fourth Quarter 2020* (report), Federal Reserve Bank of Richmond, www.richmondfed.org/publications/research/econ_focus/2020/q4 /economic_history.

Chapter 1: Where It Started

1. David McCullough, *The Wright Brothers* (New York: Simon & Schuster, 2015), 5.
2. "Remarks at a White House Meeting with Business and Trade Leaders: September 23, 1985," Ronald Reagan Presidential Library and Museum, www .reaganlibrary.gov/archives/speech/remarks-white-house-meeting-business-and -trade-leaders.
3. Sheldon L. Richman, "The Reagan Record on Trade: Rhetoric vs. Reality," Cato Institute, May 30, 1988, https://cato.org/policy-analysis/reagan-record-trade -rhetoric-vs-reality.
4. Michael Kruse, "The True Story of Donald Trump's First Campaign Speech—in 1987," *Politico*, February 5, 2016.
5. David H. Autor, David Dorn, and Gordon H. Hanson, "The China Shock: Learning from Labor Market Adjustment to Large Changes in Trade," *Annual Review of Economics* 8, no. 1 (October 2016), https://doi.org/10.1146/annurev -economics-080315-015041.
6. "Remarks: Donald Trump Holds a Cabinet Meeting at the White House— May 19, 2020," Factba.se, https://factba.se/transcript/donald-trump-remarks -cabinet-meeting-may-19-2020.

Chapter 2: Where We Are Now

1. Anne Case and Angus Deaton, *Deaths of Despair and the Future of Capitalism* (Princeton, NJ: Princeton University Press, 2020).
2. Cordell Hull, *The Memoirs of Cordell Hull*, vol. 1 (New York: Macmillan, 1948), 81.
3. Alan S. Blinder, "How Many US Jobs Might Be Offshorable?," *World Economics* 10, no. 2 (2009): 41.
4. Warren E. Buffett and Carol J. Loomis, "America's Growing Trade Deficit Is Selling the Nation Out from under Us. Here's a Way to Fix the Problem—and We Need to Do It Now," *Fortune*, November 10, 2003.
5. Milton Friedman, "The Case for Flexible Exchange Rates," in *Essays in Positive Economics*, ed. Milton Friedman (Chicago: University of Chicago Press, 1966), 157–203.
6. Michael Pettis, "Fighting Global Protection: Why the Economist Is Mistaken," Carnegie Endowment for International Peace, January 18, 2023, https://carnegie endowment.org/chinafinancialmarkets/88829.
7. Liam Gibson, "Is China's High-Growth Era Over—Forever?," Al Jazeera,

January 24, 2023, https://www.aljazeera.com/features/2023/1/24/is-chinas-high -growth-era-over.

8. For the original formulation of this theory in the context of optimality conditions in economic modeling, see R. G. Lipsey, Kelvin Lancaster, "The General Theory of Second Best," *Review of Economic Studies* 24, no. 1 (1956): 11–32, https://doi.org /10.2307/2296233.

9. International Trade Administration, "Free Trade Agreement Overview," accessed February 15, 2023, www.trade.gov/free-trade-agreement-overview.

10. David Rosnick and Dean Baker, *Trade and Jobs: Can We Trust the Models?* (Washington, DC: Center for Economic and Policy Research, 2016), https://cepr .net/images/stories/reports/trade-and-jobs-2016-04.pdf; Robert E. Scott, *No Jobs from Trade Pacts: The Trans-Pacific Partnership Could Be Much Worse than the Over-Hyped Korea Deal* (Washington, DC: Economic Policy Institute, 2013), www.epi .org/publication/trade-pacts-korus-trans-pacific-partnership/.

11. Timothy J. Kehoe, *An Evaluation of the Performance of Applied General Equilibrium Models of the Impact of NAFTA*, Federal Reserve Bank of Minneapolis: Research Department Staff Report 320, August 2003, http://users.econ.umn.edu/~tkehoe /papers/NAFTAevaluation.pdf.

12. Dani Rodrik, "The Rush to Free Trade in the Developing World: Why So Late? Why Now? Will It Last?," in *Voting for Reform: Democracy, Political Liberalization, and Economic Adjustment*, eds. Stephen Haggard and Steven B. Webb (New York: Oxford University Press for the World Bank, 1994), 62.

13. Dani Rodrik, *The Globalization Paradox: Why Global Markets, States, and Democracy Can't Coexist* (New York: Oxford University Press, 2011), 57.

14. Andy Grove, "How America Can Create Jobs," *Bloomberg*, July 1, 2010, www.bloom berg.com/news/articles/2010-07-01/andy-grove-how-america-can-create-jobs.

15. James Manyika, Katy George, Eric Chewning, Jonathan Woetzel, and Hans-Werner Kaas, "Building a More Competitive US Manufacturing Sector," McKinsey Global Institute, April 15, 2021, www.mckinsey.com/featured-insights /americas/building-a-more-competitive-us-manufacturing-sector.

16. Josh Bivens, "Updated Employment Multipliers for the U.S. Economy," Economic Policy Institute, January 23, 2019, www.epi.org/publication/updated-employment -multipliers-for-the-u-s-economy/.

17. Susan Helper, Timothy Krueger, and Howard Wial, *Why Does Manufacturing Matter? Which Manufacturing Matters?* (Washington, DC: Brookings, 2012), www.brookings.edu/research/why-does-manufacturing-matter-which-manufacturing-matters/.

18. Helper, Krueger, and Wial, *Why Does Manufacturing Matter?*, 14–15.

19. Rebecca Savransky, "Obama to Trump: 'What Magic Wand Do You Have?,'" *The Hill*, June 1, 2016, https://thehill.com/blogs/blog-briefing-room/news/281936 -obama-to-trump-what-magic-wand-do-you-have/.

Chapter 3: A Short and Selective History of US Trade Policy

1. Alfred E. Eckes Jr., *Opening America's Market: U.S. Foreign Trade Policy since 1776* (Chapel Hill: University of North Carolina Press, 1995), 2.

2. Patrick Buchanan, *The Great Betrayal* (Boston: Little, Brown, 1998), 141.

3. Henry Clay, "The American System" (1832), in *The Senate, 1789–1989*, ed. Wendy Wolff, vol. 3: *Classic Speeches 1830–1993* (Washington, DC: US Government Printing Office, 1994), 91.

4. "Republican Party Platform (1860)," Teaching American History, available at https://teachingamericanhistory.org/document/republican-party-platform-of -1860/ (emphasis added).

5. Abraham Lincoln, first debate with Stephen A. Douglas, Ottawa, Illinois, August 21, 1858, in Roy P. Basler et al., eds., 9 vols., *Collected Works of Abraham Lincoln* (New Brunswick, NJ: Rutgers University Press, 1953–55), 3:29.

6. "Republican Party Platform of 1872," American Presidency Project, University of California, Santa Barbara, available at https://www.presidency.ucsb.edu/documents /republican-party-platform-1872 (emphasis added).

7. Joseph H. Davis, "An Annual Index of U.S. Industrial Production, 1790–1915," *Quarterly Journal of Economics* 119, no. 4 (November 2004). Davis created an index to measure US industrial production in which census year 1849–50 had a value of 100. By this measure, Davis concluded that the indexed figure for US industrial production was 157.86 in 1860 and 1,783.9 in 1910. That represents an increase of 1,030 percent.

8. See Stephen Beale, "Is Trump the New Teddy Roosevelt?," *American Conservative*, March 20, 2017.

9. "Republican Party Platform of 1896," American Presidency Project, University of California, Santa Barbara, available at https://www.presidency.ucsb.edu/documents /republican-party-platform-1896.

10. Douglas Irwin, *Clashing over Commerce: A History of U.S. Trade Policy* (Chicago: University of Chicago Press, 2017), 479.

11. Hull, *Memoirs*, 1:84.

12. "1936 Democratic Party Platform," American Presidency Project, University of California, Santa Barbara, available at https://www.presidency.ucsb.edu /documents/1936-democratic-party-platform (emphasis added).

13. UPI Archives, "Rep. Richard Gephardt, D-Mo., Wednesday called the United States . . . ," September 25, 1985, https://upi.com/Archives/1985/09/25/Rep-Richaard-Gephardt-D-Mo-Wednesday-called-the-United-States/6122496468800/.

14. UPI Archives, "Rep. Richard Gephardt."

15. Sheldon L. Richman, *The Reagan Record on Trade: Rhetoric vs. Reality* (Washington, DC: Cato Institute, 1988), https://cato.org/policy-analysis/reagan-record-trade -rhetoric-vs-reality.

16. The White House, "Press Conference by the President," March 29, 2000, https:// usinfo.org/wf-archive/2000/000330/epf401.htm.

17. George W. Bush, "U.S. China Policy Must Have Clear Purpose, Strategic Vision," On Politics Archive, *Washington Post*, October 10, 2000, www.washingtonpost.com /wp-srv/onpolitics/elections/wwb2000/1018/bush/question/.

18. Ross Perot and Pat Choate, *Save Your Job, Save Our Country: Why NAFTA Must Be Stopped—Now!* (New York: Hyperion, 1993), i–ii.

19. Robert E. Scott, *NAFTA's Impact on the States* (Washington, DC: Economic Policy Institute, 2001), www.epi.org/publication/briefingpapers_nafta01_impact states/.

20. "Real Median Household Income in the United States," FRED Economic Data, updated September 13, 2022, https://fred.stlouisfed.org/series/MEHOIN USA672N.

21. "Transcript: The Democratic Debate in Cleveland," *New York Times*, February 26, 2008, www.nytimes.com/2008/02/26/us/politics/26text-debate.html.

Chapter 4: How the WTO Has Failed America

1. William Clinton, "Remarks on Signing the Uruguay Round Agreements Act," The American Presidency Project, December 8, 1994, www.presidency.ucsb.edu /documents/remarks-signing-the-uruguay-round-agreements-act.

2. Juliana Menasce Horowitz, Ruth Igielnik, and Rakesh Kochhar, "Trends in

Income and Wealth Inequality," Pew Research Center, January 9, 2020, www
.pewresearch.org/social-trends/2020/01/09/trends-in-income-and-wealth-
inequality/.

3. Quoted by Senator Brown in his floor speech. For this, see Senator Hank
    Brown, "Uruguay Round Agreements Act," *Congressional Record* 140, no. 148
    (November 30, 1994), www.govinfo.gov/content/pkg/CREC-1994-11-30/html
    /CREC-1994-11-30-pt1-PgS15.htm (emphasis added).

4. Quoted by Senator Brown in his floor speech; see Brown, "Uruguay Round
    Agreements Act" (emphasis added).

5. Office of the United States Trade Representative, *Report on the Appellate Body of
    the World Trade Organization* (Washington DC: Office of the United States Trade
    Representative, 2020), 3, https://ustr.gov/sites/default/files/Report_on_the
    _Appellate_Body_of_the_World_Trade_Organization.pdf.

6. United States Senate Committee on Finance, "Baucus Comments on Release of
    GAO Report on Trade Remedies Rulings in WTO," July 30, 2003, www.finance
    .senate.gov/ranking-members-news/baucus-comments-on-release-of-gao-report
    -on-trade-remedies-rulings-in-wto.

7. Office of the United States Trade Representative, *Report on the Appellate Body of the
    World Trade Organization.*

8. WTO Dispute Settlement Body, Statements by the United States at the Meeting of
    the WTO Dispute Settlement Body Geneva, November 22, 2019, 10–13, https://
    gpa-mprod-mwp.s3.amazonaws.com/uploads/sites/25/2021/06/Nov22.DSB
    .Stmt.as-deliv.fin_.public.pdf.

9. Thomas R. Graham, "Farewell Speech of Appellate Body Member Thomas R.
    Graham," World Trade Organization, March 5, 2020.

10. *Global Times* editorial, "WTO Holds High Banner, and Multilateralism Will
    Eventually Triumph," *People's Daily Online*, June 14, 2022, http://en.people.cn
    /n3/2022/0614/c90000-10109141.html.

11. Article XXI, General Agreement on Tariffs and Trade (emphasis added).

12. Ana Monteiro, "WTO on 'Thin Ice' with Metals-Tariff Ruling, US Trade Chief
    Katherine Tai Says," *Bloomberg*, December 19, 2022, www.bloomberg.com/news
    /articles/2022-12-19/wto-on-thin-ice-with-metals-tariff-ruling-us-trade-chief-says.

13. Karen McVeigh, "First WTO Deal on Fishing Subsidies Hailed as Historic
    Despite 'Big Holes,'" *Guardian*, June 21, 2022, www.theguardian.com
    /environment/2022/jun/21/first-wto-deal-on-fishing-subsidies-hailed-as-historic
    -despite-big-holes.

14. Doug Palmer, "Lighthizer: No One Misses WTO Appellate Body," *Politico*,
    December 10, 2020, www.politico.com/news/2020/12/10/lighthizer-wto-appellate
    -judges-444290.

Chapter 5: Our Greatest Geopolitical Threat

1. Rush Doshi, "Great Changes Unseen in a Century: The Elusive Phrase Driving
    China's Grand Strategy," *China Leadership Monitor*, September 2, 2021.

2. Andrew F. Krepinevich, *Preserving the Balance: A U.S. Eurasia Defense Strategy*
    (Washington, DC: Center for Strategic and Budgetary Assessments, 2017), 39,
    https://csbaonline.org/uploads/documents/CSBA6227-PreservingTheBalance
    _PRINT.pdf.

3. Krepinevich, *Preserving the Balance.*

4. Peter Schweizer, *Red-Handed: How American Elites Get Rich Helping China Win*
    (New York: HarperCollins, 2022).

5. David Crawshaw and Alicia Chen, "'Heads Bashed Bloody': China's Xi Marks
    Communist Party Centenary with Strong Words for Adversaries," *Washington*

Post, July 1, 2021, www.washingtonpost.com/world/asia_pacific/china-party
-heads-bashed-xi/2021/07/01/277c8f0c-da3f-11eb-8c87-ad6f27918c78_story.html.

6. Shin Kawashima, "The Development of the Debate Over 'Hiding One's Talents and Biding One's Time' (*taoguan yanghui*)," *Asia-Pacific Review* 18, no. 2 (2011): 14–36, https://doi.org/10.1080/13439006.2011.641751.

7. Robert E. Lighthizer, "A Deal We'd Be Likely to Regret," *New York Times*, April 18, 1999, www.nytimes.com/1999/04/18/opinion/a-deal-wed-be-likely-to -regret.html.

8. Department of Defense, *Military and Security Developments Involving the People's Republic of China 2020* (Washington, DC: Office of the Secretary Defense, 2020), https://media.defense.gov/2020/Sep/01/2002488689/-1/-1/1/2020-DOD -CHINA-MILITARY-POWER-REPORT-FINAL.PDF.

9. Department of Defense, *Military and Security Developments*.

10. Alastair Gale, "China Is Expanding Its Effort to Launch Weapons from Hypersonic Missiles," *Wall Street Journal*, November 22, 2019, www.wsj.com/articles/china -is-expanding-its-effort-to-launch-weapons-from-hypersonic-missiles-11637588925.

11. Matt Korda and Hans Kristensen, "A Closer Look at China's Missile Silo Construction," Federation of American Scientists, November 2, 2021, https://fas .org/blogs/security/2021/11/a-closer-look-at-chinas-missile-silo-construction/.

12. Department of Defense, *Military and Security Developments Involving the People's Republic of China 2020*.

13. "Record Number of China Planes Enter Taiwan Air Defence Zone," BBC News, October 5, 2021, www.bbc.com/news/world-asia-58794094.

14. "China-Taiwan Military Tensions 'Worst in 40 Years,'" BBC News, October 6, 2021, www.bbc.com/news/world-asia-58812100.

15. Roger F. Wicker, "Joe Biden Should Come Out and Say It: America Will Help Defend Taiwan," *Wall Street Journal*, November 19, 2021, www.wsj.com/articles /joe-biden-should-come-out-and-say-it-america-will-help-defend-taiwan-china -military-xi-11637357925.

16. Chris Dougherty, Jennie Matuschak, and Ripley Hunter, *The Poison Frog Strategy: Preventing a Chinese Fait Accompli Against Taiwanese Islands* (Washington, DC: CNAS, 2021), www.cnas.org/publications/reports/the-poison-frog-strategy.

17. Department of Defense, *Military and Security Developments Involving the People's Republic of China 2020*.

18. The White House, "Press Briefing by NSA for Strategic Communications Ben Rhodes and Admiral Robert Willard, U.S. Pacific Command," November 13, 2011, https://obamawhitehouse.archives.gov/the-press-office/2011/11/13/press -briefing-nsa-strategic-communications-ben-rhodes-and-admiral-rober.

19. Department of Defense, *Military and Security Developments Involving the People's Republic of China 2020*.

20. Derek Watkins, "What China Has Been Building in the South China Sea," *New York Times*, October 27, 2015, www.nytimes.com/interactive/2015/07/30/world /asia/what-china-has-been-building-in-the-south-china-sea.html.

21. Steven Lee Myers and Jason Gutierrez, "With Swarms of Ships, Beijing Tightens Its Grip on South China Sea," *New York Times*, April 3, 2021, www.nytimes.com /2021/04/03/world/asia/swarms-ships-south-china-sea.html.

22. Jim Gomez and Aaron Favila, "US Admiral Says China Fully Militarized Disputed Isles in South China Sea," *The Hill*, March 21, 2022, https://thehill.com /homenews/wire/598967-us-admiral-says-china-fully-militarized-disputed-isles -in-south/.

23. Snehesh Alex Philip, "Chinese Troops Challenge India at Multiple Locations in Eastern Ladakh, Standoff Continues," *The Print*, May 24, 2020, https://theprint

.in/defence/chinese-troops-challenge-india-at-multiple-locations-in-eastern
-ladakh-standoff-continues/428304/.

24. Ethirajan Anbarasan, "China-India Clashes: No Change a Year after Ladakh
Stand-off," *BBC News*, June 1, 2021, www.bbc.com/news/world-asia-57234024.

25. Josh Gerstein, "DOJ Shuts Down China-focused Anti-espionage Program,"
Politico, February 23, 2022, www.politico.com/news/2022/02/23/doj-shuts-down
-china-focused-anti-espionage-program-00011065.

26. Tom Winter and Carol E. Lee, "Chinese Consulate in Houston Was a Hot Spot
for Spying, Say U.S. Officials," NBC News, July 22, 2020, https://www.nbcnews
.com/politics/national-security/chinese-consulate-houston-was-hotspot-spying
-say-u-s-officials-n1234634.

27. James Palmer, "How a Chinese Spy Balloon Blew Up a Key U.S. Diplomatic
Trip," *Foreign Policy*, February 3, 2023, https://foreignpolicy.com/2023/02/03
/china-spy-balloon-surveillance-montana-us-nuclear-blinken/.

28. Vivian Salama and Michael R. Gordon, "Chinese Balloon Carried Antennas, Other
Equipment to Gather Intelligence, U.S. Says," *Wall Street Journal*, February 9, 2023,
https://www.wsj.com/articles/chinese-balloon-carried-antennas-other-equipment
-to-gather-intelligence-u-s-says-11675953033.

29. Sebastian Rotella and Kirsten Berg, "Operation Fox Hunt: How China Exports
Repression Using a Network of Spies Hidden in Plain Sight," *ProPublica*, July 22,
2021, https://www.propublica.org/article/operation-fox-hunt-how-china-exports
-repression-using-a-network-of-spies-hidden-in-plain-sight.

30. Megha Rajagopalan and William K. Rashbaum, "With F.B.I. Search, U.S.
Escalates Global Fight Over Chinese Police Outposts," *New York Times*, January
12, 2023, https://www.nytimes.com/2023/01/12/world/europe/china-outpost
-new-york.html.

31. Ryan McCrimmon, "China Is Buying Up American Farms. Washington Wants to
Crack Down," *Politico*, July 19, 2021, www.politico.com/news/2021/07/19/china
-buying-us-farms-foreign-purchase-499893.

32. Lauren Greenwood, *China's Interests in U.S. Agriculture: Augmenting Food Security
through Investment Abroad* (Washington, DC: US-China Economic and Security
Review Commission, 2022), 11, www.uscc.gov/sites/default/files/2022-05
/Chinas_Interests_in_U.S._Agriculture.pdf.

33. Kristina Peterson and Anthony DeBarros, "Farmland Becomes Flashpoint in
U.S.–China Relations," *Wall Street Journal*, February 6, 2023, https://www.wsj
.com/articles/farmland-becomes-flashpoint-in-u-s-china-relations-11675652368.

34. Greenwood, *China's Interests*, 12.

35. Stephen Gandel, "The Biggest American Companies Now Owned by the
Chinese," *Fortune*, March 18, 2016, https://fortune.com/2016/03/18/the-biggest
-american-companies-now-owned-by-the-chinese/.

36. "Global Emissions," Energy/Emissions Data, Center for Climate and Energy
Solutions, www.c2es.org/content/international-emissions/.

37. Ren Peng, Liu Chang, and Zhang Liwen, *China's Involvement in Coal-Fired Power
Projects along the Belt and Road* (Beijing, China: Global Environmental Institute,
2017), www.geichina.org/_upload/file/report/China%27s_Involvement_in_Coal
-fired_Power_Projects_OBOR_EN.pdf; Allison Kirsch et al., *Banking on Climate
Change: Fossil Fuel Finance Report 2020* (Rainforest Action Network, BankTrack,
Indigenous Environmental Network, Oil Change International, Reclaim Finance,
and the Sierra Club, 2020), www.ienearth.org/wp-content/uploads/2019/03
/Banking_on_Climate_Change__2020_vF.pdf.

38. "China's Global Energy Finance," Boston University Global Development Policy
Center, accessed July 15, 2021, http://bu.edu/cgef/#/all/Country-EnergySource.

39. "Wild Laws: China and Its Role in Illicit Wildlife Trade," Woodrow Wilson Center, June 2, 2016, www.wilsoncenter.org/event/wild-laws-china-and-its-role-illicit-wildlife-trade.

40. Nan Li and Evgeny Shvarts, *The Belt and Road Initiative: WWF Recommendations and Spatial Analysis* (Gland, Switzerland: World Wildlife Fund, 2017), http://awsassets.panda.org/downloads/the_belt_and_road_initiative___wwf_recommendations_and_spatial_analysis___may_2017.pdf.

41. Michael Ruchards, Naomi Basik Treanor, Xiufang Sun, and Sofia Tenorio Fenton, *China's International Wood Trade: A Review, 2011–2020* (Washington, DC: Forest Trends Association, 2022), www.forest-trends.org/wp-content/uploads/2022/06/China-Trade-Report-2022.pdf.

42. Mengyu Bai, Lixin Zhu, Lihui An, and Guyu Peng, "Estimation and Prediction of Plastic Waste Annual Input into the Sea from China," *Acta Oceanologica Sinica* 37, no. 11 (2018): 26–39, https://doi.org/10.1007/s13131-018-1279-0.

43. Blake Herzinger, "China Is Fishing for Trouble at Sea," *Foreign Policy*, November 20, 2020, https://foreignpolicy.com/2020/11/20/china-illegal-catch-fishing-biden-trump/.

44. "China 2021 Country Results," IUU Fishing Index, www.iuufishingindex.net/profile/china.

45. Kenneth Roth, *China's Global Threat to Human Rights* (New York: Human Rights Watch, 2020), www.hrw.org/world-report/2020/country-chapters/global#.

46. Matthew P. Robertson and Jacob Lavee, "Execution by Organ Procurement: Breaching the Dead Donor Rule in China," *American Journal of Transplantation* 22, no. 7 (2022): 1804–12, https://doi.org/10.1111/ajt.16969.

47. Edward Wong and Chris Buckley, "U.S. Says China's Repression of Uighurs Is 'Genocide,'" *New York Times*, January 19, 2021, www.nytimes.com/2021/01/19/us/politics/trump-china-xinjiang.html.

48. Roth, *China's Global Threat*.

49. Roth, *China's Global Threat*.

50. Roth, *China's Global Threat*.

51. "The Origin of the 'Xinjiang Model' in Tibet under Chen Quanguo: Securitizing Ethnicity and Accelerating Assimilation," International Campaign for Tibet, December 19, 2018, https://savetibet.org/the-origin-of-the-xinjiang-model-in-tibet-under-chen-quanguo-securitizing-ethnicity-and-accelerating-assimilation/.

52. United States Department of State, *Tibet 2020 Human Rights Report* (Washington, DC: United States Department of State, Bureau of Democracy, Human Rights, and Labor, 2020), 5, www.state.gov/wp-content/uploads/2021/03/TIBET-2020-HUMAN-RIGHTS-REPORT-1.pdf.

53. Javier C. Hernandez, "Harsh Penalties, Vaguely Defined Crimes: Hong Kong's Security Law Explained," *New York Times*, June 30, 2020, www.nytimes.com/2020/06/30/world/asia/hong-kong-security-law-explain.html.

54. Brendan Clift, "Hong Kong's Made-in-China National Security Law: Upending the Legal Order for the Sake of Law and Order," *Australian Journal of Asian Law* 21, no. 1 (2020): 1–23, https://ssrn.com/abstract=3749674.

55. Yaqiu Wang, "In China, the 'Great Firewall' Is Changing a Generation," *Politico*, September 1, 2020, www.politico.com/news/magazine/2020/09/01/china-great-firewall-generation-405385.

56. Paul Mozur and Aaron Krolik, "A Surveillance Net Blankets China's Cities, Giving Police Vast Powers," *New York Times*, December 17, 2019, www.nytimes.com/2019/12/17/technology/china-surveillance.html.

57. Katja Drinhausen and Vincent Brussee, *China's Social Credit System in 2021: From Fragmentation towards Integration* (Berlin: Mercator Institute for China Studies,

2021), https://merics.org/en/report/chinas-social-credit-system-2021-frag
mentation-towards-integration.

58. Roth, *China's Global Threat*.

59. Nazpari Sotoudeh and Erica Stefano, "Free Speech Risky as China Keeps Close Tabs on its Overseas Students," *Eurasianet*, September 29, 2021, https://eurasianet.org/free-speech-risky-as-china-keeps-close-tabs-on-its-overseas-students.

60. Mike Cherney, "China Sours on Australian Wine as Trade Spat Spirals," *Wall Street Journal*, August 18, 2020, www.wsj.com/articles/china-sours-on-australian-wine-as-trade-spat-spirals-11597750564?mod=article_inline.

61. "China to Halt Australian Imports in Sweeping Retaliation," *Bloomberg*, November 3, 2020, www.bloomberg.com/news/articles/2020-11-03/china-to-halt-key-australian-commodity-imports-as-tensions-mount.

62. Sonali Paul, "Australia's Top Exporting State Calls for Reset in China Ties," Reuters, June 15, 2021, www.reuters.com/world/asia-pacific/australias-top-exporting-state-calls-reset-china-ties-2021-06-15/.

63. Drinhausen and Brussee, *China's Social Credit System*, at 7–12.

64. Drinhausen and Brussee, *China's Social Credit System*, at 7–12.

65. Drinhausen and Brussee, *China's Social Credit System*, at 7–12.

66. Rick Noack, "Volkswagen CEO 'Not Aware' of Uighurs Detained in China's Xinjiang, Despite Having a Factory There," *Washington Post*, April 17, 2019, www.washingtonpost.com/world/2019/04/17/volkswagen-built-factory-chinas-xinijang-where-up-million-uighurs-have-been-detained-its-ceo-says-hes-not-aware-that/.

67. Timothy Garton Ash, "VW's Dilemma in Xinjiang Shows How the West Is Headed for an Ethical Car Crash," *Guardian*, July 28, 2021, www.theguardian.com/commentisfree/2021/jul/28/vw-dilemma-xinjiang-west-ethical-car-crash.

68. Wayne Ma, "Marriott Employee Roy Jones Hit 'Like.' Then China Got Mad," *Wall Street Journal*, March 3, 2018, www.wsj.com/articles/marriott-employee-roy-jones-hit-like-then-china-got-mad-1520094910.

69. Elaine Yu and Jing Yang, "Jamie Dimon Apologizes for Joke about JPMorgan Outlasting China's Communist Party," *Wall Street Journal*, November 24, 2021, www.wsj.com/articles/jamie-dimon-says-he-would-bet-jpmorgan-will-outlive-chinas-communist-party-11637749959.

70. Maria Abi-Habib, "How China Got Sri Lanka to Cough Up a Port," *New York Times*, June 25, 2018, www.nytimes.com/2018/06/25/world/asia/china-sri-lanka-port.html.

71. Ari Shapiro and Manuela Lopez Restrepo, "Sri Lankan Protesters Party in the President's Mansion as He Flees the Country," NPR, July 13, 2022, www.npr.org/2022/07/13/1111087981/sri-lankan-protesters-partied-in-the-presidents-mansion-what-comes-next-is-uncle.

72. Michele Ruta, Matias Herrera Dapper, Somik Lall, et al., *Belt and Road Economics: Opportunities and Risks of Transport Corridors* (Washington, DC: World Bank, 2019), 4, www.worldbank.org/en/topic/regional-integration/publication/belt-and-road-economics-opportunities-and-risks-of-transport-corridors.

73. Jacob J. Lew, Gary Roughead, Jennifer Hillman, and David Sacks, *China's Belt and Road: Implications for the United States* (New York: Council on Foreign Relations, 2021), www.cfr.org/report/chinas-belt-and-road-implications-for-the-united-states/download/pdf/2021-04/TFR%20%2379_China%27s%20Belt%20and%20Road_Implications%20for%20the%20United%20States_FINAL.pdf.

74. Joshua Eisenman, *Contextualizing China's Belt and Road Initiative*, written testimony for the USCC, US-China Economic and Security Review Commission,

January 19, 2018, www.uscc.gov/sites/default/files/Eisenman_USCC%20Test imony_20180119.pdf.

75. Morgan Stanley Research, *Inside China's Plan to Create a Modern Silk Road* (New York: Morgan Stanley, 2018), www.morganstanley.com/ideas/china-belt-and-road.
76. Lew, Roughead, Hillman, and Sacks, *China's Belt and Road.*
77. Lew, Roughead, Hillman, and Sacks, *China's Belt and Road.*
78. Lew, Roughead, Hillman, and Sacks, *China's Belt and Road.*
79. Hamima Athumani, "Officials in Uganda Dismiss Report Country Could 'Lose' Airport to China," *Voice of America*, November 29, 2021, www.voanews.com/a /officials-in-uganda-dismiss-report-country-could-lose-airport-to-china/6331909 .html.
80. Lew, Roughead, Hillman, and Sacks, *China's Belt and Road.*
81. Lew, Roughead, Hillman, and Sacks, *China's Belt and Road.*
82. Jacob Markell, "Dispute Settlement on China's Terms: Beijing's New Belt and Road Courts," Merics, February 14, 2018, https://merics.org/en/analysis/dispute -settlement-chinas-terms-beijings-new-belt-and-road-courts; Nyshka Chandran, "China's Plans for Creating New International Courts Are Raising Fears of Bias," CNBC, February 1, 2018, www.cnbc.com/2018/02/01/china-to-create -international-courts-for-belt-and-road-disputes.html.
83. Ryan Dube and Gabriele Steinhauser, "China's Global Mega-Projects Are Falling Apart," *Wall Street Journal*, January 20, 2023.
84. Alice Eckman, ed., and Françoise Nicolas, Céline Pajon, John Seaman, Isabelle Saint-Mézard, Sophie Boisseau Du Rocher, and Tatiana Kastouéva-Jean, *China's Belt & Road and the World: Competing Forms of Globalization* (Paris: IFRI, 2019), 35, http:// ifri.org/sites/default/files/atoms/files/ekman_china_belt_road_world _2019.pdf.
85. Lew, Roughead, Hillman, and Sacks, *China's Belt and Road.*
86. Richard N. Haass, "A Conversation with Prime Minister Imran Khan of Pakistan," interview with Imran Khan, Council on Foreign Relations, September 23, 2019, www.cfr.org/event/conversation-prime-minister-imran-khan-pakistan-0.
87. Tom Wright and Bradley Hope, "WSJ Investigation: China Offered to Bail Out Troubled Malaysian Fund in Return for Deals," *Wall Street Journal*, January 7, 2019, www.wsj.com/articles/how-china-flexes-its-political-muscle-to-expand -power-overseas-11546890449; Marleen Heuer, "China Increases Influence over Tibetan Refugees in Nepal," *Deutsche Welle*, August 29, 2016, http://dw.com/en /china-increases-influence-over-tibetanrefugees-in-nepal/a-19511365.
88. Mailyn Fidler, "African Union Bugged by China: Cyber Espionage as Evidence of Strategic Shifts," *Net Politics*, Council on Foreign Relations, March 7, 2018, www .cfr.org/blog/african-union-bugged-china-cyber-espionage-evidence-strategic -shifts.
89. Department of Defense, *Military and Security Developments Involving the People's Republic of China 2020.*
90. Gordon Lubold, "China's Growing Influence in Africa Seen in Arms Trade and Infrastructure Investment," *Wall Street Journal*, April 21, 2022, www.wsj.com /articles/chinas-growing-influence-in-africa-seen-in-arms-trade-and-infrastructure -investment-11650554282.
91. Kristy Needham, "China Seeks Pacific Islands Policing, Security Cooperation," Reuters, May 25, 2022, www.reuters.com/world/asia-pacific/exclusive-china-seeks -pacific-islands-policing-security-cooperation-document-2022-05-25/.
92. Phelim Kine, "The War on Drugs Puts a Target on China," *Politico*, February 7, 2022, www.politico.com/news/2022/02/07/fentanyl-china-war-on-drugs -00005920.

93. The Council of Economic Advisers, *The Underestimated Cost of the Opioid Crisis* (Washington, DC: CEA, November 2017).

94. Kaitlyn Hoevelmann, *The Economic Costs of the Opioid Epidemic* (St. Louis: Federal Reserve Bank of St. Louis, 2019), www.stlouisfed.org/open-vault/2019/september /economic-costs-opioid-epidemic.

95. Vanda Felbab-Brown, *Fentanyl and Geopolitics: Controlling Opioid Supply from China* (Washington, DC: Brookings Institution, 2020), www.brookings.edu/wp -content/uploads/2020/07/8_Felbab-Brown_China_final.pdf.

96. Felbab-Brown, *Fentanyl and Geopolitics.*

97. Robin Wright, "Russia and China Unveil a Pact against America and the West," *New Yorker*, February 7, 2022, www.newyorker.com/news/daily-comment/russia -and-china-unveil-a-pact-against-america-and-the-west.

98. Patricia Kowsmann and Alexander Osipovich, "Russian Banks Turn to China to Sidestep Cutoff from Payments Systems," *Wall Street Journal*, March 6, 2022, www.wsj.com/articles/russian-banks-turn-to-china-to-sidestep-cutoff-from-pay ments-systems-11646578489.

99. Maxim Tucker, "China Accused of Hacking Ukraine Days before Russian Invasion," *The Times*, April 1, 2022, www.thetimes.co.uk/article/china-cyber attack-ukraine-z9gfkbmgf.

100. Ines Kagubare, "Ukraine Intelligence Accuses China of Hacking Days before Invasion," *The Hill*, April 1, 2022, https://thehill.com/policy/cybersecurity /3256792-ukraine-intelligence-accuses-china-of-hacking-days-before -invasion-report/.

101. Lara Jakes and Steven Lee Myers, "Tense Talks with China Left U.S. 'Cleareyed' about Beijing's Intentions, Officials Say," *New York Times*, March 19, 2021, www .nytimes.com/2021/03/19/world/asia/china-us-alaska.html.

102. Jakes and Myers, "Tense Talks."

Chapter 6: Twenty-First-Century Mercantilism

1. "China National Nuclear Corporation," Company Profile, Chinese Defense Universities Tracker, Australia Strategic Policy Institute, https://unitracker.aspi .org.au/universities/china-national-nuclear-corporation/.

2. *United States v. Wang Dong et al.*, Indictment, Criminal No. 14-118, U.S. District Court for the Western District of Pennsylvania, May 1, 2014, 13.

3. David Stanway, "China Goes All-In on Home Grown Tech in Push for Nuclear Dominance," Reuters, April 17, 2019, www.reuters.com/article/us-china-nuclear power-hualong/china-goes-all-in-on-home-grown-tech-in-push-for-nuclear-dom inance-idUSKCN1RT0C0.

4. "Nuclear Power in China," Country Profiles, Information Library, World Nuclear Association, updated January 2023, www.world-nuclear.org/information-library /country-profiles/countries-a-f/china-nuclear-power.aspx.

5. *United States v. Wang Dong et al.*, 13–14.

6. *United States v. Wang Dong et al.*, 15.

7. *United States v. Wang Dong et al.*, 14–16.

8. *United States v. Wang Dong et al.*, 14–16.

9. Echo Xie, "China Ditches US Nuclear Technology in Favor of Home-Grown Alternative," *South China Morning Post*, September 14, 2020, www.scmp.com /news/china/society/article/3101304/china-ditches-us-nuclear-technology-favour -home-grown.

10. Tom Hals and Emily Flitter, "How Two Cutting Edge U.S. Nuclear Projects Bankrupted Westinghouse," Reuters, May 2, 2017, www.reuters.com/article

/us-toshiba-accounting-westinghouse-nucle/how-two-cutting-edge-u-s-nuclear
-projects-bankrupted-westinghouse-idUSKBN17Y0CQ.

11. *Cambridge Dictionary*, s.v. "mercantilism," accessed February 14, 2023, https://
     dictionary.cambridge.org/dictionary/english/mercantilism.
12. Laura LaHaye, "Mercantilism," Econlib, www.econlib.org/library/Enc/Mercant
     ilism.html.
13. Barry Naughton, *The Chinese Economy: Adaptation and Growth* (Cambridge, MA:
     MIT Press, 2018), 65.
14. Naughton, *Chinese Economy*, 66.
15. Naughton, *Chinese Economy*, 67.
16. David Priestland, *The Red Flag: A History of Communism* (New York: Grove Press,
     2009), 298.
17. Priestland, *Red Flag*, 299.
18. Priestland, *Red Flag*, 310–11.
19. Priestland, *Red Flag*, 299.
20. Priestland, *Red Flag*, 299.
21. Priestland, *Red Flag*, 354–56.
22. Priestland, *Red Flag*, 357.
23. Evan Feigenbaum, *China's Techno-Warriors: National Security and Strategic
     Competition from the Nuclear to the Information Age* (Stanford, CA: Stanford
     University Press, 2003).
24. Priestland, *Red Flag*, 506.
25. Priestland, *Red Flag*, 506.
26. Naughton, *Chinese Economy*, 100–101.
27. Priestland, *Red Flag*, 506.
28. Priestland, *Red Flag*, 506.
29. Naughton, *Chinese Economy*, 105.
30. Priestland, *Red Flag*, 506.
31. For a discussion of this, see Feigenbaum, *China's Techno-Warriors*.
32. Trevor R. Jones and Treston Chandler, *Sweeping U.S. Lists Seek to Restrict Trade
     and Investment That Support the Chinese Military* (Washington, DC: Wisconsin
     Project on Nuclear Arms Control, 2021), www.wisconsinproject.org/sweeping-us
     -lists-seek-to-restrict-trade-investment-that-support-chinese-military/.
33. Jones and Chandler, *Sweeping U.S. Lists*.
34. Nicholas Borst, "Has China Given Up on State-Owned Enterprise Reform?," *The
     Interpreter*, Lowy Institute, April 15, 2021, www.lowyinstitute.org/the
     -interpreter/has-china-given-state-owned-enterprise-reform.
35. Zhang Chunlin, "How Much Do State-Owned Enterprises Contribute to China's
     GDP and Employment?," World Bank, July 15, 2019, https://documents1
     .worldbank.org/curated/en/449701565248091726/pdf/How-Much-Do-State
     -Owned-Enterprises-Contribute-to-China-s-GDP-and-Employment.pdf.
36. *European Business in China Position Paper 2019/2020*, European Chamber, www
     .europeanchamber.com.cn/en/press-releases/3057/european_chamber_report
     _joins_calls_for_competitive_neutrality_and_soe_reform_to_sustain_china_s
     _development.
37. *China Enacts New National Security Law*, Covington, July 2, 2015, www.cov
     .com/~/media/files/corporate/publications/2015/06/china_passes_new_national
     _security_law.pdf.
38. Matthew Brooker, "Communist Party Cells? Nothing to See Here," *Bloomberg*,
     July 28, 2022, www.bloomberg.com/opinion/articles/2022-07-28/communist
     -party-cells-at-your-company-s-office-in-china-nothing-to-see-here; Michael

McCaul, "China Task Force Report," US House of Representatives, September 30, 2020.

39. Li Yuan, "China's Tech Rainmaker Vanishes, and So Does Business Confidence," *New York Times*, February 22, 2023.

40. Bob Davis and Wei Lingling, "Biden Administration Takes Aim at China's Industrial Subsidies," *Wall Street Journal*, September 11, 2021, www.wsj.com/articles/biden-administration-takes-aim-at-chinas-industrial-subsidies-11631295257.

41. Kenneth Rapoza, "Is This Why China's Stock Market Is Up So Much in 2019?," *Forbes*, December 18, 2019, www.forbes.com/sites/kenrapoza/2019/12/18/is-this-why-chinas-stock-market-is-up-so-much-in-2019/?sh=3798dddc79d4.

42. Matthew C. Klein and Michael Pettis, *Trade Wars Are Class Wars: How Rising Inequality Distorts the Global Economy and Threatens International Peace* (New Haven, CT: Yale University Press, 2020), 112.

43. Michael Pettis, *Avoiding the Fall: China's Economic Restructuring* (Washington, DC: Carnegie Endowment for International Peace, 2013).

44. Klein and Pettis, *Trade Wars Are Class Wars*, 115.

45. "Section 2: Vulnerabilities in China's Financial System and Risks for the United States," in chap. 2, "U.S.-China Economic and Trade Relations," *2020 Report to Congress of the U.S.-China Economic and Security Review Commission*, December 2020, www.uscc.gov/sites/default/files/2020-12/Chapter_2_Section_2--Vulnerabilities_in_Chinas_Financial_System_and_Risks_for_the_United_States.pdf.

46. Office of the United States Trade Representative, *2021 National Trade Estimate Report on Foreign Trade Barriers* (Washington, DC: Office of the United States Trade Representative March 2021), 101, 112–13, https://ustr.gov/sites/default/files/files/reports/2021/2021NTE.pdf.

47. Zhang Yukun, "China Reminds Local Governments It's Illegal to Discriminate against Foreign Companies," Caixin Global, October 26, 2021, www.caixinglobal.com/2021-10-26/china-reminds-local-governments-its-illegal-to-discriminate-against-foreign-companies-101791936.html; Allison Schonberg, *Government Procurement and Sales to State-Owned Enterprises in China*, U.S.-China Business Council, September 2021, www.uschina.org/sites/default/files/uscbc_government_procurement_report_2021.pdf.

48. Office of the United States Trade Representative, *2021 National Trade Estimate Report*, 96.

49. Office of the United States Trade Representative, *Findings of the Investigations into China's Acts, Policies, and Practices Related to Technology Transfer, Intellectual Property, and Innovation under Section 301 of the Trade Act of 1974* (Washington, DC: Office of the United States Trade Representative, March 22, 2018), 96, https://ustr.gov/sites/default/files/Section%20301%20FINAL.PDF.

50. Alex Joske, "The China Defence Universities Tracker," Australian Strategic Policy Institute, 2019, www.aspi.org.au/report/china-defence-universities-tracker.

51. Qin Hui, "Dilemmas of Twenty-First Century Globalization: Explanations and Solutions, with a Critique of Thomas Piketty's *Twenty-First Century Capitalism*," trans. David Ownby, orig. publ. in Chinese in 2015, www.readingthechinadream.com/qin-hui-dilemmas.html.

52. Yuan Yang, "Foxconn Stops Illegal Overtime by School-Age Interns," *Financial Times*, November 22, 2017; Javier C. Hernández, "China's Leaders Confront an Unlikely Foe: Ardent Young Communists," *New York Times*, September 28, 2018; Rossalyn A. Warren, "You Buy a Purse at Walmart. There's a Note Inside from a 'Chinese Prisoner.' Now What?," *Vox*, October 10, 2018, www.vox.com/the-goods/2018/10/10/17953106/walmart-prison-note-china-factory; Emily Feng,

"Forced Labour Being Used in China's 'Re-Education' Camps," *Financial Times*, December 15, 2018, www.ft.com/content/eb2239aa-fc4f-11e8-aebf-99e208 d3e521.

53. "Labor Rights in China: Some Frequently Asked Questions," Friends of China Labour Bulletin, https://friendsclb.org/labor-rights-in-china; Gary Shih, "'Everyone Is Getting Locked Up': As Workers Grow Disgruntled, China Strikes at Labor Activists," *Washington Post*, December 24, 2019, www.washingtonpost .com/world/asia_pacific/as-workers-grow-disgruntled-in-a-slowing-economy -china-targets-labor-activists/2019/12/24/28a92654-2534-11ea-9cc9-e19cfb c87e51_story.html.
54. Klein and Pettis, *Trade Wars Are Class Wars*, 113.
55. Max Masuda-Farkas, "China's Hukou System and the Urban-Rural Divide," *The Regulatory Review*, August 18, 2021, www.theregreview.org/2021/08/18/masuda -farkas-china-hukou-system-urban-rural-divide/.
56. International Monetary Fund, Fiscal Affairs Department, *People's Republic of China: Tax Policy and Employment Creation*, March 28, 2018, www.imf.org/en /Publications/CR/Issues/2018/03/28/Peoples-Republic-of-China-Tax-Policy -and-Employment-Creation-45765; Philippe Wingender, "Intergovernmental Fiscal Reform in China," IMF Working Papers, April 13, 2018, www.imf.org /en/Publications/WP/Issues/2018/04/13/Intergovernmental-Fiscal-Reform-in -China-45743; Sonali Jain-Chandra, Niny Khor, Rui Mano, Johanna Schauer, Philippe Wingender, and Juzhong Zhuang, "Inequality in China—Trends, Drivers and Policy Remedies," IMF Working Papers, June 5, 2018; National Bureau of Statistics of China, "Annual Data."
57. Lindsay Maizland, "China's Fight Against Climate Change and Environmental Degradation," Council on Foreign Relations, May 19, 2021, www.cfr.org/back grounder/china-climate-change-policies-environmental-degradation.
58. Maizland, "China's Fight."
59. Maizland, "China's Fight."
60. Maizland, "China's Fight."
61. Richard Bridle, Ivetta Gerasimchuck, Benjamin Denjean, Ting Su, Clement Attwood, and Hongxia Duan, *Subsidies to Coal Power Generation in China*, International Institute for Sustainable Development, November 13, 2016, www .iisd.org/publications/report/subsidies-coal-power-generation-china.
62. Michael Standaert, "Despite Pledges to Cut Emissions, China Goes on a Coal Spree," *Yale Environment 360*, March 24, 2021, https://e360.yale.edu/features /despite-pledges-to-cut-emissions-china-goes-on-a-coal-spree.
63. Henry Wu, "The United States Can't Afford the Brutal Price of Chinese Solar Panels," *Foreign Policy*, July 14, 2021, https://foreignpolicy.com/2021/07/14/us -chinese-solar-panels-green-tech-strategy/.
64. Bibek Bhandari and Nicole Lim, "The Dark Side of China's Solar Boom," *Sixth Tone*, July 17, 2018, www.sixthtone.com/news/1002631/the-dark-side-of-chinas -solar-boom-.
65. Johnny Wood, "China's Pollution Is So Bad It's Blocking Sunlight from Solar Panels," World Economic Forum, August 5, 2019, www.weforum.org/agenda /2019/08/china-air-pollution-blocks-solar-panels-green-energy/.
66. Wu, "Chinese Solar Panels."
67. See, for instance, Ye Qi and Lingyun Zhang, "Local Environmental Enforcement Constrained by Central-Local Relations in China," *Environmental Policy and Governance* 24, no. 3 (May 2014), www.researchgate.net/publication/260802575 _Local_Environmental_Enforcement_Constrained_by_Central-Local_Relations _in_China.

68. Sarah Eaton and Genia Kostka, "Central Protectionism in China: The Central SOE Problem in Environmental Governance," *China Quarterly* 231 (September 2017): 685–704, www.cambridge.org/core/journals/china-quarterly/article/central-protectionism-in-china-the-central-soe-problem-in-environmental-governance/42D6B6E158861C4FC2B7B76C878AFCC1.

Chapter 7: An Economic Threat

1. See Jeffrey St. Clair, "The Saga of Magnequench," Counterpunch, April 7, 2006, www.counterpunch.org/2006/04/07/the-saga-of-magnequench/; Guillaume Pitron, *The Rare Metals War: The Dark Side of Clean Energy and Digital Technologies* (Melbourne: Scribe, 2020).
2. For details on Lucent Technologies and its partnership with Datang Telecom Technology, see Craig Smith, "Technology: Chinese Tread Warily in Secrets-Theft Case," *New York Times*, May 8, 2001. For DuPont, General Electric, and AMD, see Lingling Wei and Bob Davis, "How China Systematically Pries Technology from U.S. Companies," *Wall Street Journal*, September 26, 2018.
3. U.S. Attorney's Office, "Chinese National Sentenced for Stealing Ford Trade Secrets," press release, April 12, 2011, https://archives.fbi.gov/archives/detroit/press-releases/2011/de041211.htm.
4. Center for Strategic and International Studies, *Survey of Chinese Espionage in the United States Since 2000*, Strategic Technologies Program, www.csis.org/programs/technology-policy-program/survey-chinese-linked-espionage-united-states-2000.
5. Center for Strategic and International Studies, *Survey of Chinese Espionage*; Paul Wiseman and Michael Liedtke, "Here Are 5 Cases Where the U.S. Says Chinese Companies and Workers Stole American Trade Secrets," *Chicago Tribune*, February 21, 2019.
6. The National Bureau of Asian Research, *Report of the Commission on the Theft of American Intellectual Property*, May 2013, 15, www.nbr.org/wp-content/uploads/pdfs/publications/IP_Commission_Report.pdf.
7. Sean O'Connor, *How Chinese Companies Facilitate Technology Transfer from the United States*, U.S.-China Economic and Security Review Commission, May 6, 2019, 4, www.uscc.gov/sites/default/files/Research/How%20Chinese%20Companies%20Facilitate%20Tech%20Transfer%20from%20the%20US.pdf.
8. Office of the United States Trade Representative, *2018 Special 301 Report* (Washington DC: Office of the United States Trade Representative, 2018), https://ustr.gov/sites/default/files/files/Press/Reports/2018%20Special%20301.pdf.
9. Office of the Secretary of Defense, *Military and Security Developments Involving the People's Republic of China 2020: Annual Report to Congress*, https://media.defense.gov/2020/Sep/01/2002488689/-1/-1/1/2020-DOD-CHINA-MILITARY-POWER-REPORT-FINAL.PDF.
10. Christopher Wray, "Responding Effectively to the Chinese Economic Espionage Threat," Remarks at the Department of Justice China Initiative Conference, Center for Strategic and International Studies, Washington, DC, February 6, 2020.
11. "Chinese Hackers Indicted: Members of APT 10 Group Targeted Intellectual Property and Confidential Business Information," FBI News, December 20, 2018, www.fbi.gov/news/stories/chinese-hackers-indicted-122018.
12. Ellen Barry and Gina Kolata, "China's Lavish Funds Lured U.S. Scientists. What Did It Get in Return?," *New York Times*, February 6, 2020, www.nytimes.com/2020/02/06/us/chinas-lavish-funds-lured-us-scientists-what-did-it-get-in-return.html.

13. John Hudson and Ellen Nakashima, "U.S., Allies Accuse China of Hacking Microsoft and Condoning Other Cyberattacks," *Washington Post*, July 19, 2021, www.washingtonpost.com/national-security/microsoft-hack-china-biden-nato /2021/07/19/a90ac7b4-e827-11eb-84a2-d93bc0b50294_story.html; Editorial Board, "Tough Biden Talk, Little Action," *Wall Street Journal*, July 21, 2021, www .wsj.com/articles/china-microsoft-hack-russia-nord-stream-biden-state- department-11626900081.

14. Office of the United States Trade Representative, *Findings of the Investigations into China's Acts*.

15. Wei and Davis, "China Systematically Pries Technology."

16. See James Lewis, *Section 301 Investigation: China's Acts, Policies and Practices Related to Technology Transfer, Intellectual Property, and Innovation* (Washington, DC: Center for Strategic and International Studies, April 2020), 2, https://csis -website-prod.s3.amazonaws.com/s3fs-public/publication/200422_Lewis_Invest igation_v4.pdf. ("Companies from the U.S. and other Western nations find themselves under pressure to make long-term concessions in technology transfer in exchange for market access. Chinese policy is to extract technologies from Western companies; use subsidies and nontariff barriers to competition to build national champions; and then create a protected domestic market for these champions to give them an advantage as they compete globally.")

17. O'Connor, *Chinese Companies Facilitate Technology Transfer*, 7.

18. Alan O. Sykes, "The Law and Economics of 'Forced' Technology Transfer (FTT) and Its Implications for Trade and Investment Policy (and the U.S.-China Trade War)," *Journal of Legal Analysis* 13, no. 127 (2021): 127–71.

19. O'Connor, *Chinese Companies Facilitate Technology Transfer*, 8.

20. White House Office of Trade and Manufacturing Policy, *How China's Economic Aggression Threatens the Technologies and Intellectual Property of the United States and the World* (Washington, DC: White House Office of Trade and Manufacturing Policy, June 18, 2018), 7, www.hsdl.org/?view&did=812268.

21. Christina Nelson, "Licensing in China: Challenges and Best Practices," *China Business Review*, January 14, 2014, www.chinabusinessreview.com/licensing-in -china-challenges-and-best-practices/.

22. Office of the United States Trade Representative, *Findings of the Investigations into China's Acts*.

23. Office of the United States Trade Representative, *Findings of the Investigations into China's Acts*.

24. White House Office of Trade and Manufacturing Policy, *China's Economic Aggression*, 7; Office of the United States Trade Representative, *Findings of the Investigations into China's Acts*.

25. OECD and European Union Intellectual Property Office, *Trends in Trade in Counterfeit and Pirated Goods, Illicit Trade* (Paris: OECD Publishing, March 18, 2019), https://doi.org/10.1787/g2g9f533-en.

26. U.S. Customs and Border Protection, *Intellectual Property Rights Seizure Statistics: Fiscal Year 2020* (Washington, DC: U.S. Customs and Border Protection, 2021), www.cbp.gov/sites/default/files/assets/documents/2021-Sep/101808%20FY%20 2020%20IPR%20Seizure%20Statistic%20Book%2017%20Final%20spreads%20 ALT%20TEXT_FINAL%20%28508%29%20REVISED.pdf.

27. Office of the United States Trade Representative, *Findings of the Investigations into China's Acts*.

28. Office of the United States Trade Representative, *Findings of the Investigations into China's Acts*.

29. "Economic and Trade Agreement between the Government of the United States

of America and the Government of the People's Republic of China," U.S. Trade Representative, https://ustr.gov/sites/default/files/files/agreements/phase%20 one%20agreement/Economic_And_Trade_Agreement_Between_The_United _States_And_China_Text.pdf.

30. Mark Wu, "Testimony before the U.S.-China Economic and Security Review Commission Hearing on U.S. Companies in China," February 28, 2019, www .uscc.gov/sites/default/files/Wu%20Testimony%20-%20US-China%20Econ%20 Sec%20Review%20Cmsn%20-%20Feb%202019.pdf.

31. Office of the United States Trade Representative, *2021 National Trade Estimate Report*.

32. Office of the United States Trade Representative, *2021 National Trade Estimate Report*.

33. Office of the United States Trade Representative, *2021 National Trade Estimate Report*.

34. Eric Olander, "With the U.S. in Its Sights, China Moves to Restrict Rare Earth Exports. Could Cobalt Be Next?," *The China Project*, January 19, 2021, https:// thechinaproject.com/2021/01/19/with-the-u-s-in-its-sights-china-moves-to -restrict-rare-earths-exports-could-cobalt-be-next/.

35. Office of the United States Trade Representative, *2021 National Trade Estimate Report*.

36. Office of the United States Trade Representative, *2021 National Trade Estimate Report*.

37. Paul Mozur and Jane Perlez, "China Quietly Targets U.S. Tech Companies in Security Reviews," *New York Times*, May 16, 2016, www.nytimes.com/2016/05 /17/technology/china-quietly-targets-us-tech-companies-in-security-reviews.html.

38. C. Fred Bergsten, "China Is No Longer Manipulating Its Currency," Peterson Institute for International Economics (PIIE), November 18, 2016, www.piie.com /blogs/trade-investment-policy-watch/china-no-longer-manipulating-its-currency.

39. Ana Swanson, "The U.S. Labeled China a Currency Manipulator. Here's What It Means," *New York Times*, August 6, 2019, www.nytimes.com/2019/08/06/bus iness/economy/china-currency-manipulator.html.

40. Alan Rappeport, "U.S. Says China Is No Longer a Currency Manipulator," *New York Times*, January 13, 2020, www.nytimes.com/2020/01/13/us/politics/treasury -china-currency-manipulator-trade.html.

41. Congressional Research Service, *China's Economic Rise: History, Trends, Challenges, and Implications for the United States* (Washington, DC: Congressional Research Service, updated June 25, 2019), 1, https://crsreports.congress.gov/product/pdf /RL/RL33534.

42. "Coal Mining Industry in China," IBIS World, May 23, 2022, www.ibisworld. com/china/market-research-reports/coal-mining-industry/; "Coal Mining Industry in the US," IBIS World, June 27, 2022, www.ibisworld.com/united-states /market-research-reports/coal-mining-industry/.

43. "World Nuclear Power Reactors & Uranium Requirements," World Nuclear, November 2022, https://world-nuclear.org/information-library/facts-and-figures /world-nuclear-power-reactors-and-uranium-requireme.aspx.

44. "Under Construction," Status Reports, Power Reactor Information System, IAEA, https://pris.iaea.org/PRIS/WorldStatistics/UnderConstructionReactors ByCountry.aspx.

45. David Hart, "The Impact of China's Production Surge on Innovation in the Global Solar Photovoltaics Industry," Information Technology & Innovation Foundation, October 5, 2020, https://itif.org/publications/2020/10/05/impact-chinas-pro duction-surge-innovation-global-solar-photovoltaics.

46. Annual Solar Photovoltaics Cell Production by Country, 1995–2013, Earth Policy, http://www.earth-policy.org/?/data_center/C23/.

47. Annual Solar Photovoltaics Cell Production by Country, 1995–2013.

48. David Hart, "The Impact of China's Production Surge on Innovation in the Global Solar Photovoltaics Industry," Information Technology & Innovation Foundation, October 5, 2020, https://itif.org/publications/2020/10/05/impact -chinas-production-surge-innovation-global-solar-photovoltaics

49. Hart, "The Impact of China's Production Surge."

50. "Solar PV Trade and Manufacturing," Bloomberg, February 2021, https://csis -website-prod.s3.amazonaws.com/s3fs-public/Solar%20PV%20Case%20Study%20 -%20BloombergNEF.pdf?wDUUlXhfxWtA0lLU66HdshX539MvZHDI; Latherina Bucholz, "China Dominates All Steps of Solar Panel Production," Statista, April 21, 2021, www.statista.com/chart/24687/solar-panel-global-market -shares-by-production-steps/.

51. Ugranath Chakarvarty, "Renewable Energy Materials Supply Implications," IAEE Energy Forum, 2018, 1–3, www.iaee.org/en/publications/newsletterdl.aspx ?id=455#:~:text=Rare%20earth%20materials%20such%20as,components%20of% 20renewable%20energy%20hardware.

52. Chakarvarty, "Renewable Energy Materials," 1–3.

53. Chakarvarty, "Renewable Energy Materials," 1–3.

54. "Rare Earth Element Facts," Minerals and Metals Facts, Natural Resources Canada, www.nrcan.gc.ca/mining-materials/facts/rare-earth-elements/20522.

55. Samantha Subin, "The New U.S. Plan to Rival China and End Cornering of Market in Rare Earth Metals," CNBC, April 19, 2021, www.cnbc.com/2021 /04/17/the-new-us-plan-to-rival-chinas-dominance-in-rare-earth-metals.html.

56. "Automotive Industry," Select USA, www.trade.gov/selectusa-automotive -industry.

57. 2020 Production Statistics, OICA, www.oica.net/category/production-statistics /2020-statistics/.

58. 2010 Production Statistics, OICA, www.oica.net/category/production-statistics /2010-statistics/.

59. Alice Yu and Mitzi Sumangil, "Top Electric Vehicle Markets Dominate Lithium-ion Battery Capacity Growth," S&P Global Market Intelligence, February 16, 2021.

60. Tim Colton and LaVar Huntzinger, "A Brief History of Shipbuilding in Recent Times," Center for Naval Analyses, September 2002, 18, www.cna.org/CNA _files/PDF/D0006988.A1.pdf.

61. Loren Thompson, "U.S. Shipbuilding Is at Its Lowest Ebb Ever. How Did America Fall So Far?," Forbes, July 23, 2021, www.forbes.com/sites/loren thompson/2021/07/23/us-shipbuilding-is-at-its-lowest-ebb-ever-how-did-america -fall-so-far/?sh=3157edfe6c87.

62. Thompson, "U.S. Shipbuilding."

63. Peter Edwards, "Global Cement Producer Round-Up," Global Cement Magazine, December 2020, 16, www.cfic.dz/images/telechargements/global%20cement%20 magazine%20decembre%202020.pdf.

64. Shinya Matano, "The Impact of China's Industrial Subsidies on Companies and the Response of Japan, the United States, and the European Union," Mitsui & Co. Global Strategic Studies Institute, January 2021, https://asia.nikkei.com/Economy /Trade-war/China-corporate-subsidies-swell-further-in-2019-as-US-cries-foul www.mitsui.com/mgssi/en/report/detail/__icsFiles/afieldfile /2021/02/19/2101c_matano_e.pdf.

65. Shinya Matano, "The Impact of China's Industrial Subsidies on Companies and

the Response of Japan, the United States, and the European Union," Mitsui & Co. Global Strategic Studies Institute, January 2021, https://asia.nikkei .com/Economy/Trade-war/China-corporate-subsidies-swell-further-in-2019 -as-US-cries-foul www.mitsui.com/mgssi/en/report/detail/__icsFiles/afieldfile /2021/02/19/2101c_matano_e.pdf.

66. Office of the United States Trade Representative, *2021 National Trade Estimate Report*.

67. Michaela Platzer, John Sargent, and Karen Sutter, "Semiconductors: U.S. Industry, Global Competition, and Federal Policy," Congressional Research Service, October 26, 2020, 48, https://sgp.fas.org/crs/misc/R46581.pdf.

68. "State of the U.S. Semiconductor Industry—2021," Semiconductor Industry Association, 2021, www.semiconductors.org/wp-content/uploads/2021/09/2021 -SIA-State-of-the-Industry-Report.pdf.

69. These forecasted values are derived from purchasing power parity calculations. For the data, see: Paul Heney and Tim Studt, "2021 Global R&D Funding Forecast Released," R&D World, February 22, 2021, www.rdworldonline.com/2021-global -rd-funding-forecast-released/.

70. James Areddy, "China Trumps US in Key Technology Research, Report Says," *Wall Street Journal*, March 2, 2023.

Chapter 8: Changing the Direction

1. Ana Swanson, "Trump Administration Goes After China Over Intellectual Property, Advanced Technology," *Washington Post*, August 14, 2017, www.wash ingtonpost.com/news/wonk/wp/2017/08/14/trump-administration-goes-after -china-over-intellectual-property-advanced-technology/.

Chapter 10: Making a Deal Concrete

1. Chad Bown, "Four Years Into the Trade War, Are the US and China Decoupling?," Peterson Institute for International Economics, October 20, 2022, www.piie.com /blogs/realtime-economics/four-years-trade-war-are-us-and-china-decoupling.

2. Bown, "Four Years Into the Trade War."

3. Josh Horwitz, "U.S. Business Sentiment in China Hits Record Low as Zero-COVID Persists, Survey Shows," Reuters, October 27, 2022, www.reuters.com /markets/us-business-sentiment-china-hits-record-low-zero-covid-persists-survey -2022-10-28/.

4. Trade in Goods with China, U.S. Census Bureau, www.census.gov/foreign-trade /balance/c5700.html.

Chapter 11: The Way Forward

1. Kevin Rudd, "Xi's Congress Report Lays Bare an Aggressive and Statist Worldview," *Financial Times*, October 21, 2022, www.ft.com/content/8576916d -2cf5-483f-bfe4-2238080a5c70.

2. Emily Weinstein and Ngor Luong, "U.S. Outbound Investment into Chinese AI Companies," Center for Security and Emerging Technology, February 2023.

3. Jon Bateman, "The Evolution of U.S. Thinking and Policy," in *U.S.-China Technological 'Decoupling': A Strategy and Policy Framework* (Washington, DC: Carnegie Endowment for International Peace, 2022), 12.

4. For an example of this, see "China Daily Takes Out Ads in US Newspapers to Highlight Diaoyu Claims," *South China Morning Post*, September 30, 2012.

5. Lee Edwards, "Confucius Institutes: China's Trojan Horse," Heritage Foundation, May 27, 2021.

6. Juliana Goldman, "Chinese Company Pledged $2 Million to Clinton Foundation in 2013," CBS News, March 16, 2015.

7. "Comer: Anonymous Chinese Donations to UPenn Potentially Influenced Biden Administration Policies," U.S. House of Representatives Committee on Oversight and Accountability, https://oversight.house.gov/release/comer-anonymous-chinese -donations-to-upenn-potentially-influenced-biden-administration-policies %EF%BF%BC/; Yael Halon, "Reports of Chinese Donations to Second Biden-linked University Prompt New Calls for Investigation," Fox News, February 16, 2023.

Chapter 12: From NAFTA to USMCA

1. Jeff Faux, *NAFTA's Impact on U.S. Workers* (Washington, DC: Economic Policy Institute, 2013), www.epi.org/blog/naftas-impact-workers/.

2. Richard Davies, "When a Factory Relocates to Mexico, What Happens to Its American Workers," *New York Times*, October 12, 2021, www.nytimes.com/2021 /10/12/books/review/american-made-farah-stockman.html.

3. Bill Canis, M. Angeles Villarreal, and Vivian Jones, "NAFTA and Motor Vehicle Trade," Congressional Research Service, July 28, 2017, https://sgp.fas.org/crs/row /R44907.pdf.

4. David Coffin, Tamar Khachaturian, and David Riker, "Analysis of Employment Changes Over Time in the U.S. Motor Vehicle Industry," International Trade Commission, August 2016, www.usitc.gov/employement_changes_working_paper .htm#:~:text=Over%20the%20period%20from%201997%20to%202014%2C%20 U.S.,vehicle%20industry%20declined%20from%20932%2C265%20to%20719% 2C983%20employees.

Chapter 13: USMCA

1. President Trump, "U.S.-Mexico-Canada Trade Agreement Press Conference," C-SPAN, October 1, 2018, www.c-span.org/video/?452348-1/president-trump -briefs-reporters-us-mexico-canada-trade-agreement.

Chapter 15: Europe and Japan

1. Cristina Enache, "2022 VAT Rates in Europe," Tax Foundation, January 25, 2022, https://taxfoundation.org/value-added-tax-2022-vat-rates-in-europe/.

2. Ben S. Bernanke, *Germany's Trade Surplus Is a Problem* (Washington, DC: Brookings, 2015), www.brookings.edu/blog/ben-bernanke/2015/04/03/germanys -trade-surplus-is-a-problem/.

3. "Industrial Strategy 2030," Federal Ministry for Economic Affairs and Energy, November 2019, www.bmwk.de/Redaktion/EN/Publikationen/Industry/indust rial-strategy-2030.pdf?__blob=publicationFile&v=7.

4. "Industrial Strategy 2030."

5. "Industrial Strategy 2030."

6. Matthew C. Klein and Michael Pettis, *Trade Wars Are Class Wars: How Rising Inequality Distorts the Global Economy and Threatens International Peace* (New Haven, CT: Yale University Press, 2020), 148–54.

7. Niklas Engbom, Enrica Detragiache, and Faezeh Raei, "The German Labor Market Reforms and Post-Unemployment Earnings," IMF Working Paper, July 2015, 3, www.imf.org/external/pubs/ft/wp/2015/wp15162.pdf.

8. Michael Pettis, "High Wages Versus High Savings in a Globalized World," Carnegie Endowment for International Peace, April 3, 2018, https://carnegie endowment.org/chinafinancialmarkets/75972.

9. Bojan Pancevski, "Angela Merkel's International Legacy: Cooler Trans-Atlantic Relations," *Wall Street Journal*, September 22, 2021, www.wsj.com/articles/angela -merkel-german-alliance-biden-trans-atlantic-relations-11632344868.

10. Diana Choyleva, "China Is Steadily Wiping Out German Industry," Nikkei Asia, June 30, 2022, https://asia.nikkei.com/Opinion/China-is-steadily-wiping-out -German-industry.

11. United States Committee on Ways and Means, "House Republicans Unveil 21st Century Tax Plan Built for Growth," press release, June 24, 2016, https://gop -waysandmeans.house.gov/house-republicans-unveil-21st-century-tax-plan-built -growth/.

12. Philipp Heimberger and Nikolaus Krowall, "Seven 'Surprising' Facts about the Italian Economy," *Social Europe*, June 25, 2020, www.socialeurope.eu/seven -surprising-facts-about-the-italian-economy.

13. Daniel Kochis, "NATO Allies Now Spend $50 Billion More on Defense Than in 2016," Heritage Foundation, November 3, 2020, www.heritage.org/defense /commentary/nato-allies-now-spend-50-billion-more-defense-2016.

14. See, for example, Karel van Wolferen, *The Enigma of Japanese Power: People and Politics in a Stateless Nation* (New York: Vintage, 1989); Eamonn Fingleton, *Blindside: Why Japan Is Still on Track to Overtake the U.S. by the Year 2000* (Boston: Houghton Mifflin, 1995); and Clyde Prestowitz, *Trading Places: How We Are Giving Our Future to Japan and How to Reclaim It* (New York: Basic Books, 1989).

Chapter 16: Other Major Trading Partners

1. Data via U.S. Import and Export Merchandise trade statistics, U.S. Census Bureau: Economic Indicators Division, USA Trade Online.

2. Data via U.S. Import and Export Merchandise trade statistics, U.S. Census Bureau: Economic Indicators Division, USA Trade Online.

3. Office of the United States Trade Representative, *2021 National Trade Estimate Report*, 248.

4. Office of the United States Trade Representative, *2021 National Trade Estimate Report*, 248.

5. Alyssa Ayres, "A Field Guide to U.S.-India Trade Tensions," Council on Foreign Relations, February 13, 2020, www.cfr.org/article/field-guide-us-india-trade -tensions.

6. Ayres, "Field Guide."

7. Ayres, "Field Guide."

8. Office of the United States Trade Representative, *2021 National Trade Estimate Report*, 247.

9. Office of the United States Trade Representative, *2021 National Trade Estimate Report*, 248.

10. Office of the United States Trade Representative, *2021 National Trade Estimate Report*, 257.

11. Data via World Bank database.

12. Data via U.S. Import and Export Merchandise trade statistics, U.S. Census Bureau: Economic Indicators Division, USA Trade Online.

13. Data via U.S. Import and Export Merchandise trade statistics, U.S. Census Bureau: Economic Indicators Division, USA Trade Online.

14. Data via U.S. Import and Export Merchandise trade statistics, U.S. Census Bureau: Economic Indicators Division, USA Trade Online.

15. Data via U.S. Import and Export Merchandise trade statistics, U.S. Census Bureau: Economic Indicators Division, USA Trade Online.

16. David Aller, "Korean Industrial Policy: From the Arrest of the Millionaires to

Hallyu," *American Affairs* 4, no. 1 (Spring 2020), https://americanaffairsjournal
.org/2020/02/korean-industrial-policy-from-the-arrest-of-the-millionaires-to
-hallyu/.
17. Aller, "Korean Industrial Policy."
18. Office of the United States Trade Representative, *2021 National Trade Estimate Report*, 324.
19. Office of the United States Trade Representative, "Four Year Snapshot: The U.S.-Korea Free Trade Agreement," fact sheet, March 2016, https://ustr.gov/about-us/policy-offices/press-office/fact-sheets/2016/March/Four-Year-Snapshot-KORUS/.
20. Jane Chung and Christine Kim, "How Seoul Raced to Conclude U.S. Trade Deal ahead of North Korea Talks," Reuters, March 30, 2018, www.reuters.com/article/cbusiness-us-usa-trade-southkorea-idCAKBN1H60I9-OCABS.
21. U.S. Census Bureau, "Trade in Goods with Korea, South," www.census.gov/foreign-trade/balance/c5800.html.
22. Data via U.S. Import and Export Merchandise trade statistics, U.S. Census Bureau: Economic Indicators Division, USA Trade Online.
23. Sebastian Strangio, "Vietnam, US Reach Accord on Alleged Currency Manipulation," *The Diplomat*, July 20, 2021, https://thediplomat.com/2021/07/vietnam-us-reach-accord-on-alleged-currency-manipulation/.

Chapter 17: Transcending Issues That Affect the Economy

1. International Monetary Fund, *United States: 2021 Article IV Consultation—Press Release: Staff Report: and Statement by the Executive Director for the United States*, IMF Country Report No. 21/162 (Washington, DC: International Monetary Fund, July 2021), 65, www.imf.org/-/media/Files/Publications/CR/2021/English/1USAEA2021001.ashx.
2. "New Vehicle Trade Data Visualization," International Trade Administration, www.trade.gov/data-visualization/new-vehicle-trade-data-visualization.
3. "The U.S. Auto Labor Market since NAFTA," *On the Economy*, Federal Reserve Bank of St. Louis, April 15, 2019, www.stlouisfed.org/on-the-economy/2019/april/us-auto-labor-market-nafta; "Inflation Adjusted Earnings in Motor Vehicles and Parts Industry Down 17 Percent from 1990 to 2018," Bureau of Labor Statistics, January 6, 2020, www.bls.gov/opub/ted/2020/inflation-adjusted-earnings-in-motor-vehicles-and-parts-industry-down-17-percent-from-1990-to-2018.htm.
4. Peter Sigal, "Europe Forecast to Import 800,000 Chinese-built Cars by 2025," *Automotive News Europe*, November 7, 2022, https://europe.autonews.com/automakers/chinese-electric-car-exports-europe-soar; "EU Passenger Car Imports, Main Countries of Origin," ACEA, July 22, 2022, www.acea.auto/figure/eu-passenger-car-imports-main-countries-of-origin-in-units/.
5. "China's Biggest Automaker SAIC Puts US Ambitions on Hold," *Industry Week*, April 19, 2017, www.industryweek.com/leadership/strategic-planning-execution/article/22013337/chinas-biggest-automaker-saic-puts-us-ambitions-on-hold.
6. Chris Perkins, "Import Tariffs Kill the Last Ford Focus for the US Market," *Road & Track*, August 31, 2018, www.roadandtrack.com/new-cars/future-cars/a22886625/2019-ford-focus-active-dead-us/.
7. Charles Benoit, "Leading Customs Authorities Make the Case against De Minimis Commerce," Coalition for a Prosperous America, June 6, 2022, https://prosperousamerica.org/leading-customs-authorities-make-the-case-against-de-minimis-commerce/.
8. Josh Zumbrun, "The $67 Billion Tariff Dodge That's Undermining U.S. Trade Policy," *Wall Street Journal*, April 25, 2022, www.wsj.com/articles/the-67-billion

-tariff-dodge-thats-undermining-u-s-trade-policy-di-minimis-rule-customs
-tourists-11650897161.

9. Jeff Ferry, "The Trade Deficit Is Worse Than We Thought: De Minimis Hides
    $128 Billion of U.S. Imports," Coalition for a Prosperous America, January 26,
    2022, https://prosperousamerica.org/the-trade-deficit-is-worse-than-we-thought
    -de-minimis-hides-128-billion-of-u-s-imports/.

10. Zumbrun, "$67 Billion Tariff Dodge."

11. "De Minimis Value," Avalara, www.avalara.com/us/en/learn/cross-border
    -resources/de-minimis-threshold-table.html.

12. Zumbrun, "$67 Billion Tariff Dodge."

Chapter 18: A Prescription for the Future

1. Tammy Baldwin, "U.S. Senators Tammy Baldwin and Josh Hawley Lead
    Bipartisan Effort to Restore Competitiveness to U.S. Exports, Boost American
    Manufacturers and Farmers," press release, Tammy Baldwin, United States
    Senator for Wisconsin, July 31, 2019, www.baldwin.senate.gov/news/press
    -releases/competitive-dollar-for-jobs-and-prosperity-act.

2. Terry Jones, "Has Trump Won the Debate Over Free Trade in the U.S.? I&I/
    TIPP Poll," TIPP Insights, March 27, 2023.

INDEX

Page numbers in *italics* refer to illustrations.

ABOUT THE AUTHOR

ROBERT LIGHTHIZER served in President Trump's cabinet as the United States Trade Representative from 2017 to 2021 and was a deputy USTR under President Reagan. He is one of America's most respected experts on international trade, having negotiated dozens of international agreements and practiced trade law for more than forty years. Lighthizer was born in Ohio and now lives in Palm Beach, Florida.